KENYA

KENYA

BETWEEN HOPE AND DESPAIR, 1963–2011

DANIEL BRANCH

YALE UNIVERSITY PRESS
NEW HAVEN AND LONDON

For Jennie

For information about this and other Yale University Press publications, please contact:

US Office: sales.press@yale.edu   yalebooks.com
Europe Office: sales@yaleup.co.uk   www.yalebooks.co.uk

Set in Janson Text by IDSUK (DataConnection) Ltd

Printed in Great Britain by TJ International Ltd, Padstow, Cornwall

Library of Congress Cataloging-in-Publication Data
Branch, Daniel, 1978–
   Kenya: between hope and despair, 1963–2011 / Daniel Branch.
      p. cm.
   ISBN 978-0-300-14876-3 (cl: alk. paper) 1. Kenya—History—1963– 2. Kenya—Politics and government—1963–1978. 3. Kenya—Politics and government—1978–2002. 4. Kenya—Politics and government—2002–5. Kenya—Social conditions—1963– I. Title.
   DT433.58.B73 2011
   967.6204—dc23
                                                                                        2011021877

A catalogue record for this book is available from the British Library.

10 9 8 7 6 5 4 3 2 1
2015 2014 2013 2012 2011

CONTENTS

LIST OF ILLUSTRATIONS

ACKNOWLEDGEMENTS

THIS BOOK BEGAN life in a conversation with its editor, Phoebe Clapham, in the autumn of 2007. Over the three and a half years of research and writing that followed, a good deal of assistance, advice and support was provided by a wide range of generous individuals and organisations.

The research undertaken in the UK, US and Kenya was funded by the British Academy through its now defunct small grants programme. Further assistance was provided by the British Institute in Eastern Africa during Justin Willis's and David Anderson's tenures as director. Yolana Pringle, then a graduate attaché at the institute, proved a diligent research assistant in trying circumstances in early 2008. As assistant director of the institute, Stephanie Wynne-Jones and her husband, Mike, were generous hosts and great company; Christmas Day 2007 will always be remembered fondly! In a similar vein, Will and Miriam Cunningham made my research trips across the Atlantic a pleasure with their boundless hospitality.

A number of archivists and librarians proved to be of tremendous help. The staff of the Kenya National Archives went beyond the call of duty, persevering in hunts through the stacks for lost files with great good humour and extraordinary success. At the National Archives building in College Park, Maryland, the reading-room staff patiently guided this novice through the intricacies of the US archives system. The librarians both at the Herskovits Library of African Studies at Northwestern University and in the African and Middle East Reading Room of the Library of Congress enthusiastically aided work carried out there. The George Padmore Institute in London also generously allowed for consultation of the papers of the Committee for the Release of Political Prisoners in Kenya. Several of the images for this book were located with the help of The Nation Media group's photographic service and Farah Chaudhry at Camerapix and A24 Media.

Many of the ideas contained here have been developed during and after presentations of papers of earlier drafts of chapters. Attendees of seminars and lectures at the School of Oriental and African Studies, the University of Oxford, Durham University, the University of Sheffield, the University of Leeds, the University of Birmingham, the Library of Congress and my own University of Warwick all provided useful comments and criticism. So, too, have a number of individuals in the UK, US and Kenya.

This book began when I was a member of the history department at the University of Exeter and was finished at Warwick. Colleagues at both were supportive of my work, in particular a series of heads of department. During their discussions of post-colonial African history, students at both institutions regularly forced me to develop unclear concepts and to reconsider prior assumptions.

The book has benefited from conversations over the past three years about the politics and history of Kenya and East Africa. Oliver Kisaka Simiyu, David Throup, Susanne Mueller, Jeremy Prestholdt, Rob Blunt, Ben Knighton and, especially, Jim Brennan have all, on at least one occasion, provided significant insight and assistance. John Lonsdale has been, as always, encouraging and supportive. Justin Willis read the entire manuscript, and I am particularly grateful to him for his insightful criticisms and comments. Not all have been addressed, and I am, of course, responsible for the errors, omissions and misjudgements.

Several individuals deserve particular mention for their help during the writing of this book. Thanks are due to Clive Liddiard for his diligent copy-editing. In Nairobi, Joyce Nyairo, Parselelo Kantai, Mwangi Githaru, Gitau Kariuki, Laragh Larsen and Tom Wolf were all generous with their time, thoughts and friendship. Each made sure that regular trips to Nairobi were both enjoyable and illuminating. Jason Moseley at Oxford Analytica was unhesitating in his willingness to share his knowledge, and generously provided me with regular opportunities to air my own opinions before a wider audience – something that proved invaluable when writing a book such as this.

My cohort of fellow former graduate students continue to be a source of friendship and advice. Gabrielle Lynch, Gerard McCann and Paul Ocobock read chapters, made criticisms, shared their own work and proved again, on countless occasions, to be great company. It was my good fortune that research trips to Nairobi overlapped with Gerard's own visits, while a trip to Northwestern fortuitously coincided with Paul's time in Chicago. On each occasion, a great amount of intellectual generosity was exhibited by both.

My debts to my family are too significant and numerous to detail here. Suffice to say I owe my parents, siblings, niece, nephews and in-laws (both current and future) a great deal. Four other people can be singled out for particular praise and thanks, however. As editor, Phoebe Clapham has been encouraging, diligent and patient to the last; it has been a pleasure to work with her. One of the many benefits of living in and around Oxford has been the continued ability to exploit the friendship and knowledge of Dave Anderson and Nic Cheeseman. The two are well-informed observers and unparalleled enthusiasts of Kenyan politics and history, and are unstintingly generous with their time. Both are close friends, co-editors and co-authors. Last but not least, the work on this book began a couple of days after I first met Jennie Castle. By the time of its publication, she will be my wife. In the intervening three and a half years, she has endured with good humour my frequent long absences and late nights of writing. Just one trip to Kenya during the research was no sort of compensation, but was enough for her to see why I keep returning.

Lower Heyford, Oxfordshire, April 2011

ACRONYMS AND ABBREVIATIONS

CBK	Central Bank of Kenya
CFPF	Central Foreign Policy Files
CIA	Central Intelligence Agency
CID	Criminal Investigation Department
CREST	CIA Records Search Tool
CRPPK	Committee for the Release of Political Prisoners in Kenya
DC	District Commissioner
DO	District Officer
DP	Democratic Party
ECK	Electoral Commission of Kenya
FORD	Forum for the Restoration of Democracy
GEMA	Gikuyu, Embu and Meru Association
GPI	George Padmore Institute
GSU	General Service Unit
ICC	International Criminal Court
ICJ	International Commission of Jurists
IMF	International Monetary Fund
IPK	Islamic Party of Kenya
KADU	Kenya African Democratic Union
KAF	Kenya Air Force
KAMATUSA	Kalenjin, Maasai, Turkana and Samburu

KANU	Kenya African National Union
KHRC	Kenya Human Rights Commission
KNA	Kenya National Archives
KNCHR	Kenya National Commission on Human Rights
KPU	Kenya People's Union
KSh	Kenya shilling
MP	Member of Parliament
Mwakenya	Union of Nationalists to Liberate Kenya
NAAAD	National Archives Access to Archival Databases
NACP	National Archives II College Park
NARC	National Rainbow Coalition
NCCK	National Christian Council of Kenya (1966–84); National Council of Churches of Kenya (1984–)
NEP	North Eastern Province
NFD	Northern Frontier District
NDP	National Development Party
NPPPP	Northern Province People's Progressive Party
OAU	Organisation of African Unity
ODM	Orange Democratic Movement
PNU	Party for National Unity
PC	Provincial Commissioner
PRO	Public Record Office
RBAA	Records of the Bureau of African Affairs
RG	Record Group
SLDF	Sabaot Land Defence Force
SNF	Subject Numeric Files
SWB	Summary of World Broadcasts
TNA	The National Archives
Umoja	United Movement for Democracy in Kenya
YK'92	Youth for KANU '92

NOTE ON ORTHOGRAPHY

THROUGHOUT THIS BOOK the choice of terms has been informed by accessibility. Names of ethnic groups used are those most likely to be familiar to non-specialist readers: for example Kikuyu rather Gikuyu or Agikuyu. In a similar vein, occasional mention is made of the language of Swahili rather than Kiswahili. Wherever possible, Swahili terms that are used in English-language everyday conversation in Kenya have been translated. Again, this has been done for no other reason than accessibility.

Place names follow post-independence orthodoxy. The political map of the country has, however, been redrawn on a number of occasions. References to the glut of districts created after 1992 have, therefore, been kept to a minimum. Mentions of provinces refer to those marked out by the boundaries in place between 1964 and 2010.

Approximate contemporary currency conversions are offered where necessary for information, but inflation and currency fluctuations since the 1980s make this an inexact science. Borrowing from Paul Gifford, the rough, indicative exchange rates used for conversions here are Ksh.9 to the US dollar in 1963–80, Ksh.10–40 during the 1980s, Ksh.60 for the 1990s and Ksh.70 in the 2000s.

Democracy is a really complex phenomenon. It involves the right of a people to criticise freely without being detained in prison. It involves a people being aware of all their rights. It involves the rights of a people to know how the wealth is produced in the country, who controls that wealth, and for whose benefit that wealth is being utilised. Democracy involves therefore people being aware of the forces shaping their lives.

Ngugi wa Thiong'o, quoted in 'Ngugi wa Thiong'o Still Bitter Over his Detention', *Weekly Review*, 5 January 1979

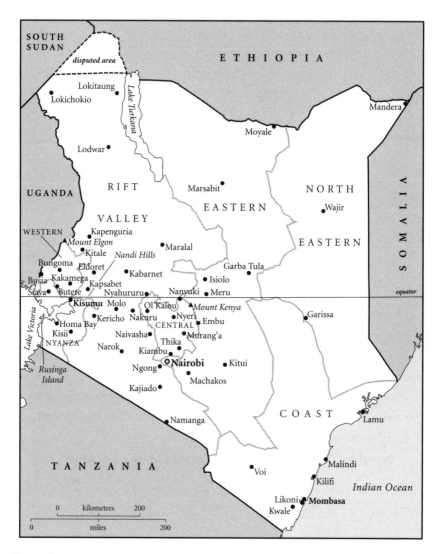

Kenya in 2011

INTRODUCTION: THE PARTY

THE BULL

In late June 1963, Oginga Odinga hosted a party at his Nairobi home. Wearing, as one American diplomat described, 'his traditional beaded cap, his Mao style, high collared jacket of fine black cotton, and black trousers', Odinga greeted each guest personally as they entered his house. The guests, all from 'the top echelon of Kenya, diplomats, guests from near-by countries, and a host of Odinga's retainers and employees from his ministry', were treated to 'huge quantities of native foods . . . served buffet style. Beans, maize, chicken, bread, potatoes, and cooked greens were the basic fare. The consumption was enormous.'[1] The hospitality was typical of Odinga, but was well within his means as a successful businessman. Always convivial company, quick with jokes and a generous host, Odinga was nevertheless a passionate nationalist politician. While not physically imposing, his forceful personality fully justified his nickname of 'The Bull'. His support for the cause of nationalism had been unshakable in the years leading up to independence.

Odinga's party was a celebration of three connected events occasioned by the imminent end of colonial rule. The first was Kenya's transition to self-rule on 1 June. Full independence would follow in

December and the country would become a republic another year later, but self-rule marked the real beginning of Kenya's post-colonial era. An election victory by the Kenya African National Union (KANU), which Odinga had helped found in 1960, was the second cause for celebration. Elections to form the first independent government had been held at the end of May and KANU had defeated its rival, the Kenya African Democratic Union (KADU). KANU's victory was not simply a victory of one party over another: it was about the triumph of one vision of Kenya's constitutional future over another. KANU and Odinga envisaged the infant nation-state as dominated by a centralised government responsible for implementing development policy. KADU, by contrast, advocated a devolved system of government, with considerable powers passed down to local authorities. Finally, Odinga was celebrating his own return to the top table of Kenyan politics. KANU and KADU had been forced to share power for the previous year as a result of constitutional negotiations with the British colonial regime. Odinga had been excluded from the cabinet under that power-sharing arrangement. With KANU's victory ensuring that the party took sole occupancy of the main government institutions, he returned to government as minister for home affairs.

For most of the Kenyan guests, this was one of the first social events for the new political and economic elite – an elite that would dominate public life right up to the present day. Drawn from across the country, and with a wide array of experience of colonial rule, the men present were involved in building a new nation. In retrospect, more important was their construction of a new ruling class. New connections were made, while old ones that had been forged at such premier schools as the Alliance High School or at university (particularly at Makerere, in neighbouring Uganda) were renewed in the years to come, at other such social events. The best education that colonialism could provide lent what one of its beneficiaries, Benjamin Kipkorir, called 'an emerging elite' with the connections, skills and knowledge 'to become Independent Kenya's rulers'.[2]

For many of the foreign guests, Odinga's party was one of their first experiences of Nairobi's social scene. Consulates were being expanded into embassies, and new diplomatic missions were being established ahead of independence. The party marked an opportunity for the new diplomatic corps to build friendships and to size up potential enemies within Kenya's new political leadership. To other foreign guests, Nairobi was a more familiar place. Several British colonial officials were making preparations to stay on in Kenya after independence as expatriate civil servants within the bureaucracy of the new nation. Other white Kenyans were also determined to stay. Although many of the white settlers living in the White Highlands were to leave the country at independence, a number did want to make a go of life in the new Kenya. To some of the guests at the party, the presence of British administrators and the economic ties to the outgoing imperial power were welcome bulwarks against the dangerous talk of some nationalists about socialism, friendly relations with the communist powers, and a redistribution of wealth from the top to the bottom of Kenyan society. On the other hand, for the nationalists among the guests and for their host, the prospect of Britain's continued influence on Kenya's affairs was nothing other than neo-colonialism.

Whatever their hopes for independence or their views of the British, all those at Odinga's home looked to the guest of honour and the new prime minister, Jomo Kenyatta, to protect their interests. Kenyatta had spent much of the previous decade in detention, falsely accused by the British regime of orchestrating the Mau Mau rebellion of the 1950s. Although innocent of those charges, his detention and previous record as a nationalist leader made him the undisputed figurehead of Kenya's African population when he was released in August 1961. Now, as guests proceeded out onto Odinga's lawn, where troupes of dancers were waiting to entertain them, Kenyatta was feted as *Mzee*, the elder, or *Baba Taifa*, father of the nation. Although his greying hair and grizzled beard betrayed his advanced years, the new prime minister was exuberant. Detention had done little apparent damage to his robust health and stature. As the dancers encouraged various politicians to join them in their performance, Kenyatta stepped forward eagerly.

He was joined by the three other figures most prominent in the final phase of KANU's successful transition from nationalist protest movement to party of government. As host and one of KANU's dynamos, Odinga justifiably joined Kenyatta centre stage. Kenyatta's new friend and ally, Malcolm MacDonald, was a less likely dancer, however. The son of Britain's first Labour prime minister, a Labour politician in his own right and a long-time servant of British diplomacy and colonialism in various positions, he nevertheless played a critical role in changing the direction of Kenyan decolonisation. He served as the last governor of the colonial era, as the only governor-general of the period between independence and the declaration of a republic a year later, and then as the first high commissioner.

Shortly after his arrival in 1963, MacDonald became convinced that Kenyatta was the best protector of British interests, rather than the most potent threat to them, as the accepted wisdom had been in London and in the offices of the colonial government in Nairobi. Kenyatta was, MacDonald thought, 'the most shrewd, authoritative and sagacious leader available to Kenya'. There were, by contrast, 'far fewer good brains in the K.A.D.U. Party' and its leader Ronald Ngala was 'rather second-rate'. The last governor thought it critical that Kikuyu supporters of KANU should hold the upper hand after independence. This was not a question of numbers: although the largest ethnic group in the country, Kikuyu accounted for perhaps only one in five of all Kenyans. Each of the other four large ethnic groups – Luhya, Luo, Kalenjin and Kamba – could boast between 10 and 15 per cent of the country's population.

MacDonald's concern was the disproportionate politicisation of the Kikuyu community. As the community that had been most integrated into the colonial economy, Kikuyu had also led protests against British rule, culminating in the Mau Mau rebellion. MacDonald believed that this tradition of protest meant that Kikuyu would not accept marginalisation after independence and would take their revenge if they were alienated by British interests, such as the European settler farmers. Moreover, that same long line of political opposition to the colonial regime, coupled with a higher level of education, meant that there were a great many more able Kikuyu political leaders and civil servants than there were among other communities. 'The only chance of peaceful progress coming to Independent Kenya was if the Kikuyu were free to assert their superior abilities in government,' wrote MacDonald later. But on arrival in Nairobi he found that existing British policy 'was to try to arrange that the General Election due to take place later in the year should result in a deadlock between the K.A.D.U. and the K.A.N.U. Parties'. MacDonald therefore 'reversed the policy of the Administration in Nairobi, and instructed that we should not seek to influence the General Election in favour of either a greater or a lesser K.A.D.U. victory'.[3] Having carefully influenced a series of elections from 1957 onwards, British colonial officials proved for one last time their adeptness at electoral management; Kenyatta was no doubt impressed.

Joining Kenyatta, MacDonald and Odinga at the forefront of the celebrations at the party was another of the architects of KANU's success. Tom Mboya, the youngest of the four men, was KANU's brilliant strategist. His talents were much needed: the arrangements for the celebration party would probably have stretched Odinga's organisational skills to the limit, and by the time he was released from detention, Kenyatta had ceased to have much interest in the machinery of politics. Like Odinga, Kenyatta after his release was an orator rather than an organiser. But Mboya was by no means an anonymous backroom operator. With the build of a middleweight and armed with a formidable intellect (and confidence to match), he earned his stripes in the bitter arena of trade union politics during the 1950s. Never a radical, he had taken advantage of the detention of militant trade union leaders during the Mau Mau rebellion to champion the cause of the poorly treated workers in the country's urban areas. 'An outstandingly modern man', as Mboya's biographer put it, he was as comfortable in front of a crowd of dock workers in Mombasa as in the offices of their employers or in the newsrooms of New York and London, where he performed a vital function as a spokesman for moderate nationalism.[4] Whereas Kenyatta represented KANU's ties to the longer struggle against colonialism that stretched back to the early 1920s, Mboya represented the younger generation of Kenyans. He and Odinga were uneasy bedfellows, but the two had done the most to launch and organise KANU, before stepping aside to allow Kenyatta to take up the mantle as its leader.

It was fitting that Kenyatta, MacDonald, Odinga and Mboya should lead the celebratory dancing at the party. Their disputes, their ideas and the constituencies and institutions they represented dominated the political landscape to varying degrees for a whole generation. And they had able assistants, too, who were the next to join the dance. Fred Kubai and Mwai Kibaki took their leaders' places with the dancers, while Achieng' Oneko dragged a reluctant Paul Ngei into the dancing. Tall, slim and clean-shaven, Oneko was normally a serious character. He was, unusually, close to both Kenyatta and Odinga. A keen political ally of Odinga, his nous and organisational skills were much needed by the more impulsive Odinga. Oneko had close personal ties to Kenyatta too. They had been in detention together throughout the 1950s, along with Kubai and Ngei, and Oneko had worked as Kenyatta's personal secretary after their release. Whereas Kenyatta came from a long tradition of constitutional protest against colonial rule, Oneko, Kubai and Ngei, together with the other leading detainees, such as Bildad Kaggia, were the strongmen of militant nationalism in the 1950s and were more forthright in their views about independence than the more conciliatory Kenyatta. Although, at the time of the Odinga party, Ngei was still outside KANU, he later joined and became a minister in the government. Oneko was already information minister, and Kibaki and Kubai were parliamentary secretaries.

Kibaki was the odd man out in this particular group of dancers. Though he hailed from one of Mau Mau's epicentres in Nyeri district, Kibaki had spent the 1950s pursuing his education rather than joining the insurgency. Trained as an economist at the London School of Economics, he gave up his academic post at Makerere to join KANU's leadership in 1960. He had much in common with Mboya, who managed the party's bureaucracy. Like his friend, Kibaki was stout in build and able in mind. The two men had clear ideas about how the economy of independent Kenya could be developed. But they were also ambitious figures who saw independence as presenting an opportunity for the younger figures within KANU's upper ranks to increase their influence at the expense of the old guard. As well as in the offices of KANU, in government departments and the parliamentary chamber, this overwhelmingly young, male group conducted the business of politics in the bars, clubs and casinos of the capital; Nairobi's social scene was decolonising as fast as its political institutions. Hotels, pubs and restaurants, previously reserved for Nairobi's white elite, became first the favourite haunts of figures like Kibaki and then, later, part of their property and investment portfolios.

Despite the celebratory mood (and the drinking and gambling that accompanied the politics of the time), Odinga's party remained sober. It was intended to be a powerful statement of KANU's unity and of the steely determination of the country's new leaders to be capable rulers of independent Kenya. Odinga's guests were impressed. 'The party was a huge success', the US diplomat present acknowledged.[5] With the benefit of hindsight, other guests came to be less sure. Among them was a young civil servant, Duncan Ndegwa. He was to rise to become the head of the civil service and, later, of the Central Bank of Kenya (CBK). Ndegwa reflects in his recently published memoirs that the only issue to unite KANU's leadership at independence was its opposition to colonialism. Terming this a 'transient unity', Ndegwa writes that, in the push for independence, Kenyatta, Odinga, Mboya and other leaders had no choice but to appear united, and so they 'temporarily buried their differences to eject an oppressive minority'.[6] Once attention shifted to governing, those divisions could not be hidden for much longer.

THE LIMITS OF UNITY

Ever since its formation in 1960, KANU had been divided along lines of ethnicity, personal ambition, regional interests and very different ideas on how the economy would be developed. Its glue was Kenyatta. 'To the vast majority of the African population Kenyatta was not only the paramount leader, but also the symbol and embodiment of their nationalism,' wrote George Bennett and Carl Rosberg in their study of the elections held just prior to Kenyatta's release.[7] He had built his reputation in the 1930s and 1940s through being the reconciler, and before his release KANU's leaders hoped the old man would provide the necessary cohesion to keep the party together. As Joseph Murumbi, who later served as vice president, argued in 1961: 'We need to exert all our efforts to get him out.' According to Murumbi, Kenyatta 'is the only person who can weld the different factions together and stop the serious split among ourselves'.[8] But age and detention had hardened Kenyatta, and, as the unquestioned leader of the nationalist movement, he was unwilling to make compromises.

While Kenyatta was a critical force in the efforts to push the British out of Kenya, the cause of building a coherent sense of a Kenyan nation was weakened by his own scepticism about the project. He thought ethnic unity to be the first priority of any Kenyan politician; only then could attention turn to building the nation. 'There is nothing wrong in bringing one's own people together,' Kenyatta said shortly before his release in 1961. 'One must put one's house in order before one can tell others to do so. I believe in the unity of all Africans, but tall buildings do not come from nowhere, they have to be built by laying one stone on top of another.'[9] He had good reason to doubt the structural integrity of his own Kikuyu community.

The original homeland of Kikuyu was up in the hills and amid the forests of the region around Mount Kenya and the Aberdare Mountains. Of all Kenya's many ethnic groups, Kikuyu had integrated best into the colonial economy, and this meant that they had spread across the colony and beyond. They worked as labourers on the vast farms owned by white settlers in the Highlands that stretched east to west from Nairobi to the Ugandan border. Kikuyu residents dominated Nairobi and joined migrants from other areas of the country working at the docks in Mombasa and in businesses around Kenya. Decades of labour migration thus created permanent populations of Kikuyu throughout the country. But one of the reasons for that outward expansion also threatened the integrity of Kikuyu ethnic unity: the overcrowded districts of Kikuyu settlement around Mount Kenya meant land there was a contentious issue. Significant inequalities in access to land lay at the heart of the Mau Mau rebellion of the 1950s, which quickly turned into a Kikuyu civil war, as supporters of the insurgency and their fellow Kikuyu opponents battled one another in the midst of a vicious British counter-insurgency campaign. To Kenyatta and others, it seemed as if the thousands of acres being vacated by departing European farmers in the 1960s were the ideal balm for the still painful wounds of the previous decade.

Kenyatta did not, however, envisage handing the farms over to Kikuyu. Although the landless population of Central Province and other parts of the country hoped the new government would redistribute the land on the basis of need, the prime minister thought otherwise. He claimed to be sympathetic to their demands. 'My only concern is the landless Africans,' remarked Kenyatta in 1961. 'We cannot ignore this problem and Government must do something to find them a place to live.' European farmers at first feared that this would entail the nationalisation or compulsory purchase of their property, but Kenyatta was no radical. 'I regard titles as a private property and they must be respected,' he promised, to the relief of the settler community. 'I would not like to feel that my *shamba* [smallholding] or house belongs to the Government. Titles must be respected and the right of the individual safeguarded.'[10] Land was, Kenyatta thought, to be paid for through the fruits of hard work and purchased by any aspiring African landowner; European owners were to be compensated at proper market values if they wished to sell, and none were to be compelled to leave independent Kenya. He explicitly ruled out the nationalisation of foreign-owned assets, including land, or the compulsory purchase of European-owned land. Kenyatta was not in any mood to provide quick settlement of the demands of the poor by seizing private assets and redistributing them to the needy. 'Nationalisation would not serve to advance African Socialism,' Kenyatta told his MPs in August 1964.[11]

In Kenya's agricultural economy, issues of land were central to the formation of development policy. Mboya was astute enough to realise that the challenge of nationhood was the challenge of development.[12] But he, Kenyatta and Odinga each had a different vision of what development meant. Kenyatta considered this to be a matter of individual endeavour and hard work. Together with foreign investment and protection of private property, these qualities would, he thought, deliver high economic growth. In turn, that growth would benefit and enrich Kenyan society as a whole, dragging the country out of poverty without the need for wholesale redistribution of wealth from the richest to the poorest. Mboya also believed in a growth-led economic model, but differed from Kenyatta in thinking that a profound redistribution of wealth would eventually be necessary. Odinga thought that resources should be redistributed immediately for the benefit of the poorest in society. He urged the government to redistribute European-owned land to landless peasants without delay.

Odinga's concern with the fate of landless peasants was not an issue of ethnic unity, as it was for Kenyatta. Odinga was Luo and had been born at Bondo, some sixty kilometres west of Kisumu and close to the shores of Lake Victoria. Like Kikuyu, Luo had been active participants in the colonial labour market. The proximity of the Ugandan border meant that many had taken up residence in Kampala, the final stop on the railway built by the British at the beginning of the century to connect the hoped-for untapped wealth of Central Africa with imperial shipping lanes at Mombasa. The docks at Mombasa were another popular destination for Luo seeking work.

Mboya knew all too well about the experience of Luo migrants in Mombasa and elsewhere. He himself had been born into just such a family, at their home close to the settler town of Thika, in present-day Eastern Province. The fertile fields of Thika and the far more arid and hot open plains and hilly outcrops running east towards the Indian Ocean that make up much of Eastern Province provided an important source of support for Mboya throughout his political career. His Luo roots and ties through his parents to South Nyanza and the area centred on Rusinga Island meant that Mboya contested leadership of his ethnic community with Odinga.

To both Odinga and Mboya, Kenyatta's ideas for the future of independent Kenya were controversial. His prioritisation of ethnic over national unity, his determination to respect private land titles, and his desire to introduce a development policy based on individual initiative rather than on state assistance were all moot. Again, as the development disputes indicate, his often dogmatic views provoked discontent within KANU. But Kenyatta equated unity with obedience; he had little time for dissent. His fellow leaders in KANU should, he thought, give him their unequivocal backing or else face the consequences. He had no time at all for those outside the party. 'I am sure for national affairs one party would be the best answer for the unity of Africans,' he is reported to have said.[13] But at independence Kenya had not one but two nationalist parties.

In its final years of colonial rule Kenya 'was a land of commotion'.[14] As elsewhere in the colonial world, there was an upsurge in political activity among Kenya's African population after the Second World War. Workers were fed up with low wages and poor housing in the towns and cities. New colonial development projects angered rural communities that were already unnerved by social changes brought about by increasing pressures on the land and other trends, such as urbanisation. Labourers on European-owned farms were caught up in waves of expulsions, as the farmers sought to mechanise their operations and push their employees off valuable tracts of land previously used to house them. With the colonial government unwilling to tolerate the mass participation of Africans in formal political parties, these grievances manifested themselves in different ways. In cities, militant trade unionism grew in strength. In some rural areas, religious sects emerged as a vehicle of political discontent. And among the Kikuyu population of Central Province, the poor neighbourhoods of Eastern Nairobi and the labour force of the white-owned farms, the Mau Mau insurgency exploded in 1952.

Restrictions on African political action began to be eased as part of the first steps towards decolonisation in the late 1950s, but colony-wide political parties were still outlawed. Instead, parties were permitted so long as they operated only in one of the colony's many districts. In many cases, this geographical constraint lent late-colonial era politics a particular flavour, in which local interests were prioritised over national agendas. With the relaxation of political restrictions and the legalisation of Kenya-wide parties, KADU was formed in 1960 as an amalgamation of many of the local parties.

The party's first president was Ronald Ngala, the most prominent political leader from Coast Province. Although small in stature, he was a determined protector of the claims of his Mijikenda peoples to control the resources of the area. The Mijikenda community was made up of several smaller groups dotted along the Indian Ocean coastline. Collectively they thought of themselves as the indigenous population of the region. The era of nationalism encouraged Mijikenda to assert that their indigeneity entitled them to determine Coast's political and economic future. They were, in the words of one local politician writing a decade later, 'struggling to assert their identity as an indigenous people of Kenya, who should be accorded first priority at the coast'.[15]

Ngala hoped that this future would include significant autonomy for Coast. But this determination clashed with the views of Coast's other great political bloc, Arabs, who thought that centuries of their economic pre-eminence – and a long history of Coast's integration into the wider Indian Ocean world – meant the region should look to the island of Zanzibar and its sultan for its political future. The Arab-led movement for secession imagined a future for the narrow, sultry coastal strip wedged between the arid interior and the ocean as separate from the rest of Kenya. Ngala's Mijikenda were also concerned about a future dominated by KANU, which they feared would mean an increase in migration from other parts of the country and competition for resources such as land. Ngala understood independence for the Coast to mean not just freedom from the British, but also an end to Arab domination and the chance to set development policy at the local level, rather than at the KANU-dominated centre.

Ngala was joined in KADU by politicians from other communities who also felt that their rights to land would likely be jeopardised by independence under KANU rule. These were communities that feared 'that if they did not establish their identity as an indigenous people once and for all, they might not be treated well when a new African government came to power'.[16] Ngala, therefore, presided over a party that was, in David Anderson's words, 'defensive in character and born out of fear'.[17] The most prominent of Ngala's colleagues was Daniel Arap Moi. A teacher by training, Moi entered politics when he was appointed to the colonial legislative council in 1955. Though this tie to the colonial regime destroyed the careers of his fellow African representatives as nationalism gathered pace towards the end of the 1950s, Moi survived. A Tugen, one of the many smaller ethnic groups that, since 1945, had steadily amalgamated with the larger Kalenjin community, Moi hailed from Baringo in the Rift Valley. He and many of his fellow Kalenjin hoped that independence would see the farms of the White Highlands pass to the groups that considered themselves to be the rightful occupiers of the Rift Valley.

Moi, other Kalenjin leaders and their Maasai counterparts feared that the migratory Kikuyu and Luo would exploit the political dominance of KANU to take over the land left vacant when the settler farmers left. A meeting of the Nandi District Independent Party resolved in 1959 that: 'The land once occupied by our fathers and mothers and now is in the hands of the foreigners should be handed back to the Nandi people.'[18] The leaders of the Nandi, the largest component of the Kalenjin, hoped to enjoy control over the fertile and open land that had supported the dairy herds and profitable crops of the white farmers and had formed the backbone of the colonial economy.

KADU hoped that control over the future of land ownership in the Rift Valley and at the Coast would be achieved through a sustained programme of devolution. The idea was a simple one. Independent Kenya would be a federation, modelled along the lines of Switzerland or the United States. The colonial-era provinces would become semi-autonomous regions, with their own parliaments and presidents. The powers of central government would be weakened, and control of resources such as land would be vested in the regional assemblies. KADU called for an independence constitution that recognised 'the integrity of their lands in the hands of the various peoples of Kenya, and their right to allocate their land to whom they wish'.[19] The policy became known as 'majimboism' after the Swahili word for region. According to John Konchellah, one of KADU's leaders: 'Majimbo means that the lands that we now have will be controlled by us, and that when Majimbo was introduced all the injustices of the past would be rectified and that the land which would be in our possession would never again be taken away from us.'[20] With the plan of KADU and the liberal settlers' party, the New Kenya Group, being backed by both the Colonial Office and the administration in Nairobi, discussion of a federal arrangement became a central point of discussion during constitutional negotiations held in London during 1961 and 1962.

KANU bitterly contested the emphasis given to regionalism during talks with the British, thinking it a policy designed to limit the power of the central government that it would almost certainly control. Its leaders backed away from attempting to win the argument around the negotiating table in London, however. The KANU delegation to the London talks in 1962 agreed, in Odinga's words, 'to accept a constitution we did not want', on the understanding that 'once we had the government we could change the constitution'.[21] The independence constitution was, then, the party's leadership told American diplomats, 'a temporary document only'.[22] Kenyatta was determined to see devolution destroyed. In an address to a KANU rally in Nairobi, he asked:

> For more than forty years now, I have been telling the Imperialist that we must rule ourselves, but he refuses; and we have been struggling with him like a man fighting a lion, and just when we have overpowered him, would you like somebody else to tell us to split our country into pieces?'[23]

After taking office following the May 1963 election, KANU therefore set about dismantling the devolved constitution agreed with KADU.

This was a fraught process. Local authorities sought to exploit the powers given to them by the independence constitution before the KANU government was able to pass amendments through parliament. Across the country, communities that had deep historical connections to places outside their supposed home regions were uprooted in the name of devolution. Notions of ethnic ownership of land were most fraught on the boundaries of the new regions. At Timau, close to the new boundary between the Central and Eastern Regions on Mount Kenya's northern slopes, Kikuyu made up three-quarters of the population, and many had spent their whole lives there. Nevertheless, by April 1964, they were being forced from their homes. As the local councillor reported, 'their houses are being burnt', and the Kikuyu residents 'removed in a very bad manner from this Division' by eager Meru officials.[24] 'Go back to your original district as no other people other than Tugen will be settled in the Sabatia Settlement Scheme,' a local official in South Baringo wrote, as he ordered the eviction of non-Tugens at Kilombe near Eldama Ravine the day after independence.[25] Luos based in Nairobi warned Kenyatta that 'there will be another Congo' should land in eastern Nyanza be granted to non-Luos.[26] After violence in Bungoma over whether or not that district would be governed by the Western or the Rift Valley regional assembly, Luhya leaders denounced the 'uncivilised tribes of Kalenjins'[27] and warned of a coming 'civil war'.[28] Bungoma remained within the Western Region and Kitale was eventually secured for the Rift Valley. Around the country, the upsurge of ethnicity, triggered in response to decolonisation and intensified by the debates of majimboism, turned violent in the months leading up to and following independence.

'I hope you will have to finish Majimbo before it spoils our Kenya', wrote Samuel Ole Kimelonganai, a representative of Maasai living in Eldoret, in a letter to Kenyatta in September 1963.[29] He need not have worried. Once full independence was achieved, Kenyatta was able to enforce his centralised vision of the constitution. His strategy to destroy the regional assemblies and force the collapse of the constitution was simple. While waiting for the legislation revoking devolution to pass through parliament, Kenyatta starved the regional assemblies of the revenues they needed to operate. By July 1964, the bank accounts of the regional assemblies were empty. 'This region has virtually no revenue,' the civil secretary in North Eastern Province wrote.[30] KADU's leadership recognised the strength of Kenyatta's position and, one by one, sought accommodation with the government. Finally, in late November 1964, KADU agreed to merge with KANU ahead of implementation of constitutional amendments that made Kenya a republic, Kenyatta a president, and the country a highly centralised one-party state.

REDISTRIBUTION, RECOGNITION AND THE IDEOLOGY OF ORDER

Prior to independence, Tom Mboya dismissed the dispute over devolution as the mere 'birth-pangs of a nation'.[31] He was wrong. Although KADU was fatally wounded by the time of independence in December 1963, the arguments underlying its battle with KANU have remained at the heart of Kenyan politics ever since. In their study of the assassination of the then foreign minister, Robert Ouko, in 1990, David William Cohen and E.S. Atieno Odhiambo highlight the significance to Kenyan history of the relationship between redistribution and recognition.[32] The terms 'redistribution' and 'recognition' are (at any rate in relation to one another) those of Nancy Fraser, an American theorist and philosopher. Fraser argues that, in the post-Cold War world, debates about redistribution have been replaced by what might more crudely be termed 'identity politics'. In her words, 'group identity supplants class interest as the chief medium of political mobilization'. Moreover, the demand for recognition of the grievances of an identity group, such as an ethnic community, 'displaces socioeconomic redistribution as the remedy for injustice and the goal of political struggle'.[33] According to Bethwell Ogot, the country's best-known historian, the decline of the left in global politics and the rise of neoliberalism witnessed in Kenya and elsewhere mean that the aim of redistribution under the banner of 'African Socialism' is dead.[34]

In this book, we will see how Kenya's leaders have encouraged political debate to centre on recognition rather than on redistribution. Mugo Gatheru, a historian, wrote at the time of independence how he hoped that the 'future Kenya nation' would be one 'in which tribalism has become only a historic memory and tribes mere ceremonial units'.[35] That hope has proved forlorn. Elites have encouraged Kenyans to think and act politically in a manner informed first and foremost by ethnicity, in order to crush demands for the redistribution of scarce resources. Initially, however, KANU represented itself as the party of redistribution. A few months after independence, Kibaki circulated a paper among various leading figures within the ruling party discussing future development policies. The critical question facing the new KANU government was, according to him, 'Will the elite which has inherited power from the colonialists use that power to bring about the necessary social and economic changes or will they succumb to the lure of wealth, comfort and status and thereby become part of the Old Establishment?'[36] Kenyatta's intolerance of redistribution meant this was pure rhetoric, but it was powerful nonetheless.

Despite Kibaki's initial promotion of redistribution, under the three presidents – Kenyatta (1963–78), Moi (1978–2002) and Kibaki himself (2002–present) – the political elite have chosen to become members of the Old Establishment. However, the need for redistribution has only grown stronger. Over the past half-century, so John Iliffe argues, sub-Saharan Africa has witnessed perhaps the fastest growth in population in human history.[37] The chief driving force for this increase lay in modern medicine's reduction of infant and child mortality. Kenya's population witnessed one of the most dramatic of changes. There were approximately 4 million Kenyans in 1950, but there are 40 million today. While the origins of the population boom lay in the period immediately after the Second World War, the first of the baby boomers did not reach adulthood and political engagement until independence in 1963. The story of Kenyan politics after independence is, then, the story of politics in a time of demographic explosion.

The results of the population boom are apparent to any visitor to Kenya. While the country is associated in the imagination of many foreigners with wide open plains, the reality of crowded towns and cities can come as a shock to the uninitiated. In the most fertile areas of the country, even rural communities can feel packed to bursting point. The most obvious outcome is competition over resources, such as land, jobs or public funding for development projects. But demographic change has also created two distinct strands of political debate.

The first of these strands is that of protest by youths and the poor. Kenya's burgeoning population swelled the ranks of the disaffected, the unemployed and the poor. By virtue of increased competition for jobs and land, many Kenyans who reached adolescence in the period after independence have found that they have been denied not just resources and dignity in the present, but also any reasonable expectation of prosperity and comfort in the future. With neither jobs nor access to land, the ever-growing number of jobless primary and secondary school graduates are reliant on their ingenuity and luck to make their way in the world. The informal sector of the economy offers many their only hope of subsistence. Their anger has been witnessed on a number of occasions since 1963, and has been channelled by political leaders seeking support for other objectives. However, the need on the part of elites to restrain protests by the dispossessed has fed into the increased importance attached to ethnicity within politics. The anger of the youth has been redirected by political elites towards supposed ethnic opponents. The demographic realities of contemporary Kenya have also consolidated conservatism as a major bloc within political debate. Those that have resources seek to protect their hold on them and to prevent any competition for land, jobs, housing and development funds.

Throughout the research and writing of this book, one of the aims has been to put some flesh on an idea first sketched out more than two decades ago. In 1987, with post-colonial political repression at a peak, the late and great Kenyan historian E.S. Atieno Odhiambo described what he termed 'the ideology of order'. Kenya's leaders, he argued, have consistently held up order and stability as necessary for economic growth and development. That fetishisation of order has been used to discredit those who dissent from the state's development policies, and to allow the state to violate its citizens' human rights.[38] That argument remains important and relevant.

Kenyans and their leaders have often represented the history of the country since independence as being characterised by peace and stability. In their efforts to depict Kenya in such terms, political leaders have played on the images of political, economic and humanitarian disaster elsewhere in the Horn of Africa and the Great Lakes region. At times this use of comparisons has been breathtaking in its hypocrisy. Proposing the motion in parliament for the constitutional amendments that made Kenya a formal one-party state in June 1982, the then minister for constitutional affairs, Charles Njonjo, stated: 'We Kenyans are happy we are making the change here in the house because Kenya believes in democracy.' 'Where in Africa', he asked, 'is an election held every five years? Nowhere.'[39] Njonjo offered Kenyans a vision of the country as an oasis of stability – a country governed by law and order – even as he snatched their basic rights away from them.

These representations have proved remarkably strong outside the country, too, as Kofi Annan showed when he arrived in Nairobi to chair peace talks during the violence that followed the 2007 elections. 'What was in my head was that we can't let this happen to Kenya!' Annan later told the journalist Roger Cohen. 'We'd seen a lot of destruction in the region – Rwanda, Somalia, Sudan, Darfur – and Kenya had been the safe haven for refugees. And suddenly Kenya itself was going!'[40] Similar attitudes were frequently expressed by Kenyans themselves during the violence of early 2008. The violence was often, although not always, depicted as a surprise, an aberration or a specific event tied to the rigging of the election, rather than as the latest episode in a much longer history of political violence.

ARCHIVES OF REPRESSION

This book makes a strong argument for viewing the violence after the most recent general election as part of that deeper history. It is intended to be accessible to the general, non-specialist reader. As such, references to secondary sources and theoretical discussions have been kept to a minimum; an extensive bibliography is provided as some compensation. Nevertheless, much of the analysis owes a great deal to other writers working on broader African politics. The authors most important to the interpretations here are Robert Bates, Jean-François Bayart, Frederick Cooper, Stephen Ellis, Jeffrey Herbst and Paul Nugent. An even greater intellectual debt is owed to the many social scientists carrying out research specifically on Kenya. The parsimonious referencing does no justice to the late E.S. Atieno Odhiambo, David Anderson, Bruce Berman, Nic Cheeseman, David William Cohen, Angelique Haugerud, Jacqueline Klopp, John Lonsdale, Gabrielle Lynch, Susanne Mueller, Godwin Murunga and David Throup. Readers interested in more analytical and detailed accounts of the events described below, or indeed alternative interpretations of them, can do no better than seek out the work of these fine scholars.

The primary sources that are used to construct the arguments are drawn overwhelmingly from what the Italian historian Carlo Ginzburg calls the 'archives of repression'.[41] The first half of the book makes much use of diplomatic sources. Reliant upon a small group of informants, sometimes prone to idle gossip, and always written with one eye on the overarching strategic aims of the foreign government concerned, such sources are far from unproblematic. The letters, telegrams and memoranda by diplomats focus on particular themes, such as corruption, personalities at the heart of government and major scandals. But more comprehensive state-level archival records, particularly after 1978, simply do not exist in Kenya or, if they do, are not easily accessible to researchers. Coupled with an understandable reticence on the part of actors involved in some of the most controversial events described below, this absence of material in Nairobi means that the diplomatic records held in Washington and London are the closest thing to a post-colonial archive that exists.

The second half of the book relies a great deal on material produced by non-governmental civil society organisations. Again, these sources should be treated with care. Civil society organisations, such as church groups and organisations of dissident exiles, were active researchers of abuses of political power in the 1980s and 1990s, but also advocates for change. This political agenda necessarily influenced their analysis and description of events in Kenya during this time. But the extent of their reach and their courage in bringing their findings to public attention were unequalled at the time. Again, the strengths of such material far outweigh its limitations.

These sources reveal one of the most interesting aspects of post-colonial political life. The corruption and violence described here has sat alongside frank and open public debate about these features of politics. Through parliamentary inquiries, judicial commissions, a relatively open press, church sermons and everyday discussion, the events that form the backbone of this book also dominated public debate at the time. And yet the ability of the ruling elites to behave in such a fashion remained unchecked. Explaining this dual experience of democracy and authoritarianism is difficult, but is probably best understood through the idea of a 'culture of impunity'. That term has been recycled endlessly over the past few years by human rights activists pushing for an overhaul of law and order and a sustained programme of constitutional reform. What the culture of impunity meant in practice was that the government's control over the police, judiciary and electoral system ensured that there was no possibility of punishment for major crimes, even if they attracted considerable attention and censure in the press. The constitution ratified in 2010 is meant to address these matters, but it is too early to assess whether or not it will achieve its aim.

The biases and tone of the archival records used are, to a certain extent, repeated here. They concentrate on the formal institutions of politics dominated by the adult men who controlled them, rather than the other men, the women and the children subject to them; the silences in those archives are echoed here. The archival material consulted necessarily drove the focus of the book towards Kenya's elites. It is therefore guilty of the charges the writer Binyavanga Wainaina makes of contemporary Kenyan journalism: 'Our media is obsessed with the soap opera of political characters. So Kenya is really just a theatre-screen where we watch a few people play drama games on stage, and clap, or cry or laugh.'[42] This is, for the most part, an account of the actions of a handful of individuals out of the tens of millions of Kenyans who have lived their lives since independence.

There is, however, a good intellectual argument for this focus on those in power and on the institutions they controlled. It is a book about statecraft and governance, and so, like most other studies of sub-Saharan African countries after independence, it is about the crisis of the post-colonial state that has been witnessed over the past five decades or so. Elites that have controlled the Kenyan state over that period must therefore be prioritised, since it was their actions, as Robert Bates argues, that delegitimised the state in the eyes of its citizens. Rather than using their control of institutions like parliament, the presidency or the judiciary to protect Kenyans and their livelihoods, elites in power have tended to use their power to seize resources, of which the most important has been land. The *symptoms* of this crisis, including ethnic division and political violence, are all too often confused with its *cause*.[43]

At various times, different groups of Kenyans have questioned for whose benefit the state operates and why they should interact with its institutions. These questions at first related to ideas of independence and sovereignty. Britain's lingering influence in Kenya's affairs and the significant role its citizens and people of South Asian descent played in the post-colonial economy were matters of great concern in the 1960s. However, the legitimacy of the state was protected during this time by its ability to deliver development to the people. This was in large part due to a favourable global economy, which saw revenues from exports bolster the public purse and therefore investment in infrastructure, agricultural improvements, healthcare and education. Once that prevailing economic climate changed for the worse, development became less prevalent and the very purpose of the state was called into question.

Rather than political power being based on contests over a strong or legitimate state, it has instead derived from control over the intersection between Kenya and the outside world. At independence, power was about mediating the relationship between Kenya and its wealthier Western allies, Britain and the US. More recently, this relationship has been as much between Kenya and private foreign investors and donors of development funds as between Kenya and foreign states. This is what Frederick Cooper calls 'the gatekeeper state'.[44] A good deal of politics in post-colonial Kenya has been about elites jostling with one another to be the gatekeepers, while at the same time trying to mobilise enough support from below to sustain their position in power.

FREEDOM

Kenyans hoped for so much more at independence. Independence Day, 12 December 1963, was one of the precious few moments of authentic unity in this complex and diverse country. Across it, every town and village marked the event with its own celebrations. Canoe races were held on Lake Victoria. At Likoni, south of Mombasa, fire-works and a marching band greeted the birth of an independent Kenya. Just before midnight on the night of 11–12 December, the lights at Nairobi's Uhuru ('Independence') Gardens were dimmed. As the final bars of the British national anthem echoed around the arena, the Union flag was lowered. A minute later, accompanied by the new Kenyan anthem and an outpouring of joy by the quarter of a million onlookers, the flag of the infant nation-state was raised. With its black third symbolising the people of Kenya; its red third the blood lost in the struggle for freedom; and its green third the country's abundant agricultural resources; with the white trim for unity and peace, and the shield portraying the country's determination to defend its hard-won freedom, the new national flag was laden with meaning for local and foreign observers alike.

From North Vietnam's diplomatic mission in Cairo came an expression of 'the great sympathy and admiration with which the people of Vietnam and the Government of the Democratic Republic of Vietnam have been following the liberation struggle of the Kenyan people under their great leader Jomo Kenyatta. The news of independence of Kenya has brought great enthusiasm.'[45] The difficult path to Kenyan independence gained the country enormous goodwill among the citizens of other new nations. The secretary of the Kulasekharapuram community centre in southern India wrote of how the centre's members had 'read with great interest the long struggle in which you and your people were involved under the able leadership of Mr Jomo Kenyatta against British imperialism and white monarchy'. 'On this happy occasion of Kenya's attainment of Independence', the letter continued, 'I wish to extend on behalf of myself and members of our glittering galaxy, congratulations and Best wishes for the progress and welfare of the Government and people of Kenya.'[46] To foreign well-wishers, Kenyan independence was reason for reflection on how much the world had changed since the end of the Second World War. To Kenyans, independence promised not just the opportunity to rule themselves, but also future prosperity and social justice.

CHAPTER ONE

FREEDOM AND SUFFERING, 1963–69

The tree of *Uhuru* planted by Mzee Jomo Kenyatta and watered by blood, sweat, toil and tears is now fully grown. I am sure I am speaking for the whole country when I say that we all derive great comfort from knowing that we enter the next phase of our history united under the leadership, guidance, and great wisdom of Mzee Jomo Kenyatta.

Oginga Odinga during the unveiling of a statue of Kenyatta at the
Lumumba Institute in Nairobi, 14 December 1964[1]

PULL TOGETHER

Colonel Pink was proud of Lamu's independence celebrations. Having brought his military background to bear as the finance officer for the committee charged by the local authority with organising the ceremonies, the owner of Petley's Hotel in Lamu town was sure the events would surpass those of many larger towns in Kenya. Distance from the capital Nairobi was to be no object. The population of the small island off the north-eastern coast participated in the independence celebrations as fully as other citizens of the new nation. Over 11 and 12 December 1963, Lamu's people enjoyed a football match, a fancy dress competition and, at the moment of independence itself, fireworks. Food was donated to the needy residents of Lamu's hospitals, sweets were handed out to the town's children, and on the water sailing races were held. But most of all, Pink was pleased with the bunting and fairy lights that adorned the waterfront. This was no mean achievement, since the town lacked mains electricity: a local businessman had generously provided a generator so that the quayside could be illuminated for the festivities.

The secret to Lamu's successful Uhuru celebrations, Pink wrote, 'is just one word "Harambee". Men and women of all races have worked harmoniously together, under the wise guidance of the Regional Government Agent and his staff, to make, it is hoped, the occasion truly a memorable one.'[2] Lamu at independence seemed to embody the new Kenya – a multi-racial nation intent on overcoming historical divisions by following Jomo Kenyatta's credo of *Harambee* – 'pull together'.

Despite their celebrations, the everyday lives of Lamu's citizens did not easily fit into the new era of nation-states, bureaucracies and international borders. The island was part of trading and social networks much older than any notions of belonging to the new Kenyan nation. Many people in Lamu, and elsewhere in the country, were unwilling to adjust those networks to fit into the framework of the new nation, or to surrender control of the movement of goods and people to the post-colonial state. Much of the population of the Horn of Africa had spent the preceding decades practising what one anthropologist and political scientist, James Scott, calls 'the art of not being governed'; moving around sparsely populated and scantly governed borderlands in order to escape state control and influence.[3]

Shariff Seyyid Ali Baskuti was typical of many of the residents of northern Kenya. Born on a small island off Kismayu in Somalia, he moved to Lamu as a child in 1939. By the mid-1960s, he was earning a living with his motorboat, transporting produce and consumer products and ferrying passengers between Lamu and Kismayu. According to Lamu's district commissioner (DC), Shariff carried out more secretive journeys, too: 'He is a ruthless spy and the enemy of the state.' The DC thought Shariff 'deserves removal or repatriation to his

Somalia'.[4] He sent lists of the names of government officials in Lamu district to insurgents known as *shifta* ('bandits') who had taken up arms against the government in Nairobi in the weeks leading up to Kenyan independence. The insurgency lasted for four years, during which time, the DC alleged, Shariff passed orders from its leaders in Kismayu to the fighters, while transporting rebels and their food supplies around the coastal areas of northern Kenya and southern Somalia. Like a great many other people in north-eastern parts of the country, Shariff was dubious about the state-building project that accompanied independence. If he felt a sense of national affinity, moreover, it was to Somalia rather than to Kenya. One (or both) of these sentiments drove Shariff, and thousands like him, to join the shifta insurgents in fighting for the absorption of much of Kenya's north-east into Somalia.

Many of those who joined the insurgency against the Kenyan state paid a heavy price. Nearly 2,000 people identified by the Kenyan authorities as being shifta were killed during the low-intensity war that lasted until 1967. Kenyatta shed no tears for those killed. At first he tried to claim that the insurgents were not even Kenyans at all. They were, he said, nothing other than Somali citizens sent by the government in Mogadishu to cause havoc and to advance its claims on Kenyan territory. 'I must see one of the raiders alive, or, if not alive, dead to be able to tell the Somalia Government that this [is] one of their people,' demanded the prime minister.[5] But Kenyatta was fooling himself if he believed his own words. Although the insurgents were supplied from Mogadishu, they were in fact overwhelmingly inhabitants of Kenya. And it was not just Somalis who took up arms. Small numbers of Turkana and members of other ethnic communities in northern Kenya also joined the fight. They were concerned not about issues of sovereignty, but about their fear of statecraft that would restrict movement and impose an unprecedented level of state regulation on their daily lives.

The insurgents were resisting processes taking place across the world as the era of European imperialism came to an end. Decolonisation everywhere opened up debates about sovereignty, citizenship and identity. The new nations of the post-colonial world were but one way in which these different ideas were expressed. Frederick Cooper, the foremost historian of African decolonisation, writes that 'the "imagined communities" Africans saw were both smaller and larger than the nation'.[6] In Kenya, KADU represented an appeal to the smaller communities of ethnicity. Ideas of belonging to larger communities proved more perishable but were in wide circulation at the time of independence. Many proud Kenyan nationalists boasted of belonging to a global Pan-Africanist community, or saw Kenyan, Ugandan and Tanzanian independence as a stepping stone on the way to the formation of an East African Federation.

Kenya's many non-African citizens had their larger communities, too. Networks of trade and family connected the country's South Asian population with a global diaspora. Some Kenyan nationalists hostile to the presence of South Asians after independence argued that such connections contradicted notions of nationhood and citizenship. The place of South Asians within Kenyan ideas of the nation has, therefore, been a recurring source of sometimes bitter debate in the post-colonial period. Fearing forced exile – an anxiety occasionally realised – and the nationalisation of their assets, 30,000 of Kenya's 170,000 or so Asians left the country in the years following independence. Arabs at the coast were similarly conscious of their ties to kin elsewhere in the western Indian Ocean littoral. At the outbreak of the 1967 Six Day War in the Middle East, Arabs in Lamu rushed to the shops to buy radios to listen to news of the conflict, while 'others wanted to enlist as fighters and others wanted to collect money in order to help their brothers in the Middle East'.[7] And while some Kenyans saw themselves as belonging to several different communities all at the same time, a great many residents of the new Kenyan nation-state did not see themselves as Kenyan at all.

SHIFTA

The new nation's internal boundaries and the distribution of power between centre and regions were settled more quickly than many had dared hope in 1963. Fears of widespread mass violence over the issue of devolution proved unfounded. But Kenyatta's government was far less successful in resolving the contest over the fate of the new North Eastern Region and northern parts of Coast and Eastern Regions. As Duncan Ndegwa writes in his memoirs, to those in power it seemed as if 'the challenge was in the north'.[8] Somalis could not be easily ignored. Despite amounting to just 1 per cent of the 8 million or so Kenyans at independence, they inhabited an area that amounted to a fifth of Kenya's total territory. The new government in Nairobi was unwilling to surrender this land to the Somali state, and so, over the next four years, the Kenyan security forces tried to bring the rebels to heel.

The experience of colonial rule had provided Somalis in the north with little reason to trust government officials or to feel affection towards the entity of Kenya. Under British rule, the arid north was peripheral to colonial interests and suffered neglect. Colonial officials were content to maintain order and expended little effort in terms of development. Somalis in northern parts of Kenya did, however, feel a pull towards the neighbouring independent state of Somalia and the notion of a Greater Somalia. Greater Somalia offered ethnic Somalis dispersed across the modern states of Ethiopia, Kenya, Djibouti and, of course, Somalia the promise that they would be brought together under one flag. The idea had first been developed at the turn of the century by a British colonial official, and then resurrected by the British foreign secretary, Ernest Bevin, after the Second World War on the grounds of economic expediency.[9]

The idea of Somali unification nonetheless gathered pace among Somalis themselves in the years that followed Bevin's statement. British and Italian Somaliland unified under the flag of the Somali Republic at independence in 1960, and it was hoped that Somalis in French Somaliland, now Djibouti, would join them. Later that year, the Northern Province People's Progressive Party (NPPPP) was formed in northern Kenya with the express aim of promoting secession from the British colony. The NPPPP proved popular, winning the support of the overwhelming majority of Somalis in northern Kenya during elections held in 1961. Leaders of Kenyan Somalis writing in March 1962 were unequivocal in their belief that they 'are members of a single Somali nation'.[10] The nationalist leaders in Nairobi were unmoved by such statements, however.

Neither KANU nor KADU was willing to negotiate the territorial integrity of Kenya. In support of their position they could point to an agreement by the regional grouping, the Organisation of African Unity (OAU), which, in order to avoid bloodshed of the sort seen in the Congo, ruled out the adjustment of colonial boundaries by independent states. Kenya's nationalist leaders had their own reasons for wanting to hold on to northern parts of the country. As the US consul in Nairobi reported in May 1963, 'Oil hopes play a role.'[11] Those hopes have not yet been realised, though exploration continues to this day. But, as the British parliamentarian and former colonial administrator in northern Kenya, Lord Lytton, remarked in 1963, 'the quarrel is not about oil'.[12] For KANU, refusal to discuss autonomy for the north was consistent with the centralist policies that also dictated its attitude towards devolution. Autonomy for the Rift Valley would have been much harder to resist had North Eastern Province been granted some form of self-rule. And the Rift Valley and the lands to be vacated by the European settler farmers were the real prize of independence, not the north.

KANU therefore remained belligerent in its opposition to Somali secession. 'We in Kenya shall not give up even one inch of our country to the Somali tribalists, and that is final,' a KANU delegation led by Odinga to the OAU stated in 1963.[13] Although a British-commissioned inquiry into attitudes in northern Kenya found great support for secession, KANU's position won the day.[14] During the negotiations with the Kenyan nationalist delegations in London, the British government accepted KANU's stance on the Somali question as part of a range of compromises made in order to guarantee protection for the settler farmers after independence.

The NPPPP and the Somali government were outraged by continuing Kenyan rule over the north after independence. In an effort to stifle the growing protests, the colonial government arrested three of the NPPPP's leaders and restricted them to remote areas of the country in March and May 1963. Later in the year, Degho Maalim

Stamboul, the party's general secretary, was also arrested. Stamboul's father, Chief Maalim Mohamed Stamboul, was later accused of organising the insurgency in North Eastern Province. When it took power in June, KANU was determined not to surrender its prize. But calls for secession only increased. In a telegram to the colonial secretary in London, the Moyale branch of the NPPPP described the prospect of rule by an independent Kenya as a 'new form of imperialism. We demand immediate secession.'[15] Telegrams and protests soon gave way to insurgency.

The insurgency was given some support by Somalia. 'We speak the same languages', said Somali Prime Minister Abdirashid Ali Shermarke in 1962. 'We share the same creed, the same culture and the same traditions. How can we regard our brothers as foreigners?'[16] Shifta fighters in Kenya were therefore given limited supplies of small arms, drawn from Somalia's ample supply obtained through its close relations with the USSR. Over the four years of conflict, shifta units used those firearms to launch isolated attacks on the Kenyan armed forces, police officers and administration officials. The small raid on the Garba Tula police post on the night of 10 February 1964 is an example of the sort of engagements that made up the Shifta War. At Garba Tula, 'a Shifta gang fired shots from close range', and 'the police returned fire in an engagement lasting about an hour but there were no known casualties on either side'. The shifta unit fled the scene after the firefight, taking with it over a hundred camels that had been stolen from herdsmen in the area.[17] The war followed this pattern of sporadic fighting between small groups of soldiers and police, on one side, and small shifta units, on the other.

Both sides frequently suffered casualties in these isolated incidents, and it was a dirty war as well as a small one. Complaints of atrocities committed against innocent civilians were common. On 6 May 1966, Gerishom Majani, the district officer (DO) in Garba Tula, was visited by a delegation led by a local sub-chief, part of the local government structure, who alleged that Kenyan soldiers had killed three people in a homestead at Kulamawe, near Garba Tula. Majani visited the homestead and found that three people, including a seven-year-old girl, had been killed. Bullet casings from standard-issue Kenyan army rifles littered the floor of the compound.[18] Shifta fighters were not necessarily much more popular, however. Having been forced to feed a group of insurgents that passed through his homestead at Kubi Turkkana in March 1965, Eketoei Ngalup later recalled how 'four of the Shifta came to me to take the cattle from my herd. I helped them to take out nine fat heads . . . I was warned not to say anything, and if I did I would be killed by the Shifta.'[19] According to one of Ngalup's neighbours, 'This threat is repeated to us very often and especially when such gang comes in.'[20] With only sporadic supplies from Somalia reaching the fighters, they eked out a desperate existence and were forced to live off the land as they crisscrossed the border region of the two countries.

Measures enforced by local administrators and security officers did little to win over support from Somalis. Areas of the province where shifta units were thought to be active were declared prohibited zones, where anyone found was to be arrested and where communal fines were issued to entire villages when shifta activity in the vicinity went unreported to the authorities. Another tactic borrowed from the colonial period was the forced settlement of Somalis into newly constructed villages built around police posts. By 1967, about 10 per cent of the population of North Eastern Province and the northern districts of neighbouring Eastern Province had been 'villagised', to use the parlance beloved of counter-insurgency specialists. Local administrators told Somalis in North Eastern Province that the new villages were meant to help their community 'abandon nomadic life and help people so that they can be kept to their own village having social amenities like schools, health services and protection'.[21] In truth, the government admitted, the purpose of this displacement of the Somali population was the 'elimination of shifta activities'.[22] By denying shifta units easy access to food supplies and intelligence, and by keeping local populations under surveillance, the government hoped the new villages would break the back of the insurgency. In the long term, the Kenyan government hoped villages would 'actually "rehabilitate" a nomad to a settled life'.[23] There was little enthusiasm for villagisation on the part of the local population, however. Instead, thousands of Somalis fled the region in an effort to escape life in the villages.

Villagisation had been used to devastating effect during the anti-Mau Mau campaign of the 1950s. The similarities between the war against shifta and the counterinsurgency effort of the previous decade were unsurprising. Through logistical and technical support for the campaign, and through training provided to Kenyan officers, the British armed forces influenced the nature of the Shifta War very heavily. Moreover, many of the local administrators involved in the conflict had prior experience of the anti-Mau Mau campaign. John Mburu, appointed as provincial commissioner (PC) in North Eastern Province in April 1966, first entered the colonial administration in 1956 as part of the counter-insurgency effort. Eliud Mahihu, the PC in Eastern Province, joined the colonial administration in 1953 to produce propaganda during the Mau Mau war.

Many of the new administrators shared the prejudices and attitudes of their colonial forerunners. The community development officer responsible for overseeing development projects in North Eastern Province, J.S. Naribo, told an audience of Somalis in August 1966 that their 'men sit idle'.[24] Earlier that month, two district officers stated that Somalis liked 'their stock more than their children'.[25] Somalia, Kenyatta once remarked, was 'scarcely able to grow its own bananas'.[26] The slow pace of development did little to rehabilitate the Nairobi government in the eyes of Somalis. By 1967, just two secondary schools had been founded in the area. Given this history of neglect and prejudice by the colonial and post-colonial state, it is unsurprising that many Somalis felt little attachment to Kenya.

The Kenyan state's authority and legitimacy ran out long before the national borders with Somalia, Ethiopia, Sudan and Uganda were reached. A civil servant posted to Garissa in September 1964 was amazed to be greeted by residents of the town with 'Hello. How is Kenya?' 'People here', he noted, 'regard the area on the opposite side of River Tana as being in "Kenya".'[27] Throughout the war, Kenyan officials promised future development funding once the insurgency was defeated. 'Anyone who wants to go to Somalia can pack up,' the new PC told a crowd on his arrival in Garissa in April 1966. 'Those who are interested to build Kenya are welcomed to build their province to be a civilised one.'[28] Such promises amounted to little. Things did not improve after the war was over either.

With Kenya's allies unwilling to supply it with the arms necessary to expand the war, and the Somali government unable to keep up its support of the insurgents due to an economic crisis north of the border, the two governments were forced to the negotiating table in 1967. With the help of Kenneth Kaunda, the president of Zambia, a peace deal respecting Kenya's sovereignty was agreed in October. Somalia's involvement in the war was over. Supplies and funds from Mogadishu dried up almost immediately. '[The] Somali Government have just suddenly cut off food supply and other equipments,' one fighter told Kenyan interrogators following his surrender. Unable to continue the war, the insurgents had little choice but to take advantage of an amnesty issued by the Kenyan government and surrender.

By January 1968, life had returned to something approaching normality in northern Kenya. The all-important cattle trade resumed, as did the pre-war easy movement of people and goods across the border. In Mandera, the local DC reported that Somalis from across the border at Bulla Hawa were 'seen daily moving to and fro to buy shop goods and other requirements freely, which reminded them of the old trade relationship before the emergency'.[29] By September, all seemed calm again in Lamu, too. 'The situation is getting back to normal,' the DC there wrote.[30] This did not mean that peace now reigned, however, or that Somalis were reconciled to the Kenyan state.

Northern Kenya remained blighted by insecurity. When shifta fighters surrendered, few did so with their weapons. Instead, as one former hostage of shifta fighters told the Kenyan security forces, 'all shiftas are returning their weapons back to Somalia'.[31] These weapons were used to arm cattle raiders and other criminal elements, and were put to use across the border. Feelings towards the Kenyan government had not improved either. According to Abdi Haji Ahmed, the MP for Garissa South in 1971, the government in Nairobi 'doesn't care if we live or die'. 'We don't get schools,' Ahmed complained, 'we don't get water. They haven't forgiven us for the shifta rebellion and we are still considered foreigners.' The economic growth witnessed in the era since independence had had little effect on North Eastern Province. 'What good does it do us to live in wealthy Kenya if we never get any of the wealth?' asked Ahmed.[32] While the Shifta War had occupied the attention of Somalis, many other Kenyans had been asking the same question.

FREEDOM AND SUFFERING

On 16 January 1964, just over a month after independence, the streets of Nairobi witnessed a public rally very different from that which had greeted the end of colonial rule. Rather than the hundreds of thousands that joined the celebrations in December, 500 men took to the streets a month later in perhaps the very first protest over the way in which the new government was going about its business. All were unemployed and each had quickly concluded that the promises of imminent social emancipation through national liberation were illusory. To the protestors, KANU's slogan of '*Uhuru na Kazi*' ('Freedom and Work') seemed like a joke in very poor taste. The men on the street instead shouted '*uhuru na taabu*' ('freedom and suffering'). They demanded that ministers sell their expensive new cars and give the proceeds to the neediest in Kenyan society. Here, then, was a clear statement of the demand for redistributive politics that quickly became a common refrain within political debate over the next five years. Yet the call for redistribution met with a telling response: public meetings were banned in Nairobi and other major towns in order to prevent similar protests taking place.[33]

The protestors in Nairobi initially had champions in the government. Figures such as Vice President Oginga Odinga, Minister for Information, Broadcasting and Tourism Achieng' Oneko and Assistant Minister for Education Bildad Kaggia were powerful voices for redistribution within the first government of independent Kenya. Steadily, however, they were marginalised. Their struggle over development policy with the likes of Mboya and Kenyatta was a matter of great interest to Kenya's former ruler and to the Cold War's superpowers. Elizabeth Schmidt argues that the Cold War in Africa was an essential part of the 'dynamics of the independence process', which contributed to the 'strong antidemocratic and leadership crises' of contemporary Africa.[34] Between 1963 and 1969, Kenyan politics were played out on the global stage. The Cold War, in turn, left its mark on the country's politics.

This started with Kenyan leaders seeking out foreign patrons to fund their political campaigns. Individual leaders found the donors that were most closely aligned to their own views on independence and development. Odinga may never have been a communist, but he was committed to a redistributive set of economic policies: 'I understood that in Communist countries the emphasis was on food for all. If that was what Communism meant then there was nothing wrong with that.'[35] He therefore looked to the Soviet Union, China and their allies for backing. Mboya was never an uncritical friend of America, particularly in relation to its actions in the Congo, but he genuinely shared American notions of liberty and believed in the importance of foreign private capital as a catalyst for economic growth. He hoped that America would 'put into practice those ideals you have always professed, to act on, not talk about, the teaching of the American Revolution'.[36] Kenyatta was content to let the British continue to exert their influence. These international connections provided Kenyans with a language and the funds to pursue their intense debate about development in the wake of independence.

KENYA'S COLD WAR

The protestors chanting 'freedom and suffering' took to the streets of Nairobi just four days after what Odinga later claimed was the true start date for Kenya's Cold War.[37] On 12 January, a political and social revolution began in the island state of Zanzibar. Events on the archipelago provided a warning to Kenya's conservative leadership and its international supporters in London and Washington of the power of the discontented underclass of East African society. To the Kenyan intelligence service, it seemed that the revolution in Zanzibar 'evolved into a straight bid by the Communists to take over the island'.[38] The revolution exacerbated a sense of instability that took hold of East Africa's governments in the first months of 1964. It was accompanied by army mutinies in Tanganyika, Uganda and Kenya. Kenya's mutiny, which took place at the barracks at Lanet, near Nakuru, was in protest against low pay and continuing British influence within the military. The mutinies in both Tanganyika and Kenya were minor and were suppressed with the significant help of British troops. Taken together, the mutinies and the Zanzibar revolution exposed the vulnerability of the newly decolonised states of East Africa to the ebb and flow of the Cold War.

In order to chart a course through the storm of the Cold War, Kenyatta's government remained rhetorically committed to non-alignment throughout the 1960s. In Kenyatta's words, 'We rejected both Western Capitalism and Eastern Communism and chose for ourselves a policy of positive non-alignment.'[39] Non-alignment was a noble aspiration, but one wholly unsuited to the particularly harsh climate within international relations at the moment of Kenya's independence. The US was alarmed by the Zanzibar revolution, which appeared to have given the communist powers a foothold in the region. For their part, China and the Soviet Union were involved in a struggle for leadership of the newly independent states ahead of the second Afro-Asian summit, due in 1965. Furthermore, China was seeking to end its international isolation and to win official recognition from newly independent states like Kenya, which did, in fact, recognise the Beijing regime rather than its Taiwanese rival.

In order to placate these various competing interests, Kenyan ministerial delegations busily set about improving relations with a whole host of regional and international states and institutions, almost as soon as the independence ceremonies were over. As part of this effort, a senior ministerial delegation was despatched to the US immediately before Christmas of 1963. The delegation included Odinga, as well as some of Kenyatta's most trusted advisers, including Joseph Murumbi. Of mixed Maasai and Goan heritage, Murumbi was appointed minister of state at independence. He had been educated in India and was one of the few members of the KANU government to have any great knowledge of Somalia or Somali society, having spent a decade across the border. The Kenyans' hosts would have been greatly reassured by the presence in the delegation of the Anglophile attorney general,

Charles Njonjo, and Kenyatta's Stanford-educated relative and minister of health, Njoroge Mungai. The ministers were accompanied by Robert Ouko, a young civil servant in the Ministry of External Affairs. The tone of the visit was captured by Murumbi's words during a speech in New York to investors. He assured them that 'your money is going to be safe. Businessmen must be allowed to make a profit and business will not be nationalized.'[40] Despite the rhetoric of non-alignment and African Socialism, Kenyatta's government was generally pro-West and pro-capitalism. The visit to the US had merely reaffirmed existing warm relations between many of Kenya's new rulers and American policymakers and business leaders.

Those relations were, in large part, the result of the extensive programme of scholarships provided to allow Kenyan students to undertake higher education in the US. As constitutional negotiations between the British government and nationalist leaders gathered pace in the late 1950s, concern grew about who would fill the ranks of the civil service. Colonial neglect of higher education meant that Kenya lacked sufficient numbers of graduates to fill the vacancies that would be left by departing British officials. To address this problem, Mboya and his American backers at the Kennedy Foundation and the US State Department drew up plans for what became known as the 'airlift': the establishment of a substantial scholarship and travel assistance programme for Kenyan students to attend universities in the US. By 1960, more than 200 colleges had signed up to the programme,[41] and between then and 1965 they hosted more than 1,000 Kenyan students.[42]

In the wake of the visit to the US, another delegation, again including Odinga, flew to China and the USSR in April and May. Just as Mboya had already laid the foundations for friendly relations with the US, so Odinga's pre-independence ties to Moscow and Beijing ensured a warm reception in both capitals for the Kenyan ministers and civil servants. In Moscow, the Kenyans signed an agreement that provided Soviet funding and assistance to build a 200-bed hospital and a technical college.[43] The Chinese agreed to provide manpower, technical expertise and a soft loan of $15 million to fund a major irrigation project in the Tana River area.[44] These agreements were of concern to some Kenyan government officials and Western diplomats alike, since Odinga had little authorisation for such negotiations.[45]

Britain was sensitive to any sign of threat to its influence over independent Kenya. Officials in London and in the High Commission in Nairobi were concerned with protecting sizeable private interests and the position of the European settler farmers. They also looked with trepidation on any sign of large-scale migration to Britain by South Asian British passport holders resident in Kenya. In Britain's eyes, Kenyatta seemed to offer the best protection for its interests and the best guarantee of political and economic stability. A series of agreements were thus struck with the new government that were intended to protect Kenyatta from a range of internal and external threats. The most extensive of these deals concerned defence. British forces had access to port facilities at Mombasa, infantry training in the Mount Kenya area and overfly rights, while the Kenyan government committed itself to using British suppliers for its defence purchases. In return, the British provided training for Kenyan forces, supplied equipment, and promised to act to support Kenyatta in case of an uprising or an invasion from Soviet-backed Somalia.[46]

The consequence of these agreements was a highly visible British presence within the security forces after independence. Half of the 300 British military trainers were issued Kenya Army uniforms and deployed with the troops around the country. A parachute company led by a British officer was formed, and the senior officers of the Kenya Air Force (KAF) came under the command of their British counterparts, while the Royal Air Force remained in the country to assist in anti-shifta operations. Inspector General Richard Catling remained in post as head of the police for the first year of independence and was then, in effect, replaced by his deputy, Lewis Mitchell. Nearly 300 British police officers remained in the force until the end of 1965.

Britain had close friends in cabinet, too. Njonjo, trained as a lawyer at Gray's Inn in London, was the most obvious. Hardly ever seen in public without a pinstripe suit and a rose in his buttonhole, the attorney general's appearance lived up to his nickname of 'Sir Charles'. As well as British tailoring, he enjoyed warm relations with Britain's diplomats. A close friend of successive high commissioners and a fervent Anglican, his enthusiasm for all things British led the Foreign Office to remark that 'the standard joke is that the Attorney General's office is the next one to be Africanised'.[47] Bruce McKenzie, Njonjo's ally in government, was another mainstay of British influence on the Kenyan government. Born in Durban and a war hero after his exploits as a pilot in the Mediterranean theatre, McKenzie moved to Kenya in 1946. He took up farming in Nakuru and made an ideal agriculture minister in the KANU government as Kenyatta sought to calm the fears of both settler farmers and the British government. He was also probably a British and Israeli intelligence agent.[48]

Other expatriates, locally known as 'retreads', filled the upper echelons of various government departments as civil servants. Outside government, too, British influence continued to be felt. Kenneth Bolton, editor of the *East African Standard* and friend of both Njonjo and McKenzie, was amenable to publishing articles about communist infiltration based on material provided by the British High Commission.[49] Bolton's active participation in the social scene surrounding politics was discomfiting for his wife, thought by the High Commission to have been a fascist in the past. 'She comes to mixed parties wearing long white gloves in order to avoid direct contact with African hands', one diplomat claimed.[50] Such examples of the continuing extreme racism of the high colonial period were rare in relations between British expatriates and their Kenyan allies.

'DOUBLE O'

There was little doubt among British and American diplomats about which individual most threatened their relations with the Kenyan government: Odinga. Commonly referred to by those diplomats as 'Double O', Odinga had close ties with their Soviet and Chinese counterparts. That partnership was far from inevitable, however. 'Odinga and his group neither understand nor have any particular sympathy for Marxist-Leninist ideology,' a British official in Nairobi wrote in the months prior to independence. The official thought that 'apart from the jargon of anti-imperialism, they do not seem to deal in the typical Marxist concepts even when talking among themselves'.[51] Odinga's relationship with the communist powers was instead born of the need for a powerful external patron. His initial advances to the Americans had been rebuffed by Washington at Mboya's request, and, until MacDonald's arrival, Britain's allies were drawn from the ranks of KADU. So Odinga turned to the communist powers instead. According to the British in August 1963, Odinga had received 'several hundred thousand pounds' from communist governments.[52]

Odinga was unapologetic. He described his ties to the communist powers as bonds of friendship based on 'mutual understanding', which meant 'my friend in Russia, China or America may accept gifts from me and likewise I can accept gifts and other assistance from him'.[53] He was particularly enthusiastic about offers of student scholarships, which allowed him to develop a source of patronage to rival the American scholarship programme built up by Mboya. In total, some 400 Kenyans had studied in communist states in the few years running up to independence, whereas by early 1965 it was thought that nearly 1,900 Kenyans were either students or had completed their studies in communist countries.[54]

Western diplomats and sections of the Kenyan government were somewhat perturbed by Odinga's scholarship programme. They assembled considerable evidence that the students sent to various countries in Eastern Europe and China often received military rather than academic training. Twenty Kenyans were sent by Odinga to China before independence to train at, in the words of the Kenyan ambassador in Beijing, 'some sort of military college' at Wuhan.[55] The ambassador's vagueness was unsurprising. The students at Wuhan and in similar institutions elsewhere had been sent secretly to their new homes by their political sponsors back in Kenya. In the USSR, the Kenyan ambassador did not know how many of his compatriots were studying in the country in 1965. Many had, he told American colleagues, 'come in "through the back door" before independence and that unknown numbers are still arriving outside the formal Scholarship Board channels which have been established in Nairobi'.[56] Lacking such information, the Kenyan government feared the worst. Special Branch thought some 300 students were undergoing training that 'overtly preached the necessity for the violent overthrow of the governments of non-communist countries. It is therefore a reasonable assumption that military training given by them will have this ultimate objective.'[57] Odinga later claimed that such projects had been agreed with Kenyatta, as 'before Independence, Britain would not agree to grant facilities for the training of African officers'.[58]

With Kenyatta exerting a firm grip over the civil service, graduates of universities in communist countries found jobs hard to come by when they returned home. Those that did complete military courses were refused employment in the Kenyan armed forces.[59] Others were suspected of having been brainwashed while abroad. Special Branch warned in May 1965:

> The presence in this country of a steadily increasing number of young men who have been indoctrinated with the principles of Marxism-Leninism and who would be prepared to take extreme measures to ensure that plans for the establishment of a 'peoples' government' are not thwarted by 'capitalist' and/or 'imperialist' stooges' ... renders the threat of possible violence to their opponents a reality.[60]

By contrast, their counterparts who returned from the US filled the offices of the civil service and the boardrooms of an Africanising private sector. The result was the formation of a cadre of intelligent, highly educated and disaffected graduates. Although already likely to be sympathetic to Odinga, their exclusion from power on their return convinced many of the need to support the radical faction within KANU.

Odinga did little to calm the nerves of the US and Britain after independence. As Washington understood it, Chinese influence over Odinga grew through 1964 and 1965. The Chinese embassy in Nairobi was becoming increasingly virulent in its verbal attacks on the US and the latter's friends in government. Moreover, the US embassy feared that the state-run broadcasting and information services over-seen by Odinga's close ally Oneko were 'now largely in USSR or Czech hands'.[61] British diplomats were more concerned with the prospect of Odinga dislodging expatriates from positions of influence over the security forces. His expulsion of Ian Henderson, a senior police officer infamous for his role in the anti-Mau Mau campaign, caused great alarm. Although Odinga later claimed to have acted under orders from Kenyatta, the deportation was believed at the time to have been Odinga's unilateral doing.[62] The British feared that Henderson's deportation would be the first step in a campaign led by Odinga to remove all British expatriates from positions of influence in the civil service and the military.

Odinga was able to expel Henderson because of the powers he enjoyed as minister for home affairs. The control of immigration procedures that came as part of his ministerial portfolio was a source of great worry to his opponents in government and the diplomatic corps. In October 1964, for instance, a Czechoslovakian plane carrying twenty-one students returning to Kenya after completing their studies in Eastern Europe landed at Embakasi airport in Nairobi. After disembarking, the students were rushed through the airport without going through the usual formal-ities. They were collected by vehicles from the Prisons Department (another institution under Odinga's ministerial control) and driven to the Ministry of Home Affairs. Four other vehicles collected cargo from the plane and delivered it to Odinga's office.[63] What British, American and Kenyan intelligence feared was that Odinga was stockpiling weapons and building up a small paramilitary force capable of mounting some sort of armed takeover of power.

Kenyatta was unconvinced. While he thought Odinga and other more radical leaders ambitious, according to an American diplomat writing in December 1964:

> Kenyatta still lacks the will and desire to move frontally. He justifies his position on the grounds that Odinga and Oneko are loyal and forthright to him personally, that he must preserve the tribal unity of the Government, and that his private suspicions

of other ambitious candidates (Mboya, Kaggia, and Ngei) require him to use check-and-balance tactics to maintain his own power.[64]

Kenyatta did not wish, furthermore, to become embroiled in a personal battle with his rival. He knew all too well from his own experience of detention that state persecution could easily create heroic figures out of political leaders. Rather than arrest or fire Odinga, the president wished the schism with his deputy, so he told MacDonald, 'to come (if and when it does come) on some action which is Odinga's own fault, and not Kenyatta's'.[65] In the meantime, Kenyatta took sensible precautions. When KADU folded and its MPs joined the government, the conservative Moi was appointed to be minister for home affairs, and thus control of immigration was removed from Odinga. Kenyatta and his supporters also ensured that the republican constitution introduced in December did not include provision for the vice president to succeed automatically, should the president die in office. Kenyatta turned next to harassment of the radical faction and began efforts aimed at undermining the institutions from which his rival derived support.

PINTO

The first move was made against Odinga's most important supporter, Pio Gama Pinto. Pinto was, so the US embassy thought, Odinga's 'brilliant political tactician'.[66] The British agreed. MacDonald described Pinto as 'a dedicated Communist, and the principal brain behind the whole secret organisation of Mr. Odinga's movement'. The high commissioner credited Pinto with having mobilised backbench opposition in parliament to Kenyatta and with leading 'other anti-Government movements'.[67] But Pinto was an important figure in his own right.

Born in Nairobi of Goan descent and educated in India, he participated in the nationalist struggle in his native Kenya, in India and in Goa. Entering the trade union movement in colonial India as a seventeen-year-old following his education there, he continued his labour activism when he returned to Kenya in 1949. As editor of the

Daily Chronicle, a trade union activist, leader of the Kenya Indian Congress and founder of the Kenya League, Pinto fought injustice and the excesses of colonial rule. Joseph Murumbi's recollection of his first meeting with Pinto was typical of the experience of many in Kenya: 'His welcome was very warm,' wrote Murumbi. 'I felt I had somehow known him for years.' Pinto's energy was perhaps what stood out most strongly, however. Muinga Chitari Chokwe, the speaker in the short-lived upper chamber of parliament, recalled the 'youthful and energetic' Pinto moving from office to office in his attempts to mobilise anti-colonial protests in the early 1950s. 'He darted like an antelope,' Chokwe recalled.[68] Pinto's involvement in militant anti-colonial politics in that period led to his arrest during the Mau Mau emergency. He spent three years in detention and a further two restricted to far-flung Kabarnet. He was finally released in 1959 and returned to the nationalist fray. Despite non-Africans being prevented from joining KANU until 1962, Pinto founded the party newspaper, *Sauti ya KANU* ('Voice of KANU') and played a critical part in KANU's electoral successes in 1961 and 1963.[69]

In recognition of his contribution to the nationalist cause, after independence he was elected by his peers to be one of a small number of so-called 'specially elected' MPs, chosen in a ballot of other parliamentarians. But he also continued to play a role within the anti-colonial efforts gathering pace in the Portuguese colonies of southern and western Africa. The connections forged in this effort gave Pinto and his fellow radical KANU leaders access to foreign support. As a result, Odinga's faction was 'much better financed and organized, and more determined to achieve their ends' than the conservative faction of the ruling party.[70] Pinto also provided his friends and allies in KANU's progressive faction with his formidable organisational skills and tactical nous in parliament and beyond.

On the morning of 24 February 1965, Pinto followed his regular routine of driving his daughter, Tereshka, up and down the driveway outside the family home in Nairobi. Tereshka was the youngest of Pinto's three children with his wife, Emma, and was not yet two years old. While he waited for the gates at the bottom of the driveway to open, three men approached the car. Pausing only to greet Pinto, the men fired shots through the windscreen. Pinto died in his car. Concerns about the motives behind the killing quickly circulated among his friends and colleagues. A half-hearted police investigation into the crime reassured no one. A few days after the assassination, Kaggia told his fellow MPs that Pinto's killing 'is not an ordinary murder. It is a political murder.'[71]

Two young men, Kisilu Mutua and Chege Thuo, were both arrested on the day of the murder in connection with the crime. Thuo was acquitted once the case reached court, but Mutua was sentenced to death by hanging. On appeal, his sentence was commuted to life imprisonment. After his release in 2000, Mutua continued to protest his innocence. The arrests did little to silence discussion of who was responsible for organising the killing. The small social circuit of clubs and restaurants in which the Nairobi elite moved was conducive to the rapid spread of rumours. Some suggested that the US had had Pinto killed, since he was an agent of communism. As the US State Department recorded:

> Other rumours center around resentment against Pinto as an Asian and speculate that he was killed because he was a major recipient of communist largesse who may have been holding out on money received, or tried to blackmail a high official, or was killed by the Chicoms [Chinese Communists] because he was moving closer to the Soviets or by Kikuyu who feared he was a threat to Kikuyu dominance.[72]

If by using the term 'Kikuyu' American diplomats meant the inner circle of mainly Kikuyu political leaders and senior officers in the security services that had formed around Kenyatta, then they were right.

In his controversial memoirs, US Ambassador Attwood wrote that Pinto was killed because he was 'Odinga's chief brainstruster'.[73] The conservative faction in government probably had Pinto killed in order to destabilise the radicals. An investigation by *The Nation* in 2000 identified the involvement of Special Branch in organising the killing.[74] In parliament in 1967, one MP alleged that Arthur Wanyoike Thungu, a member of Kenyatta's bodyguard and a KANU official in Kiambu, was 'closely associated with Pio Gama Pinto's assassination' and had been 'questioned by Criminal Investigation Department police officers at Nairobi headquarters'.[75] It was the working (but unproven) assumption at the British High Commission that 'it was probably Njonjo who procured the removal from the scene of the Chinese-orientated Pinto'.[76] The unsubstantiated allegations about the involvement of Wanyoike and Njonjo point at least to the reach of this case. In early 1965, with Kenyatta's physical and intellectual powers undimmed and his political supremacy unquestioned, it is unthinkable that any figure from within the establishment could have carried out the assassination without his approval.

Kenyatta made a concerted effort to silence all such talk. Few MPs or other Kenyans were willing to defy the president. At Pinto's funeral, his old friend, fellow Goan and comrade-in-arms in the nationalist struggle Joseph Murumbi delivered the oration. Pinto had, Murumbi said, 'made the supreme sacrifice and we can but hope that this senseless waste of a young and brilliant life will at least shock the whole country into realising that the bullet is no answer to any problem – it is an evasion'. But even Murumbi could not criticise the chief beneficiary of the murder – Kenyatta himself. Rather, he called on the mourners to 'follow the example set by our President, Mzee Jomo Kenyatta, and ensure that no bitterness clouds our emotions'.[77] Kenyatta was untouchable.

THE COUP PLOT

The aftermath of Pinto's murder was no less dramatic. On 4 April, Njonjo paid a visit to MacDonald at the British High Commission. Investigations following the murder had, Njonjo claimed, brought to light correspondence that contained concrete discussion of a coup plot. A coup attempt by the radicals, Njonjo told MacDonald, was imminent and most likely to occur on 12 April.[78] Njonjo requested immediate British military support. With the approval of the British cabinet, HMS *Albion* was despatched to Mombasa and further plans were made to place a full battalion of British troops on standby at their base in Aden.[79] In the meantime, the Kenyan authorities moved to disarm Odinga and potential supporters. On 8 and 10 April, a series of raids were made on the homes and offices of the radical leaders.[80] According to Israeli intelligence, hundreds of pistols, ammunition and 500 sub-machine guns were taken from Odinga's office.[81]

The only evidence that supports the claim that a coup was to take place is MacDonald's version of his discussion with Njonjo. Without any further documentation, it is reckless to conclude that a coup was imminent when the weight of other evidence suggests that such an event was highly unlikely. Indeed, American diplomats dismissed the likelihood of a coup in late 1964, not least because the radical faction 'give appearances of wanting to prepare for a "more orderly" takeover later', the US embassy reported to the State Department.[82] Besides Pinto's assassination, little had changed a few weeks later. The radicals enjoyed considerable support from within KANU and held key positions within government. Although Odinga did not possess any automatic right to succession by virtue of his position as vice president, his status among fellow political leaders and the country at large was second only to that of Kenyatta. The president was not even that unpopular among the radicals.

At this time, Kenyatta was commonly understood to be 'the umpire' in the struggle between them and the conservatives in the government.[83] He enjoyed close relations with Oneko, in particular, and even Odinga did not dispute the president's standing as the unquestioned leader of Kenyan nationalism. Kenyatta's animosity towards Bildad Kaggia dated back to their time in detention together in the 1950s, but outside his home in Murang'a Kaggia commanded little of the popular support needed to overthrow the president. Any suggestion of the plot being real and of Odinga's involvement must, furthermore, account for Kenyatta's apparent astonishing and uncharacteristic magnanimity. While some of Odinga's supporters were arrested, none of the leading radical politicians was. In the absence of any further evidence of a plot, this tests credulity to beyond breaking point.

Of course, it is impossible to rule out the possibility of an imminent coup. Further evidence may yet come to light; but until then it seems more plausible that Njonjo and others close to Kenyatta were paranoid and overreacted to unsubstantiated gossip at a time of great anxiety caused by the Cold War. 'Nightmares always *seem* real at the time', writes Gaddis, 'even if, in the cold light of dawn, a little ridiculous.'[84] More likely still is that the threat, such as it was, was deliberately exaggerated by Njonjo or MacDonald in order to help Kenyatta defeat Odinga's challenge. The attorney general and other leading figures within the conservative faction were perfectly capable of inflating the most obscure and unthreatening plots into full-blown alerts in order to make political capital. But whatever the provenance of the plot, the political gains of its exposure were quick to accumulate. Almost immediately, ministers made it clear to Kenyatta that they would back moves against Odinga and the vice president's faction in government.[85] Two clear factions had formed within the government: one conservative and centred on Kenyatta and Mboya, and the other radical, led by Odinga.

It became a good deal easier to convince sceptics of the threat posed by the radicals when, on 14 April, the *Fizik Lebedev*, a Soviet ship carrying a crew of military advisers and a cargo of weapons, sailed into the port of Mombasa. The connection to the coup plot seemed obvious. After all, just two weeks earlier, Thomas Malinda had alleged in parliament that 'arms and ammunition are continuously being smuggled from Communist and other foreign countries into Kenya for the purpose of staging an armed revolution to overthrow our beloved government'.[86] With Malinda's warning in mind, many Kenyans and foreign diplomats reacted with alarm to the arrival of the Soviet arms. The reality was a good deal less serious. Rather than being a covert shipment of weapons to the coup plotters, this was the fulfilment of a deal made in 1964, when the USSR had offered to supply the Kenyans with weapons after a similar request to the UK and Australia had been turned down.[87]

Njonjo and Mungai, the defence minister, initially had no intention of rejecting either the weapons or the seventeen Soviet military trainers that accompanied them. The British High Commission was of a rather different mind, however. Pointing out to their Kenyan counterparts that accepting the Soviet arms would jeopardise the defence agreements between the two countries, officials at the High Commission pressured the president to publicly reject the weapons. On 29 April, Kenyatta dutifully ordered the ship, the military trainers and the arms to return to the USSR. The arms, the president said, were 'old, second-hand, and no use to Kenya's modern army'.[88] Murumbi joked to one British official that 'he understood the equipment had been used in Russia at the time of the Russian Revolution and that he trusted this would be no precedent'.[89] The High Commission was not amused.

For all the heat generated by fears of armed takeovers, and Pinto's murder aside, Kenyatta's response to the challenge posed by his vice president remained methodical and low-key. The president continued slowly to squeeze Odinga's supporters and to marginalise the institutions controlled by the radicals. The next target was KANU itself. The party leaders who manned the branch offices dotted around the country had great sympathy for Odinga's belief that KANU should be given greater powers in government in order to enact a more redistributive policy agenda. The vice president was determined to help the achievement of these goals by founding a technical college to train party activists. Odinga thought this would strengthen the ideological coherence of the party, and also provide a highly skilled cadre of KANU members that could take on significant responsibilities of government.

Named in honour of the murdered Congolese nationalist leader, the Lumumba Institute on the outskirts of Nairobi opened its doors in December 1964. The first intake of students began their studies the following March. Construction was financed by the USSR under the terms of an agreement signed in Moscow. The library and classrooms were filled with books and other equipment donated by the Soviet, Czechoslovakian, Polish, Hungarian, Chinese, East German, Yugoslav and Indian governments.[90] The salaries of two Soviet instructors were paid by Moscow and seven of their Kenyan colleagues had trained at the Moscow Institute of Social Science.[91] Although both Odinga and Kenyatta acted as nominal patrons to the institute, Odinga's allies dominated its day-to-day running.

The government's conservatives feared that the institute would become a production line for pro-Odinga activists, who would monopolise the local and national structures of the ruling party. In response, the institute's management claimed its curriculum was inspired by Kenyatta's ideas and the KANU manifesto of 1963.[92] However, the institute quickly became associated with the radical faction. It was a favoured site for speeches by the likes of Tom Okello Odongo, then assistant minister of finance. Okello Odongo used the platform provided by the Lumumba Institute to suggest in early April 1965 that 'we must bend a little more to the Eastern Block [sic] at this moment'.[93] Such speeches were guaranteed a warm reception: neither the students nor the lecturers made much attempt to avoid Kenyatta's wrath. Some of the students formed a pressure group, issuing public statements on a range of political and socioeconomic issues. These statements included criticism of the Kenyatta government's economic policies, which were dismissed as 'nothing but perpetuation of capital exploitation in disguise'.[94] Such sentiments did little to endear the institute, its faculty or its students to Kenyatta and his supporters.

The conservative faction in the government pushed for the closure of the Lumumba Institute. Within two months of the first students entering the college, parliament voted for the Ministry of Education to take over its running. This was, in effect, a winding-up order and just one class of eighty-five students passed through the doors of the institute. When those students came to graduate in June, according to the American ambassador, the ceremony was characterised by the graduands 'shouting "Kenya and Communism!" as they received their certificates'.[95] The students were intent on one last hurrah. A month after the graduation ceremony, students from the Lumumba Institute attempted to seize KANU headquarters and install their preferred candidates as party officers. Twenty-seven were arrested, all thought by Kenyan intelligence to be 'merely pawns'. Special Branch believed more prominent radical leaders were, in fact, behind the episode. Moreover, it was thought that Wang Te Ming, a correspondent for the New China News Agency, was also involved. Twenty-six of those arrested had connections to Wang or Chinese diplomats working in Nairobi.[96]

The 'revelation' of the coup plot, the refusal of the Soviet arms and the events at the Lumumba Institute left Odinga isolated. Fellow ministers became wary of him and his intentions. As his influence within cabinet waned, so did the government's enthusiasm for Soviet aid. While the Soviets remained determined to honour existing agreements, Kenyatta's government cooled to the idea.[97] Hostility towards China was even greater. Zhou Enlai's famous observation during his visit to Tanzania in June that Africa was 'ripe for revolution' was greeted with fury north of the border. Kenyatta personally refused the Chinese premier permission to travel back to China through Kenya. A few weeks later, Wang, the journalist linked to the Lumumba Institute students, was deported for allegedly providing funds and advice to Odinga's faction. His expulsion was followed by a debate in parliament on whether or not Kenya should break off all relations with China.[98] Kenyatta had abandoned his government's commitment to non-alignment in order to retain the upper hand in his struggle with Odinga.

AFRICAN SOCIALISM

Kenya's Cold War was being played out in the context of widespread disillusionment with independence. By the time of the alleged coup plot, it was accepted knowledge at the top level of government that, in the words of intelligence sources, 'in certain areas of the country, particularly in the Central and Nyanza Provinces, the more extreme politicians are likely to attract more support than those who support the Government'.[99] While successful in the diplomatic arena, at home Kenyatta was losing the battle against Odinga. Throughout the country, local leaders sought to give voice to a pronounced disenchantment with independence. Every province and major town saw mass rallies at which one aspect or another of government policy was roundly criticised. In the cities and the large farms of the former White Highlands, intense labour disputes became ever more common. Serious famine threatened Eastern and Coast Provinces through 1965, driving discontent there. In Central Province, local politicians demanded that free grants of land be made immediately to the poor. Luhya leaders in Western Province accused Kenyatta of favouring his own Kikuyu community when appointing ministers and when allocating funds for development.[100]

The views of Willie Kamumba from Nairobi were typical of the attitudes of many Kenyans at the time. There was little in the ideas of socialism and communism that appealed to him. 'I fought the Mau Mau war', Kamumba wrote to Kenyatta. 'Now I am fighting against the Communism. We have to fight to the last minute to find that no more Communism is existing in Kenya. We all support you with all your doings now and then.' But his personal loyalty was tinged with concern about the government's failure to deliver development to the grassroots. 'We fought for our *uhuru* ['independence'] and what are we getting from this, our *uhuru*?' Kamumba asked the president.[101] A growing dissatisfaction with the government's development strategy was palpable across the country, even in Kenyatta's own Kikuyu heartlands of the Mount Kenya region. Kariuki Kagunda was a resident of Kamuya, a village in Nyeri district. His other homes in Kamuya were destroyed to make way for the construction of a coffee-processing facility. Kagunda was livid. 'Oh God!' he wrote to Kenyatta. 'Help the unlanded people!! Sir, why do you sit on that chair? Is your main work to help people, animals or plants? You are helping "Money" instead of people!' Kenyatta and his ministers were, Kagunda thought, 'just like the harlots or prostitutes . . . who throw their children in lavatories'.[102] Kagunda's and Kamumba's thoughts were representative of wider opinion.

As Kamumba suggested, socialism (or indeed redistribution) was not a widely popular ideology among Kenyans. It was, after all, out of step with many of the country's political traditions. 'Kenyans want high incomes and wealth,' writes Robert Bates. 'They want to accumulate, to invest, and to prosper; and they enjoy exhibiting the accoutrements of prosperity: good clothes, handsome homes, and properly turned out families.'[103] During a May Day rally in Nyeri in 1965, the crowds interrupted the speakers with shouts of protest against the spread of 'Communism germs [*sic*]' and by insisting that 'Communism is not food of our choice.'[104] Nevertheless, ordinary Kenyans expected to have experienced the benefits of independence and to have seen a new development strategy implemented more quickly than they had.

Odinga's potential strength lay in his ability to appeal to this frustration rather than to capitalise on any great enthusiasm for socialism and redistribution among Kenyans.

Despite Pinto's murder, Odinga's faction continued to be well organised and it formulated a coherent message designed to appeal to those disillusioned with independence. KANU's secretary in Machakos, for one, was concerned. According to the party official, Odinga and his then ally and local MP, Paul Ngei, were very active in Eastern Province, 'where they concentrate on political slogans (anti-US, anti-imperialist, pro-USSR, land reform, Soviet space achievements, etc.)'. Moreover, the machinery of Odinga's faction was also highly effective, particularly with 'lots of small cash handouts among young leaders'.[105] According to Eliud Mahihu, the provincial commissioner in Eastern Province, Odinga had a network of supporters in Embu and Meru districts drawn from the ranks of Mau Mau veterans, local KANU branch offices and the coffee cooperatives that dominated local society. With the assistance of these figures, he was steadily gaining the backing of 'those people who may have been dissatisfied' and being able to 'exploit their grievances'. In order to consolidate these gains, Odinga made particularly frequent use of generous donations to local schools as part of his efforts to build grassroots support.[106] These cash crop producers and KANU members living in and around the Central Highlands were the very people that Kenyatta considered to be his natural constituency. Urgent action was needed if men and women such as they were losing faith in his leadership and flirting with the radicals.

The conservatives therefore rushed out a pivotal economic policy paper in late April 1965.[107] The document, known in Kenya by its formal title of Sessional Paper No. 10 of 1965, was characterised by a lack of detail and a surfeit of generalities. Despite being described as 'African Socialism', the policy was in fact a development strategy based on private property and private foreign investment. That was hardly new: the commitment to foreign capital had been made a year earlier in the Foreign Investment Protection Act. Over the next six years, up to 1970, private foreign investment doubled, to a total of $92 million per annum.[108] Kenyatta attempted to describe the 1965 paper as 'a

social philosophy that could have valid meaning in practice'.[109] Kaggia
dismissed it simply as capitalism.[110]

No amount of hastily cobbled-together policy papers were a match
for Odinga's charisma and the appeal of his message of redistribution.
Kenyatta, on the other hand, was a most eloquent critic of Odinga and
his ideas. Relying on a labour ethic rooted in Kikuyu social history and
shared with many of Kenya's other ethnic groups, he directly challenged
his vice president's appeals for equality and redistribution. Belittling
Odinga and the other radicals as false prophets, Kenyatta argued that
Kenyans would have to help themselves if they wanted to drag themselves out of poverty. Poverty was, according to Kenyatta, a 'cross'
Kenyans would bear until they recognised that they were 'required to
sweat and toil, to be able to reap the maximum benefit from these opportunities' the state provided for self-improvement.[111] This message
played well with those that had profited from independence. When
visiting a cooperative-built rice mill in Mwea, Kenyatta paid 'tribute to
the discipline and hard work of the farmers on this scheme'. The cooperative's members 'have not just sat around drinking and wasting their
hard-earned money'.[112] Kenyatta was comfortable in these surround-
ings. The Mwea rice farmers had gained from the expansion in cash-
crop production that had resulted from a relaxation of colonial controls
over the agricultural sector. Kenyatta was on unsteady ground, however,
when dealing with other Kenyans who had been excluded from the
process of development. Aware that, for those who felt they had no hope
of improving their lot, Odinga's message of redistribution was more
powerful than his own mantra of self-help, Kenyatta had no choice but
to continue his efforts to minimise Odinga's ability to communicate
directly with those being left behind. The president put his faith in
economic growth continuing at a sufficient rate to convince the poorest
Kenyans that they had opportunities to improve their standard of living.

THE CONVENTION AT LIMURU

In the competition between the conservatives and the radicals, the
demise of KADU strengthened the president's hand. Despite the fierce

political battles that KANU and KADU had fought before independence, the instincts of KADU's leaders matched Kenyatta's own far more neatly than had Odinga's or Oneko's: after all, Moi, Ngala and Kenyatta all shared a valorisation of ethnicity and a suspicion of redistribution. KADU's merger with KANU in 1964 therefore provided the president with a new set of allies spread across the country. Once in government, the erstwhile opposition leaders were generally enthusiastic supporters of Kenyatta's economic policies. 'An African socialist is by nature a capitalist,' Masinde Muliro, a prominent figure in KADU and MP for Kitale East, told the *Sunday Nation* newspaper in 1967.[113] Muliro, the leading Luhya politician, had done well out of independence. The owner of nearly 1,500 acres of land and an agricultural transportation company, he was also chairman of the Maize and Produce Board that was responsible for overseeing production and marketing of the country's staple crop. But besides bolstering the strength in numbers of the conservative faction in government with men like Muliro, the demise of KADU also provided Kenyatta with the opportunity to overhaul KANU.

After the merger, former KADU branches and members had to be somehow absorbed into KANU's structures. This meant elections for positions in local branches and at the national level. As KANU's secretary-general, responsibility for managing these elections lay with Tom Mboya.[114] Mboya knew what had to be done. In the process of bringing former KADU members into the fold, members of the radical faction could be pushed out. Odinga would then be much weaker, given that he enjoyed considerable support among the existing KANU rank-and-file and in the party's local offices.

The process was a drawn-out affair. Elections in some branches began in July 1965, but the final selection of national executive positions in the newly unified KANU did not take place until nine months later. To Odinga's supporters, it appeared that Mboya was overseeing the mass rigging of the local party elections. Joseph Gogo Ochok, chairman of KANU in South Nyanza, was furious. Mboya 'has become a devil to your popular Government which was constitutionally elected', he wrote in a letter to the president.[115] Odinga ploughed on regardless.

Throughout the campaign season, he kept up a punishing schedule of fundraising and other public events in support of his allies. He was tailed throughout by the conservatives, who sought to counteract the powerful appeal of the radicals to grassroots members of the party.

Immediately after Odinga's visit to Kilifi at the Coast in November 1965, for instance, the local KANU branch convened a meeting to discuss the implications of the visit. Unusually, the meeting was attended by two MPs from outside the district: Abu Somo, the MP for Lamu, and the assistant minister for works and communications, Eric Bomett. At the meeting, the local KANU members and their prominent guests 'discussed some of the statements in Odinga's speeches and connected them with communism which they said Odinga was endeavouring to introduce to the Coast'. Bomett, a fierce loyalist of the conservatives and Moi's brother-in-law, closed the meeting by ordering Odinga's picture to be taken down from the office wall and destroyed. Abu Somo duly obliged.[116] The smashed portrait became an appropriate metaphor for Odinga's ambitions.

One by one, local KANU branch elections were won by supporters of the conservative faction. Pressure was also applied to Odinga's sources of campaign funds. Most of the radicals' funding came from Odinga's foreign friends, but the Soviet and Chinese embassies in Nairobi expected a return on their investment. These diplomats quickly recognised that the pressure from Kenyatta and Mboya made Odinga's hopes of success rather forlorn. Representatives of each of the major communist embassies were called to State House in the first weeks of 1966. There, Kenyatta told them to cease their support for Odinga or face expulsion. Odinga was informed by each in turn that his funding was being stopped. Under cover of a medical visit to Harley Street, a desperate Odinga travelled to London to talk to the communist embassies there in an effort to resume the flow of funds. He was successful, but the money came with strings attached. There was no interest among his funders in a breakaway party or a seizure of power. Instead, he was instructed to rebuild his position within KANU, in an effort to become the strongest candidate for succession after Kenyatta's departure from office.[117] The vice president's rivals were unwilling to let him remain influential within KANU, however. Instead they were determined to drive him from both government and the ruling party.

With each branch of the party having completed its elections for local officers, delegates met for a national convention in Nairobi and nearby Limuru from 11 March. The battle for control of the party between the two factions finally came to a head on the third and last day of the conference. The delegates whose election Mboya had so carefully managed were asked to vote on a motion proposing the abolition of the post of party vice president, held by Odinga alongside his cabinet position with the same title. Odinga's post was, Mboya proposed, to be replaced with eight vice presidents representing each of the country's seven provinces and Nairobi. Odinga was furious. As he addressed the delegates immediately prior to the vote, he warned that 'if the meeting proceeded with the day's business Kenya would be divided into two or more factions'.[118] The motion was, nevertheless, easily passed.

The delegates then moved on to electing officials to fill posts in the party's national headquarters. The conservatives won vote after vote over their radical rivals. Kenyatta was returned unopposed as party president. Mboya won the vote for the post of secretary-general. The eight new vice president positions were all filled by key allies of Kenyatta, including Kibaki and the former KADU leaders, Moi and Ngala. With his business successfully completed, a triumphant Kenyatta closed the meeting. The president warned 'that the Government would not tolerate one man or group of people who were bent on corrupting the masses with foreign ideologies or engaged in subversive activities'. 'Kenya had fought imperialism', Kenyatta told the delegates, 'and was determined to crush any such activities.'[119] The radical faction had been routed.

THE 'LITTLE GENERAL ELECTION'

Shortly after the meeting at Limuru closed, Odinga resigned from both KANU and the government. He did not admit defeat in his broader struggle for power, however. Instead, he established a new party, the Kenya People's Union (KPU), and was quickly joined by his fellow radicals, including Bildad Kaggia and Achieng' Oneko. For Oneko, the break with his old friend Kenyatta and KANU was a particular wrench. Nevertheless, his resignation letter was emphatic. The government had, he argued, lost 'the courage – let alone the intention – to bring about social equality'. The fight against inequality had apparently been 'the price for foreign aid'.[120] The KPU was, its founders hoped, the rightful inheritor of KANU's abandoned mantle as the party of redistribution. The government's response to such claims was scathing. Oneko's promises of a redistributive policy platform were, according to KANU's press office, entirely unrealistic given the 'factors of finance, personnel and resources which govern the pace of introducing completely free social services'.[121] As far as both sides were concerned, the formation of the KPU was the beginning of a new phase in the dispute over redistribution.

The government quickly set about trying to destroy the KPU before it took root. Sitting MPs who joined the new party were made to stand for re-election, and so twenty-nine by-elections were held across three weekends in June. These by-elections became collectively known as the 'Little General Election' and provided Kenyatta with the opportunity to destroy the infant KPU. His old suspicions of multipartyism resurfaced, but he was far from alone in thinking dissent in parliament to be undesirable. The prevailing political orthodoxy across much of sub-Saharan Africa was of unified, one-party states charged with delivering development rather than democracy. In Kenya, student leaders from Nairobi's University College, for instance, were concerned that through multipartyism 'the nation will be plunged back to the wasteful and regressive pre-independence political squabbles'.[122] The students did not, however, share Kenyatta's conviction that Odinga and the KPU should be bullied into submission.

As excitement and tension built ahead of the by-elections, the willingness of the government to rely on intimidation was apparent. In Nyanza, the heartland of support for both Odinga and the KPU, the paramilitary General Service Unit (GSU) was deployed to crush any hint of anti-government protests ahead of the elections. In the province's major towns, public demonstrations were carried out by the army to show off the strength of the state's security forces. Kisumu's KPU mayor, Grace Onyango, was unimpressed. She decried such tactics, which seemed intended only 'to frighten the Luos'. Onyango promised that the 'KPU would fight a clean fight without recourse to violence and that it was unnecessary to frighten them since they were not the type that could easily be frightened'.[123] The politicisation caused by the by-elections was readily apparent across the country. In Lamu, support for the government was overwhelming. 'Wherever you go the greeting is "*Mzee* [Old Man] and *Jogoo* [cockerel]",' wrote the district commissioner, referring to Kenyatta's commonly used title and KANU's emblem.[124] The island's towns were filled with crowds of placard-waving KANU supporters singing the party anthem 'KANU Builds the Nation'.[125] The shallowness of the unity engendered by independence was obvious.

Nowhere did the Little General Election campaign evoke such bitterness as in Bildad Kaggia's Kandara constituency in Murang'a. By supporting Odinga, Kaggia stood accused of jeopardising the Kikuyu hold over the state and its resources. Jesse Gachogo, secretary of the KANU branch in Murang'a and a senior officeholder in the party's national headquarters, led the anti-Kaggia efforts. Gachogo described Kaggia as a 'contaminated person who must be avoided by all those who do not wish to be infected by the germs of the anti-KANU and anti-Government forces, such as Kenya People's Union, "Odingaism" and others'.[126] The virulence of the language reflected the particular importance the government attached to defeating non-Luo KPU leaders at the 1966 polls.

Restrictions imposed on the KPU's campaigns were most intensive, and the abuses of the electoral process most egregious, in constituencies outside the opposition's Nyanza stronghold. Besides Gachogo's attacks on Kaggia, Moi led the assault on Oneko and other KPU MPs in the Rift Valley. Kenyatta attempted to capitalise on his nationalist legitimacy by depicting his opponents as disgruntled Luo. The demands for redistribution were drowned out by the shouts of ethnicity. But the language of ethnicity also spoke to varying experiences of the previous decade.

'There were two worlds in KANU,' thinks Bates: 'the world of Central and Eastern Provinces on the one hand and the world of Nyanza on the other'. In the 1950s and 1960s, farmers with small plots of land had expanded their production of all sorts of cash crops. The benefits of this expansion in output had been experienced the most in the Central Highlands, where higher rainfall, better infrastructure and proximity to markets in Nairobi meant that farmers could grow more, sell more and charge more than their counterparts elsewhere in the country. In Nyanza, by contrast, 'it was prohibitively costly to produce coffee or tea and prohibitively risky to raise grade cattle', writes Bates. 'But they also lacked access to major markets and quality infrastructure.' Although sugar production was expanding at this time, it took several years before the profits from that enterprise were visible on the farms and in the homes of Nyanza. That differing experience of development in large part explains the appeal of the KPU to Luo in Nyanza.[127] Because of that different recent history and the government's tactics, the opposition was ethnically and geographically isolated after the Little General Election. The most notable of the KPU's defeated candidates were Kaggia and Oneko (who lost his seat in Nakuru town), and the party after the by-elections was a rump of mainly Luo MPs representing constituencies in Nyanza.[128] Nevertheless, the KPU won nine seats, more than it could have hoped for, and polled nearly 20,000 more votes than KANU.

TWO PARTIES

Odinga's determination remained undimmed. Writing in the KPU's newsletter in June 1967, he delivered a withering attack on KANU's governance since independence. KANU was in a state of 'gradual decay'. Ministers and civil servants were no longer acting 'in the interest of *wananchi* ("citizens")', and the government was 'preaching and practising disunity and tribalism'. The fruits of independence were not being shared evenly or justly. Africanisation was taking place in small shops but not 'the major firms which actually control the economy of the country'.[129] Odinga and his supporters believed that the fruits of independence were being consumed by foreigners, particularly British investors and South Asian businessmen. The government's ties with the former colonial power alarmed many in the KPU, but so, too, did the close relations between the Americans and Mboya. George Oduya, the KPU MP for Busia North, described Mboya as 'a security risk' likely to 'commit more ruthless acts in collaboration with American CIA against the interest of the masses of Kenya and Africa as a whole'.[130] KANU had yet to alight on a way of winning its arguments with Odinga and his supporters, and so the government continued its efforts to silence the KPU.

Repression therefore continued after the Little General Election. The KPU's unexpected success convinced Kenyatta and his supporters that they needed to repress the new opposition party rather than seek cooperation. Detention, a hallmark of colonial rule, was resurrected as a tool of governance. Between August and November 1966, a series of KPU activists were arrested and placed in detention indefinitely. The government also moved to close down the KPU's channels of mass communication with the electorate. Ghulam Mohuyd-Din Paracha, the production manager of the printers that published the KPU's pamphlets and newsletters, was deported to Pakistan in March 1967. Those pamphlets and the words of the KPU's leaders presented a great challenge to the government.

Kenyatta held the government together. Oneko was right when he told the president that the party would exist only 'as long as Jomo Kenyatta leads it'.[131] Mboya aside, the president did not have a strong supporting cast. Kenyatta, therefore, had little choice but to spend the political capital accumulated during the preceding decades in his efforts to defeat Odinga once and for all. At every opportunity over the next three years, Kenyatta ridiculed and demonised the opposition party and its founders. His intellectual and personal objections to socialism and the actions of the KPU were never better spelled out than during his public address on the occasion of Labour Day in 1968. During that speech, Kenyatta described the KPU leaders as foreign-backed 'subversive men who try to confuse the workers in the towns and cities, or our hard-working farmers in the countryside, by talk that *uhuru* ["independence"] is not yet here'. He accused the KPU of extolling a vision of a Kenya where 'effort is not needed, . . . production is not necessary, and . . . a strange kind of world can be established in which all possessions and needs and services are given free'. Kenyatta critiqued the KPU with his long-held labour ethic, shared by a great many of his compatriots. Odinga and his allies, he stated, 'say nothing about the regimentation of human labour, and collapse of the human spirit, which such a theory must require. They never mention the suffering caused when something is stolen from one man in order to give it free to another.' 'They fear the dignity of honest labour,' Kenyatta said of his rivals. 'They see no future for themselves when men are free to work – and choose to work – for the rewards that can only be created by human skill and sweat.'[132] This was no simple battle for power between individuals, but rather a bitter intellectual and ideological struggle about the morality of development. Redistributive policies not only endangered economic growth and political stability, thought Kenyatta, but were also morally corrupt.

While maintaining his fierce ideological opposition to the KPU, Kenyatta also kept up his efforts to marginalise the opposition as a Luo party. Pressure was placed on its non-Luo MPs to force them to cross the floor of parliament and rejoin KANU. The first results of this strategy were seen in February 1967, when K.N. Gichoya, a Kikuyu and a senior official within the KPU, resigned from the opposition. Recognising that the appeal of the KPU was limited outside Nyanza, the opposition formulated short-lived plans in 1967 for the creation of a third party deliberately intended to attract non-Luo critics of the government.[133] The trend towards ethnocentric politics was unmistakable. Shelemiah Mbeo-Onyango, a Luo KANU MP, told parliament that 'every department is being centralized, or being taken over by one province, the Central Province or "Kikuyuized", or being taken over by one tribe, and that is Kikuyu'. But even such criticisms of Kenyatta's actions were couched in the language of ethnic grievance and threats. His colleague, Leonard Oselu Nyalick, another Luo KANU MP, thought: 'We are splitting far apart, and therefore, we are telling particularly our brothers, the Kikuyu, that the present frustration is coming out of their activities and that, unless it is arrested before it is too late, when blood comes we will not be to blame; they too, will suffer the same way we are going to suffer.'[134] Rather than heed such warnings, Kenyatta moved in for the kill.

SLAUGHTERING THE BULLS

Local elections announced for August 1968 presented a further opportunity to harass the KPU and its leaders. Kaggia was arrested for attempting to hold an unauthorised public meeting at Muriu in South Nyanza on 17 February 1968. A few weeks later he was sentenced to a year's imprisonment, reduced to six months on appeal. Odinga was, moreover, stopped from leaving the country. Restrictions preventing the opposition from holding public rallies ahead of the elections were once again imposed, forcing KPU members to hold covert political meetings at weddings and funerals. The party's fundraising effort was also squeezed. According to Oselu-Nyalick, 'Odinga always seems to have a lot of this kind of money and that is what makes him tough to beat.'[135] Cutting off this supply of funds was a priority for the government. In March, two of Odinga's supporters, Ochola Achola and Kimani Waiyaki, were accused of financing the KPU through connections in Uganda and were placed in detention.[136] Foreign sources of cash also came under close scrutiny. On 31 March 1968, the Czechoslovakian journalist, Jiří Forejt, was deported on the grounds of endangering national security.[137] Finally, the government fixed the results of the local elections. At a meeting in Nakuru on 27 July, Kenyatta ordered returning officers (in most cases district commissioners) to refuse to accept the nomination papers of all KPU candidates for the local elections.[138] KANU candidates for local office were returned unopposed across the country.

The manner of the KPU's defeat did not dampen the celebrations by KANU's leaders. In Nairobi, the president's son, Peter Muigai Kenyatta, held a victory party for members of the city's KANU branch 'at which five bulls – the KPU party symbol – each named after a KPU leader, were slaughtered and devoured with gusto'.[139] In Mombasa, some 200,000 people attended a victory celebration presided over by the president himself. Kenyatta promised the crowd that the KPU would be 'wiped out by KANU'.[140] There was no fight left in Odinga or the KPU. The party was haemorrhaging officials, MPs and members; by October 1968 just one non-Luo KPU MP remained in parliament. Odinga's communist backing dried up, too. From 1969, Soviet and other communist funders preferred to work with the government.[141] Utterly demoralised, Odinga made attempts to seek reconciliation with Kenyatta. Those efforts were rebuffed by Mboya, however, who insisted that Odinga should speak to him as secretary general of the party.[142] Instead of detente, the government continued in its efforts to destroy Odinga's base.

CHAPTER TWO

THE BIG MAN, 1968–69

Freedom, or independence, is not an end in itself. It cannot mean merely political sovereignty with a national flag.

Tom Mboya, speech to the Africa Bureau, London,
30 September 1963[1]

THE SUCCESSION

Kenyatta spent the first weekend of May 1968 at his beachside home at Bamburi, north of Mombasa. At some stage on the Sunday, he suffered a serious stroke. Heart and blood specialists and medical equipment were rushed from Mombasa to the president's home. His wife, Mama Ngina, hurried to Bamburi from Nairobi to be at the ailing president's side, along with the attorney general, Charles Njonjo, and the vice president, Daniel Arap Moi. The president's brother-in-law and minister of state, Mbiyu Koinange, had in any case been at Bamburi as usual for most of the weekend.[2] Although the president's condition was not made public, the urgency with which the dignitaries hurried to the coast alerted journalists and others to the fact that things were not at all well. By the following morning, rumours of Kenyatta's death were circulating among the domestic and foreign press corps; the *Daily Nation* newspaper even prepared a tribute supplement that was never published.[3]

Considerable efforts were made to create the impression of a minor health scare, followed by a swift return to business as usual. On 29 May, Njoroge Mungai, the minister of defence (who was also a relative of Kenyatta's and his personal physician), told MPs: 'His Excellency is in very sound health and has now assumed his official functions. All traces of the president's indisposition have now repeat now disappeared and I am sure that the whole country will rejoice in this matter.'[4] The truth was quite different. Six weeks after the stroke, the American ambassador found the president to be 'having difficulty in responding to routine questions'.[5] Kenyatta's capacity to govern had been dealt a serious blow.

With Kenyatta in convalescence for months after his stroke, power temporarily passed to two committees of senior cabinet ministers. Kenyans did not notice the difference, but the president's prolonged incapacity sparked a sense of crisis among the ruling elite. Concerns about what would happen in the event of Kenyatta's death in office were hardly new. While his exact date of birth is unknown, Kenyatta was at least seventy in 1963 and suffered from numerous serious health conditions. Just a month after independence, in fact, the British High Commission described the issue of succession as 'without doubt, the most important question in Kenya today'.[6] Kenya's allies, foreign investors and local elites all shared a belief that Kenyatta was the best guarantor of stability, control and the prevailing conditions that allowed for economic growth. Odinga's fall from grace assuaged British fears that Kenyatta's death would be followed by a turn to the left, but all knew that beneath the president the ruling elite was beset by factionalism and competing personal ambitions. Fears of a prolonged and violent struggle for the presidency in the future meant that the president's failing health was a matter of great concern to Kenyans and foreign observers alike.

James Gichuru was the conservatives' agreed successor during the first three years of independence. He had much in common with Kenyatta. He was eager to maintain good relations with the UK and US and, as a leading Kikuyu politician, seemed best placed to protect the interests of the post-colonial elite. Gichuru also enjoyed a degree of popular support and legitimacy by virtue of his strong nationalist pedigree. However, his drinking exploits and ill-health meant that, by 1967, support for his candidacy among his fellow ministers had withered away.[7] Consensus among ministers disappeared, too. Two competing candidates emerged in Gichuru's place: Daniel Arap Moi and Tom Mboya. Each was supported by powerful rival factions within the government and represented influential wider interests. Kenyatta consistently refused to publicly anoint an heir, and efforts by ministers to raise the matter in cabinet were met only with an irritable rebuff.[8] Although the president overcame his stroke and lived for another decade, the struggle to succeed him dominated politics once the KPU was defeated.

THE EVERYMAN

For all his reticence to speak in public on the matter, privately Kenyatta hoped Moi would be his successor. A day after his stroke, Kenyatta was just well enough to harangue Moi (who had been made vice president in 1967) from his sickbed over the latter's 'need to build up his image in the country as the established Presidential successor'.[9] The president knew that Moi faced a formidable opponent in Tom Mboya. Mboya was, in many respects, an archetypal citizen of modern Kenya, for whom migration was a fact of life. While he traced his roots through his parents to the ancestral home on Rusinga Island off the South Nyanza coast of Lake Victoria, he had spent significant portions of his life in Thika and Nairobi. It was in the capital that he first entered public life as a trade unionist and then politician. Mboya could, he hoped, draw on the support of this wide range of different constituencies in his struggle with Moi.

He could also call on the support of the US. Throughout the early 1960s, he received CIA funding through American labour organisations and the centrist International Confederation of Free Trade Unions. Passing through Mboya's Kenya Federation of Labour, the sums reached a peak of $1,000 a month.[10] As this relatively small sum suggests, Mboya was not funded to provide intelligence, but rather to act as a foil to Odinga.

Mboya proved to be good value for his American backers. He was a consistent and implacable opponent of Odinga's faction within KANU and then the KPU. He led the efforts to close the Lumumba Institute, oversaw Odinga's marginalisation within KANU, provided the inspiration for the 1965 development policy statement, and then harried Odinga's supporters in parliament. For their part, Odinga and his supporters, like Kaggia, saw Mboya as their primary opponent. Chinese funds were used in 1965 to break Mboya's support in his home area around the lakeshore in southern Nyanza.[11] A sustained smear campaign was mounted by the KPU in an effort to taint him as an American secret agent. Personal rivalry, ideological differences and the context of the Cold War thus conspired to set Mboya against Odinga.

The two clashed on a whole array of different stages. One of the most important was the trade union movement. The trade unions had exerted their considerable power in the 1950s through their critical role in the rise of Mau Mau and then in the defeat of colonial rule. The proven capacity of the labour movement to represent wider sentiments of discontent in Kenyan society frightened many of the nationalist leaders once they were in government. As a minister, Mboya proved no fan of political activism on the part of the trade unions. Unions, Mboya warned, 'must now play their part in consolidating independence and helping in the task of economic reconstruction. The new governments are not prepared to allow any obstruction in the economic development either from trade unions or any other group of persons.'[12] Many in the trade unions did not share his views.

Through 1964 and 1965, strikes and go-slows were common occurrences. The intelligence service believed that the Odinga-led faction 'regard domination of the trade union movement as essential for the furtherance of their political aims'.[13] Kenyatta and Mboya therefore set about nullifying the political power of the trade unions as part of their wider assault on the politics of redistribution. As fears of a general strike gathered pace in August 1965, plans for a consolidated umbrella organisation for the unions finally took shape.[14] The following month, the state-organised Confederation of Trade Unions was established. The organisation amalgamated existing labour groups, increased state control of union activity, and prevented the labour movement from becoming a vehicle for the radical political faction.

The neutered trade unions denied Mboya his own most powerful constituency. He sacrificed their support in order to help Kenyatta defeat Odinga. The efforts to rebuff Odinga in other arenas had similarly profound implications for Mboya's bid to succeed the elderly president. While he could count on considerable support in parliament from his fellow MPs, parliament's power ebbed towards the executive through the 1960s, as Kenyatta consolidated his political dominance. Similarly KANU, the day-to-day running of which Mboya oversaw as secretary general, was of little consequence in policy-making and implementation. Kenyatta feared that the grassroots membership of the party harboured radical sympathies, and so made sure it had little to do with the business of government. Mboya's bid for high office was further undermined by the limited significance of his natural support base in fast-growing Nairobi.

His parliamentary constituency of Kamukunji covered much of the city centre. But his record of fighting to improve the lot of the urban worker meant that he could draw support from across the city, and particularly in the poorer neighbourhoods to the east. The residents of eastern Nairobi had particular need of a powerful patron in government. 'Poverty in Nairobi is as old as the city itself,' remarked one of Kenya's few economic historians in 1972.[15] But the situation got worse after independence. Rapid population growth, land shortages in rural areas and other drivers of urbanisation ensured that the number of Nairobi's residents grew dramatically year on year from 1963. The potential challenges this growth posed were obvious to the city's authorities. At independence, overcrowding was already acute: average occupancy was fifteen people per dwelling in Eastleigh, for instance.[16] With no existing dwellings available and with the city authorities lacking the wherewithal to improve the housing stock, migrants to the city built homes and took up leases in the informal settlements that began to fill the green spaces of the colonial city's map.

Within a few years of independence, up to 70,000 people were living in shanty-like structures in the Mathare Valley, one of the largest of the settlements. They had a grim existence, unconnected as they were to the city's infrastructure. 'There were hardly any latrines,' council officials reported, and 'the whole place was littered with faeces and refuse'. Without access roads, rubbish collection could not take place; and without running water, most of the residents had either to draw water from the heavily polluted Mathare River or else buy it from stalls operated by the city council.[17] Fearing that the city was turning into a 'Destitute Paradise', local officials argued that the best solution lay in resettlement of the city's poor to land in rural areas.[18] Kenyatta agreed and constantly exhorted the urban discontents to 'go back to the land'.

Despite their great significance to the modern history of Kenya, the cities were no source of great political power. Kamukunji was a multi-ethnic constituency in an age of ethnic politics dominated by politicians who valorised the values of countryside. The residents of Nairobi, Kisumu and Mombasa were under-represented in parliament and generally ignored by local authorities. Mboya's urban constituency was, then, of little value to him in his efforts to lay claim to be Kenyatta's rightful successor. Other changes to the substance of political debate further damaged his hopes of succeeding. While he did not agree with the KPU's proposals for wide-scale rapid redistributive policies, he did think that redistribution was a desirable eventual goal of government after independence. The demise of redistribution as a subject of political debate thus undermined Mboya as much as Odinga.

Besides these changes to the content of political debate, changes to the practice of politics further isolated Mboya. As the president's health failed and the strength of both parliament and the cabinet weakened, Kenyatta's preferred highly personalised way of handling government business became the dominant model. Sitting in court in his private and official residences dotted around the country, the president hosted delegations from provinces and districts, listened to their grievances and issued decrees in response. For example, in July 1970, a delegation from Samburu district visited Kenyatta at his home at Gatundu, carrying with them the 'warmest greetings from our people'. After highlighting

Samburu loyalty to the Kenyan government and subsequent losses suffered during the Shifta War, the delegation requested the presence of more police in the district to improve security, the establishment of centralised villages, the creation of game reserves to protect farming interests in the district, state allocation of cattle ranches to Samburu, and greater provision of development funds.[19]

Although they had begun as spontaneous events, these visits steadily became highly regulated modes of interaction between citizens and their head of state. They were organised by provincial commissioners, and anyone who wished to join the delegation to discuss specific problems with Kenyatta could do so with the prior agreement of the president's aides. The visits were also an opportunity for Kenyatta to demonstrate his largesse. A delegation from Meru in March 1969 was presented by Kenyatta with a cheque for $33,000 to contribute towards the building of a new hospital.[20] This system of visiting delegations showed the degree to which personalised power, centred on the president himself, had become institutionalised. Moreover, these rituals of power demonstrated the entrenchment of the politics of recognition within government decision-making. The visits were a form of ethnic claim-making, with delegations led by self-appointed representatives of particular ethnic communities taking their ethnically specific grievances direct to the president for adjudication.

Kenyatta's personalised form of government was replicated in every locality around the country by the officers of the provincial administration. The provincial and district commissioners were Kenyatta's chief lieutenants. As Henry Cheboiwo, MP and KANU secretary in Baringo district, put it: 'The District Commissioner in Baringo is in fact the eye of His Excellency the President of the Republic of Kenya.'[21] Kenyatta entrusted his provincial and district commissioners with 'responsibility for nothing less than the image and the impact of government'.[22] Anxious to add substance to image, he gave considerable powers to local administrators, allowing them to chair land boards that were charged with adjudicating on boundaries and approving land transfers.[23] Members of the provincial administration eagerly exploited the ill-defined powers granted to them by the president, much to the chagrin of elected politicians. Eliud Mahihu, the provincial commissioner in Eastern Province during much of the 1960s, was particularly well known for acting in such a manner and for antagonising politicians in the area. For example, following a series of four murders in the Ngandori location of Embu district, Mahihu imposed a curfew on Ngandori in clear contravention of the constitution. The local MP described his actions as an 'unnecessary and cruel punishment on our law abiding citizens'.[24] But nothing was done to curtail Mahihu's interventions in the daily lives of the residents of Eastern Province, or to rebalance the distribution of power between the different branches of government.

Whether one looked at Kenyatta or Mahihu, politics was coming to be more and more out of step with Mboya's own approach. The personalisation of power sat uncomfortably with his own preference for machine politics. While secretary general of KANU, he complained that party members 'misuse the Office of the President too much by expecting him to be involved in every dispute and petty disagreements arising in all districts'.[25] Kenyatta, by contrast, delighted in being sought out by ordinary Kenyans and asked to dispense his personal wisdom. This personalisation of power was, the US embassy correctly perceived, a 'governing tactic' specifically intended to undermine Mboya. Kenyatta feared Mboya's talents as a far more skilled committee man and was determined to keep his young rival in his place.[26] Mboya gamely tried to keep pace. In June 1967, for example, he led a delegation of Luo leaders to meet Kenyatta at State House in Nairobi. The delegation pledged its loyalty to the president but also requested that the more repressive elements of the anti-KPU campaign be eased.[27]

Mboya did not make a very good ethno-nationalist, however. He lacked a stable ethnic base from which he could launch a bid for the highest office. The Luo community was divided along various fault lines of region, class and ideology, and its political affections were further divided by the events of the 1960s. Far more Luo regarded Odinga as their leader and representative in Nairobi than looked to Mboya. Mboya's own 'Luoness' was a matter for debate, too. He was a Suba, a group that had drifted in and out of the orbit of the larger Luo community ever since Luo migrants moved into southern Nyanza during the late eighteenth century. Although by the mid-twentieth century indistinguishable from Luo in terms of culture and language, Suba occupied an ambiguous position within the ethnic politics of Nyanza.

Mboya was in any case unwilling to abandon nationalism. In early February 1968, he told the crowd attending the opening of a school in Kericho: 'We cannot build a nation if we are divided among ourselves. We must rid ourselves of all forms of tribalism and pool together our efforts to mould a strong and prosperous nation.'[28] But with the success of Kenyatta's efforts to marginalise the KPU as a Luo ethnic party, nationalism was becoming an anachronism. When Bildad Kaggia was released from detention in 1969, even he felt unable to rejoin his former colleagues in the opposition. He had no desire to risk the wrath of his fellow Kikuyu by resuming his role within the leadership of the KPU.

Mboya's presidential ambitions were undone by the very same processes that were used to undermine Odinga. By the late 1960s he found himself to be a machine politician forced to interact with personalised power; a party man who had overseen the marginalisation of KANU during the efforts to push out Odinga and his supporters; a trade union leader who had neutered the labour movement in order to deny his great rival another support base; and a nationalist in an era of ethnic politics. But Mboya only had himself to blame. After all, he more than any other minister (with the exception of Charles Njonjo) had acted as Kenyatta's enforcer in the campaign to destroy Odinga. Nevertheless, his declining fortunes took their toll. The target of a possible assassination attempt in December 1967 and hospitalised due to a stress-related illness in May 1968, Mboya had good reason to fear what lay ahead.

THE ASSAULT ON MBOYA

Mboya's personal ambition to be president explained his willingness to inflict these wounds on himself. That ambition, his intelligence, charisma and the strong support of his fellow MPs and many ministers meant that he remained a formidable opponent to Moi in any case. As the president's failing health galvanised into action those interested in influencing the succession, he became the target of a series of clumsy attempts by his rival's leading supporters to further undermine his bid to succeed Kenyatta. Although Moi was Kalenjin, the main movers behind his campaign were Kenyatta's Kikuyu inner circle. With Gichuru's demise by 1968, this group lacked a credible candidate of its own. Moreover, they recognised that increasing discontent across the country and Kikuyu privilege under Kenyatta meant that a non-Kikuyu candidate would be more acceptable to Kenyans. Moi seemed the perfect candidate as a non-Kikuyu front for an unchanged process of elite Kikuyu accumulation behind the scenes. These efforts were led by Njonjo. Never as skilled or shrewd a political operator as his reputation now suggests, the attorney general attempted to exploit his control of the state's legal apparatus to weaken Mboya and strengthen Moi.

Beginning in early 1968 and accelerated by Kenyatta's stroke, a series of proposals were introduced by Njonjo to parliament for constitutional amendments, to minimise Mboya's chances of succeeding the ailing president. He hoped that MPs could be persuaded to raise the constitutionally stipulated minimum age for a president from thirty-five to forty years – Mboya was aged just thirty-eight at the time. The attorney general also attempted to remove parliament from the succession process. Under the existing constitution, it would elect any successor, and it was clear that Mboya could count on much greater support from MPs than could Moi. Moreover, Njonjo's draft amendments included a requirement that any candidate for the presidency needed the backing of an officially registered political party – no independent candidate would be able to stand. It was thought that the votes of KANU's membership could be manipulated in whatever way necessary to defeat Mboya. Njonjo further harboured hopes that Mboya could, in any case, be ousted from his position as the party's secretary general.[29]

Njonjo's attempted amendments met with concerted resistance in parliament. Mboya was well liked by his fellow MPs and was an able organiser of parliamentary business. In cabinet, too, he enjoyed much support. Lawrence Sagini, Jeremiah Nyagah and Ronald Ngala emerged as Mboya's strongest defenders, leading opposition to Njonjo's efforts to paint him as disloyal and a tool of American neo-imperialism.[30] Among his fellow cabinet ministers, Mboya's only opponents were Moi, Njonjo, Njoroge Mungai, Julius Kiano and Paul Ngei. Among the eight KANU provincial vice presidents, he could count on the support of five. Only Kibaki and Gichuru were thought to support Moi, who was himself the vice president for the Rift Valley.[31] As a concession to this opposition, Njonjo was forced to scrap the alteration to the age qualification. Nevertheless, his other constitutional amendments passed into law at the end of June.

Because the constitutional amendments shifted responsibility from parliament to KANU for selecting a successor to Kenyatta, the parliamentary fight over the constitution was followed by an effort to reduce Mboya's control over the party. Across the country, a series of power struggles were initiated within various KANU branches as Moi's supporters sought to remove Mboya's backers from positions of power. Instigated by claims of irregularities in the management of local branches, a series of elections were held, during which Mboya's supporters were systematically removed from their positions of influence – just as Mboya himself had overseen the marginalisation of Odinga in 1965 and early 1966. In Coast, for instance, Moi's faction mounted a bid to dislodge Ronald Ngala from his position at the head of the region's politics.[32] Jesse Gachogo, who, three years earlier, had led the onslaught against Kaggia, lost control of Murang'a's KANU branch to Moi's ally, Julius Kiano.[33] Similarly in Nakuru, where the pro-Mboya Mark Mwithaga had beaten Oneko in the Little General Election, Moi and his supporters were able to dislodge Mwithaga from control of the KANU branch.[34] The vice president's position appeared unassailable at the beginning of 1969.

Demoralised by this succession of setbacks suffered by his supporters, Mboya was resigned by early 1969 to defeat in his struggle with Moi.[35] The trigger for something of a revival of his fortunes came with a by-election held in Gem in Nyanza in May. The seat had previously been occupied by KANU's Clement Argwings-Kodhek, who had died earlier in the year in a suspicious car accident. The nomination of the KANU candidate to replace him became yet another occasion for conflict between the pro-Mboya and pro-Moi camps in government. The Moi faction successfully imposed their candidate, Wycliffe Rading Omolo. He was an unpopular choice of candidate among members of the local KANU branch office, however. He had been a KPU official in the area before he rejoined KANU and, like so many of his former colleagues, retained his hostility towards Mboya, whom he blamed for the opposition party's travails. But Mboya enjoyed significant support from KANU members in Gem because the local party office was run by his father-in-law and veteran nationalist politician, Walter Odede. Odede complained in person to Kenyatta about the nomination of Omolo, but was rebuffed. Mboya decided to stay away from Gem during the campaign and refused to lend his support to Omolo.[36]

The KPU candidate, Wasongo Sijeyo, pulled off a stunning victory in the by-election. Embarrassed by the result and fearful that it suggested a wider level of support for the KPU, Kenyatta adopted an untypically determined tone at a cabinet meeting held shortly afterwards. The president told his ministers that the infighting and battling over the succession had to cease. In particular, he stated that the government could ill afford to waste Mboya's electoral acumen. Although Mboya himself was absent from the meeting, all those present agreed to Kenyatta's proposal that he should be given full control of strategy in all future election campaigns in Nyanza. Mboya's supporters in cabinet left the meeting 'overjoyed and encouraged that President Kenyatta has decreed that [the] party should make maximum use of Mboya's talents'.[37] His position seemed to have been secured.

He was given a further boost, it seemed, two weeks later, when Kenyatta announced that parliamentary elections would be held within the year and that no further KANU elections would take place before then. Although Mboya's supporters had been soundly beaten during the branch elections held earlier in the year, he still clung on to the post of secretary general. Kenyatta's order that no further party elections take place meant that Mboya would remain in that post for another year. His remaining influence over the party in the event of the president's death and a selection process for a successor was, then, safe for the time being. But he knew that he himself was in personal danger. His opponents' efforts to lever him from control of formal political institutions had been dashed by the unexpected turn of events in Gem, and he feared that they would turn to 'informal' methods to defeat him. In late June, he left the country for a short period as rumours of assassination grew by the day. He returned home only after being given assurances, as retired member of parliament Fitz de Souza reported, from 'all Kikuyu friends that he would be safe in Kenya'.[38]

Early in the afternoon of Saturday, 5 July, about a week after his return, Mboya and his bodyguard drove to Sehmi's pharmacy on Government Road in the centre of Nairobi. Mboya parked his car outside the shop, which had already closed for the day after the morning's trade. But he knew the Sehmis well, and when they saw his car they unlocked the front door for him. Walking the short distance from his parked car to the shop front, he paused to speak to a passing friend, Barack Obama, father of the current US president. After a brief chat, Mboya said goodbye to Obama and entered the pharmacy. He greeted Mrs Mohini Sehmi warmly and the two talked with Sehmi's pharmacist before Mboya took his leave. As he left, shots were fired and he was hit twice in the chest. His assailant jumped into a car and fled the scene, while Mboya fell without speaking, first into Mrs Sehmi's arms and then onto the floor in the doorway. He was bleeding profusely and stopped breathing almost immediately.[39] His bodyguard, who had been at his side throughout but had been unable to stop the gunman, collapsed in the street in grief.[40]

Mboya was dead on arrival at Nairobi Hospital; the last desperate attempts to resuscitate him in an operating theatre proved futile. News of the shooting had spread quickly and many of his friends and colleagues flocked to the hospital soon after his arrival. So, too, did the GSU and police. Within minutes, security officers and Mboya's friends were engaged in scuffles in the corridor outside the room in which the body lay.[41] As more and more of his supporters turned up at the hospital, the crowd became overwhelmingly Luo in composition, and proceeded to shout anti-government and anti-Kikuyu slogans at bystanders. A Kikuyu priest called to administer the last rites was forcibly removed from the hospital ward by the angry mourners. When Mboya's body was taken to his Nairobi home, a number of Kikuyu who tried to pay their respects were beaten up.[42] Government ministers were unwelcome, too. Moi went to view the body but was jostled by the crowd outside the house and his car was pelted with stones as he swiftly left the compound. Even Lawrence Sagini, an old friend but now the minister for local government, was preventing from paying his respects.[43]

Emotions ran high across the country. Three days after the murder, a requiem mass was held at Nairobi's Holy Family Basilica prior to the funeral cortege leaving for Nyanza. The cathedral was full of dignitaries and up to 50,000 mourners stood outside. Soldiers, police and the GSU were deployed for fear that the emotional crowds could turn volatile and violent. As Kenyatta arrived at the cathedral in his car, some two hundred mourners surrounded the vehicle. Shouting KPU slogans and abuse directed at the president and government, they stoned his car. The security forces responded by firing tear gas. A full-scale riot then gathered pace as the mourners hurled rocks and other projectiles at the security forces and smashed shop fronts. The security forces used more tear gas against the protestors and carried out baton charges to clear the vicinity of the cathedral of mourners. The noise of the riot echoed through the basilica itself, disturbing the requiem mass.[44] Plans to have Mboya's body lie in state in the cathedral that night were quickly abandoned. As tear-gas fumes leaked into the building and overcame a number of the congregation, Kenya seemed to be falling apart.

The day after the mass, Mboya's body was driven home to Nyanza. The motorcade accompanying him on his final journey was two miles long. As it left the city and passed through Dagoretti early in the morning, the cortege was stoned by a largely Kikuyu crowd, angered by the mourners' attacks on Kenyatta the day before at the cathedral. At the same time in Dagoretti, Luo were beaten up and their shops looted by Kikuyu mobs. But once the convoy was out of Nairobi,

Kenyans came throughout the day in droves to the roadside to pay tribute to Mboya as the cortege passed by. Crowds numbering in the thousands delayed it as it passed through the towns of Naivasha, Nakuru and Kericho. When it reached Kisumu in late afternoon, further unrest broke out. Police and the GSU baton-charged the crowds of mourners and used tear gas as they attempted to get closer to the hearse.[45] Nevertheless, the people of Nyanza and many other Kenyans were determined to pay tribute to a nationalist hero. Crowds continued to line the route to the ancestral home at Rusinga Island, which Mboya's body finally reached on 11 July.

His final interment was accompanied by an extraordinary outpouring of grief by countless mourners who surrounded the graveside. One of the most prominent was Odinga, whose battles with Mboya had been quickly forgotten. Dressed in the traditional manner of a Luo elder, Odinga was received with wild abandon by the rest of the mourners.[46] Mboya's death had united Luo to an extent never seen during his lifetime. 'Mboya became a martyr and "ethnic hero" around which a sense of Luo political unity burgeoned,' writes Ogot.[47] Other former rivals were not so willing to set their grudges aside: the Chinese embassy in Nairobi ignored Kenyatta's request that all flags be flown at half mast.[48]

The Chinese reaction to Mboya's murder was no doubt influenced by Moi's immediate attempt to blame foreign communist powers for the assassination. MPs from both parties thought the government would be better served by carrying out a proper investigation, instead of political grandstanding.[49] They were not much more convinced by the arrest of Nahashon Isaac Njenga Njoroge soon after the murder. Although he had spent four years as a student in Bulgaria earlier in the decade, Njenga had not apparently acted for any reason related to the Cold War or for any other discernible motive.[50] Indeed, apart from some rather vague descriptions of the assassin that were collected at the scene of the crime, it remains unclear what evidence led the police to arrest Njenga in his office in the city centre. As he was being driven away to custody, Njenga asked the arresting officers: 'Why pick on me? Why not the big man? We did what we were told.' He refused to answer the police when they asked him who 'the big man' was.[51]

THE AFTERMATH

When Njenga's question about 'the big man' came to light during the pre-trial hearing in mid-August, it fuelled still further the widespread speculation about the assassination. As with Pinto's murder, all sorts of rumours quickly spread about the circumstances and motives surrounding Mboya's assassination. Suggestions that the KPU had been behind the murder were made by some of the party's enemies in government, and affidavits naming Oneko as the chief organiser were given to Special Branch. These were, however, rejected on account of the lack of any real evidence.[52] Given far greater credence were the rumours that Charles Rubia had in fact been the mastermind behind the murder. The government did little to quell these suggestions, and sources close to the police investigation initially made it very clear that Rubia was the prime suspect.[53]

That Rubia was hugely ambitious and saw Mboya as a block to his political aspirations was no secret. Both men had long struggled for influence over Nairobi's masses – Mboya as a trade unionist and minister and Rubia as a local politician. Rubia had first entered politics in 1955 through the city council. Having been elected mayor of Nairobi in 1962, he made such a success of the job that he was re-elected by his fellow councillors for three further terms. He eventually resigned from the council in 1967 in order to concentrate on his national political career, and it was well known that he had designs on Mboya's Kamukunji constituency. Rubia also proved to be a successful businessman and he was not averse to using his considerable wealth to boost his political efforts, most notably when he successfully usurped control of the city's KANU branch from Mboya's supporters in 1968.[54]

Rubia had at first seemed an ideal ally to Moi and Njonjo in their efforts to destroy Mboya's succession candidacy, and they supported him during his successful bid for the chairmanship of the city's KANU branch.[55] They also thought him the best-qualified challenger to Mboya for the post as the party's secretary general.[56] But they soon came to see Rubia as a threat, too. Wealthy, charismatic, popular and able, he had a unique range of skills and virtues that few of his peers possessed. Any comparison between Rubia and Moi, for instance, was unflattering to the vice president. However, Rubia overreached himself. Following his successful bid for control of KANU in Nairobi, he attempted to use his influence in the city council to block Kenyatta's daughter, Margaret, in her efforts to become mayor of Nairobi. He was unsuccessful and only succeeded in antagonising Kenyatta, Njonjo and others at the very top of government.[57] His star fell as quickly as it had risen.

Rubia was the perfect patsy, but those behind the set-up had no intention of putting him on trial. They instead hoped to discredit him through innuendo, and his rivalry with Mboya made such rumours seem plausible. Nevertheless, as Njenga's case was about to go to trial, the expatriate British police officer who was in charge of the investigation made it clear to the British High Commission that he did 'not believe that Rubia is involved'.[58] The US State Department was certain that the orchestrators of Mboya's assassination were the same Kikuyu ministers close to Kenyatta who had long opposed Mboya's succession aspirations.[59] After some doubts, the British eventually agreed. Njonjo, the High Commission alleged in 1973, 'more than probably had a hand in the death of Mboya'.[60]

Njenga was alone in the dock when the trial opened on 3 September. Few informed observers expected anything other than a verdict of guilty. The chief justice, Kitili Mwendwa, told British diplomats that 'he had no doubt that it would end with the conviction of Njenga'.[61] British expatriate police officers and senior ministers alike were certain that the defendant would be found guilty and would be hanged soon after.[62] The trial lasted just eight days and, as predicted, Njenga was found guilty and sentenced to death. He announced his intention to appeal and left court apparently carefree.[63] The appeal was heard a month later but was dismissed after just one day in court. Njenga's lawyer based the appeal around the claim that he was at worst an accessory to the murder, and hinted at a wider plot. But Njenga still refused to name names.[64] The state's prosecutor in the case, John Hobbs, admitted in private that 'it was fairly clear that Njenga was acting as the agent of a conspiracy', but that Njenga was himself guilty.[65] Njenga nevertheless remained steadfast in his silence until all legal avenues had been exhausted.

His final recourse to save his own life was to appeal to Kenyatta for clemency (though the decision was, in fact, in the hands of the chief justice). When that appeal, too, was rejected, the end was swift. On the night of 8 November, Njenga was woken by the public hangman, himself a British expatriate officer. Taken aback by the turn of events, Njenga broke down as he was taken from his cell to the scaffold and executed. The hangman was working under explicit orders direct from Njonjo. Only the commissioner of prisons, the hangman and Njonjo himself knew what was taking place. The prison chaplain, who normally attended executions, was not summoned, and the prison doctor was only present because the executioner had personally contacted him. To the British, the indecent speed, secrecy and Njenga's total surprise was 'consistent with the possibility that he had been given assurances that his life would be saved, and that he was summarily despatched to prevent him opening his mouth'.[66] According to this version of events, Njenga's silence had been bought in return for promises that the death sentence would be commuted to imprisonment. Mwendwa's refusal to issue the necessary pardon meant that those close to Kenyatta were unable to keep their side of the bargain and risked Njenga revealing what he knew of the plot as he saw out the rest of his days on death row. He had to be silenced immediately and so was executed in summary fashion.[67]

FROM NANDI HILLS TO KISUMU

The aftershocks of Mboya's assassination were felt right across Kenyan society. Ethnic intolerance increased almost immediately after the public announcement of the shooting, particularly in areas of the Rift Valley where Kikuyu had been settled in large numbers after independence: on 17 July, a group of armed Kalenjin youths from Turbo in the Rift Valley beat up two of their Kikuyu counterparts. In itself, this was not a particularly serious incident. According to the local authorities, 'tension cooled down and there is no fear at all'.[68] Local Kikuyu were not so sure.

While embellishing the details and exaggerating the level of threat – no one was killed at Turbo in July 1969 – Samwel Ngugi wrote of how 'Nandis are fighting Kikuyu to death. [They] usually scream from evening to morning. Kikuyu who are living within Kaptabei Settlement Scheme are sleeping outside at present.' Accusing local Nandi Kalenjin of burning down Kikuyu homes and beating any Kikuyu settlers, Ngugi pleaded for government protection.[69] Significant clashes were narrowly averted at Londiani through these tumultuous weeks and at Lumbwa, Kikuyu farmers sought refuge in the compounds of local administration officials in order to protect themselves from attack by Kipsigis.[70] Kenyatta's response was to further entrench the position of elite Kikuyu and consolidate the support from the Kikuyu grassroots.

The president turned to 'oathing' in order to unify Kikuyu behind him. Oathing ceremonies had begun earlier in the year, but accelerated after Mboya's murder. An adaptation of a Kikuyu dispute-resolution custom, oathing had been politicised by anti-colonial protestors in the 1940s. It became synonymous with the Mau Mau insurgency when, with its use of rituals and paraphernalia laden with Kikuyu indigenous religious symbolism, it echoed the Kikuyu circumcision ceremonies. In their oaths, Kikuyu swore to support the insurgents in their rebellion against the British. But oathing proved divisive in the 1950s: Christians thought it a pagan ritual and others decried the violence that oathers used to force reluctant Kikuyu to take the oath. Its resurrection in the late 1960s was therefore contentious.

Through 1969 and into early 1970, Kikuyu, Embu, Meru and Kamba were taken in their thousands to Kenyatta's home. One recent estimate suggests that over 300,000 people were transported to Gatundu.[71] According to one account, they swore thus:

> The government of Kenya is under Kikuyu leadership, and this must be maintained. If any tribe tries to set itself up against the Kikuyu, we must fight them in the same way that we died fighting the British settlers. No uncircumcised leaders [i.e. Luo] will be allowed to compete with the Kikuyu. You shall not vote for any party not led by the Kikuyu.[72]

The oathing was not just a matter of national politics. There were also much more localised motivations for the ceremonies. They provided an opportunity for the old guard in government to intimidate sceptical voters and get them back into line before the parliamentary elections due later in the year.[73]

Despite the fact that the ceremonies were shrouded in secrecy – very few accounts exist to this day – the scale of the operation meant it could not escape public attention. The naked political agendas at work caused resentment among existing opponents of the regime. But the large ceremonies caused great alarm across the rest of the country, too. The sense that Kikuyu were willing to fight to remain in power made many Kenyans uneasy. Others were concerned that the role of state officials in transporting those taking the oath to Gatundu and other sites suggested the Kikuyu elite had hijacked the state's institutions. In an ever more Christian country, moreover, oathing awoke arguments first made in the 1950s about the supposedly pagan nature of the practice. The main churches unequivocally criticised it and demanded that it cease immediately. Politicians followed suit. Odinga was predictably to the fore, but other prominent non-Kikuyu MPs, including ministers, also joined in. Six MPs from Eastern Province warned that 'there is going to be a physical resistance which will lead to a total breakdown of law and order' if oathing continued.[74] Oathing did, in fact, cease soon afterwards, but this was just one manifestation of the more pronounced ethnic nature of politics across Kenya at the time.

In the Nandi Hills, Kalenjin politicians set out to capitalise on the intensely ethnic character of politics in the middle months of 1969. The multi-ethnic character of the area in the west of the Rift Valley was typical of many parts of the province. The hope of a plot of land on one of the farms vacated by European settlers attracted a good deal of inward migration into the Nandi Hills after independence. The close proximity of the hills to the provincial boundary with Nyanza meant that a great many Luo had settled there since 1963, but so had Kikuyu and members of many other ethnic groups. 'We have different Tribes here,' boasted one local KANU activist in a letter to Kenyatta in 1966.[75] The presence of Kikuyu, in particular, was not something that pleased many Kalenjin in the hills, however. As the political temperature rose with Mboya's assassination, so too did resentment of the recent migrants.

In late July 1969, the local MP, Jean Marie Seroney, chaired a meeting of elders of the Nandi sub-group of the larger Kalenjin community at Kapngetuny. The resolutions of that meeting, which became known as the Nandi Hills Declaration, were a forthright example of the nature of political debate at this time. The entire Nandi district was declared to belong 'under God to the Nandi people; and every non-Nandi, whether an individual, a firm or a corporation farming in the district or in the Tinderet area is a temporary tenant of will of the Nandi'. The meeting resolved that no land transactions in the district involving non-Nandi 'shall be recognised as having any validity whatsoever', and called on every non-Nandi either to surrender his alternative ethnic allegiance or 'to remove himself and his effects from the District without any delay, lest he incurs the wrath and undying enmity of the Nandi people'.[76] The declaration was an example of a renewed and vigorous ethnic sensibility, but was also an attempt to exploit the conditions of heightened ethnic tension so as to settle disputes over access to scarce land and jobs. Seroney had his own motives, too: he was a rival of Moi, and the Nandi Hills Declaration boosted his claims to leadership of the Kalenjin community. The trial for sedition that followed as a result of the declaration elevated those claims still further.

Across the country, Kenyatta faced unprecedented challenges to his rule. But the president was not interested in reconciliation and instead fought back. He was determined to rebuild his authority, and at the same time to marginalise the KPU still further, in order to prevent the opposition from making political capital over his government's short-comings. To this end, the president undertook a series of meetings with prominent leaders from each of the main ethnic communities across the country. Towards the end of October, he began a two-day tour through the Rift Valley, Western and Nyanza Provinces to meet the people. At Nakuru and then Kakamega, Kenyatta launched virulent attacks on the KPU. None, however, compared to the president's words when he arrived in Kisumu on 25 October.

The ostensible purpose of Kenyatta's visit was to open a Soviet-funded hospital. Kenyatta had a very different goal in mind, however, and seemed to want to goad his opponents into action. Anticipating trouble, he gave his bodyguards clear and unequivocal orders prior to the visit to Kisumu to 'shoot to kill when the first stone is thrown'.[77] As his entourage arrived at the hospital grounds, he was greeted with boos and KPU slogans shouted from the crowd. Some of the 5,000 or so in attendance began stoning the president's car. As police arrested some of those involved, the situation calmed down sufficiently to allow Kenyatta to begin the opening ceremony of the hospital. Complaining that he had travelled all the way to Kisumu to open a hospital that had been built by the government, only to be greeted with protests, Kenyatta recounted a Swahili proverb: 'The thanks of a donkey is a kick.' 'These stupid people must end their nonsense and unless they do so we will deal with them severely,' he warned. He then turned on Odinga, who was also present among the VIPs. 'If it was not for my respect for you, Odinga, I would put you in prison now and see who has the power in this country. If any of your stupid supporters continue with their nonsense, we show them that Kenya has a government.'[78] The crowd was outraged.

Hecklers interrupted Kenyatta throughout his speech and KANU activists clashed with their KPU counterparts while he was still speaking. With missiles flying, the president's bodyguards rushed him to his car and fled the scene. Hostile crowds had gathered along the president's route out of the city along the Kakamega Road. They shouted insults as he drove past and many threw more stones. As the crowds spilled into the road in front of Kenyatta's motorcade, his bodyguards opened fire. The gunshots and the resulting stampede left at least eight people dead – although some accounts claim the figure was in the tens or hundreds – and scores injured. Kenyatta was driven away from Kisumu as fast as possible, heading east, back towards Nakuru. Almost immediately, he ordered the arrest and detention of Odinga, all KPU MPs and other leading figures within the party. The KPU was banned soon afterwards, and the elections held at the end of the year were restricted to KANU candidates.

CHAPTER THREE

THE FALLEN ANGEL, 1971–75

The bones we left in the forest are crying for us.

Mau Mau veterans from Mahiga to Nyeri District Commissioner,
14 November 1970[1]

LAND AND FREEDOM

'To understand Mathenge', a British diplomat wrote in March 1972, 'is to some extent to understand both the President and the Kenya Government.' As one of the president's most trusted lieutenants, Isaiah Mathenge served as provincial commissioner in Coast from 1965, and then in the Rift Valley after his appointment in 1971. From his office in Nakuru, Mathenge was Kenyatta's direct representative at the epicentre of post-colonial politics as the president set about tightening his grip on power in the aftermath of Mboya's assassination and the dissolution of the KPU. Few could therefore rival the insight he could provide into Kenyatta's thinking and the priorities that underlay his policies.

As Kenya approached the anniversary of its first decade of independence, according to Mathenge, memories of the final years of colonial rule continued to influence the president's political calculations. Of all the challenges he faced in the early 1970s, Kenyatta was, the provincial commissioner thought, particularly concerned over the question of 'the Kikuyu have-nots': 'Mainly people from the Mau Mau villages who were still without land, [the president] was desperately concerned to ensure that they were satisfied.' Kenyatta feared 'driving such groups into the forest where he would lose control of them'. From there, in his nightmares, the discontented Kikuyu could join up with unhappy junior rank-and-file in the armed forces or some other such militant section of Kenyan society. 'In any case, even without the army link they would, if driven underground, be poised to assassinate ministers and senior public servants.'[2] Mau Mau's veterans and other poor Kikuyu were the ghosts at the banquet of post-colonial Kenya. Kikuyu rivals, such as Kaggia, who threatened to mobilise Mau Mau veterans and their supporters against the president were treated with particular concern.

Mutual suspicion between the president and the Mau Mau veterans was deep-rooted. Many former Mau Mau fighters felt little affection for Kenyatta's regime from even before independence. As foreign dignitaries flocked into Nairobi ahead of the celebrations of December 1963, for instance, a group of Mau Mau veterans distributed an alternative independence address for their visitors. The self-styled 'irreconcilable ex-detainees [and] political prisoners' were in no mood to forgive and forget their enemies from the colonial period, as Kenyatta urged them to do. Nor did they have much time for the claims of the politicians to be the true leaders of nationalism. The authors of the address were 'those who fought [a] relentless battle and never gave up until the battle was won'. They were 'the people who have endured all the difficulties of humiliation during the process of time in detention and prison camps defending the right of our country [and] being ridiculed'. The veterans of the Mau Mau war were the true 'patriots of our struggle'. It was their children who 'were forced to leave school and to join their grandparents [in] full day communal labour, and consequently lost the chance to become educated'. It was the supporters of the rebellion who had their property seized or destroyed by the British security forces and their Kenyan allies, and who were forced into villages 'to die of hunger'.[3] And it was the Mau Mau veterans who, Kenyatta believed, posed one of the greatest threats to his rule after independence.

Initially that perceived threat was related to security. While the last recalcitrant groups of Mau Mau guerrillas remained in the forests of Mount Kenya, fears of a revival of the insurgency were particularly acute. Even after all those insurgents were eventually either cajoled into leaving the forests or tracked down and shot by the security forces, the threat posed by Mau Mau was not deemed to have disappeared. For the first three years of independence, Kenyan intelligence kept close watch on groups of Mau Mau veterans who, it was feared, would return to the forests to take up arms against the KANU government, should it not allay demands for land. The political threat posed by Mau Mau veterans and their supporters proved much longer-lasting.

Mau Mau veterans thought they had earned the right to enjoy at least some of the fruits of independence – a euphemism for the lands being vacated by departing European settlers. After all, had they not fought for land and freedom? To those in State House, such claims were a source of great discomfort. For one thing, the demand for free land contravened the agreements reached with the British that private property should be protected. Such claims for land further offended the ideological sensibilities of those among Kenya's new rulers who believed that land should be earned and not granted. The claims of the mostly Kikuyu Mau Mau veterans furthermore were politically indelicate in the first years of independence. There was little vacant land waiting to be redistributed in Central Province. Instead, as all participating in this debate knew only too well, the land being demanded lay in the Rift Valley and was claimed by other communities, most notably Kalenjin and Maasai.

The expectations of ex-Mau Mau and other landless Kikuyu were perhaps highest in the Nyandarua district. Formerly an area dominated by European-owned farms, much of the district was earmarked for settlement of landless Kikuyu from the other side of the Aberdare Mountains in Central Province and elsewhere in the Rift Valley Province. Finally free from colonial restrictions on movement, landless Kikuyu flocked to Nyandarua in the expectation of grants of land during the months that preceded independence. More than 26,000 applications for plots in the district were made by February 1963. Over the last weeks of 1963 and through 1964, many more Kikuyu arrived than settlement schemes of any size could accommodate. These new arrivals made short-term housing arrangements, squatted on large-scale farms still in operation, or took up residence on already-abandoned farms being prepared for inclusion in the settlement schemes. The authorities attempted to exercise some control by issuing eviction notices, but such efforts were widely ignored and resisted, with resort to petty forms of protest. By the first anniversary of independence, there were 18,000 landless people in Nyandarua district, almost all Kikuyu. Far from alleviating landlessness, independence and the attendant hopes of land grants that accompanied it initially exacerbated the problem.[4]

The town of Ol'Kalou was at the centre of these developments. According to the local KANU branch chairman, Mwangi Gitathu, the township became a desperate place in the months following independence. Previously little more than a trading centre so typical of rural areas, Ol'Kalou lacked many basic amenities and had little available housing. The town quickly became inundated with temporary shacks. There was no work either. The migrants to Ol'Kalou had 'neither any means of self supporting for themselves nor their members of families. Until date [sic], they are helplessly lying idle, hanging about like parasites with no cause to follow.'[5] Those that had moved to the town had done so in the expectation that the large European-owned farms surrounding Ol'Kalou would be subdivided and given to small farmers. However, the land was instead transferred intact as large farms, without provision for settlement, because, in the words of a government report, 'topography, soil and climate made it uneconomic to sub-divide the 120,000 acres'.[6] As a consequence, local anger in Ol'Kalou grew.

The Mau Mau War Council, a group of ex-insurgents and their families, wrote to Kenyatta in January 1964 to make their discontent clear. 'In Nyandarua District we were informed that land would be allocated to the landless but now it is the rich people who are buying land,' the group complained. 'What will you do with the poor people?' On the settler farms around Ol'Kalou, working conditions were unchanged despite independence. 'Women are overworked and in most cases their work is not recognised which results in deprival of their pay for the work done,' the veterans claimed. Attempts to farm small portions of uncultivated land around Ol'Kalou led to convictions and fines for trespass. The situation seemed hopeless. The Mau Mau veterans asked Kenyatta 'that Government settles them elsewhere or else be given permission to deal with the settlers by force'.[7] As if to back up the threat to effectively resume the Mau Mau war, the taking of oaths intended to unify and mobilise disaffected Kikuyu once again became commonplace. Threats were made to the lives of those African farmers who took over the land previously farmed by European settlers, which the landless thought was theirs. While no one was harmed, the anger of the landless Kikuyu was nonetheless palpable.[8]

Given the extent of landlessness in Ol'Kalou, it is not surprising that the local MP soon appeared as one of the most public voices calling for amelioration of the grievances of Mau Mau veterans. Like so many other young Kikuyu men born in the late 1920s and 1930s, Josiah Mwangi Kariuki, better known in Kenya simply as 'JM', found himself deeply involved in the increased political activity of the period after the Second World War. Active in the militant politics that bred the Mau Mau insurgency, he was arrested and detained in 1953. His bestselling account of his detention, *'Mau Mau' Detainee*, made him a familiar figure to both British and Kenyan audiences as the country approached independence in 1963. But he also played an important role in the founding of KANU in Nyeri in 1960 and went on to become MP for the Nyandarua North constituency, which included Ol'Kalou.

Kariuki was a successful businessman, as well as a prominent politician. His wealth was founded on wise investment of his book royalties and on the close relationships he enjoyed with the Delameres, the most prominent of the old settler families, and with Jack Block, the owner of Kenya's largest hotel group.[9] Kariuki did not hide his wealth. A smart dresser, polygamist, keen gambler and enthusiastic host, he became an integral part of the social circle that surrounded politics in the first years of independence. He did not, however, forget his connections to either his constituents or the Mau Mau rebellion.

From the very beginning of his political career, Kariuki used his seat in parliament to give voice to the suffering of the Mau Mau veterans and the widows and children of those who died in the violence of the 1950s. 'Why should the Government now turn a deaf ear to the requests of people who suffered for the freedom of this country?' he asked in one of his early speeches in parliament.[10] This was a theme he returned to repeatedly throughout his political career, as part of a broader critique of Kenyatta's land policies and the growing problem of social inequality. Despite these interests, he was no radical. In the mid-1960s, Kariuki received funds from Washington to publish a weekly newspaper to combat Chinese propaganda efforts.[11] While not a fan of Britain's involvement in the post-colonial land transfer programme, Kariuki considered Soviet influence to be a far more pernicious force in Kenyan politics. He was amenable to British investment in Kenya and broadly supportive of its foreign policy towards the wider region, including arms sales to the apartheid regime in Pretoria.[12] Nevertheless, with his policy platform of land reform, coupled with his personal charisma, Kariuki was among the most prominent and lucid critics of the government throughout the 1960s and early 1970s.

THE PROMISED LAND

Apart from token gestures, the government was unwilling to make any substantive recognition of the role of Mau Mau veterans in the independence struggle. 'The Government could not possibly have sufficient funds to compensate them all,' one civil servant informed Kamau Karugu, who had lost his home and possessions while in detention in the 1950s.[13] More significantly, any wholesale land reform programme involving the compulsory seizure of land for redistribution to Mau Mau veterans was further ruled out on the basis that it would destroy the legal integrity of title deeds.[14] The veterans were unimpressed by such sentiments. 'Did I fight to be a beggar for land?' two of them wrote in a letter to Kenyatta in 1973. 'No. I fought to own a piece of land.'[15] They were far from alone in believing that the post-colonial state had betrayed the insurgency.

Kenyatta's only retort to such criticism was to point out that much land was passing from European to African ownership. 'Don't worry, one day all our farmers will be black – one day,' he told sceptical KANU backbenchers in 1963.[16] From shortly before independence until 1970, perhaps half a million Kenyan farmers and their families were resettled on around 2 million acres of land previously owned by European settlers.[17] The newly settled farmers were thus able to participate in the extraordinary growth in the Kenyan economy over the first years of independence. Driven by an expansion in the production of almost every conceivable cash crop and livestock product, revenues of farmers nearly trebled between 1963 and 1967.[18] The wider economy was also growing on the back of agricultural output. The World Bank estimated that GDP increased by on average 7 per cent per annum for the first nine years of independence.[19] Many ordinary Kenyans were able to participate in this growing economy through access to the land vacated by European settlers and thanks to new policies designed to encourage the appointment of Africans to management positions in the private and public sectors. In short, in the words of one political scientist, 'the Kenyan regime "works" for large numbers of Kenyans', despite the obvious poverty that many still lived in.[20]

Resettlement and economic growth failed to tackle underlying structural inequalities within society, however. For instance, the interests of large-scale farming remained paramount within the strategic calculations made by the country's economic planners. Although after independence these farmers were often Africans, their position of privilege was still protected. Nor were all of those resettled equal. Some were individual farmers who took over wholesale land formerly owned by European settlers. But most were poor, previously landless and settled on small plots carved out of the major landholdings of the departing European settlers. Smaller farmers gained little from the apparent 'agrarian revolution' that saw production of cash crops increase greatly after independence.[21]

Many farmers were swamped by debt. Most of the new farmers borrowed substantial sums of money to buy their plots and improve them. A debt crisis quickly emerged, as it became clear that the new

African farmers were not able to make enough money to pay off their loans. This was a particular problem for smaller farmers, whose plots were too small to provide for their families and to generate sufficient surpluses for sale to meet the repayment terms of the loans used to buy the land.[22] Thus, rather than addressing social inequality, post-colonial land policy compounded it.

The negative effects of land policy were of particularly great significance from 1970 onwards, as the frontier of Kikuyu settlement expanded still further. A series of administrative and political decisions made this resettlement of Kikuyu much easier. Agreements with the British government allowed the Kenyan government to use money from London designated to fund the resettlement programme, without oversight, for the first time. Key civil servants and administration officers were reshuffled. Besides Mathenge's appointment in 1971, Samuel Kung'u, a Kikuyu permanent secretary in the Office of the President, was moved to the Ministry of Lands and Settlement in April 1971.[23] New sites for settlement were also identified. Kenyatta used the presidential entourage to make thinly veiled threats against British farmers who had not already sold up, while at the same time offering a quick sale on favourable terms.[24] Land titles began to be issued for supposedly protected forest reserves. More controversially, colonial legislation preventing access by non-residents to so-called 'closed districts' was revoked in 1970. These districts, which included the predominantly Maasai districts of Narok and Kajiado, as well as various tracts of northern parts of the country, were now earmarked for resettlement of Kikuyu.

The results could be seen across the country. Outward migration from Central Province in the 1960s had been sizeable; the 1969 census revealed that more than 150,000 residents of the Rift Valley Province had been born in Central Province.[25] But what followed in the early 1970s was even more extensive, and the clear political agenda at work far more explicit. In a speech in June 1971, Kenyatta announced a new wave of settlement in the Rift Valley on 150,000 acres of land. As the British High Commission recognised, this necessarily entailed further 'massive Kikuyu intrusion on to land which has been traditionally non-Kikuyu'.[26] The diplomat who wrote this was right. Inward migration to Eldoret town in the Rift Valley and settlement schemes in the surrounding area meant its population increased by nearly 50 per cent in the ten years after Mboya's assassination.[27] In the same period, the national population increased by around 3 per cent per annum. In Trans Nzoia district, the situation was even starker. Per annum population growth driven by inward migration was nearly 8 per cent in 1969–79.[28] Similar significant population increases were observed in coastal districts. The Lake Kenyatta settlement at Lamu was intended for the resettlement of those displaced by the Shifta War, as well as for landless families from Lamu and the wider coastal area. Instead, it became home to 3,600 Kikuyu.[29]

The way in which Kikuyu took ownership of this land was just as important as the fact of their doing so. Five cooperative societies, which, Kenyatta announced in November 1971, were to be allocated nearly 30,000 acres around Nakuru, were typical of the mechanism by which many Kikuyu participated in the resettlement. Kenyatta claimed during that announcement that the new settlers were to be drawn from across the country; but in truth all five cooperative societies and the 2,400 families to be settled on the land were Kikuyu.[30] Those moving onto the farms vacated by the European settlers were often shareholders in companies set up for the purpose of buying land in the Rift Valley. Most, but not all, such companies were made up of Kikuyu farmers who joined together to raise the necessary capital to purchase the large farms and then to oversee the subdivision of the land among the shareholders.

Though they allowed many who otherwise lacked the wealth to do so to participate in the land transfer programme, the land companies and cooperatives quickly found themselves suffering from inadequate management structures. Accusations of corruption and actual embezzlement of company funds became commonplace in the absence of proper regulatory frameworks, and many of the new farmers found it difficult to maintain the repayments on the loans taken out to pay for the land. While some were very successful, for others indebtedness, factionalism and discontent were rife. As cooperatives and land companies fell into dispute and mismanagement, members and share-holders appealed to the government for help. Yet it was precisely because of the state's unwillingness to become involved in development, preferring instead the mantra of self-help, that these private organisations had such difficulties. Put simply, Kenyatta's policy of 'development on the cheap' – dressed up in the rhetorical finery of self-help – placed too great a responsibility on private individuals and organisations for the delivery and management of key public goods.[31] Many of the land companies and other similar bodies could not cope with the tremendous strain.

THE KIKUYU ASCENDANCY

Many Kenyans would have agreed with Raphael Kangu, an otherwise anonymous resident of Kakamega who spent much time in late 1971 goading Kenyatta in a series of personal letters. Dismayed by the tribalism, nepotism and criminalisation of Kenyatta's government, Kangu asked if the Republic of Kenya was made up of just 'one tribe or one man with his family'. The KANU party seemed to be 'for Kikuyu only' and the Kenyan government only 'Gatundu's government'. 'What you have earned since you started to rule your tyrant government it's enough for you,' Kangu thought. It was, he concluded, time to 'let someone [else] also earn'.[32] But Kenyatta was in no mood to listen to the likes of Kangu. The expansion of Kikuyu settlement from 1969 onwards was part of the president's response to the challenges to his rule. Beginning with the 'oathing' earlier that year (discussed in the previous chapter) and continuing through his hard-line response to the protests that followed Mboya's assassination to the banning of the KPU, the president was determined to retain power by consolidating his Kikuyu powerbase. Alongside other measures, such as channelling funding for upper-level secondary education and the provision of highly skilled teachers to Central Province, land resettlement was the main way in which Kenyatta attempted to buy the support of the Kikuyu grassroots.[33] The main beneficiaries were, however, the Kikuyu elites closely connected to the state, along with other key non-Kikuyu allies, such as Moi. From 1969, the president set out to establish a Kikuyu ascendancy that dominated the main institutions in the country. Many members of the circle that formed around Kenyatta were drawn from the elite of his home district of Kiambu.

By the end of 1971, it was claimed that the cabinet was a 'suzerainty' for Kikuyu leaders and their close ethnic cousins from the Embu and Meru communities of the Mount Kenya area. Such a description was perhaps hyperbolic, but there was an element of fact. Besides occupying nine of the twenty-two cabinet posts by November 1971, ministers hailing from those three communities held every single one of the key portfolios of state: defence, foreign affairs, finance and economic planning, local government, agriculture, lands and settlement, and the attorney general. A similar pattern could be observed in the upper echelons of the provincial administration and the civil service. Four of the eight provincial commissioners were Kikuyu. In the civil service – referred to as the 'invisible government' by one backbencher in 1971 – of the twenty-five permanent secretaries, eleven were Kikuyu. Nearly half the 222 African highest earners in the civil service in 1970 and 1971 were Kikuyu.[34] In the foreign service, key diplomatic postings were reserved for members of the ascendancy. For instance, Ng'ethe Njoroge was appointed Kenya's high commissioner in London. Njoroge was the brother of Njoroge Mungai, the minister for foreign affairs, and a relative of Kenyatta. Higher education was similarly brought under the control of the president's inner circle with the appointment of Josephat Karanja as principal of University College Nairobi. Karanja's academic qualifications were impressive, including a PhD from Princeton; but of more importance were his ties to Kenyatta's inner circle. Following his appointment, Kikuyu held all the key administrative positions within the university.[35]

Kenyatta was also much concerned with the army. The force had been dominated by Kamba recruits during the colonial period. That policy had been reversed at independence, but Kamba officers continued to dominate the senior ranks. Plans to reduce Kamba representation within the officer class began to be formed in 1968 and accelerated after the events of the following year. Kenyatta was determined to remove Joel

Ndolo, then a brigadier, from his post as army commander, and replace him with a Kikuyu officer. However, aware that a token nod to national unity was necessary, Kenyatta pre-empted his move against Ndolo with the appointment of another Kamba to a senior post, and so made Kitili Mwendwa chief justice in 1968.[36] The opportunity for an overhaul of the army presented itself three years later.

On 24 March 1971, Kenyatta ordered all soldiers to return the extra ammunition supplied to them during the coup in Uganda led by Idi Amin earlier in the year. Kenyatta feared, diplomats reported, that the ammunition was being stockpiled for a possible coup attempt in Kenya. Roadblocks were erected that night by the police.[37] The trigger for Kenyatta's announcement had been the arrest and interrogation of plotters in Tanzania. Leaders of a small group of conspirators had travelled to Dar es Salaam to request support from President Julius Nyerere. They represented a group of disgruntled, mainly Luo rank-and-file that had first begun meeting the previous September, though it had now expanded to include about forty non-Kikuyu soldiers. The conspirators had identified 8 April 1971 as the day of the coup. It would, they hoped, begin with a successful assassination attempt on Kenyatta. According to the plot, the president was to be blown up as he waved the starting flag for the annual East African Safari Rally. Nyerere refused to help, however, and had Tanzanian Special Branch arrest the Kenyans.[38] When he was informed of events in Dar es Salaam, Kenyatta was furious. Speaking at the Lanet barracks close to Nakuru, he told the troops that 'the hand and the weapons used to fight the Colonialists' were ready to strike at any dissidents that threatened his rule.[39]

Court proceedings against the conspirators began in May. Over the following three months, an otherwise innocuous, hapless and vague plot by discontented non-Kikuyu rank-and-file and junior officers developed into a significant political event. The first trial of the plotters ended with twelve men being sentenced to various terms of imprisonment of between seven and nine and a half years. The plotters were mainly of Luo and Kalenjin origin, and the best known was Joseph Owino, who had previously been jailed for his part in the mutiny that followed independence, and then, after his release, had been sacked from his post as district commissioner for embezzle-ment.[40] However, the deputy public prosecutor told the court that there was a second group of plotters made up of prominent individuals. Named by witnesses during the first trial, the second group of plotters was said to have included the chief of staff, Ndolo, an MP, Gideon Mutiso and the chief justice, Mwendwa.

A plot certainly did exist, but what was presented in court by the state prosecutor was barely plausible. Even the prosecutor admitted that the plotters had 'only [a] one in a million' chance of achieving their goals. Lacking coordination, any real plan or finance, the supposed coup plot was, in the words of one American diplomat, 'of a barroom three-drink variety' rather than a credible threat to the government. To that observer and others, the revelation of a plot was due less to Kenyatta's regime being in immediate danger and more to the government's recognition that prosecutions represented an oppor-tunity for political gain.[41] Specifically, Kenyatta and his advisers were determined to exploit the testimony of the plotters that implicated Kamba senior military officers and political figures. Using the confes-sions of the plotters, Kenyatta was thus able to remove Kamba from senior positions within the military and replace them with Kikuyu, or at least more demonstrably loyal Kamba.

Almost immediately after the conclusion of the first trial, the move against Mutiso, Ndolo and Mwendwa began. Mutiso was identified in the trial of the first group of conspirators as the chairman of the planned 'revolutionary council'. More importantly, he had been a long-standing critic of the government. He was arrested on 9 June 1971 and eventually jailed for nine and a half years for his part in the plot.[42] During his trial, Mutiso in turn implicated General Ndolo, claiming that they had met on several occasions to discuss the possible overthrow of Kenyatta.[43] Ndolo was never prosecuted and was regarded by Kenyatta as 'misguided and stupid rather than vicious'.[44] Nevertheless, he had no choice but to resign. He was replaced as chief of staff by Brigadier Mulinge, whose post as army commander was then filled by Colonel Matu, a Kikuyu. Although Mulinge was a Kamba, too, he was left in no doubt of the balance of power in the military. He found himself under the closer control of a Kikuyu-dominated Ministry of Defence.[45] Promotion of Kikuyu to the middle-ranking officer class gathered pace, and Kikuyu recruitment more generally increased. Moreover, Special Branch officers were planted within army barracks to prevent future plotting.[46]

Once it became clear that Ndolo was alleged to have been implicated in the plot, Njonjo sought to bring down Mwendwa, too. According to the British Foreign Office, Mwendwa was ultimately implicated in the 1971 plot 'as a result of disobeying Njonjo's order to pardon the murderer of Mboya'.[47] Smear tactics were used to destroy the chief justice. On 27 June, a public rally was held in Uhuru Park. Billed by the government as a 'loyalty and unity demonstration', the event was presided over by Moi and consisted of ethnically constituted delegations promising their loyalty to Kenyatta and his government.[48] Banners accusing Mwendwa of treachery were placed in the crowd;[49] he took the hint and resigned.

The loyalty rally also provided Kenyatta with an opportunity to directly address the accusations of nepotism and tribalism made against his government by its critics. He was unrepentant and instead defended Kikuyu privilege:

> Some want to tell us that Kenya belongs to all the people. Granted, I know that much. But I have a question to ask: when we were shedding blood, some languished in prison and some suffering in the forests, fighting for uhuru, where were the bloody others? . . . If you want honey, bear the sting of the bee . . .[50]

The president abandoned all but the most perfunctory pretence that his was a government for all Kenyans. As his efforts to bolster his support among Kikuyu became ever more naked, so his attitude in public towards Mau Mau warmed. In a speech earlier in June, he had 'invited the crowd to declare themselves ready, and their pangas sharp, to defend Kenyatta against those who would overthrow the government'. This allusion to Mau Mau was well received by a crowd that, for a national celebration, was unusually ethnically homogeneous in its composition. For considerable efforts had been made to ensure that Kikuyu were in attendance in great numbers and were highly visible.[51] But many Kikuyu saw through these efforts to regain their affection; mere platitudes towards Mau Mau veterans had little effect on the lives of the residents of the Central Highlands and of the settlement schemes in the Rift Valley.

CORRUPTION

In the first decade of independence, many Kikuyu were angered by the exacerbation of social inequality. With good reason, they came to believe that the land transfer programme had been corrupted by elites for personal and political gain. One obvious way this took place was in cases where land was purchased from departing European settlers by the government, using loans provided by its British counterpart for the express purpose of resettling landless individuals and their families. Rather than being subdivided, the purchased land was quickly resold to key political figures that Kenyatta was keen to retain within networks of patronage.

The corruption of land redistribution was just one part of a wider picture of endemic corruption by public servants. By the government's own admission in 1967, cases of fraud involving public figures and bodies had doubled in the independence era.[52] The situation only worsened in the years that followed. 'Kenya has clearly entered its robber baron era,' wrote one American diplomat in 1972.[53] Corruption began at the very top of government. ' "Back to the land" is the traditional Kikuyu motto and [Kenyatta] is certainly taking that literally. He allegedly buys new farms for himself and his relatives on each trip to Nakuru where he apparently plans to spend at least half of each year.'[54]

International smuggling of goods was a highly profitable business, too, not least across the border to Uganda once Idi Amin's calamitous economic policies created shortages of basic commodities and drove prices sky-high. Kenyan politicians and other civil servants looked to profit from the travails of their neighbours by diverting food supplies from the domestic market to Uganda. In May 1974, for example, a petrol tanker crashed on the road to the Ugandan border, spilling its surprising cargo of contraband rice. 'There is good reason to believe', the British High Commission reported, 'that the P[rovincial] C[ommissioner] of Nyanza was controlling the operation on behalf of the vice president, using a lorry belonging to the commissioner of police.'[55] Dan Stewart, a close friend of Moi and a senior manager at the Standard Bank, alleged that the vice president was heavily involved in smuggling maize and salt to Uganda on such a scale as to cause significant shortages of both goods in Kenya.[56]

Corruption was not simply a matter of personal acquisitiveness and greed, but was rather a fundamental part of the political system. It provided the cement that bonded the post-colonial political elites and allowed non-Kikuyu leaders to remain in government and so mask, to some extent, the ethnic character of the president's rule. Wealth acquired in public and private office also provided the substance for other, older forms of alliances and patronage. Kenyatta's inner circle was tied together by marriage, private enterprise and political power. His much younger and elegant fourth wife, Mama Ngina, was notorious among diplomats and Kenyans alike on account of the allegations of corruption made against her. The daughter of Senior Chief Muhoho, one of the key allies of the colonial state in Kiambu, Mama Ngina's wealth and influence had benefited her family – and continues to do so: the most prominent of these relatives is her elder brother, George, now a key ally of Mwai Kibaki. Kenyatta's third wife, who died in childbirth, was the sister of the president's close friend and minister of state, Mbiyu Koinange. One daughter from that marriage, Jeni, further solidified the interrelationships between the Kiambu elite by marrying Udi Gecaga, the most senior Kenyan executive within the influential Lonrho multinational and member of another prominent family. The ties of interdependence and reciprocity between such individuals ensured that the elite at the heart of Kenyatta's government was unwilling to tolerate challengers.

Any efforts to halt corruption were, then, quickly quashed. A parliamentary select committee was formed in October 1971 with the express purpose of investigating the related phenomena of tribalism and corruption. The following month, Kenyatta used a regular meeting of the KANU MPs to announce that the committee would be blocked at every turn, and that the police had been ordered not to cooperate.[57] Investigations into allegations of corruption only proceeded in cases where there was a clear political, economic or personal imperative. For example, Aloys Achieng, a senior civil servant in the Ministry of Tourism and Wildlife, was suspended in June 1970 over allegations of embezzlement of public funds. Achieng had been a close friend of Mboya and, in 1969, had accused senior members of the government of having carried out the assassination.[58] He was eventually sentenced to seven years' imprisonment, later reduced to four years on appeal.[59] The Kikuyu ascendancy at the heart of the government was prepared to go to any lengths to protect its interests.

KAMAU FOR SMITH

By the early 1970s, J.M. Kariuki was the most prominent voice of criticism of the malaise into which Kenya had fallen. The assassination of Mboya and the detention of Odinga left a vacuum, and Kariuki was best placed to fill it. Even after Odinga's release from detention in 1971, the former KPU leader was prevented from participating in politics. Kariuki's supporters were the indebted and poor, the landless and land-hungry who were dismayed at the rapid accumulation of property and wealth by the ruling elite. Of all the problems facing the country at the time, his favoured issues of corruption and land policy were those that exercised Kenyans most. He was comfortable with the highly personalised form of politics and, as a Kikuyu with far greater credibility among Mau Mau veterans and the landless, was able to point out Kenyatta's hypocrisy to great effect. He enjoyed almost total support in his constituency and was returned to parliament at the 1969 elections with the largest majority in the country. Buoyed by that success, Kariuki stepped up his criticisms of the government's land policy. He urged it on repeated occasions both to cease repayments of the loan made to it by the British to compensate departing European farmers, and to cancel the debts owed by Kenyan farmers who had been resettled.[60]

Kariuki spent much of the early 1970s building a nationwide profile. By attending public fundraising events, opening schools and other public institutions, and speaking in every conceivable setting, Kariuki was determined, in the words of the US embassy, 'to convince Kenya's little men that he is their champion'.[61] As well as mastering the key rituals of grassroots politics, Kariuki also concentrated on building support within significant institutions. Each weekend, he invited two or three non-Kikuyu or Kamba MPs to his home at Gilgil in an effort to convince senior politicians that he was the only true nationalist leader. He was a common sight in the army barracks at Gilgil and Lanet as he built ties to the rank-and-file and junior officers. He diligently cultivated his support within the University of Nairobi and the Kenyatta University College over a number of years, using on-campus speaking engagements to talk openly with the students at both establishments. The ultimate aim of Kariuki's strategy was clear. As he told a senior US diplomat, he considered himself to be the 'only possible candidate as future President'.[62] His confidence was well placed. According to Peter Gicumbi, a senior official in KANU, Kariuki would win any nationwide leadership contest that was held in an open and free manner.[63]

Kariuki was widely recognised as a threat to the interests of the ruling elite. In conversation with a British diplomat, G.A. Araru, the MP for Moyale, said that he thought Kariuki 'was a better assassination prospect than a presidential one'.[64] Kariuki was far from oblivious to the personal danger that his criticism of the government caused, but nevertheless remained defiant. 'Let them put me in detention – I'll come out a bigger man than when I went in,' he stated publicly.[65] He put his faith in his close friendship with members of the presidential bodyguard, which he thought would ultimately prevent any attempt from being made on his life.[66] Most important was his close relationship with Kenyatta. He had served as the president's personal secretary in the early 1960s and, according to his aide, Oliver Litondo, had a long extramarital relationship with one of the president's daughters.[67] Moreover, although the president frequently warned him to hold his tongue or resign from his post in the government, Kenyatta was afraid to fire the most popular member of his government.[68] The president was happy, however, to let Kariuki's enemies in government try to silence him by other means.

Throughout the early 1970s, Kariuki was frequently prevented from speaking in public and had his responsibilities as an assistant minister reduced in order to restrict his opportunities to address his supporters.[69] He was a regular sight in the courts as a succession of cases were brought against him on account of his business activities. These appearances were, the British High Commission claimed, 'at the instigation of his political enemies, especially Njonjo, with the aim of discrediting him'.[70] In 1973, fearing the bankruptcy that would have disqualified him from standing for re-election, Kariuki put his own presidential aspirations to one side for the time being. In return for promises to support Moi in the succession battle (to be discussed at length in the next chapter), Kariuki struck a deal with Njonjo. For both men, this was a marriage of convenience. Kariuki gave Njonjo and the Moi faction the veneer of nationalist legitimacy and the Kikuyu votes to weaken their main rival, Njoroge Mungai. In return, Njonjo gave Kariuki the protection from physical attack and financial collapse that he needed to be able to run for parliament in the elections that were eventually held in 1974.

At first, the arrangement worked for both parties. Njonjo made sure the courts dropped a tax case against Kariuki in July 1973.[71] In return, Kariuki maintained his silence in parliament for nearly three months.[72] The following year, he supported a populist, nationalist bill backed by Njonjo that was intended to make Swahili the official language of parliament. In return, bankruptcy proceedings against him were dropped.[73] Even through this short honeymoon period, however, Njonjo kept up the pressure on Kariuki. His wife was prosecuted for involvement in ivory poaching and smuggling, and Kariuki still had to stand firm in the face of claims from creditors through late 1973 and early 1974.[74] Nevertheless, the pact lasted long enough for him to start campaigning for re-election ahead of polling in October 1974.

During the campaign period, all but one of his campaign meetings were cancelled, as the necessary permission was revoked by local administrative officers. In an effort to publicise his platform, Kariuki therefore distributed a pamphlet containing the text of the one speech he had been able to make. It was a devastating critique of the Kenyatta era. First, he addressed the development policies enacted since independence, decrying the absence of social justice as a key goal of those policies. He was particularly critical of the dominance of Central Province within development planning: 'It is no justice to spread education, health, agricultural, business and other opportunities unevenly and without regard to the interests of the nation as a whole concentrating them in certain areas only.' Corruption, too, angered him: 'It is no justice for a few greedy people with influence and connections to utilise resources of public, now Government supported or funded institutions to unfairly acquire wealth of all manner of things, houses, the best commercial premises and largest tracts of land.'[75] Indeed, such accumulation of wealth meant that 'we could not pride ourselves as we look to our record in the life of an independent nation'.[76] Continuing in a similar vein, he launched a series of stinging attacks on every conceivable aspect of the government's performance.

Kariuki's most severe censure of the government was reserved for its land policy. Recalling 'the determination with which we fought and the death of many people in Kenya' during the struggle for independence, he argued that independence had been about more than 'a mere change-over or substitution in ownership' of land. Rather, he and other Kenyans had expected independence to be accompanied by a more systematic overhaul of the land tenure system. The ownership of vast tracts of land by individuals, while thousands of others were without land, was 'socially and morally unjust and unacceptable' in the colonial period. 'It was wrong then,' Kariuki stated. 'It is socially unacceptable and unjust today. It is wrong now. I believe firmly that substituting Kamau for Smith, Odongo for Jones and Kiplangat for Keith does not solve what the gallant fighters of our Uhuru considered an imposed and undesirable social injustice.'[77] Kariuki thus gave public voice to a question that many Kenyans were asking themselves privately after a decade of independence: was this really what they had fought so hard for?

As the 1974 elections made clear, Kenyans were intolerant of the hypocrisy and excesses of the ruling elite. The government still did not permit Odinga or other former leading members of the KPU to stand, despite their release from prison and readmittance into KANU. Nevertheless, over 50 per cent of the sitting MPs lost their seats in the elections. Of those that remained, three of the most overwhelming victories for incumbents were enjoyed by Kariuki and the two other most prominent critics of the government, Jean Marie Seroney from Nandi and Martin Shikuku, the MP for Butere. Seroney's election was a personal blow for Moi, who had campaigned vigorously against his great rival for political leadership of the Kalenjin community. Seroney gave great support to another opponent of Moi, Chelagat Mutai, who won the Eldoret North seat. Leading figures in the government were given a fright. Mwai Kibaki was forced to abandon his Bahati seat in Nairobi, which he was widely predicted to lose, and instead successfully ran in his rural home constituency of Othaya in Nyeri. Njoroge Mungai, Moi's great rival for the succession and leading figure in the Kikuyu ascendancy, lost his seat in Dagoretti.

Kariuki demonstrated his clout in Nyeri, where his ally Waruru Kanja contested the seat against Peter Nderi, the brother of the director of Kenya's Criminal Investigation Department (CID). Ignatius Nderi was a key element in the security apparatus assembled by Kenyatta, and so his brother's campaign was able to operate with impunity. By contrast, Kanja's wife and another key supporter, Nyeri's mayor Nahashon Kanyi, were both violently assaulted during the campaign. The virulence of the campaign was partly explicable by reference to the past: the divisions between the two factions of Nyeri politics dated back to the 1950s, when Nderi's father, a chief, was murdered by insurgents at the very beginning of the Mau Mau war. Kanja was himself sentenced to hang for his role in the insurgency, but was later pardoned. In an indication of Kariuki's influence and the unpopularity of the ruling elite, Kanja was victorious in the election, but for safety's sake had to take up residence on Kariuki's farm in Gilgil after his victory.[78] With leading opponents enjoying unprecedented support, and with figures like Mungai and Nderi humiliated, the outcome of the elections confirmed a sense of crisis within the upper echelons of government.

GROWTH, INEQUALITY AND CORRUPTION

The prevailing sense of disquiet created by the results of the 1974 election was a constant feature of politics until Kenyatta's death four years later. The ruling elite remained unnerved by the thought of the emergence of nationwide discontent, not least as the country's economic fortunes began to change. The expectations of many Kenyans that standards of living and increased incomes would eventually be delivered if the pace of economic change could only be sustained into the 1970s were proving to have been optimistic. Kenya's political system worked so long as those commonly referred to as 'the have-nots' could hold onto some expectation of joining 'the haves'. But Kenyans were unconvinced that the government's economic policies provided them with a chance to realise their hopes of prosperity. 'Everyone admires the wealth of the rich who have lots of things, but these things are so much outside our reach that they are not given a thought,' said one resident of Nyeri. Another commented that 'income is so low that a good life is a life in which every day you have something to eat and you are well sheltered'.[79]

An influential report published in 1972 by the International Labour Organization found that the benefits of economic growth had been experienced unevenly. The expansion of the economy had increased inequality along lines of region and class.[80] The rapid economic growth was, in any case, beginning to slow in response to changes in the global economy. Although cheap oil imports from the shah's Iran allowed Kenya to ride out the early stages of the global economic downturn that resulted from the first oil crisis of 1973–74, the country was clearly vulnerable to such external shocks.[81] The trade deficit that had accumulated in the previous few years seemed to be about to become a millstone around the neck of the economy. The government failed to come to terms with increased prices for imports and stagnating revenues from the country's agricultural exports on the global market, and inflation and unemployment both increased.[82] The minister of finance, Mwai Kibaki, was frank about the situation in an interview in late February 1975: 'We are definitely facing a grim future as far as our trade balances are concerned.' He promised tough measures to rein in the trade deficit, including a reduction in public spending.[83] The government set out plans for reduced public expenditure in 1975 and made it clear that increased unemployment was inevitable.[84] Price rises for all essential foodstuffs of up to 50 per cent were announced at the end of January.

The government feared the political repercussions. Economic and social change had already contributed to unrest at both the University of Nairobi and the Kenyatta University College, which meant that both institutions were closed from mid-August 1974 to early January 1975. The need to effect some reform, even if just cosmetic, in response to such challenges was recognised at the very top of government. At the end of February 1975, Bruce McKenzie and Njonjo were convinced that the excesses of the ruling elite had to stop. With support from other figures drawn from across the divide caused by the succession struggle (to be discussed in the next chapter), the two planned to 'tell the president frankly that things had gone too far. Mama Ngina and the rest must be called to order.'[85] But little did in fact change.

Just a month after the 1974 election, there was a series of public revelations about the extent of corruption within the upper echelons of government and in Kenyatta's immediate family. The revelations centred on the illegal trade in ivory, but similar stories could easily have been told about far less newsworthy commodities, such as maize or charcoal. Illegal trading in ivory was proving a very profitable activity for the ruling elite. Private trading had been banned in 1974 in an effort to protect the country's 120,000 elephants, which were being killed at a rate of up to 20,000 a year. Despite the ban on private trading, those participating in the now illegal selling of ivory had a turnover of $10 million a year. Through bribes to persuade officials to turn a blind eye to consignments leaving the country, ivory exports continued to Europe and East Asia. The *New Scientist* magazine alleged that those profiting from this trade were closely linked to Kenyatta, his wife Mama Ngina, and his daughter Margaret.[86]

Concerned about the damage such actions were causing to elephant herds and tourism, a small number of conservationists and hoteliers joined forces in an effort to persuade Kenyatta to halt the trade in ivory. A devastating report was prepared by the anti-poaching lobby. It named Mungai, the Kenyatta family, Paul Ngei and Njonjo as participants in the illegal ivory trade.[87] The British High Commission had reached a similar conclusion, noting that the illegal trade encompassed ministers, senior officers within the armed forces, members of Kenyatta's family and the authorities ostensibly responsible for protecting wildlife.[88]

Kariuki was probably involved in the revelations about poaching and ivory smuggling. Until the election of October 1974 he had been assistant minister for tourism and wildlife and had close personal ties to Jack Block, a prominent figure in the anti-poaching lobby, who was concerned about the effects poaching would have on tourism. Kariuki's election victory (and subsequent sacking from the government) had reinvigorated him. His mandate and willingness to criticise the excesses of Kenyatta's government seemed greater than ever. He began the New Year in a zealous mood, launching a series of stinging attacks on the corruption and social policies of the government.[89] Unsurprisingly, therefore, rumours of an imminent assassination were widely circulated in political circles in early February 1975.

These rumours reached Kariuki, and subsequent events convinced him that this was no hoax or a mere warning. Aided by friends in government and the security forces, he came to the conclusion that two bomb explosions in Nairobi during February – one at the Starlight nightclub and the other at the bureau de change at the Hilton hotel – were part of an effort by figures within Kenyatta's inner circle to silence him once and for all. The night after the bombing of the bureau de change, Kariuki's car was shot at, though he was unhurt.[90] Rumours began to circulate in the press that the bombings were the work of a group known as the Maskini ('the poor') Liberation Front, which was linked to disaffected Kikuyu from Nyeri district, a constituency commonly associated with Kariuki. Throughout February, he and his close friends were under police surveillance.[91] Kariuki recognised that, at the very least, his days as a political force were numbered. Victor Riitho, a close friend, talked to Kariuki on 27 February. Riitho said that Kariuki had spoken to him 'like a man on his deathbed saying how it was important to fight for the truth whatever might happen'.[92]

On the evening of 1 March, an overnight bus to Mombasa leaving from Nairobi's Race Course Road was loaded and ready to depart when a bomb exploded on board. Seventeen people were killed outright, eight died before they could receive attention at the city's Kenyatta Hospital, and another died overnight at the hospital. Nearly seventy more people were seriously injured in the blast. It is probable that one of the plotters was killed in the explosion.[93] It was the first such terrorist incident and caused outrage across the country. But the identity of the perpetrators remained a mystery.

At the time of the explosion, Kariuki was celebrating a friend's engagement at a party in the suburb of Karen. Driving back to the city centre at around 11 p.m., Kariuki heard of the explosion and drove to the scene. Having seen the damage and bloodshed, he then headed for a casino where he was a frequent visitor, and shared a few drinks with Ben Gethi. Gethi, the commander of the GSU and another regular customer at the casino, was a good friend of Kariuki's, and the two men stayed there talking until the small hours of the morning. The next day, a concerted effort began to link Kariuki to the bus bombing. A police informer and ostensible friend of Kariuki's called and visited, trying to get the MP to implicate himself. This amateurish effort failed.[94] Nevertheless, the decision was taken by senior police officers to interrogate him in person. That evening, Kariuki met up with Gethi again at the Hilton, from where he was escorted by non-uniformed police officers for questioning.[95] He was not seen alive in public again. Later that night, he was taken to a remote spot in the Ngong Hills outside the city and shot. His body was left for the animals to dispose of, but in the event his remains were discovered the following morning.[96]

A sustained effort to cover up Kariuki's disappearance and murder began immediately afterwards. After being recovered by local policemen, his body was taken to the Nairobi mortuary. Efforts were made to conceal the identity of the corpse and so allow the authorities to bury it in an anonymous grave:[97] a false name tag was attached and the remains were moved around the building.[98] An official announcement that the mortuary was holding an unidentified corpse was made public only on the morning of 11 March, nine days after Kariuki's death and shortly before the time limit for claiming the body was due to expire.[99]

Kariuki's family had initially thought he was with a woman who was staying at the Hilton and with whom he had been having an affair in the days prior to his disappearance.[100] However, after three days without contact, the family began to fear the worst. Rumours of his murder were rife, and so it was with incredulity that many read the front page of the *Sunday Nation* on 8 March, which claimed that Kariuki was in Lusaka. The planting of this story was part of an effort to link him with subversive forces supposedly behind the bombings of the previous few weeks. Earlier that week, *The Nation* had also claimed that communist agents may have been responsible for the bombings.[101] The newspaper's editor, George Githii, had long been an ally of Kenyatta and was formerly a senior civil servant. The story was quickly discounted as friends made swift enquiries in Lusaka. Finally, Kariuki's family received word of an unidentified body at the city mortuary and on the evening of 11 March went to see if they could identify the remains. They bluffed their way past the police guard at the entrance, found his body and duly identified it. Official confirmation of his murder came the following morning.

As Bruce McKenzie made clear to the British High Commission, both the bombings and Kariuki's murder could be traced back to Mbiyu Koinange, Kenyatta's closest adviser and brother-in-law. McKenzie told the British that Kariuki had been killed 'by some of the lower echelon Gatundu thugs, on Koinange's instructions and with the President's approval'.[102] The retired MP, Fitz de Souza, gave a similar account.[103] Koinange embodied Kenya's post-colonial malaise. Highly intelligent, he had acquired undergraduate and postgraduate degrees in the US and UK in the 1930s. On his return to Kenya, he had played a critical role in the escalation of anti-colonial political action in Central Province, alongside his elderly father. He had been in London when the state of emergency was declared on the outbreak of the Mau Mau insurgency, and remained in exile in the UK throughout the 1950s, keeping the cause of nationalism alive there. He acted as a point of contact between Kenyans who sought to draw attention to their plight in the villages and detention camps and their sympathisers in the UK and across the globe. He finally returned to Kenya a hero and resumed his close political and personal relationship with Kenyatta, serving as an MP and minister from before independence. In 1966, his position as the president's right-hand man was formalised with his appointment as minister of state in the Office of the President. For all Koinange's great contribution to the nationalist cause of independence, his political horizons narrowed afterwards. His loyalty to Kenyatta trumped all other concerns, and he was second to none in his determination to protect the political domination of the Kikuyu ascendancy. He saw Kariuki as perhaps the greatest threat to that domination.

Fearing a cover-up of the sort witnessed in the aftermath of the Pinto and Mboya assassinations, MPs voted soon after the announcement of Kariuki's death to form their own select committee to investigate the murder. The select committee included figures known to be sympathetic to Kariuki, such as Rubia, and long-standing critics of the government, including Martin Shikuku, Jean Marie Seroney and Grace Onyango. Its chair, Elijah Mwangale, was another ally of Kariuki and had been beaten up by police outside the latter's home in 1974. But the committee was far from being a kangaroo court anxious to seek retribution against the government; even Moi supported its formation.

Between mid-March and early June, the committee heard evidence from 123 individuals linked to the security forces, government and the civil service. At every turn, attempts were made to block its investigations. For instance, the police refused to allow the MPs to view documents related to the enquiries into Kariuki's murder or the bombings.[104] Witnesses who appeared before the committee had, in some cases, been tortured by the police first, while others were threatened and intimidated.[105] Witness intimidation by the police, including torture and possible murder, was also reported by the British High Commission and the *Sunday Times*.[106] Police officers who gave evidence to the select committee were fired shortly afterwards.[107] Despite such obstacles being placed in its path, the committee reached findings that have subsequently been corroborated by the investigations of journalists and the contemporary archival record.

It was 'satisfied that there was some connection between the murder of JM and the bomb blasts'.[108] Moreover, it believed that the CID was 'trying to concoct evidence linking [Kariuki] with the bomb blast which killed 27 *wananchi* ["citizens"]'.[109] The obvious implication was spelled out in private by Rubia. In discussion with British diplomats, he stated that the committee had come to the conclusion that Patrick Shaw and Patrick Clarke, two British members of the Kenya Police Reserve and CID, were responsible for the bombings.[110] As for Kariuki's death, the committee recommended that a number of individuals should be subject to criminal investigation. Some were linked to the subsequent cover-up rather than directly to the murder. Others were, however, clearly accused of direct involvement. Gethi, the commander of the GSU, either 'took an active part in the murder himself' or was 'an accomplice of the actual murderer or murderers'.[111] The actual murderer, the committee suspected, was Pius Kibathi Thuo, a police officer who had, in fact, been interrogated by the CID about the murder even before Kariuki's body was identified at the mortuary. A further two suspects were also named as Peter Gicheru Njau and Peter Kimani.[112] In a quirk of fate, Kibathi's sister and Kariuki's sister worked together. According to the former, Kibathi was summoned to collect Kariuki just an hour after Kariuki had been escorted from the Hilton. Kibathi, according to this version of events, subsequently supported by journalistic investigations, took Kariuki to the Ngong Hills and there shot him dead.[113] A year earlier, Kibathi had made an attempt on Charles Rubia's life during the 1974 election campaign.[114]

The committee was equally clear that Kibathi had not acted alone, but rather had carried out the murder on the orders of senior officials within the security forces and government. Their attention was firmly fixed on Mbiyu Koinange. When the MPs visited Kenyatta to present a copy of the final report to him on 3 June, the president ordered that Koinange's name and that of the head of the presidential bodyguard, Arthur Wanyoike Thungu, be removed from the list of individuals who deserved more thorough investigation. 'When you beat the son, you beat the father', the president told the committee members. Reluctantly, the MPs did as they were told, and the final draft of the report appeared without mention of Koinange or Thungu. However, earlier versions of the report, with their names included, had already been released to certain journalists and diplomats.[115]

In an effort to divert attention from Kariuki's murder, bomb scares and further small explosions were witnessed across the country. On 5 March, for instance, a train was derailed at Voi as a result of sabotage.[116] The Kenyan public were no fools, though, and were not easily intimidated. Immediately after the announcement of the discovery of Kariuki's body, protestors took to the streets of Nairobi to make plain their anger at his death. Despite the best efforts of the police, the protests were unparalleled during Kenyatta's rule. In demonstrations at Kenyatta University College outside the city centre on 15 March, students attempted to deface the university's sign, in order to remove the president's name. Some three hundred students at Egerton College in Njoro marched the next day in protest against the murder and had to be dispersed by riot police. An arson attack was even carried out on Margaret Kenyatta's compound in Nairobi.[117] In Nyeri, Ben Gethi's home was similarly attacked.[118]

The police were charged with crushing any sign of sedition. On the night of 15 March, Wilord Gikandi Karugu and Michael Wangai Richard were sharing a drink at the Engineer Trading Centre in North Kinangop and speculating that Kenyatta was behind Kariuki's assassination. A bystander reported the two to the local police and both were arrested. Eliud Erastus Wambugu smashed and then burned a photograph of Kenyatta hanging in the Kihoto bar at Ruringu in Nyeri. He, too, was arrested. In the Pangani area of Nairobi, police arrested five men in late April for publishing and distributing seditious literature that would 'bring hatred' and 'excite disaffection against the President or the government of Kenya'.[119] But these efforts revealed the limits of state power rather than its influence; Kenyatta's legitimacy had been destroyed.

In cabinet, too, Kenyatta temporarily lost his authority. On 13 March, ministers were summoned to his Gatundu home. The president told his cabinet that the security forces believed Kariuki to have been behind the bombings, with the support of 'a group of wild young men trained in Zambia', but had subsequently fallen out with the plotters and so had been executed. The ministers were incredulous – none more so than Kibaki – and demanded to see senior police officers and question them directly about this line of enquiry. Kenyatta, astonished at the impetuosity of his cabinet, refused.[120] Cabinet reconvened a week later. Delegated by the other ministers to speak on their behalf, Moi began to suggest that Kenyatta needed to recognise the widespread discontent in the country and to take measures to address it as a matter of urgency. But Kenyatta stopped the vice president in his tracks and told the assembled ministers that only he knew how ordinary Kenyans felt about their government.[121]

Kenyatta hoped to coerce support. On 21 March, KAF jets made a number of low passes over the centre of Nairobi, while troops and police officers marched through the streets in an impromptu military parade intended as a display of strength. As Kenyatta took the salute from his security forces, thousands of onlookers stood in silence and refused to acknowledge the president's waves.[122] To ministers and diplomatic observers alike, it seemed as if the government itself was in danger of collapse. With thoughts of the fall of Haile Selassie in neighbouring Ethiopia in mind, the American embassy believed 'Kenyatta's reign appears to be reaching an end'.[123] Deputy Public Prosecutor James Karugu agreed, telling British diplomats that Kenyatta's days in office were numbered.[124] Cabinet members informally discussed the formation of a small committee of senior ministers to take over effective running of the country, with Kenyatta reduced to an honorary position.[125] In the event, he ignored any suggestion that he might dilute his powers.

THE AFTERMATH

Just a week after Kariuki's body was finally found, Kenyatta told a crowd the story of a fallen angel who was 'going bad, so God threw him away'.[126] The outrage that accompanied the discovery of Kariuki's murder provided the justification for the president to concentrate control over the security forces even more within the executive. Policing and immigration were both removed from the portfolio of the vice president and minister of home affairs, Moi, and handed over to the minister of state in the Office of the President, who was, of course, Mbiyu Koinange.[127]

Kenyatta and his inner circle then turned their attention to other potential channels of discontent. The president ordered KANU branch chairmen to expel any critics of the government from the party.[128] The government forced *The Standard* newspaper to fire its associate editor, and a culture of self-censorship took hold of the newsrooms of the main daily papers.[129] In an effort to cow Kariuki's supporters in the universities, long-dormant plans for the establishment of non-military national service for graduates were rushed into publication in early April.[130] Most significantly, Kenyatta made a concerted effort to finally destroy his long-standing critics in parliament.

Spurred on by the bravado of the select committee's investigations into Kariuki's murder, and then by the fact that parliament voted to accept its report, Kenyatta was determined to silence the legislature as a voice of dissent. Peter Kibisu, an assistant minister for the East African Community, was jailed for assault shortly after voting in parliament to accept the select committee's report.[131] Shikuku and Seroney, the leading dissident MPs, were both arrested on 15 October. The following day, all other MPs were summoned to a meeting with Kenyatta. The president warned the parliamentarians that 'hawks' were poised to strike again and that further arrests of MPs were possible if politicians did not toe the line.[132] Kenyatta was as good as his word: Mark Mwithaga, the one-time MP for Nakuru, a close ally of Kariuki and a member of the select committee that investigated the murder, was jailed for a minor indiscretion in late 1975.[133]

Free to act without meaningful sanction from either parliament or the fourth estate, the ruling elite carried on as before. Corruption at the highest levels of government continued, as three MPs and active businessmen, including Rubia, made clear during a meeting with British diplomats in July 1975. The Kenyatta family had, the MPs said, become embroiled in global organised crime. Peter Kenyatta was a partner in the International Casino, which the MPs alleged was managed by Italian Mafiosi, while the president himself was a partner with an American-Korean crime syndicate in the Casino de Paradise.[134] Even ivory smuggling, which had caused so much controversy shortly before Kariuki's disappearance, continued unabated.[135] Kenyatta's reputation was destroyed. According to Kikuyu residents of the Dagoretti constituency on Nairobi's outskirts, the president went from being known as 'The Elder' or 'The Father of the Nation' to 'The Finisher' or 'The Little Killer'.[136] Those in power were well aware that building resentment against the ruling elite could easily boil over in the event of the president's death. The process of succession therefore had to be carefully managed and dissent had to be suppressed.

CHAPTER FOUR

FOOTSTEPS, 1975–82

It is our responsibility to complete the task that our late Mzee has
left unfinished. He was one Kenyatta only. How wonderful would
it be that now in his death we would get 13,000,000 Kenyattas as
the total of our population!

Sermon by Very Rev. Charles M. Kareri at the
state funeral of Jomo Kenyatta, 31 August 1978[1]

'EXTRAVERSION'

Kenyatta collapsed and died at his beachside home in the early hours of
22 August 1978. For many, his death occasioned reflection rather than
displays of grief. While in its reaction the public did not ignore such
issues as corruption and authoritarianism, it tended to set these to one
side and instead to focus on Kenyatta's role in winning independence.
Even Odinga agreed. As Kenyatta lay in state prior to the funeral, he
went to pay his respects. After saying a prayer over the body, a tearful
Odinga spoke to the press. 'We have had very many differences, but
there is not only the one way of doing things,' he said, standing just a few
feet from the open coffin. 'My goal was his goal: nationalism.'[2] Similar
sentiments pervaded the funeral service held on 31 August in Nairobi.

The funeral also contained references to the bitter struggle for succession that had occupied so much of elite politics in Kenyatta's final years. Bishop Gitari, an Anglican church leader, led prayers for the guidance 'to choose the person of your own choice, for the leadership of this nation to continue undisturbed, so that the prosperity and stability of this nation may grow from strength to strength'. In his sermon, Charles Kareri, the representative of the Presbyterian clergy, quoted St Paul:

> I know that after my departure fierce wolves will come in among you not sparing the flock. And from your own selves will arise men speaking perverse things to draw away disciples after them. Therefore be alert.[3]

Both Gitari's and Kareri's allusions to the succession struggle were far more appropriate – if inadvertent – ways of remembering Kenyatta than were the platitudes of Odinga and other prominent mourners.

Rather than nationalism, Kenyatta's death laid bare the substance of elite politics as being about competition to control a process that Jean-François Bayart terms 'extraversion'. Bayart, perhaps the most astute and intelligent observer of contemporary African politics, argues that relationships between African states and those in the wider world are defined most of all by dependence. As a result of the colonial period, the economic fortunes of states like Kenya are determined by the vagaries of demand for its exports in the developed world. Without sufficient resources to develop their economies, Bayart argues, the states exist to act as intermediaries in this relationship. Control of the state allows for the control of inward flows of money in the form of private investment, payment for the country's exports, and aid. But control also means the state's rulers have power over the flows of goods going out to the global economy.[4]

Under Kenyatta, Kenya's extraversion meant that those who were able to act as mediators could build up great wealth and influence through legal and illegal means. By the 1970s, the elite in control of the state were just as happy smuggling Ugandan coffee or ivory poached from the Maasai Mara as they were legally exporting coffee grown in Kiambu or tea from Kericho. They and their allies owned other interests that were reliant on Kenya's ties to the global economy, such as hotel groups and banks. Acting in their political roles, members of the ruling elite also had it in their power to appoint individuals to run the marketing boards responsible for the different parts of the agricultural economy; to hire executives to sit in the boardrooms of state-owned corporations; and to set legislation and issue the various permissions and permits to allow businesses to operate. A tight web of interdependence was therefore created between the public and the private sectors, and between government and business.[5] The financial and political futures of the ruling elite depended on the outcome of the succession; they could not afford to be on the losing side.

Their anxieties were heightened by the splits within Kenyatta's inner circle through the 1970s. The earlier consensus behind Moi's candidacy against Mboya's challenge broke down. Competing commercial interests lay at the heart of the formation of two factions shortly after Mboya's assassination. Njoroge Mungai emerged as the preferred candidate of many members of the Kikuyu elite, particularly those with personal connections to the Kenyatta family. McKenzie and Njonjo were unconvinced, however. They feared that if Mungai succeeded Kenyatta, then the clique surrounding the younger man would endanger the commercial interests that Njonjo and McKenzie had built up through their ties to British investment in Kenya. McKenzie and Njonjo therefore redoubled their existing support for Moi.[6] The two factions thus acted both as competing political groupings within government, and as rival investment clubs. They fought a series of financial battles in the years leading up to Kenyatta's death. For instance, in early 1978 the two factions each sought to buy Marshalls Universal, the local agent for Peugeot, formerly owned by a British expatriate. Mungai's faction, as represented by his cousin, Udi Gecaga, and his brother, Ng'ethe Njoroge, found themselves thwarted by a consortium led by McKenzie and Njonjo.[7]

Citing Kikuyu custom, which frowned on making preparations for one's own death, Kenyatta was content to let Mungai and Moi wrestle with one another for the right to succeed him. He probably cared little which of the two emerged successful. They each represented a key pillar of the Kenyan political economy: Moi was the candidate of British influence, while Mungai represented the Kenyatta family itself. Kenyatta was concerned to ensure that the disputes over succession remained within defined social and political boundaries. Any sign of non-elite involvement, or of politically dangerous individuals threatening the ruling elite's monopoly over the argument about Kenyatta's successor, met with swift and decisive action.

MANAGING THE SUCCESSION

As novelist, playwright and academic, Ngugi wa Thiong'o was the country's best-known intellectual figure in the mid-1970s – and indeed remains so. He was also a persistent critic of Kenyatta's government, not least through his novels, which captured changing popular attitudes in the period since independence. In *Petals of Blood*, a novel first published in 1977, Ngugi wrote of how Kenya's leaders had 'prostituted the whole land turning it over to foreigners for thorough exploitation, would drink people's blood and say hypocritical prayers of devotion to skin oneness and to nationalism even as skeletons of bones walked to lonely graves'.[8] This was hardly what Kenyatta and other members of the ruling elite wanted to hear as they tried to manage the succession process.

What was worse for those in government was that Ngugi was not a lone voice, but rather part of the rising discontent among university lecturers and students. In 1969, he drafted a letter signed by sixteen other lecturers at the University College Nairobi, the forerunner of the University of Nairobi, in which the Ministry of Education stood accused of interfering with academic freedoms. Ngugi and his fellow academics were dismayed at the pressure exerted on the university authorities by the ministry in a successful effort to have a public lecture by Odinga cancelled.[9] At the time, Ngugi made it clear that his interests were much wider than simply the cancellation of a lecture or the silencing of Odinga and the KPU. Rather he considered it his duty as a public intellectual to make a critical stand against the government when the interests of the great majority were compromised by the pursuit of wealth among the ruling elite.

Ngugi was arrested at his home in Kiambu in the early hours of 31 December 1977. As he recalled in his prison memoirs:

> Armed members of the special branch who swarmed and searched my study amidst an awe-inspiring silence were additionally guarded by uniformed policemen carrying long-range rifles. Their grim determined faces would only light up a little whenever they pounced on any book or pamphlet bearing the names of Marx, Engels or Lenin.[10]

Such supposedly seditious literature – nothing that was actually illegal – was seized, and, without either facing trial or being told of the charges against him, Ngugi was taken to the Kamiti maximum security prison in Kiambu.

Ngugi knew full well why he had been arrested, however. The trigger was the staging of his popular play, co-authored with Ngugi wa Mirii, *I Will Marry When I Want*.[11] The play was staged by the Kamiriithu Community Education and Cultural Centre, a grassroots theatre group based in the village of the same name in Kiambu district. Kamiriithu was typical of many settlements that had sprung up around Nairobi's peri-urban fringe. Based around the village that had been constructed as part of the counter-insurgency effort in the 1950s, it was described by Ngugi in the late 1970s as a place where 'poverty is still the king'. The villagers were 'a reservoir of cheap labour for the new Kenyan landlords and Euro-American multi-nationals who, at independence, replaced the former British landlords in the sprawling green fields of tea and coffee around Tigoni and beyond'.[12] The community theatre group was formed in 1976 after visits from the University of Nairobi's Department of Literature, where Ngugi worked. With Ngugi on the management board, the group set about encouraging adult literacy and then the staging of plays. Over the course of 1977, Ngugi and Mirii prepared the script of their new play,

I Will Marry When I Want. Through its searing critique of politics, corruption and economic exploitation, the play became an interrogation of 'the poisoned gift of independence'.[13]

Rehearsals of the play attracted huge crowds and the premiere in October was rapturously received. According to Ngugi,

> the play was popular because it talked about landlessness in our country. I believe the play was popular because it talked about the betrayal of the peasants and workers by the political 'big-wigs'. I believe the play was popular because it talked about the arrogance and the greed of the powerful and wealthy. Again, I believe that the play was popular because it depicted the true conditions of the rural people in the rural villages.[14]

Intended as a deliberate vehicle for grassroots discontent with the post-colonial project, the Kamiriithu group hosted delegations from other communities keen on replicating its efforts. Recognising the Kamiriithu group's potential to mobilise widespread grievances through cultural activities, the authorities took steps to limit its effects: it was closed down in mid-December 1977 and a fortnight later Ngugi was in detention.[15]

Ngugi was just one of several political prisoners held in the final years of Kenyatta's presidency. Some KPU leaders remained in detention, and they were joined by other parliamentary dissenters, such as Seroney and Shikuku, in colonial-era prisons dotted around the country. The aim of political imprisonment was to ensure that the struggle to succeed the president remained one fought within the inner circle, at the heart of government. As it sought to limit popular participation in the succession debate, the ruling elite was assisted by the changing nature of the economy.

The expected recession, anticipation of which had so shaped political calculations in the months prior to Kariuki's murder in 1975, did not in fact transpire. The country instead witnessed a return to prodigious economic growth, driven by the coffee boom of 1976 to 1979. The causes of this about-turn in the country's fortunes lay not in government policy, but instead in events on the other side of the world. A sharp frost had hit the coffee-growing areas of Brazil during the southern winter of 1975. The coffee crop there was destroyed and global prices for the commodity spiked in response to the consequent downturn in supply from the world's biggest producer. In contrast, favourable rains in East Africa left Kenyan farmers well placed to exploit the misfortune of their Brazilian counterparts. Incomes for coffee farmers grew dramatically, and the rewards were visible across the coffee-growing areas of the country, and particularly in Central Province. There houses were improved through the construction of permanent stone buildings and the addition of corrugated iron roofs. Vehicles were purchased and small business ventures started.[16] This situation proved temporary, but it lasted long enough to convince a sufficient number of Kenyans of the merits of the status quo. Mungai and Moi only had to worry about one another as they clashed over the succession.

THE SCHOOLMASTER AND THE PLAYBOY

Moi enjoyed several advantages over his rival. For one thing, faced with Mungai, Kenyans across the country came to see Moi as the only real alternative to continued elite Kikuyu hegemony after Kenyatta's death. However, reliant on Njonjo as he was, Moi was no less dependent on the backing of prominent Kikuyu than was his rival. But Moi also had the stature and character of a leader. Tall, slim and upright, with a distinctive gap in his front teeth, he was not given to public displays of exuberance. He had experience, too, having served as vice president since Murumbi's resignation in 1967. Throughout his rise to that position, Moi had consistently demonstrated an adroit touch in his use of ethnicity as a tool of politics. He served his apprenticeship in the fraught environment of the Rift Valley, where he represented his home constituency of Baringo Central until his retirement in 2002. The province proved to be his powerbase and, although a member of the minority Tugen sub-group, he quickly built up his reputation as the leader of the wider Kalenjin community. The risks of such a strategy were great. For one thing, the Kalenjin community had only formed from its various smaller constituent parts during and after the Second World War. Its political unity was uncertain for much of the first part of the post-colonial period. Moreover, Moi was far from the only figure claiming to be the Kalenjin leader.

His main Kalenjin rival was Jean Marie Seroney, the orchestrator of the Nandi Hills Declaration (see chapter 2) and a leading critic of the government in parliament until his arrest in 1975. Although Moi enjoyed a close relationship with Seroney's father, who was the vice president's former teacher, he and the younger Seroney clashed on numerous occasions throughout the 1970s. Seroney accused Moi of being complicit in the settlement of large numbers of Kikuyu in areas of the Rift Valley claimed by the Kalenjin as their rightful territory. Moi had little to say in response, except to make glib protestations of his nationalism and to accuse Seroney and others like him of going 'out of their way to generate tribalism'.[17] Moi instead preferred to undermine Seroney at the local level by sponsoring candidates in elections to run again Seroney's allies in Nandi district and elsewhere in the Rift Valley. When that tactic failed, he had Seroney arrested and detained in 1975. The vice president then turned his attention to Seroney's Kalenjin supporters in parliament, who followed their patron in questioning Moi's claims to be the leader of the community. Chief among these was one of the handful of women MPs and the representative of the Eldoret North constituency, Chelagat Mutai. She was jailed for two and a half years from March 1976 for organising protests against land-grabbing in her constituency.[18]

Such tactics helped Moi eventually emerge triumphant from his battle with Seroney. But he relied on more than just repression of his rivals for victory. While Seroney gained considerable publicity with his criticism of the government, Moi's more realistic strategy of working within the system of Kenyatta's rule gained greater support from Kalenjin. Indeed, Moi ridiculed Seroney's radicalism, claiming it was simply intended to seek a form of martyrdom through detention.[19] Moi instead presented himself as a skilled political operator who could protect Kalenjin interests by remaining close to Kenyatta. His later nickname, the 'Professor of Politics', was well deserved. He organised Kalenjin land-buying companies to compete with the powerful Kikuyu efforts sanctioned by Kenyatta, but he also used patronage to build support across the Rift Valley. For many Kalenjin, furthermore, the thought of Mungai as president was enough to convince them to set aside any doubts they may have had about Moi's own candidature.

Moi's candidacy enjoyed significant support from within the British High Commission in Nairobi, too. The thinking there was that the widespread unpopularity of the Kenyatta family would result in substantial unrest should Mungai succeed. British diplomats therefore thought continued economic growth and political stability would most likely be achieved under Moi. They were under no illusions about their man, however. Speaking to a group of British investors in 1974, Malcolm MacDonald described him as 'totally thick' and warned that he 'might go seriously wrong if left to his own devices'.[20] British diplomats in London and Nairobi hoped Moi would rule as a puppet under the control of Njonjo, Kibaki and senior Kikuyu civil servants. 'Kikuyu sense may well triumph over Kalenjin sensibility', wrote one British diplomat. 'Let us hope so and do what we can to ensure it.'[21]

The reasons for British interest in the outcome of the succession struggle were obvious. Between 1977 and 1979, Britain provided more than $110 million in aid to the Kenyan government, the largest British aid package in Africa. Exports from Britain to Kenya were worth $187 million in 1977. Nor was this relationship in any apparent decline: orders of British-produced goods jumped 20 per cent in 1977. These ties were important to many Kenyan businesses, too: producers exported more to the former colonial power than was imported from Britain. To radical critics of the Kenyatta government, this relationship was nothing more than neo-colonialism, which would make the country dependent upon its former colonial ruler. To the Kenyan beneficiaries of the trade, though, it looked like good business. Moi curried favour with the latter group by positioning himself as the protector of the close diplomatic and economic ties to Britain.

A stronger rival would have exploited Moi's shortcomings. Instead, Mungai was at best the third choice as successor to Kenyatta for many elite Kikuyu, never mind the rest of the population. By the mid-1970s, James Gichuru was a spent force, and Mbiyu Koinange and Charles Njonjo were far too unpopular to consider as serious candidates; Koinange and Njonjo had to content themselves with influential back-office roles instead. Mungai's candidacy was not entirely without merit, however. A dynamic and youthful figure within the independence government, like Mboya and Kibaki he embodied the modernist appeal of KANU to voters in the early 1960s. An academic star, he qualified as a doctor at Stanford in 1957 and then returned to Kenya to establish a network of health centres around the country, before joining the first KANU government as minister for health and housing. He later served as minister of defence and, from 1969, as minister for foreign affairs. Despite his public profile, he was a playboy, far more at ease in a casino than in his ministerial office. His well-publicised wedding in 1972 was an attempt to change that public image, but was not helped by many of the jokes, made on the day by friends, that centred on Mungai's infidelity. 'From now on all your affairs must be foreign,' one speaker told him during the toasts.[22]

Mungai's candidacy was really built upon his blood-ties to the president. That relationship launched him into contention in the first instance, but as Kenyatta became less and less popular, so Mungai's own chances of succeeding decreased. He was also badly hit by the disdain that many of his own constituents in Dagoretti felt towards him. Through the early 1970s, voters there became convinced that their MP was unconcerned with their welfare and was instead rather too worried about his presidential ambitions and leisure pursuits. They dealt Mungai's hopes of becoming president a calamitous blow by turning against him in the 1974 parliamentary election. That defeat meant that, under Kenya's Westminster-style constitution, which required the president to be a sitting MP, he was out of the running to succeed Kenyatta. His reputation as an elitist with only infrequent and instrumental concern for the poor was set. He was also tainted by his close association with the elite Kikuyu inner circle at the heart of government. Even among other Kikuyu, this elite – overwhelmingly from Kenyatta's home district of Kiambu – was widely disliked. Its members were blamed in Nyeri for the murder of Kariuki and in Murang'a for the marginalisation of Kaggia and the efforts to smear Rubia.

Mungai hoped the considerable financial resources at his disposal could overcome such weaknesses. Using a large loan from the Central Bank (so British diplomats alleged), Mungai raised the funds necessary to fight for control of KANU local branch offices in 1976 by smuggling embargoed Ugandan coffee.[23] He could count on the support of some powerful friends, too. *The Standard* newspaper, owned by the Lonrho company, provided regular gushing praise for Mungai. Lonrho's financial support flowed through Udi Gecaga, Mungai's nephew. Already the managing director of Lonrho East Africa, Gecaga was made a board member of the parent company in 1973. The Gecaga family provided Mungai with further assistance in 1975, when Udi's mother, Jemimah, resigned her nominated seat in parliament to allow Mungai to resume his parliamentary career. But a nominated MP could not be president.

Mungai's lack of an elected seat in parliament was not the only constitutional impediment to his bid to succeed Kenyatta. He had little support in cabinet or parliament. Only six of the twenty-two ministers were thought to support him in 1976.[24] In parliament, the majority of MPs viewed him with disdain, and the majority of KANU members in the country backed Moi. The vice president enjoyed the support of other state institutions, too. Not least because of British and Israeli influence over the security forces, the rank-and-file in the army, police and GSU were assumed to be supportive of Moi. Their senior officers agreed: the commander of the GSU, Ben Gethi, the head of Special Branch, James Kanyotu, and the armed forces' chief of staff, Matu, considered Mungai to represent a continuation of Kiambu hegemony over other Kikuyu districts. All were from Nyeri.[25]

Mungai's effort to win the succession battle was therefore characterised by a series of efforts to circumvent the constitution and to build alternative institutions, as rivals to those whose support Moi enjoyed. He first attempted to do this through the Gikuyu, Embu and Meru Association (GEMA). Founded in 1970, GEMA was one of several ethnic associations ostensibly established to further the social welfare of its members and to protect the cultural traditions of the ethnic communities each served. Other notable examples were the (much older) Luo Union and the New Akamba Union. The groups all disavowed political activity. 'We are not gathered here to talk politics,' Mungai told a GEMA meeting in early 1973. 'GEMA is not a political body; we are not gathered here to collect weapons because GEMA is not a military organisation, but we are here to collect funds for the social welfare of the needy.'[26] Not all Kikuyu leaders were convinced, however. Kenyatta gave GEMA his blessing on its formation only in the hope that it would resemble the Ismaili social organisations – dominated by property owners but run for the benefit of the poor – and restore badly needed cohesion to Kikuyu society.[27] Njonjo correctly sensed that GEMA would likely develop into a threat to Moi, and so was an implacable opponent of the organisation from the very beginning.

Although the association had been founded by politicians, in the 1973 elections to GEMA business leaders and civil servants usurped MPs from their leadership positions. From that point on, GEMA assumed the appearance of a Kikuyu investment fund. It was led by Njenga Karume, a businessman and close friend of Kenyatta from Kiambu. His vice-chairman was Duncan Ndegwa, the then governor of the Central Bank, and the businessman Kihika Kimani became the national organising secretary. In local branches, too, businessmen took control of GEMA. In Nairobi, for example, a one-time director of Colgate Palmolive, Mwangi Mathai, became the chair of the city's branch. Mathai, Kimani and Karume quickly set about applying their commercial expertise to their leadership of the association, and in 1974 GEMA Holdings Ltd was founded. The new company set out to increase GEMA's income through returns on a wide range of investments, including large manufacturing interests and enormous rural farms. Within a year, the association had been transformed into a vast commercial enterprise.

Of the association's leaders, Kimani was the most influential. Although Kikuyu, he, like Moi, hailed from Baringo and so well understood the politics and business of land in the Rift Valley. He built his fortune after independence with the purchase of two large farms at Nakuru and Laikipia. He then turned his attention to the formation of Ngwataniro, a land-buying company established to facilitate settlement of Kikuyu farmers in the Rift Valley. By 1975, the company had over 20,000 shareholders, who provided the capital used to purchase approximately 100,000 acres of land across the Rift Valley. In Nairobi, the company's aggressive stance and its reserves of capital meant it was able to carry out a series of takeovers of profitable enterprises without resistance or any great opposition.[28] Moreover, Kimani was a public figure in his own right. He was one of the few voices that dared speak out against the establishment of the parliamentary enquiry into Kariuki's assassination, and so acquired a reputation as the most notorious Kikuyu hardliner. But he was also a keen political patron. With close ties to the Kenyatta family, Kimani had the connections, credentials and resources to ensure that his allies swept up all the district's parliamentary seats in the 1974 elections, with the exception of that of Nakuru town itself. He was therefore a direct rival to Moi in the Rift Valley.

Headed by the likes of Kimani, GEMA was meant to silence social unrest through distribution of land – the balm thought capable of healing long-standing divisions within the Kikuyu community. But it was also born out of fear. According to Njenga Karume, GEMA's chairman for much of its existence, its founders 'felt that they were under threat from the other tribes who, when combined, far outnumbered them'. The association's founders hoped it would help 'to strengthen and protect the communities they represented and which they could fall back upon in any eventuality'.[29] From the outset, then, GEMA was intended to create a reservoir of political support for Kikuyu leaders, and so strengthen the claims of a Kikuyu politician to succeed Kenyatta.

GEMA was the main plank of an effort to establish a parallel political system that shadowed the formal institutions of party and parliament. Able to hold local elections without fuss, and apparently driven by consensus and unity, it compared favourably to the moribund KANU. The group's elected leaders made sustained efforts to influence elections and other political events. For instance, in August 1976 the association supported Margaret Kenyatta, the president's daughter and incumbent mayor of Nairobi, during a mayoral contest in the council and a furore that arose after that vote was cancelled when it seemed likely that she would lose.[30]

GEMA was just as concerned with politics outside those areas populated by Kikuyu, however. From 1972 onwards, its leaders believed that closer ties to the Luo Union and the New Akamba Union could overcome the widespread opposition to the Kikuyu elite across the country. During a visit to see Kenyatta at Nakuru in 1972, for instance, GEMA's leaders asked for permission to campaign with Odinga.[31] While these efforts were quashed by Moi and Njonjo, GEMA nevertheless continued to pursue close relations with influential figures across the country. It provided significant support for Fred Gumo's successful mayoral bid in Kitale in Western Province, for example.[32] The association's leaders were trying to make GEMA and other ethnic associations seem to be the main participatory political institutions in the country, rather than parliament and KANU. The aim was clear: GEMA wanted to enjoy the constitutional privileges to determine the outcome of the succession struggle that were in the possession of other institutions controlled by Moi.

GEMA's leaders tried other ways of reducing the constitutional advantages in Moi's favour. In 1976, for instance, they organised a campaign that became known as 'Change the Constitution'. This brought together the various leading figures supporting Mungai's presidential bid to demand that the constitution be changed, so as to rescind the privileged position enjoyed by the vice president in the event of the president dying while in office. Under the existing constitution, the vice president automatically succeeded the deceased president in an acting capacity for ninety days. The fear among Mungai's supporters was that Moi would use that time to shore up his position, and deploy the considerable powers granted to the president to neutralise his opponents through fair means or foul. Although led by Kimani, Karume and other prominent Kikuyu leaders, the campaign also drew support from Moi's rivals among other communities. But this was insufficient to persuade enough cabinet ministers and MPs to back the campaign. In a sign of the strength of Moi's position, Njonjo was able to silence the clamour for constitutional change. The attorney general issued a statement that any discussion of Kenyatta's death amounted to treason. The legal grounding for his claim was non-existent, but Kenyatta agreed with his attorney general. Chastened by the president's intervention on the side of Moi, Mungai's camp was hushed.[33]

The last extra-constitutional attempt to thwart Moi centred on the Anti-Stock Theft Unit. Formed in 1974, the unit was ostensibly established to address the serious problem of cattle raiding in northern areas of the Rift Valley Province. But Joseph Karimi and Philip Ochieng depict the unit as a political militia, formed as a rival to the other branches of the security forces, which supported Moi.[34] The unit was commanded by the Rift Valley's senior police officer and close friend of Kimani, James Mungai. Perhaps 80 per cent of the two hundred or so members of the unit came from Njoroge Mungai's and Kenyatta's home district of Kiambu.[35] Mungai's rivals called for the unit's disbandment, but to no avail. When the time for action came, however, it proved inept.

THE SUCCESSION

By early August 1978, Kenyatta had surrendered all executive power. According to one British diplomat, the president's 'mental powers have continued to deteriorate and his control of everyday affairs of state has quietly passed to an informal group of senior Ministers and civil servants'. Tellingly, that group, 'which now conducts the running of the Government, is manned almost exclusively by the Vice President's supporters'.[36] Moi was not unduly concerned by the president's ill-health. He had long recognised that the succession struggle was unfolding in a most satisfactory way.[37] Indeed, his position was so strong that the murder of a key ally, Bruce McKenzie, made little impression on his campaign to succeed Kenyatta. McKenzie was killed in an explosion on 24 May 1978 as he flew back to Kenya after a visit to Uganda. Later investigations indicated that a bomb had been planted on the plane by Idi Amin's security officers. The bombing was revenge for the assistance that the Kenyan government had provided to Israeli commandos during their raid in 1976 to release hostages held by Palestinian terrorists in Uganda.[38]

It was no surprise when Kenyatta collapsed and died in the early hours of 22 August. Moi was informed of the president's death almost immediately and set out to travel to Mombasa. Even in death, power was located close to Kenyatta's person. Any plans by the Mungai faction to seize power with the support of the Anti-Stock Theft Unit were foiled immediately. The erection of roadblocks close to Moi's home was delayed and the vice president was able to travel without obstruction. Protected by the security forces, he flew to Mombasa and there, surrounded by his close supporters, was sworn in as president later that morning.[39] The moment for action by Mungai's supporters had passed.

A short announcement of Kenyatta's death and Moi's temporary rule was made at midday by the state broadcaster. A cabinet meeting was held later that afternoon under Moi's stewardship. Just twenty-four hours after the announcement of Kenyatta's death, Moi's key allies were seen in public without bodyguards.[40] Within days, a visibly relaxed Moi also felt safe enough to resume a public life. Once in office, his message to Kenyans and foreign observers alike was clear: it was business as usual. In his eulogy at Kenyatta's funeral, Moi described how 'Fifteen years ago Mzee Jomo Kenyatta led us into facing and accepting the challenge of nationhood: hard work.'[41] In the weeks that followed, Moi strove to convince Kenyans that his presidency was to be based around the same values and strategies as that of his predecessor. 'Please be assured that I will continue with the policies formulated by the founder of the nation,' the new president told a delegation from the Central Bank in September. 'It is only through continuation of his ideals and policies that Kenya will be able to maintain and advance the unity and prosperity of our nation.'[42] Moi's promise of continuity became known as *nyayo* ('footsteps'). But he gave little indication of how his government would better provide poor Kenyans with opportunities to work.

Moi was determined to establish his authority. 'I am a firm believer in discipline', the new president told a passing-out parade of the

National Youth Service. 'Discipline means rules and regulations.'[43] It soon became clear that what Moi meant by 'rules' was not the rule of law, but rather the enforcement of his personal will. In recognition of his victory, numerous delegations from across Kenya paid visits to the new president in the weeks following Kenyatta's funeral. All came to make protestations of loyalty. Even visits by his enemies became commonplace as they hoped to be spared from retribution by the new president. The Anti-Stock Theft episode gave the president and Njonjo ample ammunition to blackmail their erstwhile rivals into silence. Njonjo, in particular, revisited the incident on numerous occasions during the first months of Moi's rule, whenever it appeared that his old enemies were becoming too cocksure again. In December, for instance, the attorney general told the BBC that the leaders of the Anti-Stock Theft plot were the 'same group who were trying to amend the constitution. It is the same group who were financing this group of people who wanted to assassinate a number of people.'[44] The bedraggled Mungai and others heeded the warnings and withdrew from public gaze. With the succession settled, the task of governing began.

The most urgent matter demanding Moi's attention was the state of the economy. While the coffee boom had driven growth throughout the economy, it had been temporary and had left a legacy of high inflation for the country's new president. The new government also faced the challenge of how to sustain growth. Unlike his predecessor, Moi had few obvious opportunities to expand the economy at a rate that was sufficient to keep pace with the ever-growing population. There was no more land to be transferred from European to African hands, all export avenues had been explored, and the private and public sectors were now generally in the hands of Kenyan citizens. Yet each year, thousands more young adults left education and entered the labour market. Their demands for employment and social services constituted the most significant challenge for Moi. As an analyst at the US State Department wrote a decade earlier: 'A new combination of forces will be needed to maintain the balance and national consensus personified by Kenyatta if ideological and tribal particulars are not to destroy the harmony he has created.'[45] While such sentiments overstated the nationalism of Kenyatta, the Americans were right to perceive that Moi would have to use a very different toolkit in order to maintain authority.

Moi's promises of continuity settled lingering nerves in the board-rooms and embassies of Nairobi. Such sentiments did little, however, for the great many Kenyans who had come to see Kenyatta and his inner circle as corrupt. The new president thus set out a populist anti-corruption agenda that was designed to win widespread support. Shortly after Moi was confirmed as president in October, restrictions were enacted to ostensibly tackle tea smuggling, illegal land transfers and poaching. The appearance of reform meant that he quickly built up support among ordinary Kenyans: in contrast to Kenyatta's disas-trous last visit to Nyanza in 1969, Moi received a warm welcome throughout that province in December 1978.[46] The anti-corruption drive also gave Njonjo and Moi the pretence they needed to drive their enemies from positions of influence. The first prominent figure to be caught in the net was Bernard Hinga, the commissioner of police, in November. Hinga was replaced by Gethi, who had supported Moi throughout the succession struggle.

Under the cover of anti-corruption, Moi was beginning the process of replacing one privileged inner circle with another. He was uncon-cerned at the corrupt practices of his allies. Diplomats alleged that Kibaki, for example, was given free rein to continue all manner of dubious business deals. For instance, as minister of finance and plan-ning, Kibaki issued Fiat's local subsidiary with a licence to allow it to assemble motor cars. Fiat (Kenya) had been acquired by an investment group, allegedly including Kibaki, just prior to the licence being issued.[47] Quickly installed as vice president and leader of government business in parliament, Kibaki was the chief beneficiary of Moi's efforts to build a robust government. Moi was equally swift to move other loyal supporters into key positions. At the same time, he squeezed his main rivals. Mbiyu Koinange, for instance, was demoted to minister for natural resources shortly after Moi's position was confirmed. In a diplomatic reshuffle announced in late November, the key post of high commissioner in London passed from Ng'ethe Njoroge to Shadrack

Kimalel. Njoroge was Mungai's younger brother and had been involved in his sibling's bid for the presidency. Significantly, Kimalel was, like Moi, Kalenjin.[48]

L'ETAT C'EST MOI

Replacing Kenyatta's courtiers with his own was the first and easiest stage in Moi's efforts to topple the Kikuyu ascendancy. His next target was GEMA, and in this he was ably assisted by Njonjo, who had long harboured suspicion of the organisation. GEMA's executives soon found themselves in the dock over financial irregularities. Kihika Kimani, Njenga Karume and others were ordered to pay heavy fines for petty irregularities in the company's books.[49] Moi was particularly keen to destroy Kimani, his main political rival in Rift Valley towns like Nakuru. Kimani's supporters quickly realised that the game was up. The ordinary rank-and-file shareholders in Ngwataniro became uneasy with the lax application of regulations governing the administration of the company and realised they were on the wrong side of history. While Moi squeezed GEMA and Ngwataniro from the top, the push came from below to unseat the company directors most associated with the efforts to block Moi's succession. They voted to suspend Kimani and the other directors of Ngwataniro in March 1979.[50] Having broken the back of the Kikuyu elite's economic influence, Moi turned his attention to its political foundations. Kimani's allies were forced out of elected office in local government in Nakuru and were replaced with the president's clients. KANU branch elections were orchestrated to ensure the defeat of Kimani's supporters in the town. 'Nakuru', the new, pro-Moi mayor of the town remarked, 'is the college of politics.'[51] Kimani was taught a harsh lesson that he would not forget.

A general election held later in the year presented Moi with a further opportunity to continue his purge of Kenyatta's allies. Tainted by corruption and association with the worst excesses of Kenyatta's regime, incumbent MPs found their constituents unforgiving, and over seventy of them were defeated. In the Rift Valley, the Kikuyu MPs associated with GEMA, including Kimani, were swept from office. Although some key figures from the Kenyatta era did hold on to their seats in parliament – Mungai regained the Dagoretti constituency, for instance – most departed the scene. Peter Muigai Kenyatta, the first president's eldest son, died shortly before the polls. Jackson Angaine, Kenyatta's minister for land, and Josephat Njuguna Karanja, the former vice chancellor of the university, were both beaten. Members of the former ruling elite even turned on one another in Kiambu, where GEMA's Njenga Karume took on and defeated Mbiyu Koinange. Ethnic unity was shown to be just a means to the end of achieving power.

Moi emerged from the election in a stronger position, for several reasons. Although his preferred candidates were routed in Nyanza, and even though other awkward opponents, such as Chelagat Mutai, retained their seats, parliament was much more closely aligned to the presidency after the election than it had been before. Furthermore, Moi's allies took the place of some of the president's more implacable rivals. Seroney, for example, was defeated in his seat in Tinderet by Henry Kosgey, one of Moi's strongest supporters in the Rift Valley. Another key figure within Moi's emerging Kalenjin ascendancy was Nicholas Biwott. He did not even have to contest an election in his constituency of Kerio South. The incumbent MP chose not to run, and so Moi's aide and the wealthy chairman of the Lima farm machinery distribution company entered parliament.

Perhaps the most important outcome of the election was the opportunity it presented for reconstruction of the cabinet, as more than half of the ministers lost their seats in parliament. Only four of those who had provided the most unequivocal support for the president during the succession struggle kept their portfolios, including Kibaki and Njonjo. Other leading politicians, like Rubia, who had publicly backed Moi during the years leading up to Kenyatta's death, were rewarded with cabinet posts. The newly elected loyalists like Kosgey and Biwott were quickly promoted, too. As Moi sought to consolidate nationwide support, every one of Kenya's forty-two districts was represented in the new cabinet by either an assistant or a full ministerial post. The civil service and the provincial administration underwent similar transformations. Geoffrey Kariithi, the powerful head of the civil service, retired in September 1979. By the time the Coast provincial commissioner and key ally of Kenyatta, Eliud Mahihu, was moved sideways to be chairman of the Kenya Tea Board in May 1980, only one of Kenyatta's provincial commissioners remained in post.

A similar process occurred in the private sector, too. For those elites willing to play according to Moi's rules and demonstrate their personal loyalty to the president, the potential economic rewards were great. GEMA's influential chairman and former close friend of Kenyatta, Njenga Karume, made determined efforts to distance himself from his past. As Moi set about isolating and destroying his opponents on the left, Karume's continued statements of support for the president were rewarded with his appointment as an assistant minister. More importantly, Moi backed Karume during a dispute with Kimani over control of Agricultural & Industrial Holdings (which had previously been GEMA Holdings). During his speech to a KANU party conference in 1981, the president told Kimani that he 'should go back and rest'.[52] Kimani resigned from the company's board soon afterwards.[53] Other actors recognised the new logic of power, too. In early 1981, Lonrho East Africa's executives instigated a boardroom coup against Udi Gecaga, the chairman and chief executive. Gecaga was closely tied to the old Kikuyu establishment and Lonrho wanted to build friendly relations with Moi's regime. Mark Arap Too, a Kalenjin, replaced him.[54] As a consequence of Lonrho's decision, the company enjoyed close relations with the government. From boardrooms to the cabinet, Kenyatta's men had given way to Moi's.

Martin Shikuku, one of the most prominent backbench critics of Kenyatta's government, declared himself content with Moi's leadership. Shikuku had built his career during the Kenyatta era on his reputation as a voice of the ordinary citizen. Under Moi, he felt he was in danger of becoming redundant in that role. 'I am in a better position now,' the veteran politician told the press. 'In fact, I have no job. The job has been taken over by the president. I just follow.'[55] Besides his support for the anti-corruption drive, Shikuku was most enthusiastic about the release of all political prisoners in December 1978. Those released were, like Shikuku, at first full of praise for Moi. Even Seroney promised after his release that 'I will be second-to-none in following in the president's *nyayo* ["footsteps"]'.[56] In gratitude, he pledged to step back from involvement in the wider politics of Nandi district and the Kalenjin community more generally.[57] But the released prisoners and other former critics of Kenyatta came to realise that all was not as it first appeared in Moi's Kenya. In return for his protestations of loyalty and obedience, Seroney was allowed to stand in the 1979 elections but was defeated, as we saw above, by Kosgey. Other released prisoners and other dissidents were not even allowed to experience Seroney's humiliation. Odinga and Oneko, for instance, were barred from standing in the elections.[58] Moi's regime was no more willing to tolerate dissent than its predecessor's had been.

THE TIDE TURNS

Critics of Kenyatta's government stirred themselves for a new fight and were emboldened by the obvious shortcomings of the second president's rule. Government policies in a wide range of fields caused considerable unease. Foreign policy, for example, was once again a matter of domestic politics. Moi maintained the close ties established by Kenyatta to the Western powers. An agreement struck with the US that allowed it access to Kenyan military facilities proved to be the most contentious of all aspects of the friendly relations enjoyed with the superpower. 'Kenya is not up for mortgage or sale to foreign interests of exploitation and hegemony,' Odinga wrote in an open letter to a visiting US congressional delegation in 1982.[59] Most Kenyans were, however, more concerned with the government's handling of the economy than with its foreign policy.

Unemployment increased to nearly 20 per cent, while debt and inflation soared in the late 1970s and early 1980s. Overall inflation in 1978 was 12.5 per cent, but this average concealed significant variations. Price increases for the highest earners were thought to be just 10 per cent, but 17 per cent for the lower income groups.[60] By early 1980, growth was slowing as the cost of imports rose and demand for exports declined; by the following year, public spending exceeded income by $570 million. As the government borrowed money in order to narrow the widening trade deficit, debt owed overseas reached $1 billion in 1980 – approximately 20 per cent of Kenya's gross domestic product. A $310 million loan from the International Monetary Fund (IMF) was agreed in 1981.

Factors beyond the control of the Kenyan government contributed to the changing economic picture. The rising cost of oil in response to the second oil crisis was one such cause of economic woe, and drought in 1979 and 1980 put pressure on the all-important agricultural sector. At the same time, the global prices for commodities such as tea and coffee fell. Most important of all, every year there were more Kenyans to feed, educate and provide with medical care. By the start of 1981, some 225,000 Kenyans were entering the job market each year. Even though the economy grew at 2.4 per cent in 1980, this was far less than the rate of population growth.

The informal economy took up some of the slack. In their study of Nakuru – carried out in 1980 but written up four years later – Gichiri Ndua and Njuguna Ng'ethe demonstrated the fundamental importance of the informal economy to daily lives in Kenya's urban areas. Their survey identified nearly 1,700 distinct businesses operating outside the formal control of local authorities. Nearly 400 of these were the ubiquitous kiosks, selling all manner of household goods – from shoe polish to soft drinks. But they were joined by second-hand clothes stalls, tailors, shoemakers and cobblers, charcoal sellers and a whole host of other providers of goods and services to the 100,000 or more residents of Nakuru. Over two-thirds of these enterprises provided employment for just one person, and a quarter employed only two people. Through their enterprise, ingenuity and hard labour, Kenyans were eking out an existence for themselves.[61]

Government policies did not help them. The Kenyan shilling was devalued by a quarter of its worth in 1981 and further efforts were made to curb the demand for imports. These policies strangled industrial development, however, as the sector relied on being able to import supplies and export finished products. A combination of mismanagement and official corruption led to shortages of food and other essential items in the shops. Given control of state-owned interests, individuals close to the president were free to cannibalise those operations as reward for their loyalty. Basic staples were being smuggled across Kenya's borders for higher prices outside the country, while Kenyans went without. That smugglers were also reselling humanitarian food aid back on to the international market only made matters worse.[62] 'Between 1978 and 1979 a clique of ministers used their closeness to the centre of power to export the strategic maize reserves, and while they were at it obtained sole grain import rights,' one anonymous group of critics of the government alleged in 1982. 'The disappearance of our food must be attributed to criminal corruption plus incompetence.'[63]

Cuts to public spending agreed with the IMF produced unintended consequences or else were tempered by political considerations: government salaries were capped, which only further encouraged corruption by public officials. Similarly, matched funding from the public purse for local welfare and education projects was also reduced. This had previously been used as a source of patronage by politicians, who were instead forced to seek alternative ways in which to sustain their networks of clients in their constituencies.[64] The budgets of many state-owned enterprises were left intact. Following Kenyatta's lead, Moi had used appointments to executive positions within these organisations as a way of buying off leading critics and building alliances with important figures. His short-term political objective of remaining in power trumped any worries about the lasting effects of new fiscal and monetary policies. The public mood was changing, however. The relief with which many Kenyans greeted Moi's peaceful assumption of power was replaced with unease about the future.

The first protests against Moi's rule began on the campuses of the University of Nairobi and the Kenyatta University College in late 1979. Student activism had long been one of the main forms of dissent in the post-colonial period: between 1961 and 1980, the University of Nairobi was closed on no fewer than twenty-five occasions due to demonstrations. Students had endured a difficult relationship with Kenyatta, and so initially welcomed Moi's succession. And the president reciprocated their goodwill: in 1979 the annual march held in central Nairobi to mark the anniversary of Kariuki's assassination was allowed to pass off for the first time without police interference. Students on the march even carried banners praising Moi's government.[65] As the year progressed, however, the enthusiasm on campus for the new regime waned.

National and campus politics interlocked to a considerable degree. At the University of Nairobi, for instance, the refusal of the authorities to reinstate Ngugi wa Thiong'o in his academic post provoked much anger among the student body. The unwillingness of the university management or the government to sanction Ngugi's return to work was a reaction to his stance following his release in December 1978. Unlike his fellow former political prisoners, Ngugi was not interested in currying favour so that he could participate in the 1979 elections: he was a writer, not a politician. He saw no reason to be unduly grateful to the government for his release. When asked soon after his release if he had been embittered by his experience, Ngugi responded: 'Well, frankly, I'm very bitter. Detention without trial is nothing not to be bitter about.' But he also perceived correctly that little had changed in Moi's Kenya. His struggle to champion, in his words, 'the peasant and worker initiative' was to continue.[66] Ngugi's vigilance was well justified, as his own harassment by the authorities continued. In mid-March 1979, for instance, he and his co-author of *I Will Marry When I Want*, Ngugi wa Mirii, were arrested in a bar near Limuru for allegedly drinking after licensing hours. Both Ngugi and Mirii claimed that they had been beaten in custody and were later cleared in court.

Ngugi's travails provoked considerable sympathy on the campuses. However, it was the decision taken by the government to ban many former political prisoners from standing in the 1979 election that caused the fragile relations between the students and the authorities to finally break down. Students at the University of Nairobi took to the city's streets to protest against the decision, and the university was closed for a month to prevent further demonstrations.[67] By the time it reopened in mid-November, six student leaders had been expelled.[68] Over the following three years, protests and closures became commonplace at the two main university campuses. The unrest spread to primary and secondary schools, too. School pupils mounted a wave of strikes through 1980 over poor conditions and their treatment by their teachers.

The rise in student militancy was partly due to the declining living standards on campus. As the intake of students outstripped state funding, so accommodation became overcrowded. 'There are 8–10 in a room in condemned housing at Kenyatta University College, living in circumstances which make study nearly impossible,' it was claimed in 1982. Corruption made catering intolerable. At every level of the administration at the University of Nairobi, kickbacks and nepotism resulted in a system that meant that 'students were fed horsemeat and wildlife while the food intended for them was sold elsewhere at a handsome profit'. The higher education institutions were a microcosm of Kenyan society, and students quickly learned that 'the University offers a reflection of the looting and mismanagement taking place at all levels of society'.[69] But the student and pupil protests spoke to more deeprooted changes in Kenyan society than simply the criminal activities of its elite.

Strikes and demonstrations by school pupils and university students were just the most obvious political expressions of the population explosion that Kenya had experienced since the end of the Second World War. High fertility and decreasing mortality rates meant more Kenyans were being born and surviving infancy than ever before – Kenya was a young nation in every sense. Along with Kuwait, the Ivory Coast and Libya, Kenya's 3.8 per cent rate of population increase in 1978 was the fastest in the world. According to the World Bank in 1980, this rising population meant pressure on fertile land had increased and the incomes of parents had come to be spread ever more thinly. The demand for education grew with the rising population: close to five million children, or around a third of the entire population, were in school in 1980. Nearly a third of public spending went on trying to meet the government's commitment to provide at least a primary school education to all.[70] But as budgets came under pressure, so corners were cut. Class sizes rose, the amounts spent on catering and accommodation dropped, books became scarcer, and teachers and lecturers difficult to pay. The results could be seen in the angry faces of students during their ever more frequent protests in Nairobi.

As demonstrations continued through 1980 and 1981, Moi first tried to buy off the lecturers, who, he thought, were initiating the protests. Arguing that the hiring of expatriate consultants was a drain on precious foreign currency reserves, he urged lecturers to go into private consultancy work while continuing to be paid a salary by the university.[71] Moi's decree replicated the effects of a similar loosening of the ties by Kenyatta on civil servants earning an income in the private sector. Just as Kenyatta's measures exacerbated the trend towards gross official corruption, so Moi's encouragement of lecturers to find external incomes encouraged moonlighting and rent-seeking. The long-term effects on the quality of higher education were all too visible in the coming years, not least as academics marginalised by Moi's style of rule fled the country. Indeed, the demand for personal loyalty to the president in return for private gain quickly became the operating logic of the wider political economy. The incentives for participating in this system increased as the state's resources declined with the economy. As jobs and the opportunities to earn an income in the formal sector became ever scarcer, the inducement of an income in return for participation in this game of patronage sapped the strength of most to resist.

Student protests nevertheless continued. Believing the students' complaints to be based on little material substance, Moi asserted in March 1980 that they were being incited by radical lecturers linked to his opponents.[72] He went further later in the year, suggesting that the aim of the disturbances at the university was to provide a cover for the assassination of key leaders. 'From now on,' warned Moi, 'I shall be very careful with the University of Nairobi.'[73] As school and university protests gathered pace, dissenting voices in parliament became louder, too. Concerned that his government was coming under pressure from various directions, Moi and his senior ministers adopted a new, increasingly authoritarian tack. The president made it clear that he had no time for persistent critics of his government and that of Kenyatta. During discussions with a church group in Kabarnet in

July 1980, he asked: 'Was President Kenyatta's government a colonial one to deserve such agitators? Is my government a colonial one?'[74] Kibaki turned on journalists for their willingness to report criticisms of the government, and for their accusations of official corruption. The vice president warned critics in the press: 'They should know that we know who they are working for and for whom they are doing the job.'[75] An interview with one of the leading dissident lecturers, Peter Anyang' Nyong'o, resulted in the arrest of both the lecturer and the reporter who conducted the interview. Both were released the following day, but on the evening of their release Anyang' Nyong'o's brother, Charles Anam, was drowned in a mysterious incident on a commuter ferry in Mombasa.[76] Moi's initial populism had given way to a calculated use of authoritarianism and criminality.

Moi himself was unapologetic. Speaking to an audience of party officials, MPs and senior officers in the provincial administration in late July, he hoped that 'no one would say that I have not given many people a second chance to amend their ways and recognize their responsibilities to the nation. But I am now beginning to suspect that my approach, an approach which I know to be correct, is being regarded by some as lack of strength.'[77] Those assembled at the meeting then dutifully passed a series of resolutions clearly intended to demonstrate the president's strength. Among them was a condemnation of

> any individual or groups of persons who attempt to instil indiscipline among the young, either in the university or any other institution of learning. The government shall, therefore, from now on apply all possible measures to ensure that appropriate discipline is instilled in our young generation, and parents and party leaders are called upon to play an active role in assisting the government to this end.

Another critical resolution passed ordered the winding-up of the ethnic associations, including GEMA.[78]

Even this did not satisfy Moi. His public speeches became more vindictive against the Kikuyu elite. At rallies around the country, he condemned those who thought they had the right to power by virtue of having shed blood during the fight for independence.[79] Waruru Kanja, one of those who had fought for Mau Mau, became one of the main targets of Moi's ire. Kanja, the MP for Nyeri town and a close friend of J.M. Kariuki, had been a vociferous opponent of the efforts to change the constitution in 1976, and was no friend of the Kikuyu establishment. As a reward, Kanja was made assistant minister for local government after the 1979 elections, but he soon got into trouble with the new government. Angered at the presence in parliament of those he thought to have been implicated in some of the worst crimes of the Kenyatta era, Kanja made frequent reference in his speeches to the murders of Kariuki and Mboya. Kanja turned his ire on Njonjo, accusing him of involvement in the assassinations. He then jeopardised his imperilled position still further, claiming that Njonjo and Ignatius Nderi, the head of CID and brother of Kanja's old adversary in Nyeri, had threatened him with assassination in an effort to prevent him from talking further about Kariuki's murder. 'We should be free from intimidation,' he told parliament. 'If I am guilty I should be hanged in public, but don't take me to Ngong.'[80] Kanja was not the only Kenyan unwilling to forget what had happened in the Ngong Hills.

On 2 March 1981, students at the University of Nairobi planned to hold their annual demonstration on the anniversary of Kariuki's death. Moi ordered them not to go ahead, but the students and many of the faculty threatened to defy him. The university authorities closed the establishment to prevent the demonstration from taking place. Stanley Oloitipitip, a government minister, could not understand what all the fuss was about. 'My father is dead and everybody will die,' he quipped. 'I do not see why intellectuals should waste their time on the streets shouting about JM while he is dead.'[81] For all his flippancy, Oloitipitip knew very well why the students and people such as Kanja continued to 'waste their time shouting about JM': the criticisms that Kariuki had levelled at the Kenyatta government applied equally to Moi's.

Other politicians came to agree. Having kept his counsel after being barred from standing in the 1979 elections, Odinga was determined to return to national politics and the public stage. An opportunity to do so was created by the resignation in early 1981 of the sitting MP for Bondo, Hezekiah Ougo. Backed by the other Luo MPs, Odinga was the unanimous choice to be nominated as KANU's candidate in an unopposed by-election. He was in good cheer, then, as he addressed a fundraising event in Mombasa in early April. Speaking warmly of his relations with Moi, Odinga recounted to the audience how the president had said to him: 'Come *Baba* ['father'], join me and let us work together for this country.'[82] Moi sensed an opportunity to disarm a dangerous opponent. The president took exception to the notion that he had called Odinga '*Baba*'. 'Any other leader who thinks that he qualifies to be addressed as such by me must have lost his ground and sense of direction,' the president remarked bitterly. A week later, Moi was even more explicit. With the two men sharing the platform at another fundraiser, the president publicly humiliated Odinga. 'If over the last three or so years you have not mended your ways, you are too late,' Moi told Odinga in front of the crowd.[83] Odinga was barred from standing in the Bondo by-election.

The pettiness of the president provoked an outcry in the newspapers. *The Nation* called on him to reverse the decision to prevent Odinga from standing in Bondo. Unused to such explicit condemnation of his actions, the president responded angrily. On 20 May, five senior members of staff at *The Nation* were arrested and held for a short period of time.[84] Other examples of dissent were silenced, too. Students mounted demonstrations on 15 and 18 May, and the latter turned violent. Riot police and students clashed on the streets of Nairobi and the University of Nairobi was closed indefinitely.[85] Draconian measures were put in place to police the movements of students and lecturers. Lecturers known to hold radical views were the subject of particular harassment. The historian Mukaru Ng'ang'a, for example, was arrested a number of times for minor offences through the middle months of 1981.

In parliament, too, critics of the government came under increased pressure. Seven dissident MPs were questioned on suspicion of lodging false expense claims with the parliamentary authorities. Three of the accused responded bitterly: '[S]omebody somewhere is looking for scapegoats in the few of us that try to exercise our democratic rights of free expression and honest presentation of the people of this country as best we can.'[86] One of the seven, Chelagat Mutai, fled to Tanzania rather than risk imprisonment. Her intuition proved sound. On 24 September, Waruru Kanja became the first political prisoner of the Moi era. He was jailed for three years for failing to convert foreign currency back into Kenyan shillings following an overseas trip earlier in the year. George Anyona, a former radical parliamentarian, was the next to fall victim to the politicisation of the judicial process. He was arrested at his home on 22 October but was neither charged nor brought to court. After his wife filed a *habeas corpus* application, Anyona was finally brought to court four days after his arrest and charged with sedition, although the charges were later dropped.

THE PATH TO THE COUP

Odinga was dismayed at the course of events. By early 1982, the grandee of the left could contain himself no longer. Addressing a press conference, he was forthright in his criticism of the government. Slowing growth, increasing unemployment and an ever-widening trade deficit were caused, he argued, by 'corruption, misuse of our foreign exchange, importation of luxury goods, poor planning, over-dependence on and misuse of foreign aid and lack of a comprehensive policy on energy'. To this litany of complaints, Odinga added the close military ties with the US forged by Moi's government. He was also concerned about the alignment between Kenya's economic policy and the nascent neoliberal ideology taking shape in the offices of the IMF and the World Bank in Washington.[87] In a context of continuing student protests, backbench criticism of the government and public concern over the misuse of the judicial process, Moi made it clear that he would not tolerate further outbursts by Odinga or his supporters. While publicly mulling over the idea of restoring detention without trial, he suggested that 'maybe time has come to resort to this move'.[88]

Odinga was in no mood to listen to Moi any longer; his silence over the first four years of the president's rule had brought him no rewards. He used a visit in May 1982 to London to address the Labour Party and expand on his criticisms of Moi's rule. While refusing to mention the Kenyan government or Moi specifically, he suggested that a second, socialist party was necessary in Kenya. He continued:

> Sooner rather than later these one-party systems become non-party systems. The presidents arrogate to themselves the role of lawmaker and lawgiver. They rule by undeclared decree. They set up cohorts of sycophants around themselves and run court cabals which are united only in one intention: the exploitation of the broad masses.[89]

Back in Kenya, George Anyona took up Odinga's message. The second party was necessary, according to Anyona, 'to avoid slippage into these disastrous one-party tyrannies which are rampant in Africa today'. To Anyona and many others it seemed that KANU had become 'the biggest threat to democracy in Kenya today'.[90] Such statements were devastating in their accuracy, but nevertheless provided Moi with the ammunition he needed to silence his critics.

Sensing a crisis point fast approaching, long-standing opponents of the regime urged restraint and calm. Student leaders called on the government and KANU 'to respect the Kenya constitution, particularly that clause which guarantees the rights of Kenyans to form or belong to any political party of their choice'. Mukaru Ng'ang'a cautioned that attempts to close down formal institutions that represented dissenting voices in society would lead only to critics of the government seeking alternative outlets for their anger.[91] The government chose not to heed Ng'ang'a's warning. Instead, Moi denounced Odinga as 'engaging in divisive politics and propaganda against Kenya cabinet ministers aimed at dividing the Kenya people'. He was, Moi argued, a 'prophet of doom'. Odinga was expelled from KANU with immediate effect.[92] Any hopes that he could form the much-vaunted second party were dashed soon after. Njonjo moved a parliamentary motion to codify the one-party state within the constitution. The motion explicitly banning the founding of an opposition party was enthusiastically seconded by Kibaki. The vote that followed was unanimous – Kenya became a one-party state without protest from its elected representatives.

Even before the parliamentary vote, the government had moved to silence the most likely critics and others who challenged Moi's supremacy. Over a week in late May and early June, Anyona, Mwangi Stephen Muriithi and John Khaminwa were each detained without trial. Muriithi, the former deputy director of intelligence, was the first to be imprisoned. He used the courts to try to challenge his enforced retirement from the intelligence service and appointment as general manager of the state-owned Uplands Bacon Factory. Such reappoint-ments were typical of the way in which Moi attempted to placate former allies of Kenyatta and other potential opponents, as he levered them from positions of influence. Muriithi had no desire to leave the intelligence service, however. He paid for his impertinence with deten-tion without trial. Anyona joined him a few days later in punishment for his calls for a new party. Khaminwa, the lawyer for both men, was detained shortly afterwards.[93]

Moi connected the demands made by Anyona for a second party to university lecturers. They were, the president claimed, preaching the 'politics of subversion and violence'.[94] Accused of plotting the downfall of the government and of distributing seditious literature, academics were caught up in a wave of arrests through late May and June 1982. Following riots at the Kenyatta University College in May, Dr Al Amin Mazrui, Willy Mutunga and Maina wa Kinyatti, all lecturers at the insti-tution, were detained, and the college closed. Others soon joined them in detention. As the number of detainees swelled and the promises of further repression grew ever more boastful, some long-standing oppo-nents of the government fled into exile. Critics of the use of detention without trial, such as George Githii in an editorial in his *Standard* news-paper, were denounced as traitors. Other forums thought likely to be the setting for expressions of discontent, such as Ngugi's Kamiriithu community theatre project, were closed down.

With the space for legitimate expressions of dissent shrinking, the most committed of the regime's opponents began exploring more militant options. In *Pambana* ('Power'), an underground newspaper circulated in Nairobi during May, Moi's regime was denounced for having 'sowed unprincipled discord and enmity among our peoples, and hav[ing] looted unspeakable sums of money and national wealth'. The newspaper went on: 'All these crimes have been wrought in the name of "progress and prosperity" and inane smatterings of "love, peace and unity".' 'This is *not* independence,' it emphatically insisted, before calling on Kenyans 'to fight and overthrow imperialism and neo-colonialism and achieve the long delayed true independence'.[95] Moi was unrepentant. 'This war will now continue until we clear our homestead,' he boasted. His enemies were, the president argued, 'like rats poisoning the minds of the people and I had no alternative but to detain them'.[96] The descent into authoritarianism was complete.

THE COUP

At seven o'clock on the morning of 1 August, a Sunday, Kenyans awoke to the music of Jimmy Cliff and Bob Marley, followed by an incongruous announcement on the Voice of Kenya radio station. According to the statement, read by Leonard Mbotela Mambo, one of the station's most popular broadcasters, Moi's government had been overthrown. Mambo had been forced from his home and driven under armed guard to the radio station to make the broadcast. 'As I speak to you now, our country is fully and firmly under the control of our armed forces,' he told Kenyans. The statement prepared for him promised that 'Every care has been taken to make the revolution as bloodless as possible', before turning to a litany of grievances against the Moi regime:

> Over the past six months we have witnessed with disgust the imposition of a de jure one-party system without the people's consent, arbitrary arrest and the detention of innocent citizens, censorship of the press, intimidation of individuals, and general violation of fundamental human rights.

The resemblance between British colonial rule and Moi's regime was striking, the authors of the statement believed. The government existed only 'to terrorise and intimidate with senseless warnings. Rampant corruption, tribalism, [and] nepotism have made life almost intolerable in our society. The economy of this country is in shambles due to corruption and mismanagement.' Faced with such tyranny, 'our armed forces have heeded the people's call to liberate our country once again from the forces of oppression and exploitation in order to restore liberty, dignity and social justice to the people'. The statement promised to restore 'the freedom which our fathers and grandfathers so gallantly fought to bring to this country'.[97] With the announcement over, the reggae resumed.

The radio station had been taken over by airmen from the KAF as part of their coup attempt that had begun some four hours earlier, when they had stormed the disco at their barracks on the city's south-eastern edge. In an effort to escape the gunfire, revellers had fled the disco to call the police. The officers from the local police station who responded to the call were easily beaten off as airmen with weapons from the base's armoury fanned out from the base to the rest of the city.

The coup was not wholly unexpected. Morale within the air force had been plummeting as anger grew over the conditions of service, the lack of housing and uniforms, the poor food and relations with senior officers. Discussions between disaffected airmen about a possible coup had begun as early as 1979, with one, James Dianga, imprisoned for ten years after having been found guilty of sedition at a court martial in 1981. Dianga had set about bringing together a number of discontented airmen with a view to planning a coup attempt.[98] Other rumours of a plot had come to light in 1981 during the (separate) treason trial of Andrew Mungai Muthemba and Dickson Kamau Muiruri. The two men had been accused of attempting to form an assassination squad of military officers in order to kill Moi, but both were acquitted.

Although the trial of Muthemba and Muiruri was bound up with an effort to discredit Njonjo, James Dianga was, he later claimed, part of a second and unconnected plot – the one that came to a head in August 1982. His arrest and sentence had initially derailed those plans, however, and discussion among his former co-conspirators had only resumed in March. Led by Hezekiah Ochuka Rabala, a private in the air force based at Eastleigh in Nairobi, the plotters made contact with Odinga, and key supporters of Odinga became closely associated with the plot soon afterwards. The most significant of these political figures was Odinga's chief bodyguard, John Odongo Langi. Langi had been one of the many students sent to Eastern Europe for military training in the early 1960s – in his case to Czechoslovakia – and then excluded from recruitment into the armed forces. Similarly, Opwapo Ogai, who had been sent to Kazakhstan after having served in the Kenya Army, provided his backing for the coup. Odinga's son Raila also joined the plot and was charged with establishing a command post on the Ngong Road on the day of the coup. Paddy Onyango, another of Odinga's aides and formerly secretary general of the unofficial students' union at the university in Nairobi, provided important information about the Voice of Kenya headquarters.[99] Between April and late July, the overwhelmingly Luo plotters laid their plans.

Despite the legal proceedings of the previous year, the coup came as a surprise to the citizens of Nairobi. Most stayed in their homes as the airmen fanned out from their two bases in Nairobi at Eastleigh and Embakasi. The coup plotters from Embakasi took over the control towers at the adjacent Jomo Kenyatta International Airport and the smaller Wilson Airport. In the hours before daybreak, the airmen successively captured the General Post Office and the Voice of Kenya studios in the city centre, and then the Voice of Kenya transmission station on Ngong Road in Nairobi's western suburbs. The rebels then spread out throughout the city, from Embakasi in the south to Eastleigh in the east and Ngong Road in the west. They lacked vehicles, however, and instead relied on commandeering and stealing cars. This was not a well-executed coup.

At the Kenyatta University College on the city's outskirts, news of the coup was met with jubilation. Students danced outside the campus housing of detained faculty members, but no attempts were made to join the uprising. Kenyatta Medical School students who did try to get to the city centre turned back when they encountered roadblocks manned by members of the GSU and army still loyal to Moi. In the city centre, students from the University of Nairobi joined in the looting of shops through the main commercial districts; Asian-owned businesses were particular targets. Shouting the coup's slogan of 'Power', opportunistic individuals hijacked cars and minibuses in order to carry off their plunder.

The security forces loyal to the government had already begun their counter-attack by the time the looting started. Despite discontent in the KAF, Moi had ensured that commanders and senior officers in the other forces were carefully appointed, properly paid and well treated. Such measures ensured the loyalty of most of the security forces during the air force coup.[100] Within an hour of the coup starting, the rebels were being attacked with heavy weaponry at both the KAF's bases in the city. Outside the city, soldiers from the army barracks at Gilgil in the Rift Valley were rushed to Nanyuki, at the north-western foot of Mount Kenya, to prevent KAF airmen based there from joining the coup. Perhaps two hundred airmen fled into the forests of Mount Kenya in a forlorn attempt to evade capture. Back in Nairobi, there was little chance of escape for the plotters either.

Following an assault by loyal security forces, the airmen at the Voice of Kenya studios were defeated by ten o'clock in the morning; more than seventy of them were killed at the radio station. An hour later, it broadcast the message that the coup had been defeated and that Moi was still in power. By mid-afternoon it was apparent to the plotters that their plans had come to naught, and the looting ceased as quickly as it had begun. Property worth millions of shillings was thought to have been stolen or damaged that day. Recognising that the game was up, two of the coup leaders commandeered a transport plane, forced two senior officers to pilot it, and flew to Dar es Salaam. As daylight began to fade, Moi made a radio broadcast to reassure Kenyans that his authority had been restored. He had spent the weekend at Nakuru, but returned to Nairobi to oversee the mopping-up operation once it became clear that it was safe to do so. More than two hundred airmen and civilians were killed during the coup and another five hundred were injured, many of them innocent civilians caught in the crossfire, or people wrongly suspected of being airmen.

Within two days, nearly the entire force of over two thousand airmen had been arrested. More than a thousand members of the KAF were found guilty of sedition, treason or other such crimes, and of these twelve went to the gallows.[101] Like the plots of 1965 and 1971, the coup of 1982 presented Moi with an opportunity to consolidate his hold on power and to marginalise his rivals. The coup leaders and others suspected of being involved in the plot were speedily arrested. Raila Odinga, for instance, was held until 1988. Student radicalism was just as quickly destroyed. The University of Nairobi and Kenyatta University College were closed on 2 August, the day after the coup. As they left their residences, students were interrogated by police. Some five hundred were arrested, mainly for suspected participation in the looting. Lecturers long thought to harbour radical political sympathies were rounded up.

Moi also instigated an overhaul of the upper echelons of the security forces, in order to replace the senior officers he had inherited from Kenyatta. Despite the role of the police and the GSU in suppressing the coup, both Ben Gethi, the commissioner of police, and Peter Ndgodo Mbuthia, the commandant of the GSU, were sacked. Bernard Njiinu, previously Gethi's deputy, took over the police, and Erastus Kimaita M'Mbijjiwe, the senior police officer in the Rift Valley, became the GSU's new commandant. After four years in power, Moi had almost completed his takeover. Cabinet, parliament, the provincial administration and the civil service had been easily purged of his enemies. The private sector had come to heel quickly, too. While the security forces and higher education institutions took much longer to transform, within weeks of the coup's defeat all were under the second president's control.

The full ramifications of the coup were not clear until the following year. Accused by rivals in the cabinet of links to the coup, Njonjo was forced to stand down and was the subject of an inquiry into his activities. He had ceased to be an asset and had become a threat to Moi when he resigned from his post as attorney general and entered parliament as an elected MP in 1980. That decision sparked speculation about the scope of his ambitions, with many assuming that this was a first step in a bid for the presidency. Certainly, few tears would have been shed in Whitehall had Njonjo toppled Moi. At the very least, Njonjo wished to usurp Kibaki's position as the pre-eminent Kikuyu figure within Moi's government and build up a coterie of supporters in parliament. As Moi attempted to minimise the influence of Kenyatta's former supporters, Njonjo had made a useful totem that he could hold up in order to prove to disaffected grassroots Kikuyu that their community was not being persecuted. But by 1982, with the process of replacing Kenyatta's clients with his own supporters complete, there was little reason for the president to tolerate Njonjo's machinations and intrigues any longer. Moreover, with good relations with the US secured in 1980, there was no pressing diplomatic reason to retain the former attorney general either.

Though cleared of involvement in one treason plot in 1981, Njonjo was vulnerable in the prevailing climate of government anxiety that followed the coup attempt. Once rumours about his former ally started up again in 1983, Moi acted. A commission made up of senior judges was given a wide-ranging remit to investigate various alleged indiscretions, including connections to the 1982 coup, subsequent acts of disloyalty, corruption while attorney general, and a role in a failed South African-led coup against the Seychellois government in November 1981. The judges concluded that Njonjo had become a threat to the security of the country and that he had played a role in the 1982 coup.[102] He denied all the charges and, assuming that memories of the former attorney general's role in the defeat of Mungai would mean the Kikuyu elite would exact retribution, Moi passed the matter on to the Central Province KANU branches to adjudicate on his guilt. But Njonjo's fellow Kikuyu leaders were unwilling to play the role of Pilate. Instead, after interviewing Njonjo separately, each of the branches pronounced him innocent.[103] Njonjo escaped prison, but his career in public life had ground to a halt. So too, at last, had the succession struggle.

CHAPTER FIVE

LOVE, PEACE AND UNITY, 1982–88

We believe, however, that he will turn increasingly to repression
to maintain his hold on power, in part because of pressure from
influential hardliners in the regime. He may buy time by intimi-
dating his opponents, but he risks making new enemies and
driving diverse groups to cooperate with one another and to
consider extralegal tactics against the government.

US interagency intelligence memorandum, November 1982[1]

A DEMOCRACY OF THE TORTURE CHAMBER

As Kenya marked five years of Moi's rule and the twentieth anniversary
of independence, vast numbers of buildings and monuments were
erected, emblazoned with the second president's slogan of *Nyayo*
('Footsteps'). Though generally aesthetically unedifying, none was quite
as ugly as Nyayo House. Opened in December 1983, the dirty-yellow
skyscraper, which was quickly stained by traffic fumes, was built across
the road from the city's Uhuru Park. There, at his inauguration, Moi
had promised Kenyans that he would deliver 'love, peace and unity'.[2]
Instead, in the words of the Mwakenya dissident group, the country had
become a 'democracy of the police boots and the torture chamber'.[3]

The torture chambers belonged to the Special Branch and were located in the basement of Nyayo House. Over the next eight years, up to two thousand Kenyans underwent interrogation and torture in the fourteen cells. 'Nowhere does Moi's lack of presidential vision show as the choice of Nyayo House for housing the torture chambers,' remarked the Presbyterian cleric Timothy Njoya later. 'Nyayo House could have been a fitting monument to the President's philosophy of peace, love and unity. Instead, the building stands condemned for the grotesque activities that make it qualify as "Restricted Area". As it is now, Nyayo House has completely desecrated the legacy of Moi's vision and stands as a frightening epitaph of his Presidency.'[4]

Those tortured at Nyayo House were victims of what Ogot calls Kenya's 'decade of extreme political repression'.[5] In the wake of the coup, critics and opponents of the regime were routinely arrested and subjected to torture and imprisonment. Moreover, rather than simply being targeted at the radicals in parliament, government and on university campuses, repression was used more widely throughout Kenyan society than it had been previously. Without recourse to student politics, opposition parties or any other formal outlet for discontent, opponents of the regime were pushed underground. The state security forces followed them and became more invasive as they sought out the roots of discontent within society at large. For the first time, ordinary citizens found themselves the target of state repression, and torture and imprisonment became part of the regular engagement between rulers and ruled. Kenyans became ever more resentful of Moi's government, but because of his ability to work networks of patronage and state institutions to his advantage, the president survived without serious threat to his rule.

MWAKENYA

The best known of the dissident groups formed in the aftermath of the coup was Mwakenya (a Swahili acronym meaning 'Union of Nationalists to Liberate Kenya'). It was founded in 1985 as an umbrella group of isolated Nairobi-based dissidents who made up the last remnants of the 1982 coup plot.[6] The airman James Dianga, for instance, had been found guilty of sedition in 1981 but had been freed in 1984. After his release he was approached by a supporter of Odinga and encouraged to join Mwakenya. Dianga found the group to be a ramshackle outfit, however. It lacked effective leadership and was divided between its different ethnic constituencies. These divisions crippled it from the outset and rendered it entirely ineffectual.[7]

The group, nonetheless, made bold promises. It wanted to overthrow Moi's government as a first step towards breaking 'the stranglehold of Euro-American imperialism on our economy, politics and culture'.[8] With this in mind, Mwakenya called for an end to the military alliance with the USA. It denounced 'all foreign imperialist robbery of our wealth' and 'neocolonial puppets'.[9] The group condemned corruption, the inequity of land access, the slow encroachment of commercial ranching on pastoralist grazing areas, and the endemic problem of social inequality: 'Thus, behind the facade of skyscrapers, deluxe hotels and mansions lies the bitter reality of some Kenyans sleeping along the streets in makeshift shelters through extreme weather conditions and others dying of malnutrition and hunger.'[10] Mwakenya's talk of workers' revolts and imperialist robbery was alien to most Kenyans, but its depiction of life in Moi's Kenya was certainly more accurate than the regime's preferred image of a vibrant, stable and growing economy.

Mwakenya's only action of note was the sabotage of the Mombasa–Nairobi railway line. Nevertheless, Moi continually insisted that the ineffectual group was a serious and credible threat to national security. According to Kiraitu Murungi, then a lawyer, 'Moi's government had reached its highest level of political paranoia.' Critics of any government policy found themselves labelled 'a member of Mwakenya, and a threat to state security'.[11] Those identified as threats were detained without trial. They included Charles Rubia, who had once again fallen out of favour with the government, as well as Ida Odinga, Raila's wife, and Mumbi wa Maina, the wife of the dissident lecturer Maina wa Kinyatti.[12] The lack of any rhyme or reason for such arrests alarmed many. Rubia, for instance, was an unlikely member of an underground Marxist revolutionary group. Fearing arrest on trumped-up charges, known dissidents fled into exile.

In London, some of these exiles, including Ngugi, formed the Committee for the Release of Political Prisoners in Kenya (CRPPK). The year the group was founded – 1986 – was a particularly bleak one. By then, the group estimated that there were more than a thousand political prisoners and detainees. They included one of the CRPPK's founders, Wanyiri Kihoro. He had been studying in London prior to his return home that year, but had long been linked with the radical wing of Kenyan politics. Active in student politics at the university in Nairobi during his law studies in the early 1970s, he had delivered a eulogy on behalf of the students at Kariuki's funeral in 1975. He had then made an unsuccessful bid for a parliamentary seat in 1979, before travelling to the UK. After returning to Kenya, he lived in Mombasa. Shortly after midnight on 29 July 1986, Kihoro and his wife Wanjiru were woken by police banging on their door. After they had searched the premises, he was arrested and taken to Nyayo House in Nairobi. In the weeks that followed his arrest, he was subjected to a variety of forms of torture, before being formally detained on 10 October. He remained in detention until his release on 1 June 1989.[13]

Kihoro was typical of many of those picked up by the authorities in 1986. Those arrested often had some connection to higher education, such as former student political leaders or prominent intellectuals like E.S. Atieno Odhiambo. The police then pursued others within a suspect's social network. The scope of state repression thus widened considerably to include institutions such as the Kenya Science Teachers' College, the Mombasa Polytechnic and Egerton College near Njoro. The ties of recently recruited teachers to the university campuses and to student politics even drew the attention of the authorities to the staff rooms of primary and secondary schools across the country. Others arrested for alleged links to Mwakenya had long records of political protest. At the time of his arrest in the middle of the night of 12 March 1986, Joseph Onyangi Mbaja was the manager of Oginga Odinga's company, East Africa Spectre Ltd. Mbaja had already served a seven-year jail sentence for his part in the coup plot of 1971. Peter-Young Gathoga Kihara, jailed for four and a half years in April, had been detained by the British in 1955 and also by Kenyatta in his crackdown against the KPU in the 1960s. Details of the arrests collected by exiles in London, however, showed that the Moi government's repression did not simply concentrate on its known opponents at the university or other institutions that had long been connected to dissidence.

Those arrested, tortured and detained from 1986 onwards represented a far broader section of society than just prominent opponents of the regime. Many random arrests of alleged Mwakenya members began in January 1986.[14] The country resembled a police state, with its agents on constant guard for the smallest expression of dissent. 'The government became omnipresent: in our houses, bedrooms, schools, churches, hotels; and Moi saw real and imaginary enemies everywhere', writes Ogot.[15] Among these otherwise anonymous victims of repression were the likes of Raphael Kariuki Ndung'u, who was arrested in mid-May for 'creating disturbance by uttering words in praise of Mwakenya'; Elly John Gitau Ndabi, a fruit seller, and John Mungai Waruiru, a carpenter, who were both sent to prison for seven years after being found guilty of 'distributing seditious publications'; and Stanley Muchugia Mburu, a messenger working for the National Bank of Kenya who was sentenced to ten years' imprisonment, again for distributing banned literature.[16]

For many of the established dissidents or ordinary members of the public, arrest and detention were violent and traumatic experiences. Booked in under false names to throw family members off the scent and moved around police stations in Nairobi, the Mwakenya suspects were then handed over to the Special Branch for interrogation at Nyayo House.[17] John Gupta Ng'ang'a Thing'o, a law student, was picked up by police officers outside the law school at lunchtime on 8 May 1986, for example, and was taken to the police station in the Kileleshwa neighbourhood of the city. He was collected from the cells there in the early evening by a group of plainclothes policemen. He was blindfolded, put into a car and ordered to lie down so as not to be seen by passers-by. He was then driven around Nairobi for hours until he reached Nyayo House, just a mile from where he had been arrested. For most of the next week, he underwent torture and interrogation, before being taken to a police station and formally charged on 14 May. The next day he was taken to court. During the car journey to the court, police officers warned him that he would be tortured again unless he pleaded guilty. He did as he was told.[18]

Thing'o's willingness to confess rather than face further torture at Nyayo House was understandable. The most common form of torture there was known as the 'swimming pool'. For up to a week, the cell of a suspect was flooded with two inches of water and the suspect sprayed at regular intervals. During the ordeal, the detainees were not allowed to leave the cell and so had to urinate and defecate in the water. In his High Court appeal in August 1986, Karige Kihoro described how 'I was put in a waterlogged cell for periods of 60 hours and was continually beaten and was dictated statements alleging that I knew that some people intended to form an illegal party. I was forced to sign them as a condition of being removed from the water and having no alternative and being in pain I signed them.' Beatings were also commonplace, but were done in such a manner as to leave no permanent signs of torture on the bodies of suspects. When not being physically tortured, suspects held at Nyayo House endured further significant suffering. Even without water on the floor, cells had no furniture. The walls were painted black and the ceiling black and white. A dim light was kept on constantly. The cumulative effect, Amnesty International argued, 'contributed to the prisoners' general state of anxiety and tension'.[19]

Unsurprisingly, there were deaths in custody. Peter Njenga Karanja, a successful rally driver and businessman from Nakuru, was picked up in his home town on 6 February 1987 on suspicion of support for Mwakenya. His family were unable to find any information about his arrest for a month, until his wife discovered that he had died at Kenyatta Hospital in Nairobi on 28 February. Karanja had been tortured at Nyayo House prior to his hospitalisation and death. A postmortem found the cause of death to have been dehydration, 'laceration of the membrane supporting the small intestine, and wounds and bruises on the limbs'.[20] According to Amnesty, Karanja's body 'was found to be bruised, wounded and emaciated with skin blistering and peeling off – just 21 days after he had been seized in good health by

Kenyan Special Branch officers earlier this year'.[21] By contrast, the minister for the Office of the President, Justus Ole Tipis, told parliament that Karanja had not been tortured and had died of pneumonia and blood clots in blood vessels in his intestines.[22]

Once a confession was extracted from them, suspects were taken immediately to court without legal representation or relatives being informed. 'The High Court', Kiraitu writes, 'had become part and parcel of the state machinery of oppression.'[23] Cases were rapid affairs that might last only thirty minutes. Even in the rare case of acquittal, release did not necessarily follow. Charles Karanja Njoroge, a businessman on trial in March 1986, was acquitted but rearrested outside the court and illegally detained for a further six days. A week later, he returned to court and pleaded guilty to the same charges he had been acquitted of just a few days earlier.[24] After conviction, political prisoners were sent to one of a network of maximum security prisons dotted around the country. Most were on the sites of prisons and detention camps that were synonymous with the colonial repression of the Mau Mau insurgency in the 1950s. Conditions in these prisons were frequently little better than the suspects had endured during their interrogation.[25] Whether in prison or in detention prior to trial, systematic medical neglect of political prisoners was a recurring theme in their experience of incarceration.

Punishment did not end with release from captivity. Through the 1980s and 1990s, ever-increasing numbers of Kenyans sought exile overseas in the US, UK and Scandinavia. They included politicians such as Koigi wa Wamwere, academics like Atieno Odhiambo and other intellectuals, most famously Ngugi. Exile often followed a tough experience of life after release for Mwakenya suspects and other dissidents. Despite leaving Naivasha Prison in October 1988, Maina wa Kinyatti continued to be harassed by the police. Suffering from numerous medical conditions caused by his imprisonment, and unable to travel abroad legitimately or to find employment, Kinyatti fled to Tanzania in March 1989. He then left East Africa a month later to begin a new life in the United States. His wife was fired from her university post and evicted from her faculty housing.[26] Kinyatti and others continued their activism abroad, highlighting Moi's routine contravention of Kenyan and international human rights law.

The logic underpinning the use of torture was perverse. It was justified on the grounds of national security, since, according to Moi, the country was constantly under threat from shady fifth columnists with uncertain political goals. Angelique Haugerud, an anthropologist, has skilfully demonstrated how government officials used public meetings to convey messages of the threat posed by dissidents. Examples of dissidence, such as Mwakenya, had to be exaggerated in order to justify the abuses of human rights, which in turn allowed Moi to retain control by giving him the means to arrest all manner of opponents.[27] Moi's government claimed to be acting in the name of law and order, but the regime itself was a criminal one.

WAGALLA

The government's reliance on violence and contravention of human rights in order to retain power was most easily observed in North Eastern Province. Despite the peace deal signed in 1967 that brought the Shifta War to an end, grievances stemming from the region's marginalisation continued to be expressed. Similarly, insecurity remained a major problem for the province's residents. This was particularly true in the wake of the Ogaden War between Somalia and Ethiopia in 1977 and 1978. At the urging of both Britain and the US, Kenya stayed out of the conflict. However, the conflict did mean that increased quantities of arms flowed into northern parts of the country and that armed groups moved through the region. The government proceeded with an alien registration programme, which resulted in the arrest of unknown numbers of Somalis in Nairobi and across northern parts of the country.

Somalia's defeat in the conflict triggered a series of political developments in Mogadishu that had significant ramifications for peace in northern Kenya.[28] Faced with widespread disgruntlement and significant economic difficulties, the Somali president, Siad Barre, came under increasing pressure from various factions within Somalia. In an effort to restore control, he attempted to co-opt particular Somali clans, and so set about a weapon allocation programme, under which automatic firearms were distributed to key supporters. But these weapons were used to pursue other disputes, too, besides those that figured on Siad's agenda. Of most significance, the ready availability of weapons meant that inter-clan conflicts became bloodier and insecurity spread throughout southern Somalia, exacerbating the situation in northern and eastern Kenya.[29]

As weapons flowed across the border from Somalia and insecurity increased, the clumsy attempts by the Kenyan armed forces to disarm the locals in North Eastern Province became more frequent and violence more common. A litany of accusations of human rights abuses was compiled by local politicians in the years that followed. One KANU party official from Wajir alleged that three women had died in childbirth after being denied medical assistance while waiting in custody to be interrogated as part of a security trawl following the murder of a local official in 1980. One of the province's MPs, Abdi Sheikh, went further and claimed that up to three hundred civilians had been killed by Kenyan security forces during the crackdown.[30] Unperturbed by such complaints, the security forces continued their operations, seizing stolen cattle and ammunition, and shooting dead suspected bandits.

The security situation was further undermined by Moi's political strategy. His use of patronage as the primary means of building up networks of supporters inserted the state and its security forces into the internal politics of North Eastern Province. Moi's two partners there were Hussein Maalim Mohammed, MP for Garissa Central, and his elder brother, Mahmoud Mohammed. Maalim entered parliament in 1983 and was quickly promoted to become the first Muslim and North Easterner to serve as a cabinet minister. In the case of Mahmoud, following his vital contribution to the suppression of the 1982 coup (taken as evidence of his impeccable loyalty to Moi), he was appointed chief of the general staff of the armed forces.

The Mohammed brothers were members of the Ajuran clan. Their influence within government and the armed forces provided the clan with significant advantages over rival groups in the numerous and long-running disputes over scarce resources. Their rivals generally recognised the advantages that state sponsorship conferred on Ajuran: at a meeting held at Gurar in October 1983, for instance, elders of the Gare clan acceded to demands from Ajuran leaders to return cattle seized in livestock raids and taken across the border into Ethiopia.[31]

Members of the Degodia clan, however, were not so willing to accept the new order. Ajuran and Degodia had long feuded over control of the parliamentary constituencies in Wajir – and with it, access to funds that could be used to consolidate support within the area. (In fact, this political struggle mirrored an even longer-standing history of conflict between them over access to grazing land and water resources.)

Bolstered by access to the highest offices in the land, from early 1983 onwards Ajuran moved against their rivals in Wajir district. The atmosphere was already tense there, following the construction of a new military airstrip at Wagalla, a short distance outside Wajir town. The workforce had been transported to the site from elsewhere in the country. Angry that they had been overlooked, the local population mounted a series of protests in Wajir. Local Degodia leaders were blamed for the unrest; eleven were arrested and held without charge in the first five weeks of 1984. Five of the eleven remained in detention, including Abdisirat Khalif Mohamed, an assistant minister under Kenyatta, Mohamed Noor, the chairman of the Wajir County Council at the time of his arrest, and Ahmed Elmi, a former councillor in the town.[32]

The conflict between Ajuran and Degodia in Wajir accounted for eighty-eight lives between January 1983 and February 1984. The security forces and the local administration attempted to disarm both clans.[33] While state patronage meant Ajuran felt able to comply with the order to disarm, Degodia were reluctant to do so for fear that this would leave them at the mercy of their enemies. The conflict therefore continued. On 9 February, a Degodia raiding party attacked an Ajuran homestead, killing six people and injuring another two. Military officers immediately launched a security operation around Wajir to forcibly disarm Degodia and acquire intelligence on the raiders. Before dawn the following day, security forces surrounded Degodia settlements close to Wajir town and ordered all residents to leave their homes. Few complied, and so soldiers set light to the huts, forcing the inhabitants to flee. As they did so, all adult males were arrested, put onto waiting trucks and driven to the controversial Wagalla airstrip.[34]

According to Sugal Unshur, a councillor in Wajir town, and local MP Abdi Sheikh, five thousand Degodia were taken to the airstrip. After being beaten by army and police officers, they were made to lie naked on the runway in the fierce sun, without any food or water, for five full days. Arrested mullahs who refused to strip naked and anyone attempting to escape were shot. The two politicians claimed that others had been burnt alive by the security forces. In total, it is thought that some three hundred Degodia were killed at the airstrip. Furthermore, perhaps nine hundred of those who survived the ordeal were then, according to Unshur and Sheikh, taken under armed escort into the surrounding scrubland and shot. Aid workers in the area corroborated their account.[35] The government instead claimed that fifty-seven people had been killed while resisting attempts by the security forces to disarm them.[36]

After Wagalla, the government moved to contain any further eruptions of violence (or at least their revelation) in North Eastern. Other massacres may well have taken place as the security forces attempted to pacify the region. The diplomatic and political aspects of the state's response to Wagalla were given more attention at the time: Kenyan diplomats attempted to build closer ties with Siad Barre's regime in Somalia. The Kenyans hoped that the malcontents in North Eastern would be isolated and weakened if the two governments enjoyed warmer relations. That effort culminated in a state visit to Mogadishu in July, the first by a Kenyan president.

In North Eastern Province itself, the government attempted to restore faith in its institutions and representatives. A new provincial commissioner was appointed, peace rallies were organised and reconciliation meetings of the two competing clans were convened. An amnesty was also announced in an effort to encourage the surrender of bandits and weapons. Flows of patronage from central government to particular key individuals and clans increased. North Eastern was allocated two further seats in parliament, and a number of Somali assistant ministers were appointed to create the channels through which patronage flowed from the centre to carefully chosen clients. Jobs in the armed forces, preferential access to otherwise scarce development funding, and the appearance of access to the highest power in the land were sufficient to buy the compliance of enough Kenyan Somalis.

Perhaps more significant was the onset of famine across north-eastern Africa in 1984 and 1985. Like its neighbours, Kenya experienced what Robert Bates describes as 'a one-in-a-century drought'. While Bates documents the shortcomings of the state's response in the district of Meru, he otherwise stresses the success of the national response to the drought. The government 'procured, imported, and distributed sufficient food to feed its population. At the local level, the government located, registered, and fed the hungry'.[37] Famine relief aided pacification in North Eastern Province. Disgruntled local populations in Wajir and other areas of the province became dependent on state-provided food aid. They had no other choice. Wajir's food harvest in 1984 was just 9 per cent of what had been anticipated.[38] Compliance with the government became a matter of personal survival. By October 1984, the chief of Wajir town declared that peace had returned to the district.[39]

The move from repression to reconciliation in North Eastern Province was provoked by the response of diplomatic missions in Nairobi. Cold War sensibilities commonly restrained criticism of the Kenyan government's actions by the most important of its foreign friends. Britain and the US were willing to turn a blind eye to all but the most egregious of human rights abuses, so long as Moi remained an ally. But the actions of the armed forces at Wagalla went too far and provoked a rare display of international outcry and protest by European diplomats in Nairobi.[40] Faced with diminished domestic support for his regime, Moi knew he could ill afford to alienate his foreign friends, and so set about restoring some sort of peace in North Eastern Province with rare vigour. There were other incentives for peace in the province, too. Pacification was followed in April 1985 by the announcement of an oil exploration agreement with the local subsidiary of the Amoco Petroleum Company, for the area covered by the Wajir and Garissa districts.[41] But the government lacked the will and the resources to ensure that security and politics in North Eastern remained impervious to events across the border.

An ever-worsening civil war in Somalia ensured that incidents of banditry recurred periodically on the Kenyan side of the border. Armed attacks on buses in Kitui in 1987 and Garissa in 1989 garnered considerable attention in Kenya. Outside the country, far more concern was expressed about increasing insecurity in the country's national parks. Ivory poaching proved a valuable source of funds for Somali armed factions, but brought Somali militants into contact with tourists, conservationists and Kenyan game wardens, with predictable results. A series of fatal attacks on tourists in the eastern game parks and the murder of the famous conservationist George Adamson in 1989 drew international attention to insecurity in the region. With poaching rampant, the Kenyan government announced that all ethnic Somalis in the country were to be subject to interrogation, in an effort to identify bandits and rebels seeking refuge in Kenyan towns and villages.[42] Moreover, all Somalis resident in Kenya, whether Kenyan or Somali citizens, were required to carry special identification cards at all times.

THE NYAYO STATE

The events at Wagalla and the aftermath of the massacre demonstrate how repression was one part of a sophisticated form of rule. Like Kenyatta, Moi made good use of the provincial administration and its network of provincial commissioners, district commissioners and district officers. They were to be 'my personal representatives in their respective districts', the president told them in November 1978.[43] He also hoped that if greater local powers were given to party officials, this would increase ordinary citizens' sense of participation in the political system.[44] But Moi's most successful strategy of governance was his use of patronage. Adapting Kenyatta's own system of patronage, he extended and redirected the networks that distributed state resources from the centre to certain key allies in every district and constituency of the country.

The ability to lay claim to this flow of resources – and to maintain it – became the critical factor in local politics across the country. Katete Orwa's study of the 1983 election in the Mbita constituency of South Nyanza demonstrated the corrosive effects of such a system on local political debate. Orwa, a political scientist, found that voters and candidates had become highly parochial in their outlook. For one thing, voters were dismayed at the political system. As development funding declined along with the economic fortunes of the country, so voters quickly came to view the campaign season as the only time in which tangible financial gains could be made. 'What one gets during the campaign was the only thing one could count on,' Orwa wrote. This justifiable cynicism translated into an easy acceptance of bribery. 'Prospective voters literally demanded money,' Orwa observed. 'If a candidate failed to give it on the spot he would be told point blank that "you will not get our votes".' For those candidates that could afford to play such a game, the rewards were great. Votes were won not by stump speeches or a strong track record in parliament, but rather by the ability to 'buy support through the process of donating building material, purchase of uniforms and footballs, cash donations and, beyond these, cash payment to individuals'. The effects on the calibre of political representatives were obvious. But so, too, were the effects on the political culture of the country. Networks of patronage of the sort constructed by Moi meant that 'the electorate is being reduced to a beggary class of rural clients'.[45]

Moi's elite clients were, however, far from being reduced to a 'beggary class'. Kalenjin leaders in the Rift Valley provided him with a sturdy foundation for his government, just as elite Kikuyu had for Kenyatta. Led by Biwott, Kalenjin ministers formed an informal but influential inner circle around the president.[46] Moi used the distribution of management roles in state-owned industries and organisations to buy compliance from potential opponents and to reward existing clients for their support. For example, as both a fellow Kalenjin and a past rival of Moi, Taita Towett was given control of Kenya Airways in place of the Kikuyu grandee Eliud Mathu. But the number of potential Kalenjin economic partners with relevant commercial experience and available capital was not as large as the pool on which Kenyatta had been able to draw for his Kikuyu ascendancy. Moi had to look outside his own community for allies. In a reversal of the Kenyatta regime's uncomfortable relationship with the South Asian community in Kenya, Moi turned to it to widen his nexus of political and economic power. In early 1981, he visited New Delhi and reached a number of agreements with the Indian government to facilitate development in Kenya across a number of sectors. Such developments encouraged closer ties between elite Kenyan Asians and Moi's government.[47]

The combination of patronage and fear served Moi well in the five years following the coup. But slowly opposition built up again. Rumours and whispers about detention, torture and other abuses of human rights were rife throughout the country. 'We knew nearly everything that was going on, from Moi's personal life, to those of his sons and those of his cohorts,' wrote Njenga Karume. 'There were a few secrets, but many things were leaked and everyone was aware.'[48] The location of the Nyayo House torture cells, for example, was widely and correctly rumoured.[49] Much of this information was circulated and publicised by exiles overseas. In Europe and North America, Kenyans forced from their homeland energetically campaigned on behalf of their country's political prisoners. Led by Ngugi, various exiled Kenyan dissidents came together in October 1987 to form the United Movement for Democracy in Kenya, better known as Umoja.[50]

Condemnation of Moi's government filtered back into Kenya. Kiraitu Murungi recalls how 'behind closed doors, lawyers used to read photocopies of "subversive" articles from the *London Times*, the *Economist*, and *Newsweek*'.[51] Ordinary Kenyans discussed and criticised the government in all sorts of different settings. They sought out 'their own democratic political space, to find ways and means by which they continue to participate, withdraw, watch as spectators, run commentaries, and draw their own conclusions about political events and trends,' wrote Atieno Odhiambo in 1987. While most public gatherings required licences, funerals and weddings needed no such official sanction and so became venues for the exchange of information and opinion about the regime. In everyday conversation, people told one another rumours, they joked about the government and derided its performance. And they did so frequently on what Atieno came to call 'peoples' republics' – the ubiquitous privately owned minibuses known as *matatus*, which became the dominant form of public transport as bus services wilted along with so many other public services under Moi.[52]

As well as stories, commuters exchanged newspapers. While there was little press freedom in the 1980s, individual writers became adept at operating in the spaces left by the censors. None was as skilled in this art – or as well loved by his audience – as Wahome Mutahi, a columnist from 1982 with *The Standard* newspaper. Best known by the title of his weekly column, 'Whispers', Mutahi became the alternative chronicler of the Moi years and a master of satire and deft criticism of public authority. He spent fifteen months in jail on trumped-up charges of support for Mwakenya, but only returned to his column reinvigorated in his opposition to the Moi government.[53] Mutahi's nom de plume was apposite: for much of the 1980s, criticism of the government could only be made in whispers. But by late 1987, the whispers were once again becoming shouts of protest.

THE 1988 ELECTIONS

Moi's strategies for retaining power had run their course. His tyranny had alienated too many Kenyans and his patronage networks relied upon there being sufficient state resources to distribute to clients. As the economic fortunes of the country continued to wane, so Moi found it increasingly difficult to fund the patronage necessary to retain influence and control. Neoliberal reforms devised by the IMF and World Bank removed the state's influence over the economy and cut public spending, which in the past had been used as a 'slush fund' to build up networks of clients. In a climate of increasing poverty and state repression, street protests were witnessed in the major cities. Council workers in the capital went on strike as 1987 drew to a close. Protestors vandalised government offices and the city's police headquarters during demonstrations in Mombasa during October and November.[54]

However, the opposition remained fragmented. There were small numbers of dissidents in subversive organisations such as Mwakenya; workers and farmers disillusioned with decreasing incomes; large numbers of unemployed seeking work wherever they could find it; and elite figures who felt isolated from power. The malcontents had little in common with one another in terms of class, ethnicity or region of origin. Nor did these different groups share a common grievance around which a more coherent opposition could coalesce.

The widespread disgust over the government's handling of the 1988 elections was therefore of critical importance in galvanising these previously disparate opposition groups. The cause for concern was the practice of 'queue voting' that was used during the nomination process. Queue voting was introduced in 1986 to replace the secret ballot in KANU's internal party elections. Under the system used in 1988, voters participating in the primary elections were to select KANU's parliamentary candidates by standing behind the agent of their chosen candidate. If 70 per cent of the voters joined the line of one particular candidate, then he or she was considered to be returned to parliament unopposed. Otherwise the three most popular candidates would proceed to the election on 21 March, when the secret ballot was still to be used. Queue voting was portrayed as representing greater active participation by ordinary citizens in the nomination process. KANU's secretary general, Burudi Nabwera, claimed to be pleased that 'it will not be the secretary general who will be clearing candidates for the next election'. He told Kenyans that 'this is their election and the nomination day will be their day'.[55]

Nomination day, 22 February, produced a flurry of complaints. Electoral officials refused to allow certain agents to watch the tallying process, announced fictitious results or ignored glaring discrepancies between the number of recorded votes and the number of people present. In the words of Matere Keriri, a defeated candidate in Kirinyaga West, those managing the nomination process made 'a complete mockery of justice'.[56] Having spent much of the previous two years criticising the introduction of queue voting and the increase in presidential power, Rubia was one target for rigging by the authorities.

The nomination procedure for the Starehe constituency was blatantly fixed to ensure that Rubia's main rival was declared the uncontested candidate for the seat. The results in Starehe, Rubia believed, 'violate the very essence of our constitutional democracy and call into question the legitimacy of our claim to democratised government and about all [*sic*] our national anthem, which provides that "Justice is our shield and defender" '.[57] Other key political figures, embittered by their experiences, joined Rubia in his vocal protests over the conduct of the 1988 elections.

Twenty-five candidates immediately launched petitions claiming that they had been cheated of victory. Perhaps most notable was Martin Shikuku, the veteran dissident politician.[58] Kenneth Matiba, a former civil servant from the Kenyatta era and a well-known Kikuyu businessman, was also angered by the queue system. He claimed that support by the administration for his rival, Julius Kiano, prevented him from winning the 70 per cent needed to be declared the unopposed candidate.[59] Masinde Muliro, a veteran Luhya political leader, joined Rubia, Shikuku and Matiba in his condemnation of queue voting and his demand for the restoration of the secret ballot.[60]

The supporters of these elite politicians, who were among the most prominent public figures in the country, were dismayed at the outcome of queue voting. In the towns of Butere and Kakamega in Western Province, thousands of Shikuku's supporters marched through the streets in defiance of an order by the police and administration officials to return to their homes. Other protests were witnessed in Taveta in Coast Province, Mombasa, Nairobi, Kisumu and Kiambu.[61] Kenyan exiles in London demanded fresh elections in accordance with international standards of democracy.[62] At home, Mwakenya 'declares null and void the results of the recent stage managed general elections and pledges to continue [to] challenge the political legitimacy of the newly formed puppet government of President Moi and his KANU clique'.[63] The government dismissed such complaints. One minister claimed that those complaining about queue voting were 'doing nothing but inciting our people to hatred and violence when there is no cause for such violence and/or hatred'.[64] Others were less sure.

1 Jomo Kenyatta (centre), Mwai Kibaki (left) and Tom Mboya (right) celebrate KANU's election victory in May 1963.

2 KANU leaders including Achieng' Oneko (far left), Oginga Odinga (centre with cane) and Tom Mboya (far right) at a function in 1963.

3 Mboya's assassin, Nahashon Isaac Njenga Njoroge, during his pre-trial hearing, August 1969.

4 Residents of Nakuru mourn Mboya as his cortege passes through the town, 9 July 1969.

5　Kenyatta's bodyguard and other officials try to protect the president as the riot begins during his visit to Kisumu, 25 October 1969.

6　Kenyatta celebrates with members of the Ndeffo group of Mau Mau veterans after allocating 75 families land in 1971, during the aftermath of public revelations about the coup plot.

7 JM Kariuki addresses a church congregation (undated).

8 Ministers, students and other mourners during prayers at JM Kariuki's home in Gilgil prior to his funeral, March 1975.

9 People searching for relatives missing after the Kenya Air Force coup consult photographs of unidentified bodies held at the city mortuary in Nairobi, 11 August 1982.

10 One of those jailed for their alleged support of Mwakenya, Nelson Akhalukwa Mvuwa, is led away from court, 2 January 1987.

11 President Daniel Arap Moi with the British Prime Minister, Margaret Thatcher, in Nairobi, 4 January 1988. Note Kibaki, then vice president, in the background.

12 Oginga Odinga and his son, Raila, after the latter's release from detention in 1991.

13 Members of the security forces watch DP supporters after a campaign rally in Nairobi, 27 December 1992.

14 William Ruto (left), Uhuru Kenyatta (centre) and Kalonzo Musyoka (right) during a rally at Uhuru Park in Nairobi to celebrate Ruto and Kenyatta's return to Kenya after their first pre-trial hearing at the International Criminal Court, 11 April 2011.

15 A Kalenjin militia member during the post-election violence, Trans Mara district, 1 March 2008.

THE GENESIS OF CIVIL SOCIETY

The government's intransigence over the issue of queue voting consol-idated opposition to Moi's regime. The churches emerged at the forefront of this effort. In the two decades following independence, their involvement in politics had been stymied by external pressure from the state and by internal disputes over the extent to which men of the cloth should concern themselves with such worldly matters. By the mid-1980s, though, individual church leaders had become convinced of the need to jettison this stance. Men like Timothy Njoya, a senior Presbyterian clergyman, instead began public and frequent criticism of the government's human rights record in 1984.[65] Other clergy were less keen to speak out in defence of suspected Mwakenya dissidents or coup members. But queue voting was another matter altogether.

After queue voting was introduced for KANU's elections in 1986, a wider array of religious voices began to speak out regularly against the government. In a letter to the president, for instance, the Catholic bishops pleaded for greater public debate on issues of political signifi-cance and for a reconsideration of queue voting.[66] By the time the 1988 general election came around, the churches' opposition to the practice was well established. Bedan Mbugua, the lay editor of the *Beyond* church magazine, wrote that 'democracy in Kenya has slipped a step downward, putting the country onto the path of self-destruction which many African countries have followed'. The magazine was banned as a result, but the clergy did not let up. Whether from the pulpit or in the national press, church leaders from across the various denominations were unequivocal in their denunciation of the conduct of the nominations and elections. The then bishop of the Catholic diocese of Nakuru, Ndingi Mwana'a Nzeki, stated 'his fear for the future of true democracy in our country' and his alarm over 'a party and government that is increasingly intolerant of the people's views and wishes'.[67] Nzeki's Anglican counter-part, Alexander Muge, agreed. Then the bishop of Eldoret, he described queue voting as 'intimidative political rallies'.[68] Once the election was over, the likes of Muge continued their attacks.

The flagrant misuse of queue voting and the unwillingness of the government to accommodate the concerns of the clergy pushed church leaders to pursue a wider range of concerns. For instance, in a 1988 pastoral letter, the Catholic hierarchy asserted its commitment to a 'God-given mission of human development and of promoting justice, love and peace'. 'The situation of growing injustice should not be', the bishops believed.[69] The Anglican Muge, in particular, proved a charismatic and forthright commentator on political matters through the second half of the decade. His vitality and populism allowed issues that were commonly talked about in the Marxist-inspired language of the dissident under-ground or within closed networks in Nyanza or North Eastern Province to be given a much wider airing. Put simply, Christianity transformed public debate of politics in post-colonial Kenya. It provided its adherents and leaders with a common language and a set of idioms that cut across Kenya's many ethnic vernaculars and cultural traditions.

Church leaders were not easily silenced. For one thing, Moi made no secret of his own Christian faith and could hardly be seen to be gagging the clergy. While other forms of political dissidence were silenced relatively easily by using legislation to restrict freedom of speech and public meetings, freedom of religious practice was far more difficult and contentious to curtail. Church leaders were conscious that they enjoyed a privileged position within society and were determined to exploit it. They offered searing critiques of the government. Believing that 'the people of this country live under threats, fear and tyranny', for instance, Muge likened Kenya under Moi to apartheid South Africa.[70] Even when domestic press restrictions were used to limit reporting of their words, Muge, Njoya and the other church leaders skilfully used foreign media outlets to distribute sermons and other literature criticising the government.[71]

The single greatest advantage enjoyed by the church leaders was, however, the religiosity of Kenyans. Although at independence prob-ably a minority of the 8 million or so citizens of the new nation were Christians, by the 1980s perhaps 80 per cent of the population were baptised. 'I would challenge anyone in Kenya to tell me anybody who has that kind of audience every week in this country', the vice chancellor of the University of Nairobi remarked in 1984.[72] With young people and educated members of the population disproportionately represented within the ranks of post-colonial Christianity, the cultural impact of that evangelical growth was significant. As Ngugi remarked in 1970, 'As a Kenyan African I cannot escape from the Church. Its influence is all around me.'[73] Once reluctance within the churches to engage with secular issues was overcome, church leaders were second to none in their criticism of the government.

The church leaders were joined in their public denunciations of the government's actions by a handful of lawyers. This was hardly surprising: the Protestant umbrella body, the National Council of Churches of Kenya (NCCK) and the Law Society of Kenya had, after all, long worked together on areas of common interest and both had called for public discussion of queue voting when the controversy erupted in 1986.[74] For obvious reasons, lawyers who had acted as the defenders of political prisoners were to the fore of this effort. Men like John Khaminwa, who was detained in 1982 for his defence of Anyona and Muriithi, had seen the physical and mental effects of torture at first hand. The dissident lawyers had also, in several cases, been trained in Nairobi during the height of campus radicalism.

Like the church leaders, the lawyers found that the treatment of political prisoners was not an issue on which popular discontent could be galvanised. Complaints about issues such as *habeas corpus* for political detainees and the torture of suspects meant little to many Kenyans. Concerns about such matters were typically expressed in the parlance of human rights, with little thought given to 'translation' into a language that was more understandable to the wider public. As Kiraitu Murungi, one of the lawyers involved, put it in his memoirs:

> Whenever I visit my home in the rural areas most of the talk there is about rain, drought, livestock and which people in the village are sick. All the United Nations declarations, conventions and pompous declarations of human rights have not been heard of by the majority of our people. They are of no consequence in our villages.[75]

Many of Kiraitu's figurative villagers did not, in any case, sympathise with the plight of individuals labelled as subversives.

The coalescence of opinion over the conduct of the 1988 elections between the churches and the lawyers was mutually beneficial. The churches provided the lawyers with a wider audience and a medium for communication; the lawyers, for their part, brought two vital elements to this relationship. First, the elite backgrounds of the lawyers and their defence of political prisoners supplied a link between civil society activism and political opposition of various shades. Secondly, lawyers like Paul Muite, Kiraitu Murungi, Gibson Kamau Kuria, Gitobu Imanyara and Pheroze Nowrojee developed the criticisms of the queue-voting system into a broader debate about constitutional reform. 'We cannot hope to safeguard democracy in this country through undemocratic methods,' Murungi argued in November 1988.[76] The ideas that, first, Kenya's ills were caused by its constitution and, second, that salvation lay in constitutional reform were seized upon by church leaders. Constitutional reform became the mantra of civil society in Kenya for the next quarter-century.

By late 1988, a new political alliance was taking shape outside the institutions of government – one based around demands for constitutional reform and driven by civil society. But the hold of the government was still sufficiently strong to make it very difficult for these aspiring reformers to imagine what form democracy might take in Kenya and elsewhere in the region. One lawyer writing in mid-1989 thought that 'the system of a one-party state has outlived its usefulness in Africa'.[77] Few at that time agreed: rather than replacing the one-party state, the possibilities for reform seemed limited to some sort of overhaul to make it more transparent and accountable. 'Nobody wants political earthquakes,' Murungi told his fellow lawyers at a conference held in Nyeri in November 1988.[78] But within months the first tremors began to be felt. The epicentre was not in Nairobi, Mombasa or Kisumu, but rather in Berlin, Warsaw and Bucharest.

CHAPTER SIX

THE WAR OF ARROWS, 1989–94

We cry out for democracy, good governance, transparency, repatriation of our funds from foreign banks, and a better economy. We cry out for an end to political murders, arson, displacement, and homelessness – all committed in the name of Moi's regime. Where there is truth, there is victory; but it can never come easily or freely. We cannot justify keeping quiet when the Moi regime incites Kenyans against one another, when bows and arrows are piercing and killing our people.

Wambui Waiyaki Otieno, 1998[1]

THE NEW ORDER

Speaking at a religious conference held just days after the fall of the Berlin Wall, a political scientist, Kabiru Kinyanjui, told his audience:

The events of the last few weeks in Eastern Europe challenge not only our thinking, language and world-view, but also our understanding of freedom and the basic quest for justice and peace. The thinking which shaped post-Second World War Europe and the world in general has collapsed. A new order is emerging.[2]

He was right: in the weeks that followed, the demands for political reform, inspired by events in Eastern Europe, grew ever louder in Kenya and across the African continent. Kinyanjui also accurately predicted that this new era demanded a new language of politics: 'Those who have often suppressed legitimate voices for justice, democratization and peace in Africa, by terming these forces "communists", should also think afresh on these issues. They will now be hard-pressed to find other scapegoats!'[3] Only Kinyanjui's optimism was misplaced. Although a new age of democracy seemed imminent, Kenya's leaders found other scapegoats with ease.

Kinyanjui was not a public figure and so Moi was not troubled by his words. Timothy Njoya, the Presbyterian cleric, was another matter. When Njoya used his sermon on New Year's Day in 1990 to call for an end to the one-party state, the president moved to try to silence all talk of multipartyism. 'Those who talk about two or so parties have something missing in their heads,' Moi stated. The advocates of multipartyism like Njoya 'have their own masters abroad: they tell them to say this and that'.[4] His desperate attempts to paint Njoya and his ilk as foreign-backed subversives demonstrated the president's vulnerability to political liberalisation.

In late 1989 and early 1990, Moi did not have to look hard to find evidence of widespread discontent with his government. Student demonstrations at the University of Nairobi in November 1989 turned violent, and striking workers at Ruiru, a suburb of the capital, rioted over missing pay soon afterwards. Even more troubling for the president was an emerging opposition that straddled the ethnic divides that Kenyatta and Moi had done so much to create. Dismayed by the queue-voting saga and encouraged by the efforts of the lawyers and clerics, prominent political figures once again found their voice. Among them were wealthy Kikuyu politicians. Some, like Rubia, had long records of opposition. Others, like Kenneth Matiba, were recent converts to the cause. Although a minister in Moi's government, Matiba was alienated by the queue-voting episode. In their marginalisation, the likes of Matiba and Rubia found common cause with other political veterans from across the country and from different points on the political spectrum. Odinga was the most prominent, but others included the Luhya politicians Martin Shikuku and Masinde Muliro. The national leaders shared their opposition to political imprisonment and torture with what remained of the radical faction on campuses, in exile and in the prisons. Connecting these different groups were human rights lawyers like Kiraitu Murungi and Paul Muite, whose defence of political detainees and whose ties to the Kikuyu elite made them ideal intermediaries. Most importantly, the churches provided this network with a public and accessible voice.

The opposition at first also had the changing global political climate in its favour. The donors of Kenya's aid had not previously worried much about issues like corruption and democracy. The British high commissioner in 1975, for example, was insistent that it was futile to think 'that the provision of aid should in some way be used to force the Government of Kenya to put their house in order'.[5] Cold War *Realpolitik* had trumped democracy and human rights at every turn. But with the Cold War over, Kenya's anti-communist stance lost its relevance. Its strategic importance, which derived from its relative proximity to the Middle East, was lost with the Iraqi invasion of Kuwait and the opening up of military bases in the region for US forces. Kenya's position within geo-political calculations in Washington, London and Brussels was now peripheral.

The end of the Cold War also changed the foreign policy objectives of Kenya's erstwhile friends. Foreign partners were no longer willing to turn a blind eye to the excesses of the government in Nairobi. Instead, taking their lead from the IMF and the World Bank, the US, UK and other European donors prioritised political reform as a condition for future aid. According to Barber Conable, the World Bank's president, the key to economic growth in countries like Kenya lay in what he called 'good governance', which 'must be provided to complement policies that promote market mechanisms and entrepreneurship'.[6] Good governance was a euphemism for multiparty elections. By any measure, Kenyans were not subject to good governance. With insecurity rampant, the economic gains of the 1960s and 1970s stuck in reverse and political repression continuing, the country was instead experiencing a crisis of governance. The clumsy cover-up of the murder of the British tourist Julie Ward in the Maasai Mara game reserve in September 1988 seemed to outsiders to encapsulate all that was wrong in Kenya. The country was, in the words of one Australian newspaper, an 'African Paradise Lost'.[7]

FREEDOM CORNER

The potential power of a new alliance between opposition leaders and foreign diplomats was demonstrated in the first weeks of the post-Cold War era. The country's leaders had become accustomed through the 1980s to grabbing public land for private gain. But even by Kenyan standards, the plans to build a new headquarters in Uhuru Park for the ruling party and the *Kenya Times* newspaper, co-owned by KANU and Robert Maxwell, were brazen. The park was one of the few green public spaces in the city and was publicly owned. Foreign diplomats were alarmed at the proposed cost of the building: at $200 million, the building was a flagrant act of profligacy at a time when donors were expected to pick up an ever-larger share of public expenditure. American and Japanese diplomats made their disapproval clear to the Kenyan government. Under intense domestic and international pressure, the construction project was abandoned in late January 1990.

The campaign against the project was led by Wangari Maathai, the head of the Green Belt Movement. Her prominence demonstrated how much politics had changed by the late 1980s and early 1990s. As the state withered in response to the neoliberal edict of donors, space was left for social movements and other civil society organisations to emerge. These were further encouraged by the changing priorities of donors, who now came to see groups like the Green Belt Movement as more transparent and accountable recipients of development funds than the government. As civil society stepped onto the main stage of public debate, so too did Kenya's women.

The previous marginalisation of women was no accident. Instead it was linked to their representation within the radical strands of nationalism at independence. With men often away from home in search of waged labour, the burden of unpopular rural development projects introduced in the late 1940s and early 1950s fell disproportionately on women. Similarly, in Central Kenya at least, it was women who faced the brutal realities of day-to-day life during the anti-Mau Mau counter-insurgency campaign. This bitter experience of colonialism politicised many: 'women were the revolution'.[8] At first there was a channel for this discord, in the shape of the Women's Wing of KANU. But, like other more radical elements of the party, the Women's Wing was margin-alised. Politicians, most notably Moi, instead encouraged women to join the Maendeleo ya Wanawake organisation ('The Development of Women'). The Maendeleo ya Wanawake had been formed in the 1950s and was intended to inculcate in women the skills needed to be modern mothers and housewives, rather than political leaders.

There were some exceptions to this story of women's marginalisa-tion. We briefly met Grace Onyango, who served as mayor of Kisumu before she entered parliament, and Chelagat Mutai, Moi's nemesis in the 1970s, in earlier chapters. But those wishing to join the handful of women MPs faced considerable obstacles. Wambui Otieno was one of the most prominent of these aspiring political figures. She had played an important role in the Mau Mau insurgency, was a keen nationalist activist and a member of the Kikuyu political aristocracy, but even she was unable to win parliamentary elections in 1969 and 1974.[9] Wambui was then a national figure, but is now most commonly associated with the protracted and well-publicised dispute over the body of her husband, Silvanus Melea Otieno. After his death in 1986, Wambui and her husband's extended family clashed over where the body should be interred. In the following six months, the case went through a succes-sion of legal challenges before Otieno was buried at his ancestral home in Nyanza, rather than in Nairobi, as Wambui insisted had been his wish. As Atieno and Cohen explore in their articulate book on the subject, the episode revealed much about ethnicity, the law and moder-nity.[10] To Wambui, her inability to simply bury her own husband said a great deal about why women were unable to exert greater influence within Kenyan society. 'Political participation aside,' she writes, 'culture is the greatest constraint on African women's advancement.'[11]

For all the challenges that Wambui and others like her faced, however, there were spaces for women to exert an influence on public life. Across the country, self-help groups and cooperatives dominated everyday lives after independence. Women played disproportionately influential roles within these institutions, as the example of Nakuru in the late 1970s demonstrates. The town was host to a wide array of different groups dominated by women. Women's church, dancing, discussion and investment groups met regularly. A women's welfare association helped families meet the cost of burials, education or legal action. Nakuru women also joined the Ikobe Farmers' Cooperative, together with others from across the eastern part of the Rift Valley. The society's members raised money to buy a 500-acre farm at nearby Molo. Similarly, the Kangei na Nyakinyua ('Mothers and Children') Consumers' Cooperative was established in 1969 with the aim of buying a commercial property in Nakuru town, the revenue from which would then support a welfare fund.[12] It was precisely these sorts of groups that became the platforms for debate about development and reform that energised local communities during the push for multipartyism.

Maathai was then typical of these changes. She was no stranger to politics. Her husband, Mwangi Mathai, from whom she was divorced in 1979, had been a key player within GEMA and an MP – indeed, he defeated Wambui Otieno for the Lanagata seat in 1969. Wangari herself had attempted to stand in the 1979 elections, but her nomination papers had been rejected. From the mid-1980s, however, she became the country's most prominent environmental campaigner. As head of the Green Belt Movement, she campaigned against deforestation and other activities that threatened the livelihoods of the rural poor. From its founding in 1977 to the mid-1990s, more than 50,000 people joined the organisation, as members spread across the country. They planted and tended trees in an effort to encourage reforestation and provide a sustainable source of household fuel. But the group also became embroiled in defence of women's access to land. Such a stance inevitably intertwined with politics, and Maathai became a figurehead for complaints about land theft. She soon joined the pro-democracy campaign as her environmental and political activism became inseparable.

Maathai and her supporters returned to Uhuru Park in February and March 1992. Whereas their previous protest there had been against the attempted theft of the park itself, this second demonstration was explicitly political. She and her supporters staged a hunger strike in an effort to bring about an end to political imprisonment. Many of the protestors were the mothers, wives and siblings of political prisoners. They camped on the corner of Uhuru Park, directly opposite Nyayo House – a site that quickly became known as Freedom Corner. Although police raided the camp after just four days, the women kept up their vigil there until the release of the remaining political prisoners. 'We remained united together until our children were released', wrote Rael Kitur, the mother of the political prisoner Tirop Kitur. 'Every single day, at the Freedom Corner, we sang and prayed.'[13] The campaign built Maathai a national reputation as a fierce advocate of political reform and the extension of human rights. By contrast, images of policemen beating the women protestors, many of whom bared their breasts in an effort to shame the police officers, led to yet more public condemnation of the regime. As Maathai wrote: 'What the mothers were saying to the policemen in their anger and frustration as they were being beaten was "By showing you my nakedness, I curse you as I would my son for the way you are abusing me." '[14] Although the practice of political imprisonment was briefly resurrected in 1994, the women at Freedom Corner demonstrated how the state was weakening: it was no longer able to restrict the emergence of new social movements.

Part of the success of individuals like Maathai and of the groups they worked with was their ability to take advantage of new forms of mass communication. The state's control of radio and television and its strong indirect influence over the newspapers meant that dissenting views had been communicated only with great difficulty. Mwakenya, for instance, relied on pamphlets, published in small print runs and distributed only in Nairobi and its environs. 'It's the silence that hurts', Maathai argued in January 1990. 'That's how you create a dictatorship.'[15] As part of the wider reduction in the state's influence over Kenyan society and economics, however, that silence was broken in the months that followed. Opportunities to establish new newspapers, television stations and, most importantly, FM radio stations were eagerly seized upon by entrepreneurs. The Kenya Television Network, for example, was established in 1990 as a private competitor to the state-run Kenya Broadcasting Corporation. These different media outlets were then taken up by Kenyans as new arenas in which to debate the performance of the government and to consider alternatives to Moi's rule.

'WHO KILLED BOB?'

In the early 1990s, the biggest challenge facing Moi was how to survive in this era of social movements, international support for reform and liberalised media. Despite this new combination of challenges, the government tried to respond in the usual ways. Restrictions on the press and the use of political imprisonment had served Moi well over the past twelve years. Editions of magazines containing articles condemning the government for its position on multipartyism were therefore impounded, and particular efforts were made to harry perhaps the single most influential journal of the time, *Nairobi Law Monthly*. This magazine, edited by Gitobu Imanyara, regularly featured articles by opposition leaders and pro-reform lawyers and was to become a leading voice for critics of the government. Imanyara was detained for three weeks in July 1990, and his lawyer, Pheroze Nowrojee, was charged with contempt of court the following month.

To maintain the cohesion of the ruling elite, the government nevertheless turned to another well-rehearsed method of asserting its supremacy. On 15 February 1990, the partially burnt body of the foreign minister, Robert Ouko, was found, close to his home near Kisumu, with a bullet wound in the head. Ouko had been an important figure in the ensemble of post-colonial politics. An intelligent and affable figure, he had been a civil servant through the first years of independence, before moving into government as an elected MP. After the banning of the KPU, he played a key role in efforts to bridge divides within Luo politics. He was, however, no great liberal nor an instinctive reformer: in November 1989 he told a press conference in Norway that Amnesty International, a consistent critic of Moi's human rights record, 'had become one of the leading peddlers of half-truths and outright lies'.[16] Ouko was, however, astute and recognised that change of one form or another was needed in Kenya.

Ouko had gone missing three days before his body was discovered. He had just returned from a visit to the US, where he had accompanied Moi and other senior ministers in discussions with State Department officials. His relations with his colleagues in cabinet and with the president had soured in the months leading up to his death. Ouko and Biwott, in particular, had very different views on the continuing corruption within the highest levels of government. Kenya's rulers, Ouko thought, were no longer immune to criticism from abroad about their corrupt habits. Instead, he believed that official corruption was an impediment to future good relations with donors, including the US. His views were confirmed by the cold reception that Moi and his ministers received in Washington during their visit in February 1990. Biwott, on the other hand, thought that the regime could ride out the storm. Moi was inclined to agree with his closest political ally. Ignoring the difficulties the delegation in Washington was experiencing in securing guarantees for future development aid, Biwott was determined that the networks of patronage and corruption that sustained the Moi government should remain intact.

Soon after Ouko's body was discovered, the authorities claimed he had committed suicide by first setting fire to himself and then fatally wounding himself with a gunshot. This none-too-plausible account fooled few and protests swiftly followed. In an attempt to calm the situation, Moi ordered that a further investigation be carried out. John Troon, an officer with Scotland Yard, was summoned to recommence the investigation. Troon persuaded Iain West, one of Britain's most prominent pathologists, to accompany him. Once their investigation was complete, the two men concluded that, in West's words, 'Robert Ouko was shot by another individual and . . . his body was subsequently set on fire.'[17] Troon pushed for the prosecution of Hezekiah Oyugi, the permanent secretary in the Office of the President, and Nicholas Biwott. Although both Oyugi and Biwott were arrested shortly afterwards, they were quickly released for lack of evidence and

Troon's report was suppressed. Biwott – 'the most feared and hated man in Kenya', according to the US ambassador, Smith Hempstone – and Oyugi – who 'controlled a nationwide network of intelligence agents, informants, and thugs' and 'held the power of life and death over virtually every Kenyan – were at least forced to resign from government.[18] Jonah Anguka, a former district commissioner and long-time associate of Ouko, was also arrested and held on remand for three years before being acquitted in 1994. Anguka later claimed to have been 'a very easy and vulnerable target for the government to sacrifice as a lamb to cover up the Ouko killers'.[19]

Numerous investigations have failed to establish exactly who did kill Ouko, and why. Hempstone believed that he had most likely been seized at his home in Koru, tortured at CID headquarters in Nairobi, and then taken to State House in Nairobi. There, Hempstone writes, 'Moi is said to have personally beaten Ouko' because of slights the president felt he had suffered during their trip to the US. The following day, Hempstone alleges, Ouko was returned to State House 'and hurled to the floor in front of Moi'.

> Someone – most accounts say it was Biwott – then pulled a pistol from his pocket and shot Ouko twice in the head in front of Moi. The president, it is said, then ordered the body returned to Koru by CID helicopter and burned in an attempted to conceal the nature of his injuries.[20]

Hempstone's allegations are impossible to prove. 'We cannot fix a final narrative of Robert Ouko's demise,' concede the authors of perhaps the most searing account of the political culture of Moi's Kenya, which includes an intelligent analysis of the controversies surrounding Ouko's murder.[21] The suspicious deaths of a number of witnesses have made that task even more difficult. However, most Kenyans were certain who was to blame. Although crowds chanted 'Who killed Bob?' during demonstrations held across the country, they knew who was really responsible. To those listening to the shouts of the protestors it was clear that the long-established tactics for suppressing dissent and seeing off the challenge of rivals were out of date. A new approach had to be found.

SABA SABA

With the Cold War over and events like Ouko's murder exposing the government for the corrupt, inept body it was, Charles Rubia and Kenneth Matiba thought the days of the one-party state were numbered. As the two veterans argued in April 1990, 'If that system has gone in most of the countries of the world, Kenyan leaders had better accept the inevitable changes which are bound to come.'[22] They embarked on meetings with Oginga Odinga, his son Raila and faithful ally Achieng' Oneko to discuss the next step towards restoring a multi-party constitution. The opposition leaders laid plans for a mass rally to be held at the Kamukunji grounds in Nairobi, the site of many a historic demonstration during the colonial era. They settled on the date of 7 July (7/7 or *Saba Saba* in Swahili, as the events of that day have become known). As the day of the demonstration approached, support for the reform movement built up momentum. According to one former political prisoner, Kariuki Gathitu, customers in bars ordered beer 'by saying *mbili mbili kama kawaida* (two as usual). It came to be understood as meaning two and not one party.' In Gathitu's local Venus Bar in the Shauri Moyo area of Nairobi 'the song *Reke Tumanwo* (enough is enough, let us part company) played non-stop'.[23] The president was scared. 'The days of mercy are gone,' Moi warned. 'I will have to swing into action against these people.'[24] But when the authorities refused to issue a licence to allow the rally planned for 7 July to go ahead, it hardly mattered to pro-democracy activists: such patently bureaucratic obstacles seemed anachronistic.

Not even a crackdown against the opposition's leaders could dampen the enthusiasm of their supporters. In the days leading up to the planned rally, Matiba and Rubia were arrested and detained. The lawyers John Khaminwa and Mohamed Ibrahim joined them in detention, along with Raila Odinga and Gitobu Imanyara. Gibson Kamau Kuria, another of the prominent human rights lawyers, escaped arrest by seeking refuge at the US embassy before fleeing the country. Nevertheless, by early afternoon on 7 July, thousands had gathered at Kamukunji. They were determined to celebrate their defiance of the government, but the euphoric atmosphere dissipated. As one eyewitness testified, 'Trouble started when people saw the CID, and started pointing at them, getting angry and saying they had come as spies. They decided to drive them away.'[25] In response, riot police charged the crowd. As the protestors fled and fanned out across the city, rioting began. Pro-democracy supporters sang their support for multipartyism, demanded the release of Matiba and Rubia, and gave the two-finger 'Victory' salute that had quickly become the symbol of the pro-democracy movement. The police retorted with tear gas. Over the next two days, the violence spread throughout Nairobi's outlying neighbourhoods and suburbs. Public transport workers joined the protests and went on strike, bringing the city to a standstill. By the Monday, violent anti-government protests were witnessed in the major towns of Central Province and Nakuru. In response, Moi issued orders permitting the security forces to use lethal force to crush further demonstrations. In all, over twenty protestors were killed and more than a thousand were placed in detention during the protests and the violent crackdown that followed.

The authorities were unrepentant. The demonstrators were, senior government officials claimed, participating in a Kikuyu plot orchestrated by Matiba and Rubia to take over the government. 'What we are seeing today is absolutely tribal,' Biwott claimed on 7 July itself.[26] Few agreed. To church leaders, the violence of early July seemed 'symptomatic of deeper problems of poverty and lack of participation in the affairs of the nation'.[27] Although the clergy and other supporters of reform hoped that *Saba Saba* would prove to be a turning point, the event marked only the beginning of a new chapter of political violence. The crushing of the demonstrations sent a clear signal to party hardliners that violence was no longer reserved for use against troublesome Somalis or isolated dissident figures. Instead, it was an acceptable part of the toolkit of every politician desperate to retain his seat in parliament. The rhetoric of such individuals clearly became more vitriolic in the aftermath of *Saba Saba*. William Ole Ntimama, the controversial Maasai political heavyweight, called on his constituents to violently attack any supporters of multipartyism who had infiltrated the district of Narok. This was a none-too-subtle reference to Kikuyu residents in the district who were thought to provide the backbone of support for the opposition movement. Two people were killed in a village in Narok shortly afterwards, as hundreds of Ntimama's supporters hunted for pro-democracy fifth columnists.[28] He and other leading figures in KANU were bent on defeating the opposition and ensuring their survival by turning Kenyans against one another.

THE RETURN TO MULTIPARTYISM

Throughout 1990 and 1991, the government attempted to deflect support for the opposition by promising internal reform of KANU. But the party did not exist in any meaningful way, and as such was incapable of undertaking the reforms necessary to appease the demands for democracy. Oginga Odinga, ever impatient, attempted to force the pace of change. He made a short-lived effort to establish a new party in February 1991, but was blocked from doing so by the government. In August he tried again. Together with fellow veterans Masinde Muliro, Martin Shikuku and George Nthenge, Odinga announced plans to establish the Forum for the Restoration of Democracy (FORD). They were, they told journalists, 'at the forefront of the struggle for independence' and 'the fathers of the independence constitution upon which the freedom of Kenya and the liberty of the citizens was founded and safeguarded'.[29] FORD had the backing of the wide array of opponents to Moi's rule that had coalesced over the previous few years. The president reacted in predictable fashion, denouncing FORD as an 'illegal political organization aimed at creating political instability'.[30] Muliro was briefly arrested, but was quickly released, and other well-known opposition leaders, such as Raila Odinga and Paul Muite, were harassed by state security officers. But these tactics no longer worked.

FORD's leadership was arrested ahead of a major rally in Nairobi in mid-November, but this only provided the excuse for demonstrations in support of multipartyism around the country. The leaders were taken to their home areas for bail hearings, and there they were greeted as returning heroes. In Kiambu, the police had to use tear gas in an effort to clear thousands of Paul Muite's singing and chanting supporters from outside the courthouse. Gitobu Imanyara had his bail hearing in Meru, where the proceedings in the courtroom could hardly be heard above the pro-FORD songs and cheers of his supporters. Like many Kenyans, Wambui Otieno was impressed by the demeanour of Muite and other young FORD leaders as they stood trial. 'In them I could see the old spirit we had when we fought for independence,' she writes in her memoirs. 'As I watched their determination, I knew that I would not be alone anymore, others would join me in telling Moi the truth.'[31] The defiance of FORD's leaders and the support they received from local populations seemed further evidence of the inevitability of multipartyism's eventual triumph.

The final proof of democracy's imminent success appeared to come on 26 November. After much debate, foreign governments finally reached a consensus on using aid as leverage to support multipartyism in Kenya. As the finance minister and vice president, George Saitoti, flew to Paris to meet representatives of donor governments, Moi made a desperate attempt to prevent the aid tap being turned off: he ordered the arrest of Biwott and Oyugi for the murder of Ouko. But it was too late. Saitoti was told that new aid deals with foreign countries were suspended for six months and that future aid 'would depend on clear progress in implementing economic and social reforms'.[32] Moi took the hint and on 3 December it was announced that the one-party system was to be dismantled.

Moi made no secret of his distaste for the decision. Just days before the constitution was finally amended to allow more than one party to operate, he spoke at a rally in Nairobi about 'multi-partyism and all that rubbish'. Describing democracy as 'a luxury' that 'Africans cannot afford', the president warned Kenyans against listening to the opposition's leaders: 'What some of them want you to do is to fight, and I do not want my citizens to fight.'[33] The meaning of Moi's words was clear. Kenya's poverty and ethnic divisions, the president thought, made violence inevitable without a strong, centralised, one-party state; democracy for Kenya meant ethnic bloodshed. The president did his best to make these words seem prophetic in the months and years that followed.

Half-hearted it may have been, but Moi's announcement was nevertheless greeted with joy and relief by pro-reformists. At the first mass FORD rally permitted by the authorities, Oginga Odinga addressed a vast crowd at Kamukunji and told them 'Today we are tasting freedom.'[34] But campaigners also recognised that political reform was only one step towards demolishing the edifice of authoritarianism. The Catholic bishops welcomed the resumption of multiparty politics in their New Year letter of January 1992. 'A new era is starting in our country,' they wrote.[35] But the bishops also called for an end to the gross corruption, abuse of human rights, manipulation of the constitution and incitement of violence.[36] They could not help but notice that these abuses of power and criminal acts were becoming more rather than less frequent as momentum for reform gathered.

THE VIOLENCE BEGINS

As talk of multipartyism gathered pace, an older (but just as fraught) discussion resurfaced. As a subject of national political debate, majimboism had been moribund since shortly after the absorption of KADU into KANU back in 1964 (see the introduction to this book). It was reignited by Noor Abdi Ogle, an MP in Wajir and a close ally of Biwott. During a speech in parliament in July 1991, Ogle explicitly connected implementation of majimboism with the survival of KANU and the one-party system. According to him, devolution would meet most Kenyans' demands for change, and so its implementation would remove the popular support for multipartyism. Ogle and others hoped that devolution would therefore allow both KANU and the one-party state to survive in a global age of political change. A few weeks later, Ogle's thoughts were echoed by Joseph Misoi, a Kalenjin MP, assistant minister and ally of the president. Ogle and Misoi found support from other key supporters of the regime, including Eric Bomett, the MP for

Nakuru, and Shariff Nassir, the veteran Coast politician and chairman of the KANU branch office in Mombasa.

Senior Kalenjin political leaders held a series of public meetings in the Rift Valley Province during the weeks that followed. Led by cabinet ministers and MPs, including Henry Kosgey, these meetings produced a variety of resolutions. Warnings were issued to FORD's leaders to stay out of the Rift Valley, and to ordinary Kenyans, other than Maasai and Kalenjin, to stay put in their own provinces. Bishop Manasses Kuria was dismayed: 'This is a system that Kenyans rejected almost 30 years ago. The very idea of reviving it to counter multi-party demands had all the elements of mischief. Anything that is likely to cause disharmony, strife and chaos is evil; it is satanic.'[37] Kuria's concerns reflected a broader awareness of the threats of violence posed by the advocates of the new majimboism.

Those threats were first made good at Meteitei Farm in Nandi district during October 1991. The farm was typical of many areas of the western Rift Valley. It was a former settler-owned property that had subsequently been subdivided among smallholders and their families. It was multi-ethnic, too. Given the proximity of the farm to Nyanza Province, a great many Luo took up residence there – to the chagrin of local Kalenjin, who thought the land was theirs by right. Besides those disputes, Meteitei had been blighted for years by disagreements and resentment over the way in which plots had been allocated on the farm. Kalenjin residents of the area felt that they had been doubly wronged, and in 1991 they had their revenge. As the violence began, Luo families were forced from their homes by Kalenjin youths. Within days, the violence spread quickly from Meteitei to other similar settlements in Nandi district, and then into the neighbouring districts of Kericho and Kisumu. By the end of November, six people had been killed in the clashes and nearly 22,500 displaced. Schools were closed, homes destroyed and property stolen.

The political context of the violence was immediately apparent. Church leaders rightly recognised that the violence was far from spontaneous. 'These tragic happenings are orchestrated', the Catholic bishop of Nakuru, Raphael Ndingi Mwana a'Nzeki, stated bluntly.

Those responsible were the politicians campaigning for majimboism in their 'irresponsible statements made in Kapsabet, Kapkatet, Kericho and Narok'.[38] Everyone knew that any future election would likely be decided in the Rift Valley, given that the province accounted for nearly a quarter of all the seats in parliament. But with the opposition dominated by Kikuyu, Luhya and Luo leaders, KANU's leadership feared that populations belonging to those groups in the Rift Valley would swing behind FORD. This worried both the president and his MPs from the province. The Rift Valley was therefore declared a 'KANU zone'. Loyalist leaders from the Kalenjin, Maasai, Turkana and Samburu communities (commonly referred to collectively by the acronym KAMATUSA) declared themselves to be representatives of the indigenous population of the province. They demanded the expulsion of Luhya, Luo and Kikuyu residents. This was nothing short of 'ethnic cleansing in the Rift Valley'.[39]

For individual MPs and candidates in the Rift Valley, the strategy was appealing, since they could rid their constituencies of likely opposition supporters. For the president, violence offered a way of pushing out supporters of rival candidates from entire provinces. Amendments to the constitution made it necessary for the successful candidate in the forthcoming presidential contest to gain not just the most votes nationwide, but also at least a quarter of the votes cast in five of the eight provinces. If likely opposition supporters were expelled from the Rift Valley in large enough numbers, it would be that much harder for any of Moi's rivals to reach that benchmark.[40] The government was not simply interested in arithmetic, however. It also wanted to discredit the whole notion of democracy. 'Since multipartyism came, you can see tribal clashes have started,' Moi told Kenyans in late January 1992. 'I warned of such violence earlier.'[41] He hoped that voters would exact retribution on the opposition for bringing unnecessary suffering to the country, and so allowed ethnic violence to take hold. This is what the political scientists Patrick Chabal and Jean-Pascal Daloz term 'disorder as political instrument; the deliberate instigation of violence by states for political ends'.[42]

The politics of the violence was well understood by its targets. Opposition leaders suspected that the Youth for KANU '92 group

(known widely as YK'92) was involved in the incitement and organisation of violence. YK'92 was led by Cyrus Jirongo, a businessman with
close ties to the Moi family who was alleged to be involved in
numerous corruption scandals through the early 1990s. According to
one arson victim in Nandi, 'My uncle was told if you are not for the
FORD meeting then you are one of us – if you are one of us, you must
help burn the houses.'[43] As elections due the following year drew
closer, the violence spread across western Kenya. 'This was the most
tension-backed Christmas', wrote one resident of Kakamega:

> As people celebrated the Lord's birthday, houses could be seen
> burning, having been set ablaze by arsonists . . . It was a war of
> bows and arrows . . . Several people have been killed and quite a
> number have been injured.

Another described how

> On the roads people are walking with arrows and spears, and
> women are carrying bundles, going for refuge somewhere. It is
> Nandis vs Luhyas, although it is everywhere. The few Nandis
> caught say they have been sent by powerful people in the
> government.[44]

Twelve people were killed in Kakamega, around a hundred were
injured and hundreds more displaced.

It is surprising that more people were not killed, given the ferocity
of the attacks. Church workers witnessed an assault on Luhya residents
of farmland around Endebess, to the east of Mount Elgon, on
26 December. At 8 p.m., bullets were fired at the targeted homes and
the attackers made 'a war cry'. Hearing the Kalenjin youths
approaching, the mainly Luhya targets fled their homes. A hail of
arrows caught those who were slow to evacuate their homes, but as the
youths arrived they found most of the houses empty. The invaders set
about looting the houses for abandoned possessions, and then they
torched homes, grain stores and crops in the fields. When some of the

residents returned to the scene the following morning, almost nothing remained of their homes. They had no choice but to head to the small towns of Kimondo and Endebess. There thousands of refugees struggled to build shelters out of whatever materials they could find in burgeoning shanty neighbourhoods.[45]

Opposition leaders and prominent voices from civil society called on the government to provide protection to the communities being attacked. Masinde Muliro pleaded with Moi to 'restrain people of the Kalenjin community from political thuggery in Western Kenya' – but to no avail. Indeed copious evidence was building up of the state's involvement in the violence. As the Catholic bishops argued:

> There has been no impartiality on the part of the security forces in trying to restore peace. On the contrary, their attitude seems to imply that orders from above were given in order to inflict injuries only on particular ethnic groups . . . It is difficult for the government to exonerate itself from the responsibility of these violent clashes.[46]

A parliamentary select committee inquiry conducted in early 1992 was fierce in its condemnation of all sections of the government. Provincial administration officials 'directly participated or encouraged others in perpetrating acts of violence. Security officers and the judiciary acted in a reluctant fashion against those responsible for the violence and 'were partisan in several cases when dealing with clash situations'. State-run media outlets 'did not give comprehensive information to the public'. Finally, the parliamentary report stated unequivocally that politicians incited the violence.[47]

The government obstructed all efforts to investigate properly and to stop the violence. The speaker in parliament, Jonathan Ng'eno, blocked four separate attempts to have parliament discuss the issue. Ng'eno was subsequently implicated in the training and equipping of perpetrators of the clashes.[48] The indifference at the very top of the government to the plight of victims was mirrored throughout the security forces and the judiciary. One victim of the clashes in Nandi district told the press:

Most of the police here are Nandis – they watch or collaborate. I
went to the sub-chief, who tells me to go to the chief, who tells
me to go to the DO [district officer]. I go to the DO and police
who tell me to go away.[49]

Police and local officials at Koguta, a settlement scheme along the
main road connecting the centre of the tea industry at Kericho and the
lakeside city of Kisumu, taunted victims of the attack there with
the ironic two-fingered salute of FORD and told them: 'Let the
FORD help you.'[50] Victims were treated little better by the courts,
which commonly released perpetrators on bail and handed out minor
sentences to the more than one thousand individuals charged with
involvement in the violence. In any case, the corruption and political
manipulation of the judicial system had long since eroded the faith of
Kenyans in the courts. As one victim of the violence on Mount Elgon
put it: 'We did not think of using the courts. We never thought
about it.'[51] Journalists attempting to investigate the clashes were
harassed, emergency legislation was used to restrict access to sites
affected by the violence, and human rights activists were prevented
from operating unimpeded in those locations. The regime was fighting
for its life.

Numerous investigations into the violence highlighted how government vehicles were used to transport raiders around the affected areas.
This indicated that MPs and local administrative officials were responsible for organising and facilitating the attacks.[52] At Sondu in Nyanza,
for example, the youths who were probably responsible for the attacks
on Luo residents were not local Kalenjin. They were instead transported to Sondu from the neighbouring Rift Valley, most likely from
Moi's home area of Baringo.[53] The raiders were frequently paid for
their efforts: one witness told a later parliamentary inquiry that he had
received 'Ksh.1,000 [$16.67] per every person killed and Ksh.600 [$10]
per each house burned'.[54] Though sparked off by such outsiders,
however, the violence quickly became internalised within communities. Put in disconcertingly simple terms, the violence proved popular
with many members of Kalenjin communities in the Rift Valley.

LAND, ETHNICITY AND VIOLENCE

Political violence of the sort witnessed in the Rift Valley, Western and Nyanza Provinces is often the result of an alliance between national elites and local people. While it may be easy to blame Moi and his ministers for the violence of the 1990s, that does not explain why many ordinary Kenyans participated in or tacitly supported the clashes. In trying to explain this violence, to focus solely on the impending election and the arena of high politics risks depicting those who participated in it as puppets in a macabre piece of political theatre. Viewed from the bottom up, the clashes were a way of resolving grievances over land.

Those grievances were made up of at least two historic layers. The deepest stratum was the memory of colonial dispossession. The settlement of European farmers and the annexation of land from Africans in the early part of the twentieth century remained a powerful issue within local political debates in the Rift Valley. For instance, Kalenjin leaders justified their efforts to push Luhya out of Trans Nzoia district by proclaiming that it had belonged to the Pokot sub-group of Kalenjin before the colonial conquest. Pokot elders pursued this claim in representations to the Kenyan and British governments, as well as to the United Nations working group on indigenous peoples. In letters to the British High Commission, the Pokot elders referenced colonial-era maps as they sought compensation and restitution for what they described as their 'expulsion' from grazing areas that now lay within the boundaries of Trans Nzoia.[55]

The bitterness created by the colonial annexation of land was exacerbated by the post-colonial settlement programmes. Communities such as the Samburu, Maasai and various sub-groups of the Kalenjin community believed that, instead of allowing them to return to the land stolen from their parents and grandparents, the Kenyatta regime had consolidated their dispossession by allocating that land to Kikuyu farmers after independence. A Kalenjin informant told Africa Watch that 'at independence Kenyatta gave all the land to the Kikuyu and the Kalenjin got nothing, so now the Kalenjin must take land back'.[56] Many Kalenjin, Samburu and Maasai feared that a victory for the opposition would herald an expansion in Luhya, Luo and Kikuyu settlement in the Rift Valley.

Besides this broad history of land disputes, the violence of the 1990s was made up of a series of more localised contests over access to land. It is easy to explain why, in seeking to resolve these disputes, Kenyans turned to violence rather than to well-established state institutions or legal mechanisms: those institutions and mechanisms had fallen into disrepute. The differences between the Kenyatta and the Moi eras tend to be greatly exaggerated by critics of the latter; but in certain respects there were indeed some critical variations in the ways policies and institutions worked before 1978 and after. Land policy was one such area.

Whatever one thinks of the way in which settlement of the Rift Valley and other parts of the country was carried out, it was at least done with a semblance of organisation and was backed by a bureaucracy. As a result, landholders could feel secure that their claim to the land was safe. As one 1971 study of this very question found, property owners 'did not feel very insecure, or worried about losing large portions of their land'.[57] But that confidence was eroded over subsequent decades. By 2001, an inquiry led by the rehabilitated Charles Njonjo found that the government had overseen a 'breakdown in the administration of land laws as a whole and abuse of office by public officials dealing with land matters'.[58] The result was that:

> The public has lost faith and confidence in the existing land dispute settlement mechanisms and institutions, because they are characterised by delays, incompetence, corruption, nepotism, political interference and overlap of roles or functions, leading to conflict, confusion and unnecessary bureaucracy especially when there is a low participation of the local people in land disputes resolution mechanisms.[59]

Without recourse to formal state institutions to resolve land disputes, many Kenyans turned to other ways of trying to settle their differences.

The crisis in land tenure was of the Moi government's own making. As the economy declined and the state and its public sector shrank, land became a valuable currency with which Moi's regime was able to buy the support of key partners. The grabbing of land for the purposes of political patronage was as naked in the 1990s as it had been at any stage since the colonial era; Jacqueline Kloop terms it a time of 'land grabbing mania'.[60] Moi's government ruthlessly exploited the very uncertain hold many of its subjects had on their land. Across the country, tens of thousands of people depended for their access to land on unwritten agreements struck decades before. As a major drive began in the late 1980s to formally register landholdings and to issue land titles, local authorities and powerful individuals seized the opportunity to dispossess Kenyans in urban and rural areas. In the Trans Mara area of Narok district, for example, Kisii and Luo families were expelled from land they had worked for the previous two decades. Large numbers of Kisii resided on either side of the boundary between Kisii and Narok districts. Kisii farmers had taken long leases or had purchased land from Maasai on an informal basis: neither the lease agreements nor the land purchases were supported by official paperwork.[61] In his parish close to the boundary between Kisii and Narok districts, Father John Kaiser watched during 1986 and 1987 as 'thousands of the Kisii people pass[ed] through Nyangusu and Ramasha carrying whatever belongings they could, probably to start life all over again – as refugees'.[62] Behind them, the land they left was quickly grabbed. Between 1989 and 1993, more than 837 title deeds were issued in Trans Mara, and plans were laid for a massive expansion in the subdivision of group ranches and the demarcation of individual plots of land.[63]

Such scenes were witnessed across the country. Alexander Muge, the bishop of Eldoret, denounced the 'brutal and lawless' evictions seen on Mount Elgon, in Nyeri and in Nairobi itself.[64] Under the pretence of concern over security and sanitation, a series of informal settlements dotted around the capital were destroyed in the final weeks of 1990. Nearly 1,500 businesses, mainly small kiosks and shops, were demolished and more than 45,000 people displaced. Within hours, formerly bustling neighbourhoods were in ruins. In most cases, demolition was swiftly followed by the erection of fences and the sale for private development of what had been publicly owned plots of land.[65]

Migrants who had moved into districts in the Rift Valley after independence were particularly vulnerable to forcible expulsion. Like the
Kisii residents of Narok, most victims of the clashes did not have title to
the land from which they were displaced. Whether because of delays to
surveys, corruption and ineptitude within the local administration, beset
as it was by graft and nepotism, or simply because the farmers had not
yet repaid the loans used to buy the land (but which needed to be settled
before a land title could be issued), the victims of the violence were in a
weak position.[66] In Nakuru district, many of those who had bought land
as part of a much larger cooperative or had been issued land by the big
land-buying companies such as Ngwataniro still had not had their plots
formally demarcated or had title deeds issued to them.[67] In the Uasin
Gishu district, which encompassed Eldoret town, more than 40 per cent
of the total land mass had not been demarcated.[68]

In many places, registration of land ownership occurred at the same
time as multiparty politics resumed. In Nandi district, more than
38,000 title deeds were issued between 1989 and 1993.[69] At Meteitei,
the site of the first outbreak of violence, the issuing of land titles was
already under way, but was only completed after the clashes began and
non-Kalenjin families had been forced to leave. This pattern of prior
conflict, disputes over land and uncertainty about the future was a
feature of a number of locations where the clashes were most intense.
At Owiro, also in Nandi, a survey of the landholdings of the mainly
Luo residents was just beginning when the violence ignited. At Kotetni
in Kericho, a survey of the holdings of the local population of mainly
Luo families had been carried out prior to the violence there, but land
titles had not yet been issued. The same was true at Kunyak, Ochoria
and Buru Theselia in Kericho, and Koguta and Kotetni in Kisumu.[70]

For many Kalenjin, Maasai, Turkana and Samburu, the issuing of
land titles in the Rift Valley threatened to make permanent the presence
of groups they considered to be outsiders. Those fears were heightened
by the prospect of FORD winning the forthcoming election, which
KANU's supporters thought would herald a consolidation of the position of Kikuyu, Luhya and Luo in the province. But besides posing a
threat to the self-proclaimed indigenous population of the Rift Valley,

the elections also presented an opportunity. Politicians were flush with campaign funds (some raised through the corruption deals discussed in the next chapter), and their aim of expelling the 'outsiders' for political reasons was in line with the hopes of many of their constituents. An ethnically cleansed Rift Valley fitted the objectives of the president, his MPs and their supporters. The years 1991 and 1992 seemed to represent a last opportunity for the self-proclaimed indigenous population of the Rift Valley to force those they saw as aliens off disputed land.

THE ELECTION

Although the violence was closely tied to electoral politics, there was a pause in the clashes around the time of the December election itself. The arrival of election observers and greater international attention increased scrutiny of Kenya's affairs. Areas affected by the violence were put under curfew and were subject to extensive police patrols. The hiatus allowed some sort of 'audit' of the damage: around 300,000 people had been displaced and more than 1,500 had been killed in the fourteen months leading up to election day. Children made up three-quarters of all those displaced, and their education was devastated as schools closed and families were forced to take up residence in temporary camps. The dislocation of families from their crops increased dependence on purchased food-stuffs and removed a valuable source of income. Households that took in displaced relatives and friends also found their incomes stretched.[71] The abandonment of farms meant that food was in short supply. A United Nations Development Programme report described 'the contrast in the landscape between cultivated fields with intact and inhabited homesteads with that of fallow, weed infested fields surrounding destroyed homesteads'. It was, the author wrote, 'a truly depressing sight'.[72] After attacks on Kikuyu residents of Gitwamba, at the foot of Mount Elgon, the once thriving market in the trading centre became moribund. Local dairy production was wiped out and land prices collapsed to less than a third of their values prior to the violence.[73] The effects of the violence could be seen on the beaches and in the game parks, too. Visitors stayed away and the tourist revenues shrank by more than half.

With the conflict paused, attention shifted to the election itself. In the heady days following Moi's announcement that multiparty politics were to resume, the chances of a KANU victory seemed remote. But as the opposition proved incapable of remaining united, the prospects of Moi and KANU remaining grew. FORD was afflicted by several divisions. The first was generational: right from the time of its foundation in 1991, the small group of veteran politicians who had established the party felt threatened by the so-called 'Young Turks' – the professionals from the worlds of academe, journalism and law, such as Peter Anyang' Nyong'o, Paul Muite and Gitobu Imanyara. The second division emerged as FORD's membership expanded in the wake of the decision to legalise opposition parties: the party's dissident roots were in danger of being swamped by Kikuyu conservatism, as figures like Njoroge Mungai joined it, regarding FORD as the best vehicle for a renaissance of the Kenyatta era. Such figures had little in common with the party's founders and endangered its reformist image.

Aside from its internal problems, FORD proved unable to retain its monopoly on opposition. From January 1992, it faced a rival in the Democratic Party (DP). The DP was founded by Kibaki, following his resignation from the government and KANU. He had been a disconsolate passenger in the government after his demotion from the position of vice president in the wake of the 1988 elections. He had nevertheless remained a public supporter of Moi and had famously dismissed FORD's chances of defeating KANU as 'trying to cut down a fig tree with a razor blade'.[74] He did think, however, that KANU had to undergo reform to become more accountable and transparent if it was to survive as the ruling party. Moi was unimpressed, however, and made plans to fire his oldest ally; Kibaki resigned instead.

The DP garnered much elite Kikuyu support, but was hampered in its bid to build wider backing. In Karume's account of its founding, the party was simply a vehicle for the ambitions of its leaders, who had thought that KANU was doomed but who were too late to have any chance of playing leading roles in FORD. There was 'no possibility of becoming party leaders in FORD because it was already like a top-heavy, overloaded ship that was bound to sink under the weight in due course'.[75] Kenyans were rightly cynical about Kibaki's motives, and the DP suffered further from unflattering comparisons between his late conversion to multipartyism and the courage demonstrated by FORD's leaders. Although John Keen, a veteran Maasai politician, was among the party's founders, the alignment of the DP and the old Kikuyu elite hardly reassured voters outside of Central Province that the new party represented a break with the past. Moreover, it was unashamedly elitist in its outlook. It was, as a political scientist and later key supporter of Kibaki, Kivutha Kibwana, remarked, 'a party the World Bank should like'.[76]

Despite the emergence of the DP, a united FORD remained a likely victor in a free and fair election. That unity was by no means assured, however. As the election approached, the question of who was to be the party's presidential candidate became more pressing. For many of FORD's members, the party's founder, Oginga Odinga, was the natural choice. Others disagreed and thought Kenneth Matiba deserved the privilege. Matiba had been absent from the day-to-day business of politics since his arrest shortly before *Saba Saba*. His health had suffered while he was in prison, and after his release he travelled to London for specialist treatment and a long period of convalescence. He finally returned to Kenya on 2 May 1992, to be greeted as a returning hero. 'Hundreds of thousands of jubilant supporters lined the road leading from the airport into the city,' Karume recalls. 'A tourist or visitor who was not familiar with Kenya's politics might have thought it was the pope who was arriving.'[77] With his return, Matiba brought the tensions within FORD to the surface. His overwhelming support among Kikuyu was not matched elsewhere in the country, but he was reluctant to be anyone else's running mate in the forthcoming elections. By contrast, Odinga could claim to have nationwide support and saw the election as a chance to make good a political career marked by frustration and defeat. Neither man was prepared to give way.

There was little in the avuncular Matiba's policies or life history that suggested he would redress the problems of poverty and inequality. He had served as a senior civil servant under Kenyatta before leaving government to head up East African Breweries, the producers of Kenya's ubiquitous lagers. In that role, and in other corporate positions, he had attracted a great deal of publicity. Similarly, he had made good use of a spell leading the Kenya Football Federation to maintain his position in the public eye before he returned to politics as an MP in 1983. He was an unabashed member of the Kikuyu elite, and his ideas about the economy and society had much in common with those that had been espoused by Kenyatta: 'The economy can only be salvaged by ourselves through hard work.'[78] Radical remedies for inequality were unsuitable, because 'what benefit do you get of destroy[ing] something good?' Matiba saw his goal as building 'an enabling climate for the creation of wealth'.[79] He understood the struggle for democracy and the power struggle within FORD in terms of the boardroom and the market. 'I have always believed in competition,' he wrote:

> It works so well in business and industry where it enables the customer to get the best product, the best service and the best value for his money. In opposing Odinga or anybody else, I want to demonstrate that the spirit of competition in the business world can work in politics as well.[80]

But Matiba's message did not help him to reach out beyond his Kikuyu supporters.

Odinga's much longer personal history of opposition and promises of social justice were of far greater appeal to Kenyans at large, but by the early 1990s even he had dropped his cherished ideas of redistribution. Having learned bitter lessons from his past, Odinga was anxious to avoid divisive issues and to retain FORD's broad base. As he told the *Nairobi Law Monthly*, he knew only too well that the FORD coalition could easily suffer from 'cracks which will always emerge due to individual movements'. Odinga therefore attempted to emphasise widely shared concerns, most notably corruption. Corruption 'is one of the major problems which FORD will have to deal with'. He also recognised that international support was essential if Moi was to be toppled, and so was careful to avoid alarming diplomats with any allusions to his past political battles: 'The investors would like to deal with people who are honest and sincere in handling the affairs of the country. They would like to get returns from their investments in our country.'[81] Odinga had mellowed in his old age.

With the announcement of the date of the election imminent, FORD finally split in two in October 1992. Odinga led FORD-Kenya and Matiba FORD-Asili ('the original') into the December elections. As David Throup and Charles Hornsby note in their encyclopaedic account of the period:

> Only a united FORD, with Matiba and Odinga working in harness for victory, might have stood a chance of defeating KANU with its control over government patronage and the state machinery given that the DP would already split the opposition vote.[82]

A victory for KANU and Moi, unthinkable just a few months before, was now likely. The government was careful to leave nothing to chance, however. As Maathai complained in an open letter to Moi after the results were declared, the 'Electoral Commission, the State mass media and the Civil Service' were all used 'to rig Your Excellency back to power'.[83] The campaign was marked by significant corruption, intimidation and other malpractices. High numbers of KANU candidates were able to stand unopposed, the Electoral Commission was seen to be in the pocket of the government, and the officers in the provincial administration continued to serve their political masters rather than the Kenyan people.

Moi and KANU were therefore able to survive the election held on 29 December. The president faced down the challenge from Matiba, Kibaki and Oginga Odinga, despite winning just 36 per cent of the votes cast in the presidential election – his three rivals split the opposition vote. In the parliamentary polls, the ruling party was even more successful, with KANU returning 100 MPs, the two FORDs winning 31 seats each, and 23 seats going to Kibaki's DP. The opposition parties rejected the results, but had no way of contesting them in the courts. Dismayed but undeterred, supporters of reform, like the lawyers Maina Kiai and Gibson Kamau Kuria, called on 'Kenyans who cherish truth, freedom and justice' to 'once again harness all their resources to ensure that their country joins the community of democratic nations'.[84] The patience of Kenyans was being tested, however.

THE SECOND WAVE

The fragile peace brought about by the holding of the elections remained in place until March 1993, when a high-level delegation from the IMF and the World Bank left the country after a visit to assess the pace of economic and political reform. Once the election observers, journalists and economists had returned home, the violence resumed. Oscar Kipkemboi, the chairman of YK'92 in Nakuru district, promised it would only end once all Kikuyu had left the Rift Valley. Oginga Odinga begged Kalenjin to cease their attacks on their neighbours and urged the attackers to think again if they believed they could push all non-Kalenjin out of the Rift Valley 'through a war of arrows'.[85] Kalenjin leaders paid little heed to such warnings.

At Londiani, the Presbyterian pastor, Solomon Kamau, was one of those Kikuyu targeted by Kalenjin youths. His home was looted and then burnt to the ground on 22 June 1993. He understood the message, telling the NCCK that 'this harassment is meant to scare off the non-Kalenjin who have refused to bow to the eviction crusade in the Rift Valley'.[86] A burst of arson attacks against Kikuyu families living near Eldoret on the night of 10 July 1993 came after Jackson Kibor, the local chairman of KANU in the district, told a *harambee* meeting (see chapter 1) at a primary school that all Kikuyu should be forced to leave the area. In the days that followed, there was an intensification of theft and arson attacks against Kikuyu living around Eldoret.[87] Over a hundred people lost their lives and 15,000 fled their homes in Molo, near Nakuru, as attacks on Kikuyu there began in August 1993. Along the Narok and Kisii district boundaries, Maasai youths continued to target Kisii communities. New arrangements were put in place in Narok district to allow the local administration to monitor land sales, so as to prevent non-Maasai from buying land in the area.[88] The violence reached West Pokot in late October and early November

1993, and was prompted by a series of announcements by the local MP and cabinet minister, Francis Lotodo, who announced that non-Pokot should leave the district.[89]

The renewed violence was particularly bad on Mount Elgon. Gangs of Sabaot youths, together with their ethnic kin, the Sebei from across the border in Uganda, targeted non-Kalenjin living on and around the mountain in an effort to seize land and create ethnically homogeneous districts and parliamentary constituencies. Those expelled from their homes on Mount Elgon were forced to take refuge in temporary shelters, in schools and in church compounds. At Kapkateny in Bungoma district, Africa Watch investigators found a hundred refugees from the clashes on the mountain living together: 'In a one-room shed of approximately twenty by sixty feet, the displaced population lives in cramped, unhygienic conditions. People have nothing but potatoes and maize meal given by the churches.'[90] Rather than alleviate their suffering, the government urged the displaced to return home.

Government advice to go back to the farms paid no heed to the reality of life in areas affected by the clashes. No effort had been made to disarm those responsible. 'Without the return of guns, we are not well', said Judith Kundu, who had been expelled from her home on Mount Elgon. She had attempted to return to her home on the mountain, but had been forced out for a second time.[91] Others who tried to return found their former homes occupied, either by those responsible for the violence or by others expelled from other parts of the surrounding area. On Mount Elgon the situation was further complicated by the settlement of Sebei on the farms left behind by the targets of the clashes. With the encouragement of local Sabaot leaders, some 350 individuals – descendants of the 10,000 or so Sebei who had left Kenya in the 1930s in search of land – crossed the border from Uganda to make good what they considered to be their historic claim to the land on the mountain's slopes. The Sebei were determined to resist any attempts by the rightful owners of homes and farms to return. Peter Wafula, an elderly man, and his wife Teresa tried to return to their land at Ite in early March 1993. The Luhya couple were shot dead, despite the presence of police officers.[92]

The government was still determined at all costs to prevent investigation of the violence and of the plight of its displaced victims. Affected areas were closed off to outsiders to frustrate prying eyes, and sustained efforts were made to silence high-profile voices of criticism. As part of this effort, Father Tom O'Neil was banned from saying mass at his church in Enoosupukia in Narok. O'Neil was outraged by the expulsion of Kikuyu residents of the area, many of whom held title deeds for land they had farmed since the late 1960s. Their expulsion followed a declaration by the local MP and minister for local government, William Ole Ntimama, that Kikuyu in Enoosupukia were illegal squatters. Ntimama demanded that they leave the district immediately. 'Kikuyu had oppressed the Maasai, taken their land and degraded their environment', he told parliament. 'We had to say enough is enough. I had to lead the Maasai in protecting our rights.' Over three days in mid-October, Maasai youths mounted a series of raids on Kikuyu homes around Enoosupukia in which seventeen people were killed and 30,000 forced from their homes.[93]

Around a third of the refugees from Narok formed a camp at Maela in Nakuru district, where they lived in dismal conditions. Having already gained considerable publicity for his denunciations of the evictions, O'Neil took up the cause of the plight of his former parishioners. He was ordered to leave the country. The government had good reason to be embarrassed by the situation. Rather than alleviate the suffering of those lacking shelter, proper food supplies and medical support, the authorities tried to close the camp at Maela. The 10,000 or so displaced Kikuyu there were served with an eviction order soon after they arrived. The first effort to enforce that order resulted in the destruction of homes in the camp and the eviction of around 6,000 people. Nevertheless, 4,000 men, women and children remained; they had nowhere else to go. But the government was determined to make them leave, and so blocked deliveries by humanitarian groups of food, medicines and blankets. But still the refugees remained.

Finally, two days before Christmas 1994, the camp was cleared. Its American Catholic chaplain, Father John Kaiser, watched as the local administrative official ordered the residents to leave behind their possessions and to board trucks. As they did so, the official told them they were being taken to the 'Promised Land'. Around them, local KANU activists destroyed their temporary shelters and stole or burnt their meagre possessions. The trucks left the camp and headed for the escarpment of the Rift Valley and Central Province beyond. There they 'were simply dumped by the roadside or on a football stadium, in the middle of the night'.[94] The 'Promised Land' was in fact just another desperate corner of Moi's 'land of dread and desolation'.[95]

CHAPTER SEVEN

THE GOLDENBERG YEARS, 1993–2002

The blood of innocent Kenyans continues to flow in the river of time. Is it the blood of a collapsing order gasping for breath as it crumbles into a state of anarchy? Or is it the blood of convulsive maternal pangs giving birth to a new and better Kenya? Let the choice be ours![1]

Alamin Mazrui, 1997

THE DEATH OF ODINGA

On 20 January 1994, Oginga Odinga suffered a heart attack at home in Kisumu. He was quickly transported to hospital in Nairobi, but died there that same day. Odinga's advanced age – he was eighty-two when he died – and poor health did little to diminish the grief that many felt. Even Moi was magnanimous for once: 'Kenya has lost a great son, a nationalist and a patriotic citizen.'[2] The president glossed over his rival's role in the restoration of multipartyism, but Odinga's supporters and allies were less willing to forget his leadership of the reform movement. 'He offered his body, mind and resources in the service of justice [more] than anyone else,' Timothy Njoya remarked in an interview shortly after Odinga's death.[3] During the funeral, as Odinga's body was being lowered into the ground, the tens of thousands of mourners present made the two-fingered salute of support for FORD.

'Odinga's life-long objective was to make Kenya a more humane, more just and more tolerant society,' argues Ogot. 'He will also be remembered as a person who kept faith with the people, a leader who lived by the principles he preached, a great nationalist and Pan-Africanist and one of the founding fathers of the Kenya nation.'[4] His unquestionable courage during the last years of colonial rule, the repression of the KPU, his detention and in the push for multipartyism was inspirational. In each of those moments, Odinga galvanised support for movements that might otherwise have crumbled in the face of government aggression. But his legacy is more complicated than Ogot suggests. Odinga's vision of nationalism based around redistribution or democratisation centred on social justice was never matched by political nous. On countless occasions, he was outsmarted by otherwise mediocre rivals, never mind the likes of Mboya, Kenyatta and Moi. Acts born of impatience, inflexibility and poor judgement often cancelled out potential gains for his favourite causes.

Odinga's final lapses came regrettably soon before his death. In 1993, with the opposition in tatters and having finally reached the end of his tether, with a political life spent almost entirely out of office, he began talks with Moi about joining the government. More seriously, he became embroiled in the single largest corruption scandal in Kenya's post-colonial history. Six months before his death, Odinga admitted to having accepted a campaign donation worth nearly $60,000 from the businessman Kamlesh Pattni. The donation to Odinga was part of wider allegations about Pattni's role in an enormous corruption affair known as the Goldenberg scandal. Revelations in the local and foreign press over the next four years meant that the scandal cast a shadow over all political debate. Goldenberg, moreover, typified the way in which politics were conducted in the final eight years of KANU rule. These were, as one account of the period puts it, the 'Goldenberg years'.[5]

GOLDENBERG

In the early 1990s, in an effort to encourage export industries in Kenya and boost foreign currency reserves, the government ran a scheme designed to reward exporters. It agreed to pay companies a bonus of 20 per cent of the value of exported goods if they exchanged the foreign currency earned into Kenyan shillings. There was, in addition, a programme of export credits, intended to tide exporters over during the period between shipping goods to foreign customers and receiving payment.

Goldenberg International, co-owned by Pattni and former head of the Special Branch, James Kanyotu, was set up in 1990. The company promised the government that it would earn around $50 million in exports of gold and diamonds, and was granted a monopoly over exports of those two commodities, despite the fact that the country has no diamond reserves and very little gold.

But in fact commercial exploitation of mineral resources had precious little to do with the real reasons for the company's foundation: Goldenberg was actually formed so that the government could build up its 'war chest' ready for the 1992 election. For the Goldenberg scheme revolved around exploiting the bonus payment and the export credit schemes for the benefit of the company's owners and, importantly, their friends in government. Rather than gold or diamond mining, the company's revenues came from the CBK: essentially, it was guaranteed a bonus of 35 per cent under the government's export incentive scheme and extended export credit scheme.

Fraudulent claims for the export credits and bonuses, based on non-existent sales, soon began to arrive on the desks of officials at the CBK. At one stage in early 1993, the funds transferred to Goldenberg amounted to Ksh.7 billion ($120 million) or 7 per cent of the money in circulation in the Kenyan economy. However, as the auditor-general soon noticed: 'No evidence has been seen to confirm that the gold and other precious metals claimed to have been exported and for which compensation was paid, originated and were processed in Kenya.'[6] Despite such reservations, billions of shillings flowed from the central bank to Goldenberg between 1990 and 1993. Goldenberg's funds were handled by the Delphis Bank, owned by Ketan Somia, Pattni's friend and a close associate of Moi, Saitoti and Biwott. Goldenberg itself owned the Exchange Bank, which in 1992 and 1993 used the revenues gained in the export scam to engage in currency speculation.

Writing in July 1993, John Githongo remarked that Goldenberg 'is shaking the very foundations of Kenya's economy'.[7] The shilling plummeted, losing about half its value against sterling in the eighteen months leading up to the public revelations about Goldenberg in mid-1993. The increase in money in circulation drove inflation to an annual rate of over 40 per cent in August 1993.

By then, the true nature of Goldenberg had begun to emerge. As the scandal developed, officials and businessmen close to the regime who were involved in Goldenberg began to fear defeat in the election and so used the company to plunder the economy for private gain while they still had the chance.

Newspaper investigations and questioning by opposition leaders began in early 1993. The original source of the information was a CBK employee, David Munyakei. Alarmed by the sums leaving the central bank for Goldenberg's accounts, Munyakei approached senior management. They did nothing. 'I initially thought that the government was not aware what was going on at the CBK,' he later told Billy Kahora.[8] Munyakei turned to politicians instead. He met the opposition MPs Paul Muite and Peter Anyang' Nyong'o on a number of occasions. The two politicians began to expose what was going on through leaks to the press and then by asking questions in parliament. Munyakei, however, was quickly uncovered as the source of the information, jailed for a short period, sacked from his job and forced to flee Nairobi for a new life in Mombasa.

The international and local press stoked up pressure on the government to investigate the Goldenberg scandal properly. The scrutiny of the IMF and the World Bank led to the closure of the Exchange Bank and the forced retirement of the central bank's governor, Eric Kotut. Despite the revelations, the opposition was hamstrung in its efforts to expose the truth about Goldenberg, for it soon emerged that many opposition leaders had, like Odinga, accepted Pattni's money.[9] Others, including Muite, were alleged to have been involved in the affair, too.

In the months that followed, Odinga attempted to block his supporters from investigating the Goldenberg affair.

Although Musalia Mudavadi had called a halt to Goldenberg's plundering when he took over as finance minister in January 1993, he consistently demonstrated an unwillingness to investigate the company further. Saitoti, Mudavadi's predecessor in the Ministry of Finance, remained as vice president and stubbornly denied any wrongdoing in the affair. Goldenberg was too big to hide, but too important to investigate properly. While the public quickly came to know the basic details of the scandal and could guess at the enormity of the sums involved, they did not see those guilty of such gross corruption punished for their crimes. Indeed, the beneficiaries of the scandal felt little need to hide their wealth. Instead Pattni erected an enormous monument to the scandal in the form of a gauche five-star hotel in central Nairobi. By contrast, David Munyakei died in poverty in July 2006: the Goldenberg whistleblower was unable to afford medical treatment for a relatively minor gum disease and came to suffer a number of subsequent illnesses and complications.

In Kahora's masterly account of his life and times, Munyakei becomes a Kenyan everyman – transitory, forced to move from place to place to find work, but with a flexibility of identity to fit whatever situation he found himself in. Whether in Narok, Nairobi or Mombasa; among his mixed Kikuyu and Maasai family; with his Taita girlfriend or Swahili wife; as a Christian or Muslim; in the city or in the countryside, he found the ways to survive in a complicated and hostile world. He was thus like generations of East Africans before him, exerting what John Lonsdale has termed 'agency in tight corners' in an effort to make the best of often harsh physical, political and economic climates.[10]

This history of mobility and multiple identities was, however, coming to an end in the Rift Valley at the same time as the Goldenberg scandal unfolded. The bitter violence of the multiparty era led to a new emphasis on notions of identity that emphasised autochthony, the notion of belonging to a particular place or, in everyday parlance, of being a son of the soil. Older notions of what it meant to be Kikuyu or Luo, for example, were formed during long histories of migration. By the early 1990s, these identities were more commonly anchored in a particular place – in these cases in Central and Nyanza Provinces, respectively. But these newer notions of ethnicity conflicted with the realities of people's lives and made no allowance for those living outside their supposed home provinces and districts. Victims of the ethnic clashes were continually urged to return home, but as Ogot asks, 'what is *nyumbani* ['home'] for the large number of Kikuyu people evicted from the Rift Valley?'[11] Many of those expelled from their homes in the early 1990s were third- or even fourth-generation migrants who had no connection to their presumed home of Central Province; they certainly had no land there. KANU's leaders were not greatly troubled by such questions. Instead, the violence continued.

THE VIOLENCE RETURNS

The revelations about Goldenberg deflected a good deal of attention from the plight of the victims of the violence before and after the 1992 election. Incidents of violence had become rarer by 1994 in any case. The 1992 election was a memory and, with the next polls only due in 1997 and thus not yet on the horizon, the political and financial fuel for the clashes was missing. But once party membership drives began again in 1995, the bloodshed started to increase. Kikuyu looking to go back to their homes in Burnt Forest were told that they could return so long as they promised to vote for both Moi and KANU in the 1997 elections. On 7 March 1995, police officers and Kalenjin youths had a six-hour gun battle through Trans Nzoia and Bungoma districts. Over the next three months, ten people were killed during clashes along the boundary between the two districts. 'If Kenyans think the killing of people in the name of so-called tribal clashes is over, then they are in for a rude shock,' the Catholic priests in the Ngong diocese warned in March 1995.[12] The pattern set earlier in the decade began to be repeated.

By October 1995, speeches in favour of majimboism were again being made by leading KANU politicians in the Rift Valley. The sense of impending conflict around the rest of the Rift Valley was palpable. Sure enough, the still relatively isolated cases of arson, theft and murder started to spread from the epicentres of Molo, Kitale and Bungoma. In Kapenguria, Pokot raiders clashed with Turkana, and the multi-ethnic farms of southern Nyanza witnessed waves of arson attacks throughout the remainder of 1995 and into 1996. Once voter registration began in mid-1997, security concerns were further exacerbated. Twenty-seven people were killed in the Kerio Valley in the northern Rift Valley as Pokot supporters of local KANU politicians drove 10,000 Marakwets, thought likely to vote for opposition candidates, out of the area.

Attention soon shifted from the Rift Valley to Coast Province. Isolated incidents of violence had been witnessed in Coast earlier in the decade. The targets were, as elsewhere, the communities of migrants to the area, and the perpetrators were largely self-proclaimed representatives of the indigenous population of the province. Mijikenda militias had attacked Luo and Kamba residents in a small number of episodes around the 1992 election, but Coast had not witnessed violence on anything like the scale of the Rift Valley. In 1997, the violence was much greater, however.

The worst of it was centred on the town of Likoni and Kwale district to the south. Around half a million people lived in the affected area. The population was made up of members of the Digo and Duruma ethnic groups, both parts of the larger Mijikenda community, as well as migrants and their descendants drawn from the Kamba, Kikuyu, Luo and Luhya communities. Migration to Coast from upcountry areas of Kenya pre-dated independence and colonialism, but post-colonial migration into Kwale and Likoni had placed particular strain on the social and political fabric of the area. Sustained inward migration to Kwale, for instance, had driven average annual population increases of between 3 and 4 per cent throughout the 1960s and 1970s. Migrants, mainly Kamba from Eastern Province, took up places on large settlement schemes in the district. Others were attracted to the area to seek work in the burgeoning Diani Beach resort or in Mombasa city itself. All along the coastline, 'the issue of land ownership has been at the centre of local politics', wrote Karuti Kanyinga.[13] But as well as the farmers and the labourers, migration included administrators and investors. Coastal communities were largely excluded from positions of power within the local administration and from the riches made by investors in the luxury hotels and resorts that sprang up among the mangroves and palm forests that line the beach. A pronounced sense of grievance therefore mounted among Digo and Duruma communities over the decades from 1963, leading them to ask 'the question that dogs so many citizens of the coast: Why are the Mijikenda so oppressed?'[14]

According to one local resident and migrant, by the 1990s 'the prevailing animosity' was that 'the upcountry people should return to their home-regions'.[15] Tension between local and migrant populations was visible in a variety of different forms. The influence of migrants over the local administration meant, many Mijikenda believed, that little consideration was being given to local, Muslim sensibilities and culture when decisions about the licensing of hotels, bars and other entertainment were being taken. 'The loud music from the bars is now in stiff competition with the Islamic call to prayers,' one Muslim resident complained.[16] Besides the issues of ethnicity and migration, such sentiments also pointed to the increased politicisation of Kenya's Muslims. Despite making up around 20 per cent of the population, the mostly Sunni Muslim community had exercised little political clout in the past. However, mobilisation around revisions to family law led to greater engagement by Muslims in public debate in the 1980s. The Islamic Party of Kenya (IPK) was formed in 1992 in an effort to mobilise the Muslim vote (if such a thing could be said to have existed), but garnered little support. It was, in any case, undermined by divisions in Coast around ideas of migration and belonging. The IPK, with Moi's encouragement, came to be viewed as the party of Arab Muslims who had migrated to the coast at various periods, while the rival United Muslims of Africa association represented itself as the voice of indigenous African Islam in the province.

These issues of indigeneity and migration were more obvious in debates about those who had moved to Coast from other parts of Kenya during the post-colonial period. The immediate political implications of that recent history of migration became clear once voter registration was completed in June 1997. As elsewhere in and around Mombasa, the migrant vote seemed set to determine the outcome of the election. Local and national KANU leaders feared that the ruling party would be unable to hold on to parliamentary seats in contests against opposition candidates tied to the dominant migrant groups in the area. Threats began to be made even before voter registration was finished. A Luo man recounted to the Kenya Human Rights Commission (KHRC) how he had been told: 'This time you will go and vote in your home-areas.' Once registration was complete, guns were brought into the area and preparations began for the attacks on migrants. Local unemployed youths were recruited and trained following oath-taking meetings held at night. Ex-servicemen from the local communities played a crucial role, too, in the process. Investigations into the training and equipping of the youths revealed the involvement of local political leaders, KANU activists and local Mijikenda businessmen.[17] The late Karisa Maitha, then a DP MP in Mombasa, alleged that the violence was orchestrated by Rashid Sajja, a nominated KANU MP, Nicholas Biwott 'and some other associates of theirs at State House'.[18]

The trigger for the attacks was the arrest of one of the leading plotters in August. Five hundred of his comrades stormed the police station at Likoni in an effort to release him. The attackers then raided the police station's armoury before turning their attention to migrants living in the vicinity. Over the days that followed, the violence spread along the towns and villages on the coast south of Mombasa, into the city itself and then northwards. The bloodshed lasted until November, when the security forces finally brought the area under control. The violence was similar in form to that witnessed in the Rift Valley. The initial raids in mid-August were led, human rights investigators claimed, by non-Mijikenda, who withdrew from the scene once the momentum of the violence had built up. Around a hundred people were killed, mostly Luo. Homes and businesses were destroyed by the raiders and the victims were forced to find refuge elsewhere. Again, the police did little to curb the violence. Police officers at Nyali told those who had received threats: 'You cannot get assistance here. Just go and organise yourselves into groups.'[19] Army and navy officers deployed to respond to the initial outbreak of violence in August were quickly called back to their barracks, and the suspected leaders of the attacks were released after having been arrested by the police. The economic effects were severe, as migrants fled and tourists stopped coming to the beaches.

Again, however, viewed from the perspective of its planners, the strategy was successful. Up to 100,000 people left the Kwale area ahead of the election, and few of the remaining migrants attempted to return to vote. As one of those refugees put it, 'Many of us heard that we would be attacked against if we dared return. So, what is of greater value, life or voting? So, we just decided to leave that matter [of voting] alone.'[20] KANU retained the three seats it had won in Kwale in the 1992 elections. As the KHRC report on the violence in Coast noted, Moi and KANU retained strong support in the province from local communities. Fear of the supremacy of Kikuyu, Kamba, Luo and Luhya migrants from elsewhere in the country outweighed any concerns many coastal voters had about Moi and his government. But the violence was not simply about winning particular seats. Instead, as the KHRC recognised, the purpose of violence was still to create a much wider sense of chaos linked to the holding of elections. This allowed Moi to continue to depict his opponents as a dangerous, destabilising force within society.[21]

'Something very wrong is happening in Kenya,' the Catholic bishops wrote in a pastoral letter at the end of August 1997. The bloodshed in Coast seemed to have triggered 'the terrible spirit of violence and cruelty which plagues our country'.[22] At the scene of some of the very first clashes in 1991 and 1992, cattle raiding and arson attacks became commonplace through September and October 1997. Villages along the boundaries between Nyanza and Rift Valley Provinces quickly became deserted. 'Nobody can afford to remain in the village because the raiders can strike any time,' said one resident of the area.[23] Although the campaign period remained more peaceful than had been the case in 1992, violence peaked significantly in the days leading up to the election. It was worst in the northern Rift Valley.

There Pokot youths, egged on by Lotodo's inflammatory speeches and ministerial protection, sought to extend their community's land hold-ings and political control. On Christmas Eve, twelve people were killed as Pokot youths attacked Marakwet homes near Tot in the Marakwet district. The justification for the attack was that two leading Marakwet figures had declared their support for the opposition. Those behind the Tot massacre hoped that voters in Marakwet would be intimidated into supporting KANU and Moi. One local clergyman bemoaned the fact that 'Pokots were expected to strike and yet no security measure was taken to stop the attack'.[24] As in 1992, violence suited the regime as it fought for its life during the election campaign.

THE ELECTION

When the country went to the polls on 29 December 1997, Moi again faced a divided opposition. Oginga Odinga's death had led to a power struggle within FORD-Kenya between the veteran leader's son Raila and Michael Kijana Wamalwa. Not only did Raila have the family name, but Wamalwa had been tainted by allegations of involvement in the Goldenberg scandal. Nevertheless, Wamalwa, a Luhya, refused to surrender control of the party, and so Raila formed his own National Development Party (NDP). FORD-Asili collapsed under the weight of bickering between its two principals, Matiba and Shikuku. Matiba even decided to boycott the presidential election altogether in protest at the government's manipulation of the process. Kibaki's DP was undermined by its decision to open talks with leading Kalenjin, Maasai, Turkana and Samburu elders over the Rift Valley violence. This left the party open to criticism that it had abandoned its Kikuyu supporters. Safina ('Ark' in Swahili), a newly formed party, was up and running just a month before the December election and suffered from considerable harassment of its leaders. These included Richard Leakey, the famous paleoanthropologist, and Paul Muite, who again was tainted by association to the Goldenberg scandal.

Not content to rely on the opposition's penchant for self-destruction, Moi set about working the electoral system in his favour. Although a body known as the Inter-Parties Parliamentary Group had been set up by Moi and the opposition parties to discuss constitutional reform that would allow for fairer elections, he successfully manipulated it to ensure its ineffectualness. The group was unable to introduce restraints on presidential power or limits on the privileges enjoyed by incumbents during election campaigns. Moi and KANU therefore had the usual range of tools open to them in their efforts to manipulate the outcome of the election. The state-owned media were again used as a propaganda tool, the police harassed opposition supporters, and the provincial administration put bureaucratic obstacles in the path of rival leaders seeking to organise rallies and membership drives. While blatant manipulation of the results of the 1997 election was less evident than in 1992, Charles Hornsby argues that the 1997 polls 'were far more chaotic administratively'.[25] As with so much other chaos in contemporary Kenya, the ultimate beneficiary was Moi.

Moi comfortably won the presidential election, with just over 40 per cent of the vote; Kibaki was second with 31 per cent. As in 1992, it is clear that, had the votes cast for the other opposition candidates been added to Kibaki's, a single candidate would have defeated Moi with ease. As it was, Raila Odinga came a distant third, followed by Wamalwa and Charity Ngilu, the Social Democratic Party candidate and the first woman to stand in a presidential election. In the parliamentary election, KANU again won a narrow majority, with 107 of the 210 seats up for grabs. While local and international observers declared themselves satisfied that the final results were acceptable, it was clear to other commentators that: 'The general election was stolen yet again!'[26] But with foreign governments reluctant to declare the elections null and void for fear of provoking instability and further violence, Kenyans had little choice but begrudgingly to accept the result and prepare for five more years of Moi and KANU.

THE AFTERMATH

Moi promised voters 'a calmer and more confident Kenya where endless confrontation no longer dominates the domestic agenda; a nation where political differences do not mean personal antagonisms'.[27] Voting in 1997, however, only worsened the already fraught situation in many parts of the country. Once the election results became known and ethnic voting patterns widely circulated, various individuals and communities set out to settle scores and punish groups seen to have been treacherous.

Violence between Kikuyu and Samburu in Laikipia began in early January. Cattle raids and arson attacks were mounted by Samburu youths. That they wore T-shirts distributed during the election campaign and emblazoned with KANU slogans left little doubt about the motives for the attacks. One Kikuyu refugee told a church group that 'the moment we refused to vote for Kariuki and President Moi, we straight away knew that clashes would come to this place'.[28] Similar scenes were witnessed at Njoro in Nakuru district. There Kikuyu youths fought back and targeted local Kalenjin households. Kikuyu-manned roadblocks were set up on the highway connecting Njoro with the town of Mau Narok, and Kalenjin travelling along the route were dragged from their vehicles and attacked. In all, more than 300 Kalenjin families were forced from their homes in Njoro during January 1998. 'This is just related to the elections,' one Kalenjin refugee told church workers who visited the refugees camped at Kiginor primary school. 'The Kikuyu are fighting because they did not want to accept that President Moi actually won the elections.'[29] More than a hundred people were killed in Njoro in the four weeks that followed Moi's victory. Despite pleas from church and opposition leaders, the violence continued in the following weeks and months.

In places where clashes had been witnessed before, local populations widely anticipated further conflict. In the absence of adequate protection by the security forces, local residents often took matters into their own hands. In Trans Nzoia, where Pokot youths had long targeted local Luhya, villages had formed vigilante groups. Following a raid on Chorlem village in the district on 27 February, local vigilantes from Chorlem and neighbouring Kapkoi tracked the Pokot raiders to a home in the area, where they found seven individuals. The raiding party surrendered but were beaten to death by the vigilantes. The incident at

Chorlem made the conflict much worse. Rather than bringing an end to the raids, vigilantism drove demands for revenge by Pokot. By early April, Lotodo and his ilk elsewhere had forced 30,000 people from their homes and had overseen the killing of more than 120 people in the period since the election. Lotodo was able to operate with impunity. Despite the two men's uncomfortable personal relationship, the president refused to listen to any claims of Lotodo's involvement in the clashes in West Pokot, Trans Nzoia and Marakwet. 'Lotodo is an innocent man who has no problem with everyone in Kenya,' the president claimed.[30]

With parts of the country beset by bitter fighting, events of the morning of 7 August 1998 led to a tragic and brief moment of national unity. At 10.30 a.m., a truck was driven into the car park at the rear of the US embassy in central Nairobi. Security guards tried their best to stop it entering the embassy compound, but its occupants opened fire on them, threw a grenade and then detonated the bomb on board. Glass and rubble rained down on the busy Haile Selassie Avenue, which runs along the southern edge of the city's central business district, and Moi Avenue, a block away from the blast site. While the embassy itself remained standing, the Ufundi building next door collapsed and others close by were severely damaged. The attack left 213 people dead, 201 of whom were Kenyans. Within days, Al Qaeda claimed responsibility. Kenyans temporarily set their own bitter divisions to one side as the country came together in grief and outrage. Such unity proved short-lived, however.

Violence resumed in the northern Rift Valley in December 1998, for instance, and claimed the lives of around 300 people in the months that followed. The ready availability of firearms made these disputes more deadly than at any previous time: in part due to ongoing conflicts elsewhere in the Horn and Great Lakes regions, by 2002 around 11,000 guns were coming onto the Kenyan black market each year. As the supply increased, so the price of firearms and ammunition fell on the black market. In 2001, Human Rights Watch found guns to be available for as little as $65.[31] The availability of cheap weapons made cattle rustling a highly profitable business. The large cattle raids witnessed in the northern Rift Valley at the end of the 1990s and the beginning of the next decade were followed 'within two to three days' by 'lorry loads of cattle . . . being transported out of the Kerio Valley'. The cattle were transported to slaughterhouses around the country, indicating that the raiders were seeking immediate cash returns, rather than putting the cattle into their own herds.

The combination of the commercialisation of cattle rustling and access to weapons was deadly. In March 2001, fifty-three Marakwet, mainly women and children, were killed by Pokot raiders at Murkutwo. The victims were attacked in revenge for a cattle raid by Marakwet youths a month earlier. As the cattle stolen were sold almost immediately after the raid, Pokot looking for vengeance were unable to reclaim their stolen livestock and so instead attacked the villagers of Murkutwo.[32] Lotodo tried to deny responsibility for such events. 'I am not a cattle rustler,' he protested. 'How can a person aged fifty-nine who has a belly engage in cattle rustling?'[33] However, in Kenya's brand of democracy, the politicians who were successful included those like Lotodo who could organise and arm private armies, mount illegal operations like cattle rustling, and force members of other ethnic groups out of their constituencies. By the final years of Moi's rule, the country had entered a constant state of insecurity.

For this, Moi's government bears ultimate responsibility. In July 1999, Justice Akiwumi released the report carried out by the judicial commission under his chairmanship into the clashes of the 1990s. Its conclusions were devastating. The report set out in detail the perpetration of violence by politicians, KANU officials, district officers, district and provincial commissioners and officers in the security forces. The report went so far as to name sixty-four individuals who deserved further investigation, including the ministers Nicholas Biwott and William Ole Ntimama, the former provincial commissioner in Coast, Wilfred Kimalat, and the ex-district commissioners of Kwale and Mombasa.[34] Every branch and level of the government was implicated in the clashes of the 1990s, but Moi's regime refused to abide by Akiwumi's recommendations. Its official response dismissed the findings of the report as being based on 'hearsay, rumour or gossip'. Moreover, the government specifically rejected the recommendations for further investigations, claiming that the commission had found no new evidence that would be sufficient to allow for prosecutions.[35]

MUNGIKI

The growth of insecurity created the conditions for the expansion of other forms of violence throughout Kenyan society. Justus Ogembo, an anthropologist who has examined a spate of murders of people believed to be witches in Kisii in the early 1990s, argues that, with the start of the clashes, 'law and order broke down and gave the people the opportunity to gratify their long-held fears and hatreds'.[36] This Hobbesian vision was partly true: by instigating and perpetuating the violence, and then refusing to punish the perpetrators, the government legitimised violence more generally as a means of settling all sorts of political, social and economic grievances. But besides 'long-held fears and hatreds', new grievances emerged in an era of supposedly free and fair elections and markets.

Through conditional aid packages in the late 1980s and early 1990s, the IMF, World Bank and foreign donors had set about encouraging the Kenyan government to implement reforms intended to boost economic growth. Kenya's combination of fast population growth and a stagnant economy needed urgent attention. The IMF believed that 500,000 jobs needed to be created each year if school leavers were to be absorbed into the workforce. Moreover, the economy needed to grow by up to 8 per cent per annum for a full decade if unemployment was to fall by just 5 per cent over that whole period. The foreign experts identified expanding exports of agricultural and horticultural products as the engine for this much-needed growth. Regulations and bodies that allowed the government control over a wide range of activities within the rural economy were relaxed and the production of export crops, such as flowers and vegetables, was encouraged. Although some benefited a great deal, for many this was a difficult time. The balance of trade actually worsened, external debt increased and growth slowed.[37] The liberalisation of the rural economy also produced unexpected outcomes beyond the sphere of economics.

In Kibaki's Nyeri district, coffee farmers had a traumatic experience of the new economic order. The late 1990s was a hard time for the producers of one of Kenya's key export crops and the mainstay of the local economy. Inclement weather, an outbreak of the coffee berry disease and a widespread infestation of army worms led to a significant drop in production between 1997 and 1999. The political and economic climates were no kinder. Local coffee cooperatives had, until 1996, been directly controlled by government through the commissioner of cooperatives. As part of the economic reforms carried out in accordance with the structural adjustment programme, the cooperatives became self-governing. Such reforms did not, however, result in any great benefit to either producers or consumers of coffee from Nyeri. Instead, output levels fell, the quality of the crop declined, and the revenues of farmers shrank.

Without alternative sources of income, small farmers felt these negative effects particularly keenly, and so agitated for reform of the cooperatives, which they felt were run for the benefit of larger farmers. The small farmers wanted to negotiate a deal with the Thika Coffee Mills, but the larger farmers in control of the cooperatives preferred the existing arrangements with the Kenya Planters' Cooperative Union. According to Kiraitu Murungi, this was 'a liberation struggle between the exploiters and the exploited; between the oppressive coffee elite, and the oppressed coffee farmers who are seeking to remove the robbers from their backs'.[38] As the dispute escalated through 1999, rival farmers stormed production facilities: one person was killed and many injured. The dispute, which became known locally as the 'coffee war', had significant indirect effects, too, as declining revenues from coffee in the wake of the dispute led to a drop in household incomes and therefore school enrolment across Nyeri. By 2000, the effects of the crisis, coupled with sustained drought, resulted in a significant shortage of food in Nyeri and elsewhere in Central Province. In Nyeri and its neighbouring district, Nyandarua, 250,000 people were thought to be in need of emergency aid.

From the very beginning, Kibaki, the MP for Othaya in Nyeri, and other leading politicians in the district were embroiled in the dispute. While sympathetic to complaints about the failings of the existing management of the coffee cooperatives, Kibaki and most of the Nyeri MPs from his DP spoke out against the small farmers. Kibaki was fortunate that any semblance of redistributive politics had long since disappeared from the national debates. His poorer constituents in Othaya did not let the opposition leader's stance on the coffee wars influence their voting habits: they had little choice but to continue to support Kibaki and his fellow elite politicians. However, the poor of Nyeri and many other Kikuyu sought to make their economic grievances and political disillusionment clear in other ways, outside the realm of formal electoral politics.

Their urban counterparts reached a similar conclusion. The era of structural adjustment was a difficult one for the poor in the cities – indeed even more so than in the countryside. Food prices rose in response to both the lifting of fixed prices paid for agricultural goods and poor policy decisions. Household budgets were also stretched by the introduction of fees for basic medical and education services. Corruption and spending cuts in local and national government further hampered the delivery of basic essential services, such as water, electricity, policing and rubbish disposal. Even as the cost of living rose, the inhabitants of Nairobi and the other major cities in the country found it ever harder to find work, as public sector employment was slashed. As the legitimate functions of local authorities and national government withered away, other actors stepped into the resulting vacuum.

Having abandoned hope that Moi's regime or the World Bank could provide the means for prosperity, many Kenyans turned instead to Pentecostalism. It was not hard to find: Pentecostal churches took over almost every public space in towns and cities for daily prayer meetings, Sunday services and regular mass revival events led by American or Nigerian celebrity pastors. Pentecostal churches were also founded at an astonishing rate in rural areas, and religious broadcasting took up a good deal of the newly liberalised radio and television spectrums. The

Pentecostal message spread throughout Kenyan society due to the accompanying rise in the popularity of gospel music.

To take the words of Stephen Ellis and Gerrie ter Haar about the place of religion within contemporary African politics more generally, Pentecostal churches provided one of the main ways in which Kenyans could talk about 'a world in which power is seen as being too often an instrument of evil people who use it to destroy peace and harmony'.[39] According to their message, the churches provided their congregations with a mechanism to improve their lives. 'Use your mouth to confess prosperity, wealth and abundance', Pius Muiru, the founder of the Maximum Miracle Centre, one of Nairobi's largest Pentecostal churches, told his congregation. 'Let your mouth become the gateway to your destiny. Think rich.'[40] While church members were not necessarily wealthy, the message of many preachers was 'unashamedly about victory, success, and achievement, with health and finance prominent'.[41]

The rise of Pentecostalism, as James Smith observes, was also marked by a particular concern for the occult and the figure of the devil: 'Demons pervade everything, whether people realize it or not, and any kind of economic progress, individual or social, requires that they be expunged.'[42] The ability of the wealthy to continue to increase their riches even as the country got poorer led many to ask how wealth was really accumulated. Kenyans also questioned how it was that an unpopular incumbent regime could remain in power, despite the introduction of multiparty elections that were supposed to have made politics more transparent and accountable. Pentecostalism and its ideas about devils and demons provided compelling answers that ideas of democratisation, development and human rights could not. As one writer put it in her account of a vision in 2000, the devil was at 'State House [the president's official residence] and it is eating the nation and His Church'.[43] Pentecostalism's message of aspiration and accumulation did not appeal to all, of course. But those who felt unable to even dream of wealth had their own ways of speaking about the state of politics and society in Moi's Kenya.

In rural and urban areas of the Central Highlands, young disenfranchised Kikuyu joined the group known as Mungiki ('the multitude' in

Kikuyu) in great numbers during the 1990s and early 2000s. Mungiki began as a rural commune at Gitwamba in Baringo district in 1985. According to one of its founder members, Maina Njenga, it was formed 'when a number of people, me among them, saw visions by which we were commanded by a divine power to call upon the Kikuyu and all Africans to go back to their roots'. As Njenga told a journalist in 1998:

> I was a student at Jomo Kenyatta High [in Nakuru] when I saw the vision. God was calling upon us to forsake the ways of the white man. He was saying that we had sinned against him by rejecting all the values that always held us together. This is why we are suffering.[44]

Through its initial emphasis on indigenous religious beliefs and an assertion of independence from Western cultural values, Mungiki represented an appeal to ethnic unity that many Kikuyu felt would lead to the restoration of their control over positions of power. Mungiki members were, in the words of one of its leaders in Thika, 'the true sons of the Mau Mau'.[45]

Mungiki became infamous for its support of the controversial practices of oathing and female circumcision (now commonly referred to as 'female genital cutting'). Such practices were out of step with prevailing religious attitudes by the 1990s, given that the evangelisation of Kenya was now all but complete. Matu Wamae, an MP in Nyeri, denounced Mungiki as 'retrogressive, dangerous and backward. It is taking the people of Central Province back to practices that they abandoned 40 years ago.'[46] However, Mungiki's cultural politics have proved chameleonic. Besides its commitment to indigenous religious beliefs, the group's leaders and followers have also experimented with Islam and, more recently, Pentecostalism. Nevertheless, once the group and its practices entered the public eye in 1997 with a court case that led to the jailing of fifty-seven of its members, the stereotypical image of Mungiki followers being snuff-using, dreadlocked Kikuyu traditionalists entered the public consciousness.

Mungiki was not rooted in the past, but instead was a product of the troubled present. It was a response to social divisions within Kikuyu society and the failure of elite Kikuyu politicians to do much about those inequalities. 'We have a duty to mobilise and bring economical, political and social changes in society so that the masses can control their destiny,' asserted Ndura Waruinge, the group's national coordinator, in 2000.[47] Maina Njenga saw the group as providing a voice for the demands of the poor 'for good governance to attain justice and prosperity'. Njenga spoke out against unemployment: 'You can't have peace when people are jobless . . . You can't have peace when you demolish shanties without giving people an alternative.'[48] This appeal to poor Kikuyu was matched only by the power of Mungiki's calls for ethnic unity.

Across the country, multiparty elections and the violence of the 1990s drove an upsurge in ethnic sentiments. Mungiki represented itself as an expression of Kikuyu unity in the face of the threat from Kalenjin in the Rift Valley. Local pockets of Mungiki activists were involved in the formation of vigilante groups to protect Kikuyu families during the clashes of the 1990s. Its ranks were then swelled by displaced Kikuyu, forced by the violence to take up residence in the eastern Rift Valley, Central Province and Nairobi. George Nyanja, an MP for Raila Odinga's NDP, told one television news programme: 'Why I support Mungiki is that I have been told the objective is to unite the Kikuyu people.' Many Kikuyu shared Nyanja's belief that this 'is a noble idea'.[49]

Mungiki was not just a product of the ethnic substance of politics in the 1990s; it was also an outcome of the increasing role of militias in political contests. The violence and insecurity that accompanied the 1992 and 1997 elections meant that groups like Mungiki existed in every town and city. Politicians sponsored private armies and militias for self-protection and to attack rivals – the Baghdad Boys, for instance, provided security for Luo political leaders in Kisumu throughout the multiparty era. A number of Kikuyu MPs attempted to use Mungiki in a similar fashion. In return for providing these services and enjoying the protection of powerful political patrons, Mungiki was able to expand the scope of its operations and acted first and foremost as a criminal gang.

Gangs had become a fact of life in Nairobi and its satellite towns as law and order diminished through the 1980s and 1990s. While jobs, welfare and affordable sanitary housing were in short supply, guns were easily available. One survey estimated that there were around 5,000 illegal firearms in the city by 2001.[50] Much gang activity centred on public transport networks plied by private minibuses. As policing became less and less effective, gang members established protection rackets along major routes and in the termini dotted around the city. In 2001, any new owner wishing to operate a minibus had to pay a fee of between Ksh.30,000 and Ksh.80,000 ($430–$1,150) to whichever gang controlled the route on which the vehicle was to operate. The start-up fee was only the beginning of the extortion. Peter Gashogu owned a vehicle that operated on one of the commuter routes. He described how 'City routes have been hijacked by strangers who have established turf where minibus operators are blackmailed to part with huge sums of money.' Once the minibuses had left the relative safety of the city centre, 'groups of untidy young men station themselves in strategic places where minibuses pick [up] and drop commuters'. Drivers and conductors would then be forced to hand over Ksh.5 ($0.07) per passenger or face the consequences.[51] With fares costing perhaps just Ksh.40 ($0.60) on such routes, the effects of this extortion were devastating for owners and their crews.

Turning to the police was pointless. Corrupt to the point of becoming indistinguishable from the criminals, the police were indifferent to the plight of the minibus owners. Gashogu complained that: 'If we go to the police, they offer no assistance. In fact the police force is part of the problem we have to face daily.'[52] Police roadblocks, ostensibly erected to help prevent the operation of gangs and other criminals, were nothing but unofficial toll booths, as commuter vehicles paid further fees to the officers in order to proceed without being issued with a ticket for some minor misdemeanour.

The gangs were unrepentant. 'We earn an honest living and we have every right to operate on this stage', said Joseph Obok, a gang leader in

Githurai. 'Being jobless youth, we got tired of staying idle all day and decided to come here and eke out a living for ourselves.'[53] Obok belonged to Kamjesh, the dominant gang controlling many of the minibus routes. Kamjesh's returns from this business attracted envy from Mungiki members, who from 1998 attempted to seize control of the protection rackets from Kamjesh, one neighbourhood at a time. For nearly two months from September 2001, for instance, Mungiki and Kamjesh engaged in a bloody gang war for control of minibus routes in Dandora. 'Gangsters are slaughtering our people like chickens and police are taking no action!' complained a representative of the Dandora minibus owners.[54] Seventeen people were killed as the two groups repeatedly clashed in the streets. Throughout Dandora and adjacent neighbourhoods, crime and violence soared during the weeks of the gang war. With the backing of its political patrons, and able to call on seemingly inexhaustible support from youths from the nearby informal settlement of Mathare and elsewhere in the city, Mungiki emerged victorious.[55]

Having won control of Dandora, Ndura Waruinge publicly announced that Mungiki would move on to seize control of all Nairobi's major commuter routes. Recognising that resistance was futile and that the authorities were not going to intervene, minibus owners began to seek their own accommodations with Mungiki. For example, a delegation representing the owners of minibuses operating from Nairobi, through Thika town and then on to Murang'a, held a meeting with Mungiki leaders in a Nairobi hotel in November 2001 to negotiate terms. The owners of the 200 or so vehicles agreed to pay Ksh.500 ($7.00) per minibus per day to Mungiki in return for the group's protection. Similar deals were struck with owners on other routes within the city and on those connecting the city to Mount Kenya region and the eastern Rift Valley. Throughout this area of the country, perhaps 500 minibus stages were now under the control of Mungiki.

The profitability of this exercise drew attention to Mungiki's increasing economic clout. Speaking on a Sunday morning news programme shortly after the end of the Dandora minibus war, Waruinge claimed that the group had accumulated over Ksh. 800 million

($11.5 million) in subscription fees from its membership base alone. He went on to assert that Mungiki now had over four million members. Whether or not the figures were accurate, it is unquestionable that Mungiki had emerged as a shadow state in Nairobi and its surrounding area.

As Waruinge's announcement on national television suggested, Mungiki's leaders were no longer concerned with maintaining even the slightest semblance of legality or worried about publicising its activities. Although police operations were periodically mounted against the gangs, such efforts were ineffective, suspects were commonly released quickly, and little effort was made to arrest the gang leaders. 'Has the Government given up on the maintenance of law and order and allowed Mungiki to reign without any intervention?' Eric Gor Sungu, the opposition MP for Kisumu town, asked in parliament.[56] As John Githongo remarked in his newspaper column: 'There is clearly more to Mungiki than meets the eye.'[57] Mungiki's place in the puzzle of Kenyan politics became easier to understand once Moi's intentions for the end of his term in office became clear.

Under the revisions made to the constitution when multiparty politics resumed, term limits were imposed on the presidency. Future presidents were to be restricted to two terms of four years, but this provision was not retrospective. Thus Moi was able to serve two further terms in office. By 2002, however, his time was up. Although he was at first unwilling to nominate a successor, it became clear in 2001 and 2002 that his preferred choice was Uhuru Kenyatta, the son of the first president. This was a position supported by Mungiki's leaders. 'We would rather vote President Moi and KANU back to power than the doomed opposition alliance,' Waruinge told the press in March 2002.[58]

Moi was not particularly concerned with winning Mungiki's endorsement for Kenyatta, however. Of far greater importance was the gang's contribution to the more widespread state of insecurity that Moi and his supporters had worked so hard to create through the 1990s in their efforts to discredit the electoral system. Moreover, Mungiki was a challenge to elite Kikuyu politicians at the head of the opposition. Within Kikuyu society – so those in government thought – Mungiki offered the potential to divide voters along class lines, as the poorer sections of the community turned to the gang rather than to elite politicians in their search for solutions to the many problems they faced in daily life. To other Kenyans, it was depicted as yet another example of a presumed Kikuyu tendency to embark on violence in order to grab power. This played on memories of Mau Mau, the oathing controversy of 1969 and the efforts made by Mungai to block Moi's succession in 1978. The net effect, Mungiki's invisible patrons hoped, was to damage the electoral strength of figures like Kibaki. And even if Moi ran out of patience with Mungiki, the group had insurance: Waruinge claimed in November 2001 that Mungiki had more than 7,500 police officers in its ranks.

Free to expand its operations without much police interference, Mungiki did so. As well as the minibus sector, the group sought to exploit other key urban services that had been abandoned by the municipal authorities. Of greatest significance was Mungiki's vigilantism, which replaced long-forgotten local policing. The gang ruled its neighbourhoods through fear. On 1 February 2002, for example, four people were killed by more than forty gang members in the Kibarage informal settlement of Dandora. The homes of the four victims were apparently selected at random, and the male head of the household ordered out of the house and then killed. Mungiki members knocked on the door of Celestine Ogunja and demanded that her husband come out. Ogunja was a widow, however, and so the gangsters instead went next door and ordered her neighbour outside. 'I warned him to not go outside but he did not heed my advice and they killed him in cold blood,' Ogunja recalled.[59] As day broke the following morning, hundreds of residents fled Kibarage. In towns with large Kikuyu populations throughout the Central Highlands, local residents began forming vigilante groups to protect themselves, their homes and their businesses from burglaries and other criminal acts carried out by Mungiki members.

Clashes between these vigilantes and the gangs soon became commonplace. In the Kariobangi neighbourhood of Nairobi, the local vigilante group was known as the 'Taliban'. In the early hours of 2 March the Taliban was patrolling the marketplace in Kariobangi. They came across Mungiki members boarding vehicles to take them to a ceremony to be held later that day in Nyandarua. Fighting broke out between the two groups and three people were killed, including two Mungiki members. At half past eight the following evening, a large number of Mungiki members were taken by lorry into Kariobangi and dropped off along the busy Kamunde Road. Josephat Kinuthia watched from his apartment window as the gang members exacted revenge for the death of their comrades the previous night: 'I saw very many people, numbering about 300. They all menacingly brandished pangas [machetes] and pick axes as they went about their orgy. It was a terrifying sight to watch people being hacked to death.'[60] Most of those killed were Luo, who, with Luhya and Somali, made up the bulk of the 50,000 or so residents of Kariobangi. As one witness, Steve Otieno, recalled: 'I overheard them asking for their victims' identity cards and what tribe they came from. Sometimes they did not wait long for one to say his name or flash an ID card. They just attacked.'[61] In about thirty minutes of violence, the Mungiki members killed twenty-three people and seriously wounded twenty-eight. Many of the bodies were mutilated by the Mungiki men before they disappeared down side roads.

Moi was insistent that the government was not to blame for the Kariobangi massacre. Placing responsibility for the attack squarely on the police, he stated: 'I don't want to hear that anyone has been hurt because KANU has the power.'[62] The group and another seventeen like it were explicitly outlawed, and Waruinge and David Mwenje, the Embakasi MP and one of Mungiki's patrons, were both arrested, along with many other rank-and-file members. The crackdown against Mungiki lasted just a few days, however. Waruinge and Mwenje were both quickly released from custody and gang members carried on their activities in the city and throughout the Central Highlands.

THE LOGIC OF DISORDER AND CORRUPTION

In August 2002, the country looked ahead with fear to the impending election. Wanyiri Kihoro, the MP for Nyeri town and a former political prisoner, demanded that the president make sure Mungiki 'are kept off the streets'. He went on: 'President Moi has a duty in the twilight of his presidency to steer this country away from chaos and disorder so that he can have his retirement in peace.'[63] As Kihoro knew all too well from his days in Nyayo House, Moi and his supporters were prepared to go to any lengths to remain in power. 'Nobody prefers violence,' a police spokesman said after a weekend of clashes in Thika between Mungiki members and the police in 2001.[64] He was wrong: Moi for one preferred violence. In their race to the bottom, the president and his allies dragged the country down with them.

Corruption and insecurity soared at the cost of Kenya's democracy and economy. From the top to the bottom of society, those that thrived in Moi's final decade in power were the agents of disorder, who built their political powerbases, economic wealth and social status on their ability to manage and exploit the conditions of violence and criminality. Thuggery, the management of private militias and the ability to distribute the spoils of office around networks of clients became essential parts of the political system. Even as donor-funded civil society activism and press freedom grew by the day, there was little room within formal politics for those with alternative visions of politics, based upon reason, peaceful debate and negotiation.

Those that set out to draw attention to the abuses of power by the country's leaders continued to be harassed. Wangari Maathai, for instance, kept up her fearless campaign against land-grabbing throughout the 1990s. Her opposition to private development of the Karura Forest on Nairobi's outskirts led again to her being beaten up by state security officers and ridiculed by the president. Others paid a higher price. Father John Kaiser, the American Catholic priest we met in the previous chapter, had proved a courageous critic of the government during the clashes of the 1990s. In 1999 he testified to the judicial inquiry into the violence and implicated several leading government figures in the organisation of the bloodshed. The following year, Kaiser championed the case of Florence Mpayei, who alleged she had been raped by Julius Sunkuli, a cabinet minister. On 24 August, Kaiser's body was found close to the Nakuru–Naivasha highway in the Rift Valley. He had apparently been murdered, despite the claims of the government. The situation was dire. 'Kenya faces its severest crisis ever,' the opposition MP James Orengo wrote that month. 'Total collapse is now a real possibility.'[65] It is unsurprising, then, that so many Kenyans came to believe that the only hope for the rebirth of their country lay in the fall of KANU and Moi.

CHAPTER EIGHT

NOTHING ACTUALLY REALLY CHANGED, 2002–11

When you rattle a snake you must be ready to be bitten.

John Michuki, minister for internal security, 2 March 2006[1]

THE SUCCESSION

Less than a week after the Kariobangi massacre of early March 2002, Moi held a rally in the neighbourhood. He used the event to anoint a group of the so-called 'Young Turks' within KANU's leadership as the pool of candidates to succeed him after his retirement at the election later in the year. Moi paraded Musalia Mudavadi, Raila Odinga, Uhuru Kenyatta and William Ruto on the dais. In front of the large crowd at the rally, Moi turned to each and asked: 'If I leave for you [the] leadership, will you kill? Will you protect the country? Properly?'[2] Six years later, all of Moi's anointed successors stood accused of participating in the violence that engulfed the country from the final days of 2007 to the end of February 2008. While none in fact did succeed him, Moi did at least identify some of the men who would shape politics in the decade that followed. Of the four, Odinga, Kenyatta and Ruto, in particular, joined Mwai Kibaki in dominating the political stage up to the present. Along with Kibaki, Moi's men of the future helped keep Kenya stuck in its past.

Of this group of leaders, Kibaki and Odinga were the best known in 2002. Both had stood as presidential candidates in 1997, and it was clear that Kibaki would be one of the main contenders in the forthcoming election. He had remained steadfast in his appeal to Kikuyu conservatism, but Odinga's politics had undergone significant change in the period since he first stepped into the public eye in the early 1980s. A more imposing figure than his father, Raila shared the older man's skills as a public speaker. His political agenda by 2002 owed something to his father, too, though it was in many respects quite different. He had, it is true, inherited his father's mantle as the leading Luo figure, but had jettisoned the radicalism. Kenya after the Cold War, structural adjustment, Moi and Kenyatta was no place for ideological discussions of redistribution.

Nevertheless, Odinga's radical past was too attractive for his rivals to ignore. His family ties, education in East Germany and links to the 1982 coup were frequently offered up as evidence of his unsuitability for power. Kalonzo Musyoka, for instance, later warned US diplomats that Odinga would be 'another Chavez' if he got into power.[3] Although this had been meant as a derogatory remark, Odinga was flattered by such comparisons. Despite frequent claims to be the representative of the youth and the marginalised, he lacked all the political conviction and ideological substance of the Venezuelan leader. He failed to escape his dependence on his Luo support base, and his politics were as pragmatic as those of any other politician. Despite his father's experience, and having been a political prisoner himself, Odinga merged his NDP with KANU in March 2002 in the hope of winning the party's presidential nomination in return for delivering the Luo vote.

William Ruto stood on the stage at Kariobangi much more as the inheritor of Moi's leadership of the Kalenjin than as a potential presidential candidate in 2002. He had emerged as a significant figure within Rift Valley politics in the previous decade. He first came to public attention as a leader of the YK'92 group of KANU activists ahead of the first multiparty election. As we saw above, this group was alleged at the time to have been responsible for the harassment of opposition candidates and their supporters, and for the perpetration of ethnic violence. The experience served Ruto well and provided a platform for a successful bid to win his local parliamentary seat in Eldoret in 1997. Once in parliament, he was rapidly promoted through the government and was appointed minister for home affairs in August 2002. Controversy continued to dog him, however. He was later accused of participating in illegal land transactions in 2001, and court proceedings were continuing at the time this book went to press.[4]

Ruto's appeal to voters in the Rift Valley was built on two planks. The first was an unashamed ethnocentrism: he deliberately set out to portray himself as the defender of Kalenjin interests once Moi passed from the scene. The second was his claim, based solely on his age, to be an instinctive champion of the marginalised youth (he had been born in 1966, compared to Kibaki in 1931 and Odinga in 1945). Ruto cited the two themes of ethnicity and generation in justifying his support for Uhuru Kenyatta as Moi's successor. He played on and encouraged Kalenjin fears of retribution and isolation in the wake of Moi's retirement. A pact with the Kikuyu and support for Kenyatta would, Ruto argued, protect Kalenjin after 2002 if Kenyatta won the election.[5] Kenyatta's relative youth – he was forty-one years old in 2002 – was used by Ruto as further evidence of the suitability of the first president's son to become the third.

Ruto was careful to follow Moi's lead at this stage. The outgoing president remained the undisputed Kalenjin leader, and his younger colleague had no desire to isolate himself from mainstream opinion in the Rift Valley. Moi, as we saw in the previous chapter, had made no secret of the fact that he favoured Kenyatta as his successor. Indeed, Moi's enthusiasm seemed to exceed Kenyatta's own willingness to be a political leader. With the exception of Beth Mugo, Uhuru's cousin, most of the extended Kenyatta family had stayed out of politics after Jomo's death in 1978. Uhuru, the second of Jomo and Mama Ngina's four children, seemed set to follow suit. He busied himself with the family's vast business interests until 1997, but then, with Moi's encouragement, he stood for election in his local parliamentary constituency. Despite the family name and the backing of the president, he suffered a humiliating defeat in that election. Moi did not lose interest, however.

Kenyatta was appointed to head up the state-run tourist board as a consolation for his election defeat, before entering parliament as a nominated MP in 2001. Project Uhuru, as the succession campaign became known, gathered pace soon afterwards. Moi's strategy was obvious to all. He hoped that Kenyatta would divide the Kikuyu vote, thus weakening Kibaki's support. But Moi also expected the opposition to be divided again anyway, meaning that the successful candidate would only have to win perhaps a third of the votes. With the outgoing president's endorsement sufficient for Kenyatta to win KANU's power-base of the Rift Valley, a decent share of the Kikuyu vote would likely be enough to see Uhuru home if faced with several opponents.

Many in KANU had their doubts about the wisdom of having Kenyatta on the presidential ticket. However, while he remained in office, Moi's opinion was supreme. On 14 October 2002, then, KANU delegates from across the country gathered at the Kasarani sports complex in northern Nairobi to witness Kenyatta's coronation. More than 4,500 delegates filled the indoor arena. The building shook to their chants of 'Uhuru na Kazi' ('Freedom and Work'), the party's slogan since independence but now a particularly apposite one. Accepting the party's nomination, Kenyatta assured the delegates that 'I intend to serve you, the party and this great nation with devotion, discipline, vigour, courage and undivided loyalty.'[6] Few of his rivals were present to hear his acceptance speech, however. Moi's strategy had backfired, instead dividing the ruling party and unifying the opposition.

Once it became clear that Moi was steadfast in his support for Kenyatta, several leading figures from within KANU began talks with the opposition parties. KANU loyalists who had declared in public their desire to be the presidential candidate, such as the vice president, George Saitoti, and the minister for foreign affairs, Kalonzo Musyoka, were humiliated by Moi's actions. They also recognised that Kenyatta was unlikely to win the presidential election. They therefore sought out the most likely victor, in order to maintain their positions of influence. This was characteristic of the two men; the US ambassador's later description of Musyoka as 'an opportunist interested primarily in advancing his political ambitions' had long applied.[7] Odinga was no less an opportunist and no less slighted by Kenyatta's nomination. Unlike Musyoka and Saitoti, however, Odinga was not tarnished by a long career in KANU or by alleged involvement in the worst incidents of corruption and ethnic violence. The merger between his NDP and KANU was a short-lived affair. Between the start of the arrangement in March 2002 and its collapse in October, Odinga had little time to become tainted by association, and he remained a credible presidential candidate.

As Odinga began talks with other opposition leaders, careful negotiation was necessary in order to avoid the self-defeating divisions of 1992 and 1997. After extended private discussions, Odinga and Kibaki struck a deal. The Nyeri man would stand as the undisputed presidential candidate of a united opposition coalition, but would serve only one term. Ongoing discussions about constitutional reform would, it was agreed, be hurried to a conclusion within three months, in order to create a new post of prime minister for Odinga. Odinga's supporters were also promised half the seats in cabinet. With that, the National Rainbow Coalition (NARC) was formed. On the day of the Kenyatta nomination, KANU's defectors joined other opposition leaders on a stage at Uhuru Park in the city centre. To the cheers of spectators, Odinga declared 'Kibaki *tosha*' – literally 'Kibaki is enough', but meaning 'Kibaki is the one'. With those words, Moi's mystique and seemingly unshakable grip on Kenya was broken. 'The whole country, it seemed, woke up and decided to take things into our own hands,' recalls Binyavanga Wainaina, a leading figure in a new generation of writers and intellectuals. 'In one day, Moi's 24 years of power started to crumble.'[8]

THE SECOND LIBERATION

Come election day in December, NARC was a formidable force. Each of the main ethnic groups and regions was represented in the coalition's leadership, with the exception of the Kalenjin, who remained in line behind KANU and Moi. The breadth and unity of the opposition movement convinced many that NARC represented an opportunity for real change, and the likelihood of victory dissuaded its leading members from breaking into competing factions. NARC demolished the weary cynicism many Kenyans felt towards their political system after a decade of democracy without change. 'Everywhere I went, I heard the same words,' Wainaina recalled. 'Roads. A new constitution. Taps. Water. Electricity. Education. The usual tribal chauvinism and crude political sycophancy vanished.'[9] Not even the terror attacks on a Mombasa hotel, which killed thirteen people, and the simultaneous attempt to shoot down an Israeli passenger jet on 28 November, could derail the campaign. Nor could the serious injuries sustained by Kibaki in a car accident in early December, after which Odinga ran NARC's campaign in the final weeks running up to voting.

The result of the election was overwhelming. Kibaki won nearly two-thirds of the votes cast in the presidential election and NARC's constituent parties took 132 of the 222 seats in parliament. There was no scope for KANU to dispute the results or for Moi to stage a last-ditch effort to hold on to power. For once, polling was relatively peaceful.

Once the results were announced, however, such matters were far from the minds of NARC's supporters. The hundreds of thousands of people who flocked to Uhuru Park on 30 December to witness Kibaki's swearing-in were overjoyed at the result. Despite still being restricted to a wheelchair while he recovered from the injuries sustained in his car crash, the new president addressed the crowd. He promised that he would not dash the hopes of the country, which saw NARC's victory as a national rebirth: 'NARC will never die as long as the original vision endures. It will grow stronger and coalesce into a single party that will become a beacon of hope not only to Kenyans but to the rest of Africa.'[10] Those watching the ceremony on televisions in homes and bars around the country were overjoyed. In Kericho, Joseph Odhimbo announced 'Our frustrations have come to an end.' In Kibaki's home town of Othaya, his supporters ceremonially smashed one of the ubiquitous portraits of Moi that hung in every place of work and every public building. Across the rest of the country, the old portraits of Moi were taken down quickly and replaced with the smiling face of the third president.[11]

Ruth Odari watched Kibaki's inauguration from her home in Kisumu. As she told *The Nation*: 'We have what we asked for. I would like to ask [NARC] to live up to the promise of providing free primary education and to revive the economy.'[12] Her wish was granted almost immediately, with an announcement of the abandonment of fees in state-run primary schools. When the new school year began in January, primary schools were deluged with 1.3 million new pupils seeking to take advantage of free education. Although it led to over-crowded classrooms and greater strain on other school resources, the policy was very popular.

The new government's energetic attempt to put right many of the problems it had inherited impressed commentators. 'We have been very encouraged by what we have seen in the last two months', Gary Quince, the head of the European Union's diplomatic mission in Nairobi, stated in March. Moribund marketing boards for agricultural produce and other state-run enterprises were reinvigorated as Moi's clients were shown the door and replaced by eager new appointees. 'The main theme of the new leadership is economic recovery and investment is key to that', the head of one local economic think-tank said. A wave of redundancies swept through the judiciary and senior ranks of the civil service in the name of anti-corruption. The anti-corruption campaigner and journalist John Githongo was appointed to head up the anti-corruption drive within the government. 'The government is more decent, capable and public minded,' argued Mwalimu Mati, a senior figure in the local office of Transparency International.[13] Beyond the sphere of formal politics, it also seemed that things really had changed. Under the new dispensation, the already vigorous press blossomed and cultural activities of all sorts soared. The non-profit sector experienced a boom, too. As one study of the sector put it in 2007, 'using anecdotal estimation, there are well over one million non-profits in Kenya'.[14] The extent of public debate of politics in a variety of settings and forms was unprecedented. The Institute for Education in Democracy, a Nairobi-based organisation, argued that Kenyan politics were now built on 'solid democratic principles' and 'the democratic space has greatly expanded since 1997'.[15]

The new cabinet bolstered NARC's nationwide appeal. Each province and all major ethnic groups were represented by at least one cabinet minister. The near-universal support that the NARC government enjoyed in early 2003 soon showed signs of stress, however. For one thing, the health of the elderly president was a cause for concern. He was rumoured to have suffered strokes while in office, absent from public events for extended periods of time, and prone to slurring his way through speeches; it was not always clear who was running the country. The secrecy surrounding the death of the vice president, Michael Wamalwa, did not help either. He died in a London hospital in August 2003, most likely of an AIDS-related condition, but right up until his death Kenyans were assured that all was well. More seriously, opposition to the government first emerged in relation to anti-corruption measures. The forced resignations of civil servants and judges were regarded among Moi's Kalenjin as vindictive acts by a Kikuyu president. 'How are Kenyans expected to respect the government if it continues to undo good things of a legitimate government?' asked Musa Sirma, the MP for Eldama Ravine in the Rift Valley. 'We are demanding fairness in whatever is being done in this nation.'[16] The government soon gave other Kenyans good reason to doubt its competence and honesty. In Parselelo Kantai's acclaimed short story based on this moment in recent Kenyan political history, the metaphor of pungent fish is a recurring trope. By the end, 'the stench of rotting fish is everywhere now'.[17] The metaphor was apposite.

VOMITING ON THEIR SHOES

For all the rhetorical boasts of change and reform, the new government was unwilling to fundamentally address corruption. A devastating report commissioned from the Kroll risk consultancy group and delivered in April 2004 sat on the shelf until it was leaked three years later. The report alleged that Moi, his relatives and key supporters, including Biwott, had looted the Kenyan economy to the tune of nearly $2 billion.[18] Despite its own initial optimism, Transparency International thought the government's anti-corruption strategy 'is not taken very seriously'.[19] Behind the scenes, the newly appointed ministers and their supporters had quickly eased themselves into positions at the top of corruption networks. The apparent hypocrisy of the government, whose ministers continued to attack Moi's regime for its corruption, angered many in KANU. 'Some people are now shy to talk about the present graft but are happy to talk about the past,' said the KANU MP Maoka Maore in April 2004.[20] Maore and other MPs were concerned about emerging details of inflated deals struck with companies for various goods and services related to immigration and defence.

The press picked up the scent. In the months that followed, the public learned of a series of suspect deals involving huge sums of public money paid to fictitious companies, including Anglo Leasing (Anglo Fleecing, as it became popularly known). By July, the government's anti-corruption policies were widely recognised to be in tatters. The British high commissioner, Edward Clay, denounced the 'gigantic looting spree' that was under way. After claiming that corruption accounted for around 8 per cent of Kenya's GDP, Clay proceeded to condemn Kibaki's ministers, who 'have the arrogance, greed and perhaps a desperate sense of panic to lead them to eat like gluttons'. This gluttony caused ministers, Clay claimed, 'to vomit all over our shoes'.[21] The scandal was poisoning Kenya's diplomatic relations with donor governments, but also relationships within the government.

While journalists, MPs and foreign diplomats asked searching questions about the extent of the Anglo Leasing scandal, John Githongo was busy conducting internal inquiries within the government. When appointed, his connections to both civil society groups and the Kikuyu elite in NARC seemed to make him the ideal candidate to lead the drive against corruption. Githongo's subsequent travails have been well documented in Michela Wrong's excellent book on the scandal, but are worth briefly revisiting here.[22] He first became aware of the Anglo Leasing affair in early March 2004. In the weeks that followed, he and his staff steadily unpicked the tangled threads of various different bogus contracts and kept senior ministers and Kibaki informed of their progress. From the very start, Githongo was aware of the political implications of the scandal. He quickly assembled evidence of the involvement of senior ministers and civil servants in the scandal, including Vice President Moody Awori, Justice Minister Kiraitu Murungi and Defence Minister Chris Murungaru. Those individuals soon began their efforts to derail Githongo's investigations. On 10 May, Murungi warned him to make sure his inquiries did not 'knock out key political people'. The likes of Awori and Murungaru were, the justice minister claimed, 'key players at the very heart of government'. A week later Githongo began to receive threats to his personal security.

In Githongo's account of his conversations with the principal actors in the affair, their frankness is startling. Murungi described to Githongo how Anglo Leasing was being used to provide the resources needed to fight the next election, due in 2007. But it is also clear that the scandal was at least as much about the financiers of mega-corruption forming new relationships (and renewing acquaintances) with the new NARC government. Instead of the transition of 2002 bringing about real change, it provided an opportunity for the same shadowy figures as were behind Goldenberg and a whole host of other such scandals in the 1990s to profit. Just as Saitoti and Musyoka fled KANU to NARC when they realised that the ruling party was about to be defeated, so too did the former government's partners in crime. Murungi alleged 'implicitly and explicitly' to Githongo that Kibaki 'knew all about these shenanigans'. However remarkable Murungi's candidness may have been, the most astonishing thing about Anglo Leasing was its scale. By October, Githongo had reason to believe that 'we were sitting on roughly $700 million worth of contracts – some of them highly dubious. If one brought in the even murkier and more secret military ones, then the figure was over $1 billion.'[23] Further serious threats to Githongo's life followed. In January 2005, once it became clear that Kibaki knew the full extent of the scandal but was unconcerned, Githongo resigned from his post. Fearing for his life, he spent the next three years in Oxford.

Ordinary Kenyans were no less disillusioned with the NARC government. Insecurity remained high across much of the country, since the new government had neither disarmed local communities nor taken steps to reduce the chances of violent conflicts breaking out. Over two weeks in January 2005, more than fifty Kenyans lost their lives in various clashes between communities over grazing, access to water and cattle raiding. 'All those Kenyans who murder their fellow human beings will be brought to justice,' Kibaki warned.[24] The police force was incapable, however, of investigating these incidents, and the government showed little interest in resolving the local disputes that had underpinned the electoral violence of the 1990s. The continued ready availability of weapons was a matter of particular concern. 'We have a big challenge in mopping up guns,' an assistant minister in the Office of the President, Mirugi Kariuki, admitted in parliament.[25] Despite such statements, little effort was made to put words into action. Instead, armed groups continued to hold onto their weapons and local disputes were militarised. The potential consequences were brutally demonstrated in Marsabit district on 12 July, when Borana cattle raiders attacked the Gabra village of Turbi. Over fifty people were killed, many of them children at Turbi's primary school. As the press arrived in the aftermath of the massacre, one local civil servant told them: 'We have asked our people not to bury the dead before the outside world can come and see that the Kenyan government can't protect its own people.'[26] Across the country, Kenyans were becoming all too aware that the government was unable to fulfil the most basic of tasks entrusted to it in 2002.

The failure to enact change was partly a result of the simple fact that the government included many of those responsible for earlier misrule. Amos Wako, for example, had served as attorney general since 1991 and had proved an able defender of the powerful. Back in 1993, the KHRC had published a scathing critique of Wako's first two years in office, chronicling his silence on the prosecution of key opposition figures and abuses committed by the government and the security forces. The author of the KHRC's report, Maina Kiai, reminded his readers of Wako's maiden speech in parliament in 1991: 'No man, save the President, is above the law.'[27] More than a decade later, the US ambassador, Mark Bellamy, thought 'Wako is the main obstacle to successful prosecutions of any kind in Kenya'.[28] Other members were throwbacks to the Kenyatta era. John Michuki, who served Kibaki as transport and then later as internal security minister, had been appointed to the provincial administration during the Mau Mau emergency and had been a senior civil servant under the first president. He retained his outmoded colonial attitudes to government, justifying the government's need to limit human rights because 'The African mind does not accept authority.'[29] This was no new generation of political leaders, but rather a government made up in part of individuals who had learned their political skills in the disorder of the past.

Even some of those sitting in government for the first time proved unable to resist the opportunities presented by power. When the people of Mai Mahiu, one of the communities affected by the violence of January 2005, sat down at a reconciliation meeting in early February, the chairman was the internal security minister, Chris Murungaru. 'Everyone will be pursued as an individual,' Murungaru told the residents of Mai Mahiu when warning them of prosecutions for murder.[30] But while Murungaru spoke in public about peace, it was alleged that he acted very differently in private. According to Githongo, he habitually made threats to life and, as we shall see, was accused by the US embassy of being a lynchpin in drug trafficking networks.

Despite these shortcomings, revelation of the failings of the NARC government was slow. The euphoria of the 2002 election was only broken when the Anglo Leasing scandal came to public attention. The delay in widespread awareness of the nature of Kibaki's regime can be explained partly by a decline in the influence of civil society groups. While these had acted as watchdogs during the 1990s, human rights groups, professional bodies and other NGOs were ironically weakened by the success of the multiparty effort. By 2002, figures like Wangari Maathai, Paul Muite, Peter Anyang' Nyong'o and Kiraitu Murungi, who had played such important roles in the push to end Moi's authoritarian rule, sat in parliament rather than outside the political system. Leading figures from civil society – for example Githongo – flocked into the civil service. This brain drain weakened the quality of civil society leadership in the aftermath of 2002, but also restrained criticism of the government from many of the once forthright critics of human rights abuses who now sat in parliament. The alleged involvement in some of the worst examples of abuse of power under Kibaki by a few individuals formerly associated with civil society activism further discredited their erstwhile colleagues. Kiraitu Murungi, Githongo's adversary but once one of the most courageous human rights lawyers, was the most obvious such individual.

A changing of the guard took place in the churches, too. The clergy who led the protests against the government in the 1980s and 1990s had, for the most part, departed the scene by 2002. Their replacements lacked the same courage and conviction to continue speaking truth to power. The nature of religious public engagement changed as a result of other developments, too. A greater concern for expanding influence and the rise of Pentecostalism meant clergy even in the established churches became more interested in personal morality than the constitution, and in the threat of Islam and Satan than the dangers of authoritarianism.

The most prominent abandonment of discussion of political affairs was that by David Githii, the moderator of the Presbyterian Church. Elected in 2003 on a promise to make the Church seem more relevant to Kenyan youths, he instead spent much of his two terms in office until 2009 occupied with a campaign to remove what he claimed were satanic and Masonic symbols from churches. After the destruction of numerous irreplaceable stained-glass windows, artefacts and even monuments in honour of dead family members in some of Kenya's oldest church buildings, Githii's campaign was brought to a halt by a government plea and the opposition of congregations and prominent churchgoers, including Muite and Njonjo. The Presbyterian leader was not to be deterred, however, and wrote a book detailing the extent of Satanism throughout the country and the symbols used to adorn public buildings. Besides accusing MPs of habitually dabbling in witchcraft, Githii argued that various images around the parliament buildings and its grounds 'suffocate the Parliament with symbols dedicated to the Devil'.[31]

Throughout Githii's campaign, he was opposed by Timothy Njoya. 'He is wrong and he must stop these teachings,' Njoya stated in unequivocal terms in December 2004.[32] But this veteran campaigner for reform was not to be distracted by such matters. Although his fellow activists from the 1980s and 1990s had either left the public stage or joined the government, the cleric was determined to keep up his vigil against the abuse of power. He was alarmed by what he saw in the first two years of Kibaki's presidency. 'We now know what "NARC" means,' Njoya argued in 2005. ' "Nothing-Actually-Really-Changed"!'[33] Promises of eradicating corruption proved hollow, and insecurity was as endemic as before, but Njoya was particularly frustrated by the direction of constitutional reform. A national review commission headed by a constitutional expert, Yash Ghai, had started its work prior to the 2002 election. After the election, constitutional change became an expectation rather than an aspiration. Delegates to the commission, representing every conceivable interest group in the country, thrashed out their differences in public. With proceedings televised, carried by radio and extensively reported in the newspapers, Kenyans were able to hear delegates discuss a wide array of issues.

The two most contentious matters up for discussion were the powers given to the president and the question of devolution. These issues were not simply theoretical; they were of intense and immediate relevance to NARC. As we saw above, in return for his endorsement of Kibaki as NARC's presidential candidate, Odinga had been promised swift constitutional change that would lead to the creation of the post of prime minster. But, by June 2003, it was clear that the constitutional review process was no closer to completion than it had been at the time of the election. Enraged both by the direction in which the country was heading under Kibaki and by his disavowal of the promises made prior to the 2002 elections, Odinga's supporters had had enough. When one of the leading figures in the constitutional review process, the political scientist Crispin Odhiambo Mbai, was murdered in his home in unexplained circumstances in September, everything seemed to point to the new president's determination to keep his monopoly on power. Talk soon began of the need for a 'third liberation'.

The coalition was in a terminal state for two years, from mid-2003. It finally collapsed when the constitutional review process reached its conclusion with a referendum in November 2005. Although the constitutional review commission advocated significant devolution of power from central government to local authorities and a reduction in the powers of the president, Kibaki's faction in government had the last say. The attorney general revised the draft constitution before it was put to the public in a referendum, and clauses promising devolution and the dilution of presidential power were removed. Kibaki and his supporters hoped the allure of a new constitution would be sufficient to meet demands for reform, regardless of the document's content. 'There is no possibility of acquiring consensus for the best constitution,' claimed the minister for trade and industry, Mukhisa Kituyi. 'We have a document which broadly reflects public consensus. We cannot agree on everything. Let us complete the Constitution and get on to do other things.'[34] But such sentiments underestimated the strength of feeling in the country.

While Kibaki's faction in the government campaigned for acceptance of the draft constitution, they faced a broad coalition backing the 'No' campaign. Peter Anyang' Nyong'o, a minister in the NARC government and ally of Odinga, denounced the draft as 'a bad and fraudulent constitution made by a small group of people mesmerised by power who think the rest of Kenyans are foolish'.[35] Odinga and his supporters joined with KANU, as well as with other disaffected members of the government. With no presidential nomination at stake, it was easy for Odinga, Kenyatta and Kalonzo Musyoka to share the limelight as the leaders of the 'No' campaign. Taking their cue from the symbol of an orange allocated to the 'No' vote on the ballot paper – and inspiration from the Orange Movement in Ukraine – the opposition forged a new political coalition that became known as the Orange Democratic Movement (ODM). The 'No' campaign was triumphant in the referendum. It claimed 57 per cent of the vote and was backed by a majority of voters in seven out of the eight provinces. Only in Kibaki's own Central Province did the 'Yes' campaign win a majority.

Kibaki's faction cared little about whether or not the draft constitution was supported in the referendum – it was no hardship to be saddled with the old constitution and its protection of presidential power and central government. The president and his supporters therefore accepted the result of the referendum. That indifference had also influenced the nature of the campaign: vote rigging, harassment of opposition supporters and violence were all notable for their absence. But this relative harmony was widely misinterpreted. Coming in the wake of the peaceful transition from KANU to NARC in 2002, optimists viewed the referendum as evidence of the consolidation of democracy. Instead, it was a reflection of the calculations made by Kibaki's supporters. Money and effort would, they believed, be better spent ensuring that their man remained in power after 2007.

THE CRIMINAL STATE

A Kibaki victory in 2007 seemed highly doubtful after the referendum, however. Riding a wave of popular support, the leaders of the ODM left the government to join the opposition ranks in parliament; NARC was no more. Instead, Kibaki was left with a rump of supporters largely drawn from the Kikuyu, Embu and Meru communities of the Mount Kenya region. Denounced by critics as the 'Mount Kenya mafia', members of the inner circle had good reason to hold on to power. To lose office would mean to surrender great wealth and, potentially, to risk prosecution for their increasingly commonplace criminal activities. Some gestures towards reform were made. Chris Murungaru, who had served as internal security and transport minister during the NARC government up to 2005, was fired from the cabinet. A few weeks after the reshuffle, he was alleged in Githongo's widely distributed dossier to have been one of the key players in the Anglo Leasing scandal. Generally, however, Kibaki attempted to consolidate his faction's grasp on power. For instance, the president promoted hardliners from within his own Kikuyu community. Njenga Karume, the former GEMA leader, took up a new appointment as defence minister following a cabinet reshuffle in December 2005. John Michuki moved from transport to internal security. The elderly, conservative and Kikuyu president was remaking government in his own image.

The influence of the hardliners was quickly demonstrated. On 25 February 2006, *The Standard* published a story describing a meeting between Kibaki and Kalonzo Musyoka. Musyoka was at that time in the opposition ODM, and the paper suggested that the meeting was an attempt by Kibaki to undermine the alliance that had defeated him in the 2005 referendum. The story caused a stir, given the political sensitivity of the subject, and both Kibaki and Musyoka denied that the meeting had taken place. In an ominous development, the journalists who wrote the story were arrested and interrogated. In the early hours of 2 March, a team of armed men stormed *The Standard*'s offices in central Nairobi. Office staff were physically assaulted, mobile phones were stolen and computers taken. The newspaper's sister television station, KTN, was taken off the air. At the same time, another armed group stormed the newspaper's printing plant and destroyed copies of that day's edition which were awaiting collection and distribution.

The Standard reported the following day that the raid was planned by the internal security minister, John Michuki, the CID director, Joseph Kamau, and Kibaki's personal adviser, Stanley Murage. Michuki was unrepentant. 'When you rattle a snake you must be ready to be bitten', he told reporters. Other ministers were horrified by events. According to Musikari Kombo, the minister for local government, the attack on *The Standard* was 'extreme, sinister and barbaric'.[36] While similar statements of outrage were repeated, detailed comment about the raid was limited. 'We are all being blackmailed,' one leading political figure told the US embassy, as he outlined the lengths to which the police and the president's staff were prepared to go to keep discussion of the raid out of public debate.[37] The disproportionate use of force in ostensible response to a routine piece of speculative political reporting caused many Kenyans to ask what was really behind the raid.

These questions became louder with the broadcast of CCTV footage from inside the building that housed *The Standard* newsroom. The videotape showed two white men leading the raid. The two, it emerged at a press conference they held on 13 March, were brothers: Sargasyan and Margaryan Artur. They claimed to be Armenian, but others suggested they were Bosnian, Czech, Russian or Ukrainian nationals. They had arrived in the country separately in late 2005 and quickly set about gaining the paperwork they needed to set up business in Kenya. Both were granted work permits and they registered a series of companies. Among the directors of one of these companies were the personal assistant to Mary Wambui (the polygamous Kibaki's second wife) and Wambui's daughter, Winnie Wambui. Both of the brothers also possessed Kenyan passports that had been reported stolen from the immigration headquarters in Nairobi, and security passes giving them access to all areas of the Jomo Kenyatta International Airport.

Those closely connected to the raid on *The Standard* alleged that the brothers were used to destroy evidence of the involvement of Kibaki's family in corruption and narcotics smuggling. A journalist at the newspaper told the US embassy that 'police contacts warned him weeks earlier that foreigners had been imported to protect the First Family from public corruption charges'. Those arrested at the media group's buildings on the night of the raid reported how police officers involved 'told them that they were looking for papers implicating both presidential wives in corruption: Official First Lady Lucy in the Anglo-Leasing scandal and Unofficial Wife Two Mary Wambui in cocaine shipments'.[38] The Arturs were alleged to have been involved in drug trafficking, too. While in Kenya they imported various containers through Mombasa, which the parliamentary report into the episode alleged 'may well have contained drugs'.[39]

The two were finally deported on 9 June. MPs regarded the deportation as 'suspicious . . . [it] appeared to be a cover-up of their true identities and activities in Kenya'.[40] With their expulsion, the curtain was brought down on a 'tale of hired thugs of questionable nationality, prominent Kenyans, massive corruption, blackmail, threats, and narcotics trafficking schemes' that one US diplomat thought 'reads like a script that Hollywood would reject as unbelievable'.[41] Given that, as the MPs' report alleged, it was 'abundantly clear that the two brothers were conmen and drug traffickers' and that they clearly 'enjoyed protection by the high and mighty in the Government', the parliamentary inquiry recommended further investigations into a number of senior figures. These included John Michuki in connection with the role of the Arturs during the raid on *The Standard*, and the head of the civil service, Francis Muthaura. Joseph Kamau, the head of CID, was also singled out by the MPs for further investigation. But it was the connection between the president and the Arturs that most alarmed the MPs.

Included in the list of individuals recommended for further investigation on account of their obvious close associations with the two Armenians were Kibaki's special adviser Stanley Murage, Kibaki's wife Mary Wambui, and their daughter Winnie Wambui. Although Kibaki ordered Kamau and five other officials to be suspended for their part in the affair, the president also refused to make public a report into it by Shadrack Kiruki, a former commissioner of police. Likening it to Watergate, the MPs saw the whole affair and the cover-up as evidence of the pernicious effects of an over-powerful presidency and a criminalised political system. 'What did the Head of Government know?' the MPs' report asked. 'When did he get [to] know it and what did he do?'[42] The affair of the Artur brothers was not, however, the only indication of official complicity in criminal activities at the highest level of government.

Following a seizure of cocaine worth nearly $66 million in December 2004, an informant to the US embassy stated that Murungaru was among 'the real guilty parties'.[43] The investigation and prosecution of that case, which was probably linked to the Arturs, too, was marked by sustained political interference, the harassment of police officers, and even the murder of a senior policeman in Mombasa. To critics of the government, Kibaki and his ministers seemed to have lost all sense of reasonable conduct. Shortly after the raid on *The Standard*, Odinga addressed mourners at a funeral in Siaya, close to Kisumu. 'I have repeatedly told President Kibaki to move out of office,' he told the crowd. 'He has no moral authority to continue clinging to power when his key lieutenants have either stepped down or been adversely mentioned in graft cases.'[44] Both the drug case and the saga of the Armenians demonstrated the profoundly criminal nature of the regime; it had presided over Kenya's descent into narco-statehood. Kenyans had learned a harsh lesson in the meantime. 'To rid a country of an authoritarian regime or dictator is not necessarily to move it fundamentally beyond authoritarianism,' Bethwell Ogot later remarked.[45] Kibaki's opponents could at least look forward to the 2007 elections with optimism.

THE CAMPAIGN

As the election approached, Kibaki's supporters pinned their hopes of victory on the performance of the economy over the previous five years. 'After two decades of stagnation and decline, the Kenyan economy has shown consistent growth in the last few years,' the World Bank reported in August 2007.[46] Poverty, the government claimed, was declining. Statistical evidence supported that argument, with the number of Kenyans living in absolute poverty declining by 6 per cent in the decade from 1997. However, it was also true that Kenya, again according to the World Bank, remained 'a highly unequal society, with exclusion and disadvantage reflecting stratification by class, gender, and region'. Inequality was worsening particularly quickly in urban areas.[47] This ambiguous economic picture provided the backdrop for the 2007 elections.

'You can trust Kibaki', the president's campaign literature promised. Kibaki headed the new Party for National Unity (PNU), but was the presidential candidate for a wide array of other parties, too. Emphasising the economic growth witnessed over the previous few years, the president's campaign for re-election represented him as a safe bet. The election was, according to Kibaki's speech as he launched his campaign, 'about sound, wise and proven management of public affairs that will improve the welfare of all our people and create wealth in our beloved country'. 'Kenya is better than it was five years ago,' the president claimed, 'and will be far better off five years from now under PNU.'[48] *Kazi iendelee* ('The Work Goes On'), PNU's slogan promised voters.

The collapse of NARC was a disaster for Kibaki and his hopes of re-election. Moi and Kenyatta had both faced revelations about gross corruption on a scale similar to the Anglo Leasing scandal and both had emerged with at least some legitimacy intact. For all that they practised ethnic politics, the first two presidents were careful to ensure that sufficient numbers of elites from a wide range of ethnic groups enjoyed the benefits of power. Ministerial jobs, appointments to head up state-owned industries, and licences for trade and manufacturing were all used judiciously to buy the cohesion of national elites. In the wake of the referendum defeat, Kibaki instead consolidated power in his inner circle, in which trusted Kikuyu, Embu and Meru allies wielded tremendous influence. None was as important as the head of the civil service, Francis Muthaura from Meru, appointed in 2005. When making such decisions, age, class and status were just as important to Kibaki as ethnicity. Former economics students from Kibaki's time at Makerere University, for instance, were disproportionately influential in the inner circle. Many shared the president's love of golf: Amos Kimunya, the minister of lands and settlement, was the chairman of the exclusive Muthaiga golf club, and John Michuki owned the Windsor golf hotel and country club just outside the city. Michuki had long been an ally of Kibaki. The two men had gone to school together and had worked alongside one another in government in the 1960s and 1970s. Kibaki's ties to Jomo Kenyatta's regime were further represented by his close relationship with George Muhoho – a relationship that survived Kibaki's defeat of Muhoho's nephew, Uhuru Kenyatta, in the 2002 election. The president's second wife, Mary Wambui, completed the inner circle.

Viewed from the clubhouse at Muthaiga, Kenya's political history had a powerful message for those surrounding Kibaki. Each had bitter memories of the 1980s and 1990s, when it seemed as though Kikuyu influence was restricted and the opportunities for wealth limited as a result. Kibaki and his supporters were not willing to repeat that experience. They were heartened, therefore, by a clear weakening of the opposition as the election drew closer. The ODM coalition broke down as Kibaki successfully courted KANU and Uhuru Kenyatta, who promised to back the president. A month later, Kalonzo Musyoka announced his intention to run as a presidential candidate and formed his own party, ODM-Kenya. Odinga was left as the candidate for ODM, but still opinion polls suggested he had a comfortable lead over his rivals in the presidential election.

Much of that appeal derived from the way in which Odinga and the ODM highlighted the failure of Kibaki's government to address inequality. Accepting ODM's nomination, Odinga promised 'that the lives of the desperately poor, who make up more than half of our population, become lives worth living'.[49] 'They must not be allowed to work for the few at the expense of the many', ODM literature warned of the PNU. While Kibaki stressed economic growth, Odinga emphasised the rising cost of basic essentials.[50] The emphasis placed by Kibaki on economic expansion caused many Kenyans to ask who was reaping the benefits of that growth. 'To the people of the Rift Valley nothing has moved,' said ODM candidate Zakayo Cheruiyot. 'When PNU says *kazi iendelee* they feel spited.'[51]

Odinga constructed a set of alliances that covered the entire country. From Western Province, he could count on the support of Musalia Mudavadi. Having stayed in the KANU fold in 2002 and been punished by his constituents in Western Province for that decision, Mudavadi was determined to make sure he picked sides wisely this time around. William Ruto, who saw Moi's support for Kibaki as presenting the perfect opportunity to dislodge the former president as the lynchpin of Kalenjin politics, represented the Rift Valley in the ODM's leadership. Joseph Nyagah, a Nairobi-based MP who hailed from the eastern side of Mount Kenya, was the representative of both the city and Mount Kenya in the Odinga-led coalition. Charity Ngilu, who, like Ruto, saw backing Odinga as one way of challenging her local rival Musyoka, was Eastern Province's representative. Najib Balala from Coast completed the regional sweep of the ODM's leadership. Despite this nationwide coverage, the ODM eschewed a nationalist-style campaign and instead focused on a series of local grievances specific to each province and ethnic group.

To Luo in Nyanza and elsewhere in the country, the ODM was about punishing Kibaki for his betrayal of Odinga in 2003 and was an opportunity to correct decades-old political grievances related to the persecution of Raila's father, the banning of the KPU, the murder of Mboya and the more recent killing of Ouko. 'For Nyanza, there is probably no other election in Kenya history which carries as much significance as this one,' wrote the journalist Gitau Warigi a few weeks before polling day. 'Everywhere, the mood is pregnant with anticipation. And that anticipation is for a result which to most locals is pre-ordained.'[52] The expectation of an ODM victory was shared in other regions of the country.

In the Rift Valley, the ODM seemed the best vehicle for devolving power to local authorities in order to protect the demands of self-proclaimed indigenous groups for land over those consistently described as 'outsiders'. As Ntimama put it in a television interview: 'the government has done very little indeed on the land policy and we need something more to be done and we need our people, you know, to get their security or title . . . which we don't have'.[53] Kibaki's government was furthermore accused of deliberate neglect of Kalenjin in order to punish them for Moi's marginalisation of Kikuyu. William Cheptumo, the ODM candidate in Baringo North, believed that '2002 was a watershed in the country and particularly for our community. People lost their jobs and for once in our history, we looked lost without a clear identity.'[54] Fears of Kikuyu domination were widely shared by people in other parts of the country.

In Coast, such concerns fed into grievances over regional inequalities in terms of access to education, healthcare, sanitation and electricity, and served to enhance the ODM's appeal. 'I will ensure that development issues are decided by the local people,' promised Odinga at an ODM rally at Tiwi on the Indian Ocean. He then outlined how he would make sure that 60 per cent of all public spending was controlled by local authorities rather than by central government.[55] With the Islamic influence in Coast Province particularly strong, the ODM also appealed to concerns about the Kibaki government's participation in global counter-terrorism operations. Kenyan citizens had been the subject of renditions to Ethiopia for interrogation over alleged links to international terrorist networks.[56] 'We agreed that President Kibaki is not going to be our candidate because of the renditions,' said Sheikh Abdi of the National Muslim Leaders Forum, as he announced his group's endorsement of Odinga.[57]

Kibaki's best hope for political survival lay in galvanising almost total support from Kikuyu voters and those of other closely linked ethnic communities, such as Embu and Meru. This task was made easier by the ODM's promises of devolution if elected. The return of majimboism to public debate alarmed many, as it reminded Kikuyu of the bloody experience of the 1990s and the threats of violence from the

1960s. Kikuyu church leaders, for instance, denounced the ODM's policy. 'We are the ones who bear the brunt when land clashes break out,' Githii told other clerics at a meeting in October. They agreed, describing devolution as 'a monster that the devil would use to cause bloodshed in the nation'.[58] On its own, however, fear of devolution was insufficient to overcome the divisions of class, gender and region that split the Kikuyu community and which threatened to weaken Kibaki's bid for the presidency.

The second part of Kibaki's strategy to win the overwhelming backing of Kikuyu voters was to confront Mungiki. Having made use of the gang to boost Kenyatta's run for the KANU presidential nomination in 2002, Moi's government had no further use for it in its last weeks in office. Under Kibaki, the police had moved against Mungiki in the first months of 2003 and arrested some of its leaders. An uneasy truce had held over the next four years, but Mungiki's position of dominance in the poorest neighbourhoods of Nairobi and other urban centres across the Highlands remained unchecked. As the country approached the 2007 elections, however, the gang's position posed greater problems, and so an anti-Mungiki offensive began in May 2007. The police made little allowance for due process or human rights. 'We will pulverize and finish them off,' stated Michuki, the internal security minister. 'Even those arrested over the recent killings, I cannot tell you where they are today. What you will certainly hear is that so and so's burial is tomorrow.'[59] At the city mortuary in Nairobi, victims of gunshot wounds overwhelmed the facility between early June and late October. In total, the bodies of more than 500 young men, almost all of them Kikuyu, were recovered by the authorities in Nairobi and its satellite towns. Eyewitness testimony and further investigation led the Kenya National Commission on Human Rights (KNCHR) to find that 'extra-judicial executions and other brutal acts of extreme cruelty have been perpetrated by the Police against so-called Mungiki adherents'. Moreover, the KNCHR thought that killings may have been part of 'official policy sanctioned by the political leadership, the Police Commissioner and top police commanders'.[60] The police death squads were meant to destroy

Mungiki as a credible voice of dissent against Kibaki's presidential bid and to shore up support from other Kikuyu who had tired of Mungiki's intimidation, violence and criminality.

THE ELECTION

Voters went to the polls on 27 December. In the weeks that had preceded the election, opinion polls suggested that the gap between the two main presidential candidates had narrowed significantly. While the atmosphere in many polling stations was tense, and though numerous bureaucratic delays occurred in several locations, voting itself went relatively smoothly and peacefully. While any hope of a swift declaration of the result was quickly shown to be optimistic, there seemed little initial reason for concern about the management of the election. The next day the International Republican Institute, one of the few foreign observer groups in the country, gave the election its provisional approval.[61] As attention switched from voting to counting, the mood across the country began to change. Over the following three days, great confusion was created by the process of tallying and reporting the results. All official results were meant to be announced at the press centre set up by the Electoral Commission of Kenya (ECK) at the Kenyatta International Conference Centre in central Nairobi. But delays in announcing results from the presidential election caused great frustration.

As the delay lengthened, so suspicion of government malfeasance grew. Supporters of the government (or at least members of ethnic groups thought to be its supporters) living in areas dominated by the opposition quickly came to fear that they would be the target of violent protests against any rigging. In Busia, on the Ugandan border, on 28 and 29 December local opposition activists warned Kikuyu residents that they were to be evicted imminently.[62] Despite the delay, expectations of an Odinga victory were also growing. On the basis of the first batch of declared results, which came overwhelmingly from ODM strongholds, Odinga's supporters thought their man was on his way to State House. Crowds in Kisumu celebrated what they believed was a victory for Odinga. The main newspapers agreed, and the morning editions on 29 December effectively called the election for him. By the afternoon of the same day, the situation had changed. As Samuel Kivuitu, the chairman of the ECK, began to announce a series of results from Kibaki's heartlands, ODM leaders in attendance at the tallying centre tried to stop him. They claimed to have concrete evidence of rigging from the constituencies being announced. These constituencies, it later turned out, were those from which the European Union observers' mission reported irregularities.[63] After listening to representations from all parties, Kivuitu decided to postpone the announcement until the following day and instigate an overnight investigation of the results.

The first protests began shortly afterwards in Kisumu, Mombasa and Nairobi. Control was quickly regained by the police, but tension remained high across the country into the following morning, 30 December. One of Kericho's Kikuyu residents, Dr Njoroge, waited for the results: 'By the third day we were all very anxious and afraid.'[64] In Nairobi, a security cordon was put in place around key government buildings and the building where the results were being announced. The media and observers waited there for much of the day for the final declaration, which everyone now expected would announce Kibaki as the winner. ODM members made one last attempt to block announcement of the result before the building was cleared. Taken to a secure room with only the state broadcaster for company, Kivuitu finally announced the results in the late afternoon. Kibaki had, he reported, won the presidential election by more than 200,000 votes. He then hurried the short distance to State House to deliver the certificate declaring the result to the president. A swearing-in ceremony was hastily organised and, as the sun set, Kibaki began his second term in office.

It was with incredulity that Kenyans watched these events unfold live on television. An election that had been called for Odinga just a day before had now been won, so it was claimed, by Kibaki – and by a surprising margin. The president's supporters celebrated the unexpected victory, but elsewhere violence erupted almost immediately. In

Kericho, 'within no time we now started seeing fire in the town, people shouting and screaming and we could see smoke all over the town. We soon heard gunshots and this continued into the night.'[65] In the hours that followed the results, some supporters of Odinga attacked individuals and groups they thought had supported Kibaki. Some of this was spontaneous: 'It was terrible and every person who was perceived to be from a particular tribe was kicked out of his house and the house set on fire,' recalled Salome Njeri. She and her family, Kikuyu residents of Busia, fled to the local police station, where they spent the next eight months.[66]

In the two months that followed the disputed election, at least 1,133 Kenyans were killed, thousands of women raped and property widely destroyed. The violence took three forms. The first – and, in terms of fatalities, statistically the least significant – constituted protests against the result itself. As the reports of domestic and foreign observers made clear, the elections were at best marked by significant irregularities, the extent of which made it impossible to declare a true winner; at worst they had been fixed. According to ODM's spokesman Salim Lone, 'The robbery was blatant.'[67] For his part, Kibaki was insistent that 'he won the election fairly'.[68] The truth was somewhere in between: rigging took place on both sides, the paper trail was retrospectively tampered with, and the margin of victory for either candidate was almost certainly tiny. As the US embassy's analysis put it: 'We do not think it will ever be possible to tell definitively who actually won the election.'[69] But it is important to note that confusion and obfuscation of the result was a deliberate policy of the PNU. The ECK had been packed with Kibaki's allies earlier in the year: nineteen of the institution's twenty-two members had been appointed by the president. Nine of the appointees were labelled by ECK Chairman Samuel Kivuitu ahead of the election as 'the riggers'.[70] Moreover, as the American ambassador reported, the tallying centre in Nairobi was the subject of a break-in on the night the election result was declared. 'We do not know what was taken or altered,' Ranneberger wrote, 'but since there was heavy police security around the ECK, we can only conclude that it was an inside job.'[71] Kibaki fiddled and Kenya burned.

Although the ODM won the most seats in the parliamentary elections, this was of little comfort to the supporters of Odinga. The ODM's leaders put a plan for civil disobedience into action, calling on Kenyans to protest against the result of the presidential vote. Looting and vandalism were reported in Nairobi, Mombasa and Kisumu. In some places this was particularly targeted at businesses and other property owned by Kikuyu, on account of that community's support for Kibaki and the PNU. The extent of these protests was, however, limited. A massive security operation was mounted to prevent the civil disobedience campaign gathering pace. Sites for demonstrations were blocked off and, with live television and radio broadcasts suspended, it became difficult for the ODM's leaders to communicate plans for mass action.

The second strand of the violence was the response to the protests. Through the first two weeks of January, the police and other security forces used disproportionate force to quell demonstrations against the election result. It became apparent almost immediately that live ammunition was being used against the protestors, as police officers brutally cracked down on any demonstration of support for the ODM in major urban areas. As one twenty-seven-year-old woman from the Manyatta informal settlement in Kisumu put it: 'The police were shooting indiscriminately. I saw them but there was no time to escape. I found myself in hospital.'[72] Another eyewitness, Joel Cheruiyot of Kapsoit, described how: 'I think that the government used excessive force even on innocent people who were going about their own business . . . In fact the police used to force people to close their shops by using live bullets or by beating people. There are ladies who were raped but are silent.'[73] A later investigation into the violence found that 405 people had been killed by the police. 'Among the victims were some who were ostensibly going about their lawful business when they were hit by bullets and many more whose wounds confirmed that they had been shot from behind,' the investigation concluded.[74] The actions of the police can be easily explained with reference to the long history of political control over the security forces, their habitual use of extreme violence in response to challenges such as Mungiki, and a tradition of disregard for human rights and the law.

The third strand of violence proved the most pernicious. Almost immediately after the declaration of Kibaki's victory, planned attacks were mounted on homes and communities. The fact of the disputed election was used to reignite a much older conflict over land, power and wealth. 'The fire this time', Billy Kahora later called it in his editorial in the influential *Kwani?* literary journal.[75] In areas of the Rift Valley and Western Provinces affected by the clashes of the 1990s, armed militia attempted once again to force out ethnic groups considered to be outsiders.

Michael Mwangi, a retired headmaster living in North Kinangop, had lived through the ethnic clashes there in April 1992. As elsewhere, the violence following the 2007 election began almost immediately after the result was announced. However, it gathered pace and intensity in the days that followed. 'Burning of houses started on the night of 31 December 2007 and 1 January 2008,' recalled Mwangi. Through early January, farms close to his home were attacked by Kalenjin militia, and the police seemed powerless. Eventually, the army was deployed in the area, but many Kikuyu residents were told to take refuge at the local police station. As they left their homes, Kalenjin youths burned and looted their property. 'Homes were burning while the police just watched,' Mwangi claimed. Like so many others, he took in people fleeing the violence. But with up to 500 people camping out in his compound by the end of January, his home became a target for the local Kalenjin militia. With his farm surrounded by militia members one night and his house on fire, Mwangi was saved only by the last-minute arrival of police officers.[76]

Eldoret and its surrounding countryside was the epicentre of the post-election violence. The targets of the violence were the non-Kalenjin population of the area – mostly Kikuyu. Within just five days of the announcement of the election result, nearly ninety people had been killed in the area. Around 50,000 people had been forced from their homes in the same short period. However, with roads out of the area blocked with burnt-out cars and rocks, and with Kalenjin militias marshalling unofficial checkpoints, those forced from their homes sought refuge in communal buildings such as churches and schools, as well as in the compounds of police stations and administrative posts. Some 400 people sought protection at the Kenya Assemblies of God church in the village of Kiambaa, less than fifteen kilometres from Eldoret. The Kikuyu residents of the area had, in some cases, been living at Kiambaa for forty years. 'I was born and brought up here,' one later told reporters. 'My parents settled here after buying land and I do not understand why political issues have caused a rift between us and our brothers from other communities.' At 10 a.m. on New Year's Day, the women at the church were making lunch. 'We were preparing *githeri* [maize and beans] for the more than 400 people who had sought refuge in the church when a group of youths brandishing weapons charged at us', recalled Margaret Wanjiku. The attackers set light to the church and, according to Wanjiku, in a matter of minutes the church building was a burnt-out shell.[77] At least thirty-five people were killed in the attack, including infants and the elderly. William Ruto later attempted to clear Kalenjin youths of involvement. In conversations with US officials, he claimed 'the cause of the incident was an accidental kitchen fire during preparations for lunch'.[78]

The violence at Kiambaa and elsewhere was, in part, the result of a form of identity politics that we have encountered on several occasions in this book. Kikuyu were commonly depicted as outsiders, without legitimate claim to the land in the Rift Valley that they occupied. Milka Kiarie, a resident of Molo who had been a victim of the clashes in 1992 and 1997, was forced from her home on 26 February. She later described how Kalenjin militia members 'came and told us that we had to leave since it was their land which they were given at independence and the Rift Valley belonged to them'.[79] But such a view ignored the multi-ethnic, mobile history of modern Kenya. 'I have nowhere to go,' said one survivor of the Kiambaa church massacre. 'I am ready to go back to what used to be my home depending on how things shape up.'[80] Such sentiments were courageous, but also rooted in fact. Kikuyu belong to the Rift Valley just as much as Kalenjin, Maasai and Samburu.

In 2008, when asked about the origins of the post-election violence, the civil society leader Gladwell Otieno said: 'It's about resources, it's about land, it's about tribe, it's about so many issues that successive governments have not addressed.'[81] That was true, but in the heat of the moment, of all these different factors it was ethnicity that was seized upon by many Kenyans in an attempt to understand events. Politicians came under pressure from their constituents to provide support and protection for ethnic kin across the country. While the police and other security forces were used to crush protests against the election result, the same officers were far less able to protect families in areas affected by the communal violence. To Michael Mwangi, 'It looked like the government had been overthrown. Three-quarters of the policemen were on the ODM side.'[82] Reuben Cheruiyot, a book-seller in Londiani, lost his business in the violence, even though 'My shop was just 50 metres from the police station.'[83] When her home in Molo was attacked, Milka Kiarie went to the local police station. Some of the police officers 'tried to help but some of them were not assisting because they were favouring their side as most of them were Nandis'.[84] In order to fight back, Kibaki's inner circle turned to Mungiki.

Mungiki members, who had been the target of state repression just months before, now became the PNU's soldiers of fortune. Credible rumours of Mungiki members being used to crush protests in Nairobi's poorest neighbourhoods were circulated from the very first days of the crisis. However, more substantial evidence exists of the state's complicity in Mungiki's violence in the Rift Valley. According to the BBC's Karen Allen, 'meetings were hosted at the official residence of the president between the banned Mungiki militia and senior government officials'. Although the government denied these reports, Allen's sources told her that Mungiki members 'were given a duty to defend the Kikuyu in Rift Valley and we know they were there in numbers'.[85] Other journalists found similar evidence of state involvement in Mungiki's actions. 'Kikuyu politicians and businessmen hired group members for reprisal killings in Nakuru and Naivasha at the height of the post-election violence', *Africa Report* claimed in 2008. 'For Ksh.300 ($5) per person for a gang of 50, politicians were able to hire Mungiki to wreak revenge on the Kalenjin youth militias that had driven tens of thousands of Kikuyu families from their farms in the Rift Valley.'[86] Mungiki's targets were not the rival Kalenjin militias involved in the violence against Kikuyu communities in the western Rift Valley, but rather Kalenjin and Luo residents in the towns of Nakuru and Naivasha.

Mungiki's assault in Naivasha began on 27 January. Over the preceding days, Luo and Kalenjin residents of the town had received warning messages of imminent attacks. A police officer told the BBC how he and his fellow officers had been given orders to allow a convoy of minibuses through police checkpoints along the main roads connecting Nairobi to the two Rift Valley towns. 'We were ordered not to stop the vehicles to allow them to go,' the policeman said. The minibuses were 'packed with men' and 'I could see they were armed'.[87] News of the arrival of these strangers on the evening of 26 January was widely circulated around Naivasha. The following day, Mungiki's attacks began. 'I remember the merciless killing of innocent Kenyans by armed attackers,' recalled Jane Achieng, a forty-nine-year-old widow. 'What I saw was too inhuman.' Achieng owned sixteen properties that were rented out to tenants working in the town and the surrounding flower farms; all her houses were destroyed on 27 January. Achieng fled her burning home and eventually made her way to Busia.[88] Other Kalenjin and Luo sought refuge in the grounds of Naivasha's prison.

In total, more than 500,000 Kenyans were forced from their homes in the first two months of 2008. Many took refuge with friends, relatives and, in some cases, complete strangers. Although not as newsworthy, astounding generosity and instinctive humanitarianism were as much a feature of the crisis as was the violence. Some people took extraordinary risks. Mama Kiplagat, a 29-year-old woman living in Burnt Forest, took in her Kikuyu neighbours – a widow and her three children. 'If Kalenjin had realized I had helped a Kikuyu, they would have even killed me,' she later remarked. 'It was very risky and I was in danger because of suspicion and even feared that my children would betray me if they knew about it.'[89] Hundreds of thousands of Kenyans nevertheless had no choice but to head to the camps set up for the victims of the violence.

Kenneth Kamau was one of those forced to seek refuge in the camp established at the main stadium in Naivasha. A Kikuyu, he had fled from his home in Narok after being attacked by Maasai youths on 12 January.

Suffering from serious wounds, Kamau was first taken to hospital and then to the Naivasha camp. 'At the camp we have a lot of problems,' he commented. 'When it rains the camp gets flooded. Some of us have disabilities and are unable to take shelter and it gets really cold. Since the Red Cross left, it takes time before we get food. At times we have to wait for a month or two to get food.'[90] Kamau and the other tens of thousands of people displaced by the violence were quickly forgotten by the government. Eighteen months after the violence erupted, nearly half of the displaced people were still awaiting resettlement. Even now, three years after the violence, camps dot the landscape of the Rift Valley and homes remain abandoned. The government's treatment of the displaced has been scandalous. Camps have been forced to close and the payments promised to help relocate or rebuild old homes have been delayed – and have sometimes never materialised at all.

ENDING THE VIOLENCE

By late January 2008, the situation seemed bleak. 'We are operating in crisis mode,' one police insider told US diplomats.[91] The police force was stretched thinly and its officers were not, as we have seen above, necessarily determined to do much to end the violence. Soldiers were deployed in a few areas, but their loyalty to the government was untested. However, a combination of domestic and international pressure brought an end to the conflict more quickly than many had dared hope. International efforts to broker a solution had begun in the very first days of the crisis. Travel bans were imposed on individuals suspected of instigating the violence, for example. In early February, the businessman Joshua Kullei, the MPs Henry Kosgey, William Ole Ntimama and Zakayo Cheruiyot, and the former MP Musa Cherutich Sirma were banned from travelling to the US because of their alleged incitement, organisation or funding of militia violence against Kikuyu in the Rift Valley. At the same time, the MPs John Mututho and Kabando wa Kabando, the former MPs Njenga Karume and James Kimathi, and the businessman Richard Ngatia were banned because of allegations of various forms of involvement in Kikuyu militia attacks.

ECK commissioners Kihara Muttu and Jack Tumwa were both, furthermore, banned from travel to the US for allegedly 'accepting bribes to fix [the] election results tally at ECK headquarters'.[92] Alongside these bureaucratic efforts, a series of foreign dignitaries attempted to broker peace.

Hapless efforts by Jendayi Frazer, then the US assistant secretary of state for African affairs, came to naught. John Kufuor, the president of Ghana, visited the country to no great effect, but did persuade his compatriot Kofi Annan to lead an African diplomatic mission. Together with Graça Machel, the wife of Nelson Mandela, and the former president of Tanzania, Benjamin Mkapa, Annan arrived in Nairobi on 22 January. Over the next five weeks, he chaired regular meetings of delegations from both sides in the dispute.

From early on, the proposed solution from the mediators was a power-sharing government. But with both delegations of negotiators made up of hardliners – most notably Ruto from the ODM and Martha Karua from the PNU – reaching agreement proved difficult. The PNU's negotiators blamed the ODM for the violence, accusing the opposition of trying to 'blackmail' its way into government.[93] Finally, Annan decided to meet face to face with Odinga and Kibaki. 'I couldn't let them hide behind the mediators any longer,' Annan told one journalist.[94] Supported by Mkapa and the current Tanzanian president Jakaya Kikwete, Annan met the two main leaders on 28 February. After five hours, a deal was struck. A coalition government would be formed and Odinga would be appointed to the new post of prime minister. Ministerial posts were to be divided up equally between the two parties. 'Better half the loaf than no bread,' remarked Odinga.[95] The violence ceased quickly.

The power-sharing government was finally sworn in six weeks later. Besides Odinga's promotion and the expansion of the cabinet to accommodate its new ODM members, the power-sharing agreement included a package of reforms intended to prevent any future recurrence of violence. Two independent inquiries were also commissioned. The first, chaired by the retired South African judge Johann Kriegler, was to examine the conduct of the election itself. The second, headed by the Kenyan judge Philip Waki, was given the remit of investigating the causes of the violence. A committee of international and local experts was appointed to draft a new constitution, and a truth commission was set up to address long-standing historical grievances, such as the violence of the 1990s. Finally, agreement was reached to investigate, try and prosecute the perpetrators of the violence that followed the 2007 election.

Politics after the violence ceased were dominated by this ambitious reform programme, but there was little in the performance of the coalition government to inspire Kenyans. 'Half-hearted and vague', according to Parselelo Kantai, the power-sharing deal meant only the 're-orientation of power at the centre among rival political elites, but elites nonetheless'.[96] The agreement was blighted by two debilitating contradictions. First, those responsible for the violence were entrusted with resolving it. There was little reason to believe that they had the capacity to build peace or enact the reforms necessary to prevent any future recurrence. Secondly, the merits of designing and implementing measures intended to reduce the chances of a future recurrence of violence in the long-term had to be weighed against the short-term political expedient of keeping the coalition together, thus preventing an immediate return to conflict. These short-term considerations trumped the reform agenda at every stage.

Key institutions showed no sign of having learned any lessons from the violence either. The security forces and their political masters immediately demonstrated a willingness to use disproportionate violence without due regard for human rights in order to crush any security threat. Once the post-election violence was over, the police, GSU and army turned their attention to Mount Elgon. There a distinct low-intensity conflict had been rumbling on for the previous two years. Historic land grievances drove local politics, and politicians sought to exploit these for personal political gain. In 2006, disgruntled Sabaot, who felt short-changed after successive attempts to resettle the population of the area, formed the Sabaot Land Defence Force (SLDF). This militia soon allegedly became linked to the aspiring politician Fred Kapondi. Kapondi contested the 2007 election and,

Human Rights Watch claims, used the SLDF during his campaign.[97] In two years of bloodshed, until April 2008, up to 200,000 people had been displaced from their homes by the SLDF, more than 600 people had been killed and many more beaten, abducted and sexually assaulted. Once the election and the violence elsewhere were over, the security forces, including the army, were charged with eradicating the SLDF. This they did with gusto between April and June 2008. Up to 4,000 suspected militia members were detained during the operation, and many of those were allegedly tortured. Others were even less lucky: around 220 people were allegedly killed by the armed forces.[98]

There was little willingness on the part of the government to consider its conduct of the election either. The PNU, the US ambassador remarked, consistently refused

> to truly own up to the fact that the flawed election results were the impetus to the crisis. They seem almost oblivious to the vote tallying problems, treating it as a minor detail that can be brushed aside and dealt with through legal means.[99]

Even the final report of the Independent Review of Election Commission led by Kriegler was, according to one human rights consortium, 'a half-baked job that attempts to cover up offences committed by people who deserve no such protection'.[100] Rather than interrogating the political culture of elections, Kriegler's commission focused entirely on bureaucratic procedures. The final report refused to attribute blame to any party, with the exception of the ECK, and so the review sustained the Government of National Unity through its most contentious dispute. Few members of the government had much to gain from a close analysis of how the election had been managed. While Kibaki and his supporters had the most to fear from a forensic analysis of events at the tallying centre, a glance at the large turnouts in many constituencies won by ODM leaders suggested that irregularities could be found there, too. The only faction that pushed for greater discussion of the conduct of the election was that made up of those alleged to have been the orchestrators of the ethnic violence in the Rift Valley. Presenting the violence there as a spontaneous response to the theft of the election was a way of rebutting the accusations of their involvement in the planning of the bloodshed.

In contrast to the inquiry into the management of the election, the independent committee chaired by Philip Waki that investigated the violence produced a robust report that apportioned blame without fear or favour. Ruto complained that the report was 'rubbish' and 'unfairly incriminating'.[101] Impartial observers disagreed. 'This is a report whose authors intend it to have real meaning – to end the impunity that it so clearly highlights with respect to the politically instigated clashes of the 1990s and political violence in general,' wrote Muthoni Wanyeki of the KHRC after the report was published.[102] However, its extensive efforts to contextualise the violence within a longer history of police brutality, the use of militias by politicians and profound inequalities within Kenyan society were quickly lost in a furore over the names of those whom Waki's report suspected of masterminding the violence. Those names, written on a list, placed in a sealed envelope and handed to Kofi Annan for safekeeping, were the subject of much subsequent speculation.

The process of constitutional reform was another example of the way in which the presumed political need to keep the flawed coalition intact undermined the long-term objectives of peace and stability. All agreed that constitutional reform was unfinished business: the retention of the existing constitution was intolerable to almost every Kenyan. But there was little agreement on what the new constitution should look like. Two key issues continued to divide both the government and the wider population. Devolution of power to local authorities was seen by many in the ODM as essential to solving the problem of an over-centralisation of power. To the PNU's leaders and supporters, devolution was a constitutional cover for ethnic cleansing and provided succour only to the ethnic warlords. The role of the president was similarly divisive. Many in the PNU supported retention of the powerful presidency. The ODM's leaders wanted to see the powers of the presidency restrained either by the continuation of Odinga's temporary post of prime minister or by bolstering other institutions in government, thus enabling them to act as checks and balances on the executive.

A committee made up of constitutional experts from Kenya and overseas was charged with producing a draft document that worked through these seemingly intractable disputes. The committee handed over its suggested draft to the politicians in November 2009. In the months until a final version of the draft was tabled ahead of an August 2010 referendum, political leaders negotiated with one another about the contents of the document. A final version was published three months before the referendum. The draft constitution promised a greater separation of powers between the executive, the legislature and the judiciary. A second chamber was to be added to parliament and legislators were to be given greater powers of oversight over presidential appointments. However, a strong presidency was retained, and there was to be only limited devolution of power to new county councils. The much-anticipated decentralisation of power would not happen.

Despite the fact that the draft constitution failed to measure up to the expectations of constitutional reform that had been expressed so fervently over the previous two decades, many of those who had been in the vanguard of the push for reform supported it at the referendum. To civil society leaders, MPs who had long been linked to the reformist position and other observers, it seemed likely that 2010 represented the last opportunity for meaningful reform. Pro-reform campaigners set their reservations to one side and campaigned enthusiastically for the 'Yes' vote. 'This constitution will help us fight poverty, ignorance and disease and dictatorship,' Odinga told crowds at a rally in Nairobi in May.[103] Such promises could never be kept by any constitution, never mind the wordy and complex document presented to Kenyans.

Rather than tackling the obvious limitations within the draft constitution, the 'No' campaign was built around narrow political self-interest. Ruto believed that campaigning against Odinga represented his best opportunity for a tilt at the presidency in 2012. The two former allies had fallen out, and Ruto had entered an informal alliance within the government with the vice president, Musyoka, and the deputy prime minister, Kenyatta. However, with popular support firmly behind the

'Yes' campaign, neither Musyoka nor Kenyatta was willing to oppose the draft constitution. They, too, joined Odinga and President Kibaki in half-hearted campaigning for acceptance of the draft document. Ruto and his fellow Kalenjin MPs were left isolated in the 'No' campaign. They predictably picked on land as an issue to galvanise support, arguing – without any basis in fact – that the proposed constitution jeopardised Kalenjin claims to the Rift Valley. 'We will not accept to suffer while people sit on our land,' Ruto's ally and Mount Elgon MP Fred Kapondi told the crowd at the launch of the 'No' campaign.[104]

Although politically exposed, Ruto was nevertheless able to find partners for his 'No' campaign. Jettisoning the churches' longstanding support for constitutional reform, various Christian leaders opposed the draft. Their grievances hinged on the continued provision for Islamic family courts (which, the church leaders claimed, unfairly privileged Islam over Christianity) and on the new constitution's tolerance of abortion (in very rare cases). The proposed constitution 'violates the rights of some religious groups' and was 'offensive to the Christian community', claimed the NCCK general secretary, Canon Peter Karanja.[105] Voters offered a stern rebuke to Ruto and the clergy. Over two-thirds voted to accept the draft constitution. Odinga had seized the initiative and now sought to make hay. Having already been demoted to the post of higher education minister, in October Ruto was suspended from the cabinet. But worse was to follow.

By late 2010, no individual had yet stood trial for their part in the bloodshed three years before. Both the perpetrators and the organisers had escaped justice. Efforts to establish a tribunal to try the main organisers of the violence failed to get through parliament, not least because many MPs feared prosecution. The existing court structure had, on several occasions in the past, proved itself incapable of coping with such incidents. For once, however, Kenyan politicians were not in complete control of their own affairs. From the very beginning of the violence, human rights groups appealed to the International Criminal Court (ICC) to investigate alleged crimes against humanity committed by the state security forces and some of the ODM's leaders. The ICC's prosecutor, Luis Moreno-Ocampo, was moreover keen to take up the

Kenyan case. In urgent need of a successful prosecution to prove the ICC's worth, Moreno-Ocampo opened an investigation.

Building on the findings of the Waki commission and reports into the violence compiled by human rights groups, Moreno-Ocampo delivered his conclusions in December 2010. He announced that he would request the ICC to issue summonses to six individuals in two distinct cases. In the first, Moreno-Ocampo accused William Ruto; Henry Kosgey, the minister for industrialisation and the ODM chairman; and Joshua Sang, a broadcaster and executive at the Kalenjin-language radio station Kass FM, of crimes against humanity. In the second case, Francis Muthaura, the powerful head of the civil service; Uhuru Kenyatta, the deputy prime minister and minister of finance; and Mohammed Hussein Ali, the former police chief, were accused of the same charges. According to Moreno-Ocampo:

> These were not just crimes against innocent Kenyans. They were crimes against humanity as a whole. By breaking the cycle of impunity for massive crimes, victims and their families can have justice. And Kenyans can pave the way to peaceful elections in 2012.[106]

The prosecutor also made it clear that there were many more than six organisers of the violence, and that he expected the Kenyan authorities to prosecute perpetrators within the local court system.

PLUS ÇA CHANGE

Throughout the period after the election, Kibaki and Odinga consistently made vague, intangible promises of reform. 'We are going to act,' Kibaki assured US diplomats in June 2009.[107]

There is precious little evidence to suggest that a fundamental overhaul of politics and governance has taken place in the four years since the disputed election. Instead, the recurring themes of this book – corruption, assassination and ethnic chauvinism – have been all too frequently observed. The power-sharing government has been blighted by a succession of corruption scandals. Although not on the scale of Goldenberg or Anglo Leasing, these have ranged from the illegal sale of maize reserves to profiteering from the sale of Kenyan embassies overseas. Though corruption allegations made in 2010 led to the suspension of Ruto and the forced resignation of the foreign minister, Moses Wetangula, there has been no evidence of a sustained war on corruption within the government. In March 2009, according to Aaron Ringera, the head of the Kenya Anti-Corruption Commission, 'Every mover and shaker' in government was taking part in a 'feeding frenzy' of corruption.[108] As Wrong's book extensively documents, Ringera himself was embroiled in efforts to sabotage Githongo's investigation of the Anglo Leasing scandal and in the threats made against his life. Ringera's characterisation of the coalition government was echoed by his successor, Patrick Lumumba. According to *Der Spiegel*'s reporting of the US diplomatic cables released by Wikileaks in December 2010, Lumumba 'is convinced that there is hardly a single minister in the country's bloated, 42-member cabinet, that doesn't use their position to line their own pockets'.[109] As before, however, corruption has existed alongside other expressions of misrule.

Human rights have continued to be transgressed as part of the everyday business of government. On 6 March 2009, Oscar Kamau King'ara and John Paul Oulu were shot dead in their car while travelling through central Nairobi to a meeting with the KNCHR. The pair had run the Oscar Foundation, a civil society group, and had recently provided a UN investigator, Philip Alston, with evidence of police involvement in the illegal extrajudicial murders of Mungiki suspects. In a letter to senior government officials sent in October 2008, King'ara had described the killings as 'systematic and widespread' and as targeting 'a certain population for extermination'. He accused the police of acting with 'impunity and tribal bias with all intent to exterminating them [the suspects] from the face of the earth'.[110] Such accusations were repeated by other figures. For instance, Sally Kosgei, an ODM minister, told US officials that the police were 'permitted to utilize extrajudicial killings to control organized gangs such as the Mungiki, which threaten to disrupt Kikuyu politics by operating in the heart of Central Province'.[111] King'ara and Oulu were killed just hours after a government spokesman dismissed the Oscar Foundation as a mouthpiece for Mungiki. No arrests followed.

The ideas that underpinned politics have remained intact, too. The reaction to another shooting, this time of Moses Ole Mpoe in December 2010, demonstrates how the events of 2008 and earlier episodes entrenched certain attitudes related to ethnicity, land and citizenship. Mpoe was a campaigner for the restitution of lands seized from Maasai grazers in the colonial period. By the time of his death, he had switched his attention to the resettlement of those displaced by the violence of 2007–8. Mpoe and other Maasai leaders were opposed to plans announced by the government to purchase nearly 2,500 acres in Narok district, to be allocated by the state to those displaced by the post-election violence. Mpoe considered this to be another example of state-led theft of Maasai resources. He was, however, shot on 3 December while sitting in his car close to Nakuru town. Mpoe's MP, William Ole Ntimama, termed the killing a political assassination intended to silence opposition to the relocation of the displaced. 'We are trying to maintain peace,' Ntimama claimed, 'but we don't want the Government to push us to accept the 2,400 foreigners in our midst. It will be unfortunate if the police fail to nail the killers.'[112] Ntimama's words, his pre-emptive justification of possible ethnic violence against mainly Kikuyu displaced victims of the post-election violence and his characterisation of fellow Kenyans as 'foreigners' show how far Kenya has yet to go before the events of 2007–8 can be treated as history.

THE LEOPARDS AND THE GOATS

THE PARTY (AGAIN)

In August 2010, the Odinga residence in Nairobi hosted another party, on this occasion to celebrate the outcome of the constitutional referendum. Some things had changed: it was Raila rather than Oginga who greeted the guests, and the Kamba dancing troupe had been replaced by 'a bevy of beauties'. But some things remained the same. The younger Odinga was no less generous a host than his father had been. Guests were treated to a buffet table covered with 'chicken, lamb and beef' and 'beer, wines, spirits [and] soft drinks'. Ida Odinga, Raila's wife, welcomed the visitors. 'We are celebrating a great day,' she told them. 'We appreciate your hard work in ensuring "Yes" emerged victorious. Those who will come after us, including our grand children, will definitely say we did a good thing by giving them the new Constitution.' The air of celebration dominated the other speeches, too.

'I feel so proud to be a Kenyan,' Raila told his guests. 'When called upon at this critical time, they were not found to be wanting; they rose to the occasion.' As his father had done in 1963, Odinga shared the limelight with a Kenyatta. Uhuru kept his remarks brief, telling the party-goers: 'I don't care what you do or say today, nothing will make me angry.'[1] Just as memories of Mau Mau and thoughts of shifta or majimbo were banished from Oginga's celebration of self-rule in 1963, so those present at Raila's party hoped the referendum victory meant that a page had been turned on the post-election violence of early 2008. But that history was not so easily escaped: within months Kenyatta had received a summons from the ICC for his alleged role in crimes against humanity.

In the days following the referendum and ratification of the new constitution, it was common to hear Kenyans refer to these events as a 'new start'. 'After half a century of trying, Kenyans have bequeathed unto themselves a constitution that marks the birth of the Second Republic,' wrote the former minister Mukhisa Kituyi in late August.[2] There was little reason to believe him. Moreno-Ocampo's announcement in December 2010 of the six accused in the ICC's investigation into the post-election violence has a far better claim to mark the end of the first republic. The state's institutions and the ways in which politics had been conducted since independence had been shown to have failed utterly. The only way that Kenyans could expect to check the abuses of power of those in high office and find justice was through external intervention. The fragility of independence and the weakness of the nation-state were laid bare for all to see.

The celebrations at Odinga's Nairobi home in August 2010 were far removed from the reality of life for most Kenyans. The displays of wealth and power made this an event as distant from the average resident of Eldoret or Kajiado as a party in Knightsbridge or the Upper East Side. But homecomings are another matter altogether. Decades of labour migration have scattered Kenyans around their country, and now that education and the search for work take them overseas in ever greater numbers the celebrations marking the return of a family member are one of the rituals of everyday life. Three such homecomings in recent years tell us a great deal more about the state of Kenya than the self-congratulation of Odinga's party.

THE KENYA WE WANT

On 30 May 2003, Mau Mau veterans, political leaders, representatives of the local and international press and hundreds of ordinary citizens flooded Nairobi's main airport and the surrounding area: Stanley Mathenge was coming home. The excitement was understandable, as Mathenge had not been seen in Kenya for nearly fifty years. A leading light in radical politics, he had been a key figure in the emergence of the Mau Mau insurgency in the 1950s. Fearing arrest in October 1952, he fled from his home in Nyeri to the forests of the Aberdare Mountains. There he became one of the military leaders of Mau Mau's 25,000 or so forest fighters. Over the next three years, he and his followers kept up the fight against British colonial forces and their Kikuyu loyalist allies. But by 1955, the rebels in the forest were suffering. Aerial bombing, factionalism among the guerrillas themselves, the cold and wet of the high-altitude forests and harassment from police and army patrols made for a miserable existence. Mathenge wanted to pursue talks with the British authorities, but his fellow leader, Dedan Kimathi, refused. Mathenge knew then that his position was hopeless. With the net tightening around the last few hundred forest fighters, he led a break-out. With up to twenty-nine supporters, the general attempted to escape from the Aberdares and flee to independent Ethiopia. The last anyone saw or heard of them was as they left their camp high in the mountain forest on 23 July 1955.

Their deaths seemed certain. It was with great amazement and no little joy, therefore, that Kenyans greeted the news in January 2002 that Mathenge had apparently been found in Ethiopia. Joseph Karimi, a Kenyan journalist, was said to have been tipped off about his whereabouts by George Kilimo, a Kenyan resident in Ethiopia. Not only had Mathenge and his followers survived their long trek to Ethiopia, but there the Mau Mau general had thrived. After settling on a large farm on the rural fringe of the Ethiopian capital, Addis Ababa, Mathenge had remarried and was a grandfather many times over.

Mathenge's discovery could not have been more timely or symbolic. There seemed no better omen for Kenyans working for the second liberation than the return of a hero from the first. In Mathenge's home in Nyeri, the news was greeted with joy. 'This is Mathenge, no doubt about it,' said Muraya wa Muthai, a Mau Mau veteran and former comrade-in-arms, speaking to a journalist after seeing a photograph of the old man.[3] The news set in train a number of visits by dignitaries to

Ethiopia. Each returned home sure that they had met the Mau Mau hero. When his wife, Miriam Muthoni, also returned from Addis Ababa in October 2002 saying she was sure that the old man was Mathenge, there seemed no doubt.

The homecoming had been fixed to coincide with the annual celebration on 1 June of the anniversary of self-rule, and Mathenge was to be guest of honour for the presidential address and the military parade in Nairobi's Nyayo Stadium. Wearing a new grey suit and a brown flat cap, he entered the arrivals hall at Nairobi airport to the accompaniment of songs from the independence era sung by the assembled crowd. In a welcome address on behalf of the government, the MP and former dissident Koigi wa Wamwere declared it to be 'the greatest day for this country since independence'.[4] Then, in those first confused moments on Kenyan soil, the return of Stanley Mathenge turned from triumph to farce.

'I'm no Kenyan, I'm no Kenyan,' Mathenge told his escort. Looking bewildered, he asked the Ethiopian ambassador in Amharic: 'What am I going to say [as] I don't know their language [or] good English?' The ambassador suggested that Mathenge give a short address, which the diplomat then translated into English. 'I hear that my mother and General Mathenge were brother and sister,' the old man said. 'So I am half Kenyan and half Ethiopian. I am happy to be back among my people.'[5] His words were disconcerting enough. That he could speak neither Kikuyu nor Swahili, the lingua franca of Kenya, was even more troubling, considering that Mathenge had been thirty-seven years old in 1955. Having finished his short speech, Mathenge and his Ethiopian family were escorted to a waiting government Mercedes and driven to their suite at the Panafric Hotel.

The scenes at the airport were sufficient for the government to withdraw Mathenge's invitation to the Madaraka Day celebrations. With the country in uproar, a press conference was held. Answering only questions put to him in Amharic, the old man said that he had been born in Ethiopia close to the Kenyan border, and unequivocally denied that he was the Mau Mau general.[6] That was enough for his minders, Kilimo and Karimi. The two men whisked the old man away to his room before any further damaging questions could be asked. For the next week, the country was gripped by this identity crisis and the press was denied any further access.

Perhaps the most tragic characters in the saga were those who had fought with the real Mathenge. Mau Mau veterans undertook a pilgrimage from their homes around the country to the Panafric Hotel in central Nairobi to meet the man they had fought with and who had led them in the forests during their struggle against British rule. Sitting on the veranda outside the hotel's restaurant, the assembled veterans spoke to the press about their experiences during the war, their memories of Mathenge and their thoughts on the identity of the old man from Ethiopia. Some thought the man was the general, but most disagreed. His lack of height could be put down to the ageing process, but the absence of a distinctive gap in his front teeth, the disappearance of a scar on his neck, a darkening of the skin and the apparent loss of ten years were sufficient for most to recognise that Kenyans had been the victims of a hoax.

It transpired that it was not Mathenge at the Panafric, but instead Ato Lemma Ayanu, an Ethiopian farmer with at best indirect family links to Kenya. Exploiting divisions within the Mathenge family in Nyeri, the government's naivety and the public's optimism, Ayanu's handlers had sought fame and fortune by claiming to have solved one of the great riddles of Kenyan history. In the small hours of 7 June, and having run up a $16,000 bill at the hotel, Ayanu left the country on an early-morning flight to Addis Ababa. Little was to be heard of the Ethiopian or his handlers again.

The willingness of so many to suspend their disbelief requires some explanation. The 1950s and early 1960s are commonly thought of as being a golden age of nationalism, when Kenyans pulled together for the common good and politicians strove for political and economic freedom rather than personal gain. Mathenge therefore appeared to offer a tangible link to that past and help the country meet the common plea for greater national unity.

Such calls took on fresh urgency after the violence of early 2008. From politicians, through civil society leaders, to international figures,

Kenyans were constantly told that nationalism was the only way out of the chasm into which the country had fallen. Many of the subsequently enacted reforms, such as the establishment of a Heroes Day national holiday and the formation of the National Cohesion and Integration Commission to monitor the words and actions of politicians, explicitly set out to encourage a greater sense of nationalism among Kenyan citizens.

Yet nations are not easily created and are, history suggests, projects undertaken by strong states. The Mathenge/Ayanu affair is a useful warning of the deceptive simplicity of nationalism and, as such, suggests that pause for reflection is due when nationalism is offered as an easy cure for Kenya's ills: history that appears simple, without ambiguity or contradiction, is, rather like the reappearance of Mathenge, too good to be true. The historical record of the late 1950s and early 1960s is not just one of a march to independence. It is also one of fractious contests over access to state resources and the drawing of boundaries that accompanied the achievement of independence. Nationalism, moreover, fails to capture the full range of identities that Kenyans exhibit, besides being Kenyan. They are also youths and elders; rich and poor; men and women; Luo, Kikuyu or members of any one of the other tens of ethnic groups; Muslim and Christian; Arab, African and Asian; citizens of the world and fierce sons of the soil. In short, as Peter Wafula Wekesa argues, Kenyan nationalism 'masks the historical reality defining our dynamic and diverse experience'.[7]

Borrowing from Naipaul, Kahora labels recent state-led efforts to inculcate a sense of national identity 'fairy tales'.[8] The same criticism can, however, be made of the stories Kenyans tell themselves about ethnicity. Kenya may not be a nation, but nor is it simply 'a collection of ethnic states living uncomfortably within a set of borders delineated under colonialism'.[9] The long history of ethnicity in Kenya (and East Africa more generally) is of accommodation, of open boundaries and of movement, rather than of indigenous peoples. A dangerous myth of purity and autochthony has taken hold among the residents of the Rift Valley in particular, and must be demolished as a matter of urgency.

Nevertheless, the centrality of ethnicity to politics needs to be confronted. Ethnicity is not an intrinsically bad thing. More discussion could take place about how to harness the capacity of ethnicity to act as a restraining force on misbehaving elites – a process John Lonsdale famously terms 'moral ethnicity'.[10] As Tom Young writes, 'if ethnic identity is good for certain things, draw on it or adapt it, don't try to suppress it'.[11] Viewed from the grassroots, ethnicity seems to work. Kinuthia Macharia's study of the role of ethnicity in Nairobi's informal sector in the late 1980s makes for illuminating reading in this regard. Macharia was interested in finding out why members of certain ethnic groups dominated the ranks of workers in particular sectors of the informal economy. Garment manufacturers, for example, were generally Luo, while lamp makers were Kikuyu (and indeed were drawn from a very small area of Murang'a district). Women who sold food from semi-permanent kiosks to workers in the city's Industrial Area were overwhelmingly Kikuyu, while Luo women controlled the sale of food on the streets outside factory gates.

Underpinning these arrangements were two factors. The first was networks: ethnicity provided a way in which information about new opportunities could be shared. Women selling food found out about available spots because 'a friend told them about the space appropriate for food selling'. These networks also extended to training. One of the Kikuyu lamp makers from Murang'a told Macharia, 'when I learnt the skills, I continued to teach other people in my home area, mainly friends and relatives'. But ethnicity also provided something otherwise missing in the unregulated and unpoliced informal economy, and in a formal economy marked by corruption: trust. The sense of common identity and of reciprocal ties between members of the same ethnic group meant that ethnicity allowed for the extension of credit between different workers in the informal sector. Moreover, customers had more trust in the goods and services they were buying if they were purchasing from someone from the same ethnic group.[12]

In Macharia's account, ethnicity was a powerful response to the shortcomings of the formal economy, the labour market and the state. People who would otherwise not have access to credit, wages or social security support were able to eke out a living by making the most of their ethnic networks. From that account, we can extrapolate a broader idea about how ethnicity worked in post-colonial Kenya. In the absence of redistribution, ethnicity provided a way in which Kenyans could access and protect the scarce resources of land, jobs and political power. The networks of kin encouraged by ethnicity provided for access to plots of land, work and housing on a reciprocal basis. The networks of patronage meant that, if their political leader became an MP or a minister (or even president), then the roads in their district might be repaired, the moribund local factory rejuvenated or the village school expanded. Ethnicity was not irrational and nor was it an expression of traditionalism; instead it was a logical response to an experience of the modern world in which resources are scarce – a symptom rather than a cause of Kenya's ills.

THE KENYA WE HAVE

Confronting ethnicity rather than dreaming of nationalism was perhaps part of John Githongo's message on his return home in August 2008. After three years in exile (see chapter 8), and feted like Mathenge as a returning hero, he might have been forgiven for adopting a celebratory tone in his first press conference back on Kenyan soil. The prodigal was in a reflective mood, however. As he considered the devastated political and social landscape in the aftermath of the post-election violence, he did not try to make light of the enormous challenges facing the country in the years ahead. 'There are no saints in this story,' he told the assembled journalists, 'and I do not pretend to be one.' Rather than sloganeering or offering trite solutions to the country's malaise, his only advice was: 'We are going to have to make do with what we have – it's imperfect.'[13]

Githongo's determination to have a frank discussion about such matters was refreshing. Kenyan public debate is often marked by moments of intense openness followed by extended periods of silence. The aftermath of the violence of 2008 was one such moment, but anger and hope quickly gave way to pessimism and pragmatism. 'I wake up to the Kenyan morning and look around,' Kahora writes, 'and the new day seems to forgive the recent past, and mostly because the public life is one of amnesiac collusion, a physical fact without regret or hope.' This 'amnesiac collusion' is built on the need of ordinary Kenyans to get on with the business of living and the need of their rulers to get on with the business (in every sense) of government. A succession of conferences entitled 'The Kenya We Want' have been convened at various moments of crisis during the post-colonial period, but Kahora notes, ' "The Kenya We Live In" is something that is never broached in public spaces'. People 'talk about what we want as we skirt the real'.[14] So, to take on Kahora and Githongo's challenge, what does Kenya have?

Most importantly, Kenya has profound inequality. By accident of birth, the chances of a newborn surviving and then thriving in modern Kenya vary greatly. A child is nearly four times more likely to die before his or her fifth birthday in Nyanza Province than in Central Province. The population of Western Province has less than half the health facilities per head that Central Province has. Girls in the Rift Valley are half as likely to attend secondary school as their peers in Central Province. Less than a third of the population of Nyanza has access to the clean water that more than nine in ten residents of Nairobi have. Even within provinces, inequalities between ethnic groups are evident. Kikuyu in the Rift Valley have, on average, twice as many household assets as members of other communities in the province.[15] Some variation is to be expected, given the differences in climate, altitude, soil fertility and extent of integration of different parts of the country into the regional and global economies. Nevertheless, the need for ameliorating redistributive policies is stark.

In common with so many countries in the aftermath of the Cold War, Kenya has lost the ability to talk about redistribution. Matiba was no 'voice of the common man', but even he realised that the refusal to discuss redistribution in such an unequal setting was a problem. Even as he dismissed redistribution as a policy, he admitted 'we have never considered this problem seriously as a nation and discussed it openly'. Inequality was, he conceded, no accident, but rather 'we are responsible, ourselves, for what has happened'. He acknowledged that 'we have not made an effort to give the matter serious attention'.[16] It is not surprising, therefore, that the poor and marginalised turn to ethnicity to protect what little they have and to try to gain more land or jobs or whatever else it is they need to survive. The politics of recognition have trumped redistribution.

This is no accident: this book has shown the lengths to which Kenyatta, Moi and Kibaki went to crush voices calling for redistribution. These voices were at first coherent and measured, such as the KPU, JM Kariuki or the university students and lecturers in the late 1970s and 1980s. As assassination, repression and detention silenced the champions of redistribution in formal politics, so the demands for it moved to the informal political sphere and became angrier and more indecipherable. Mungiki and other recent episodes of violence are the result.

Kenya has a schizophrenic political system that reflects the place it occupies in the shadows and spaces between the forces that define the modern age. On the one hand, it has a vibrant civil society and a free press that routinely exposes corruption scandals and demonstrates the links between senior political figures and electoral violence. On the other hand, groups like Mungiki thrive and its politicians are accused of crimes against humanity. This simultaneous experience of open debate of politics and existence under a government that has exhibited its authoritarian tendencies on numerous occasions is typical of the paradoxical nature of life in Kenya since 1963. Kenyans experienced independence, but not all enjoyed the rights and benefits of citizenship; they have witnessed economic growth, but have not necessarily been able to find work; they have participated in development projects that have not necessarily delivered improved standards of living; and they have voted in elections without experiencing democracy. It is, to quote Kahora again, 'a half-made place' that the positivist language of big themes of recent history – decolonisation, development and democratisation – fails to describe accurately.[17]

Decolonisation did not end external influence in Kenya's affairs, and nor did it liberate a great many Kenyans in the fullest sense of the term. Kenya's politics is not best described as democratising, but rather as a hybrid form of democracy and authoritarianism. It oscillates and has peaks and troughs, but it has been that way since before independ-ence. Kenya's developing economy is, in fact, producing extreme vari-ations in the experience of everyday life – from pastoralists in West Pokot, for example, to finance and technology executives in Nairobi who inhabit thoroughly globalised spaces. The point is not that Kenya is calm or chaotic, peaceful or violent, economically vibrant or desti-tute, democratic or authoritarian, but rather that it is all those things simultaneously. If one is fortunate to stand on the right side of the line dividing any of those conditions, then Kenyan society seems empow-ered and dynamic. If not, then it is a place characterised by exclusion.

Though it has these potentially debilitating conditions, Kenya also has things in its favour. The agency of Kenyans themselves is the country's greatest resource. Writing a few months before the 2007 elec-tion, Wainaina celebrated the ingenuity of its entrepreneurs, the creativity of its intellectuals and the underlying commitment to democ-racy on the part of the citizenry, whatever its rulers may be up to. Kenyans, he argues, no longer have to concentrate on the pessimism of commentators who emphasised corruption, crime and violence: 'We have learned to ignore the shrill screams coming from the peddlers of hopelessness. We motor on faith and enterprise, with small steps. On hope, and without hysteria.'[18] This book, it must be confessed, muffles the sounds of enterprise and hope. But as the examples of independence and the movement to restore multiparty democracy demonstrate, Kenyans have the capacity to overcome tyranny. They will not be helped by their current political leaders.

THE FIRE NEXT TIME

Our third homecoming is that of Njeeri wa Thiong'o, the wife of Ngugi, a few days before the 2007 election. Like Githongo's return, Njeeri's required great courage. Three years before, she had accompanied her husband on his first trip back to Kenya since going into exile in 1982. The visit in 2004 ended in tragedy, however. The couple were attacked in their rented apartment in Nairobi and Njeeri was raped. Among those accused of the attack was Chege Kiragu, Ngugi's nephew. He was later acquitted, but in 2007 stood for election in Ngugi's home constituency of Limuru, on Nairobi's outskirts. Njeeri therefore travelled to Limuru from the family home in California to deliver a message from Ngugi to the voters.

On the Sunday before the election, she visited churches in Limuru to deliver the message in person. It was controversial. The author gave his backing to Kibaki, claiming that 'the last five years of Kibaki's rule, 2002–2007, have been the freest in Kenya's history'. Such sentiments were thrown back in Ngugi's face as the tragedy of the election played out in the days that followed. The real focus of the letter, though, was the parliamentary election, rather than the presidential battle. He urged voters to cast their ballots for 'a person of known integrity', and not Kiragu. 'Do not allow a leopard to guard your goats,' the message urged.[19] The point was driven home rather more powerfully than Njeeri or Ngugi would have hoped. As Njeeri left the Presbyterian church where she had spoken, youths in one of Kiragu's campaign vehicles tried to block her path and threatened her. She was unharmed but it was a narrow escape.

Despite the drama of Njeeri's visit and the endorsement given to Kibaki by Ngugi, the letter raised a more important point. The most immediate problem Kenyans have in forcing a change to the nature of politics is that, come election time, there are often, but not always, only leopards to choose from. The leopards have made violence seem a normal part of the political process. One witness to the violence in early 2008 remarked: 'The violence was also there in 1992, but that was the normal tribal clashes. We don't know what causes the clashes. It just happens. We cannot say it is caused by elections. One tribe suddenly rises against another and there is loss of life and property.'[20] The banality and normalisation of violence are, however, products of the political system, or at least those that inhabit it. So long as thugs and criminals are privileged in their efforts to win seats in parliament or on local councils by the inability of the courts and police to arrest and prosecute, thuggery will remain an essential part of political life.

Even politicians seen as reformers are forced to play the game. After the 2007 election, Boni Khalwale received much praise for his chairing of parliament's Public Accounts Committee. Using that position, Khalwale, MP for Ikolomani in Western Province, led efforts to expose official corruption. He rightly won plaudits for this effort. He is, according to US Ambassador Ranneberger, 'a politician worth watching' because of 'his willingness to take on vested interests and talk truth to power'. But, as Ranneberger had to concede, Khalwale was fined in the run-up to the 2007 election 'for hiring a youth gang to intimidate a rival candidate's supporters'.[21] Rather than just the activities of a few morally bankrupt individuals, such things are systemic and fundamental to the operation of politics. Only when the leopards are dislodged will Kenya finally enjoy the fruits of independence. Kenyan politicians have by now proved that they are utterly incapable of halting political violence or stopping corruption.

Little hope should be invested in the ability of American, British or European diplomats to instil change either. Western governments have been far from neutral actors in Kenya's political history, but have instead tended to side with incumbent figures and parties at moments of dispute. 'Donors' primary concern appeared to be the avoidance of any path that could lead to a breakdown of political and economic order', writes Stephen Brown.[22] The influence that Western governments exert over Kenyan politicians is in any case declining – since 2002 China's interests in Kenya have grown considerably. Kenyans will themselves have to bring about the change.

Equity in access to justice, the provision of basic services and the availability of economic opportunities are, according to John Githongo, the 'primary democratic outcome Kenyans seek'.[23] Kenya may never be prosperous or be a nation; but armed with a government that it deserves, it can be a state whose citizens live side by side in peace and enjoy equal opportunities. Compared to the rhetoric of the nationalist parties of the 1960s and the politicians of the multiparty era, these may seem unduly modest goals. But such a state has proved elusive since Kenya came into being with the colonial conquest at the end of the nineteenth century. Peace and equality are worth fighting for.

BIBLIOGRAPHY

Abantu for Development. *The Other Side of Prison: The role of women left behind*, Nairobi, 2004

Abdi Sheikh, S. *Blood on the Runway: The Wagalla massacre of 1984*, Nairobi, 2007

Adar, Korwa. 'Kenya: Governance, accountability and human rights practice in the post 1992 and 1997 multi-party electoral dispensation', Writenet paper no. 12/2000, April 2001

Adar, Korwa and Isaac Munyae. 'Human rights abuse in Kenya under Daniel Arap Moi, 1978–2001', *African Studies Quarterly*, 5(1) (2001), available at: http://web.africa.ufl. edu/asq/v5/v5i1a1.htm

Adhiambo Mbeo, Mary and Oki Ooko-Ombaka (eds). *Women and the Law in Kenya: Perspectives and emerging issues*, Nairobi, 1989

Africa Watch. *Kenya: Taking liberties*, New York, 1991

— *Divide and Rule: State-sponsored ethnic violence in Kenya*, New York, 1993

African Rights. *Kenya: Shadow justice*, London, 1996

Ajulu, Rok. 'Thinking through the crisis of democratisation in Kenya: A response to Adar and Murunga', *African Sociological Review*, 4(2) (2000), pp. 133–57

— 'Politicised ethnicity, competitive politics and conflict in Kenya: A historical perspective', *African Studies* 61(2) (2002), pp. 251–68

Akare, Thomas. *The Slums*, London, 1981

Alila, Patrick, Kabiru Kinyanjui and Gatheru Wanjohi. *Rural Landlessness in Kenya: Dynamics, problems and policies*, Nairobi, 1993

Amario, Fai. *Fai Amario's Kamiti Notebook: Prison memoirs of a Kenyan industrialist*, Naivasha, 1999

Amnesty International. *Torture, Political Detention and Unfair Trials*, London, 1987

Amutabi, Maurice. 'Crisis and student protest in universities in Kenya: Examining the role of students in national leadership and the democratization process', *African Studies Review*, 45(2) (2002), pp. 157–77

Anderson, Benedict. *Imagined Communities: Reflections on the origins and spread of nationalism*, London, 1983

Anderson, David. 'Vigilantes, violence and the politics of public order in Kenya', *African Affairs*, 101(405) (2002), pp. 531–55

— *Histories of the Hanged: The dirty war in Kenya and the end of empire*, London, 2005
— ' "Yours in the struggle for Majimbo": Nationalism and party politics of decoloniza-tion in Kenya, 1955–64', *Journal of Contemporary History*, 40(3) (2005), pp. 547–64
— 'Majimboism: The troubled history of an idea' in D. Branch, N. Cheeseman and L. Gardner (eds), *Our Turn to Eat*, Berlin, 2010, pp. 23–52
Anderson, David and Emma Lochery. 'Violence and exodus in Kenya's Rift Valley 2008: Predictable and preventable?', *Journal of Eastern African Studies*, 2(2) (2008), pp. 328–43
Anguka, Joshua. *Absolute Power: The Ouko murder mystery*, London, 1998
Anonymous, *Independent Kenya*, London, 1982
Anyang' Nyong'o, Peter. 'State and society in Kenya: The disintegration of the nation-alist coalition and the rise of the presidential authoritarianism 1963–78', *African Affairs*, 88(351) (1989), pp. 229–51
— (ed.). *30 Years of Independence in Africa: The lost decades?* Nairobi, 2002
Association of African Women for Research and Development. *Women's Political Leadership in Kenya: Involvement, challenges and the way forward*, Nairobi, 1998
Atieno Odhiambo, E.S. 'Democracy and the ideology of order in Kenya' in M. Schatzberg (ed.), *The Political Economy of Kenya*, New York, 1987, pp. 177–202
— 'The formative years: 1945–55' in B.A. Ogot and W. Ochieng (eds), *Decolonization and Independence in Kenya: 1940–93*, London, 1995, pp. 25–47
— 'Foreword: A critique of the postcolony of Kenya' in Wambui Waiyaki Otieno, *Mau Mau's Daughter: A life history*, Boulder, CO, 1998, pp. xi–xiii
— 'Ethnic cleansing and civil society in Kenya 1969–1992', *Journal of Contemporary African Studies*, 22(1) (2004), pp. 29–42
Attwood, William. *The Reds and the Blacks: A personal adventure*, New York, 1967
Badejo, Babafemi. *Raila Odinga: An enigma in Kenya politics*, Lagos, 2006
Barkan, Joel and Michael Chege. 'Decentralising the state: District focus and the politics of reallocation in Kenya', *Journal of Modern African Studies*, 27(3) (1989), pp. 431–53
Bates, Robert. *Beyond the Miracle of the Market: The political economy of agrarian develop-ment in Kenya*, Cambridge, 2005
Bates, Robert. *When Things Fell Apart: State failure in late-century Africa*, Cambridge, 2008
Bayart, Jean-François. 'Africa in the world: A history of extraversion', *African Affairs*, 99(395) (2000), pp. 217–67
— *The State in Africa: The politics of the belly*, Cambridge, 2009
Bayart, Jean-François, Stephen Ellis and Beatrice Hibou. *The Criminalization of the State in Africa*, trans. S. Ellis, Oxford, 1999
Bennett, George and Carl Rosberg. *The Kenyatta Election: Kenya 1960–1961*, London, 1961
Berman, Bruce. *Control and Crisis in Colonial Kenya: The dialectic of domination*, London, 1990
— 'Ethnicity, patronage and the African state: The politics of uncivil nationalism', *African Affairs*, 97(388) (1998), pp. 305–41
— 'Ethnicity, bureaucracy and democracy: The politics of trust' in B. Berman, D. Eyoh and W. Kymlicka (eds), *Ethnicity and Democracy in Africa*, Oxford, 2004
Bevan, David, Paul Collier and Jan Willem Gunning, with Arne Bigsten and Paul Horsnell. *Peasants and Governance: An economic analysis*, Oxford, 1989
Bienen, Henry. *Kenya: The politics of participation and control*, Princeton, 1974
Black, Ian and Benny Morris. *Israel's Secret Wars: A history of Israel's intelligence services*, New York, 1991
Blundell, Michael. *A Love Affair with the Sun: A memoir of seventy years in Kenya*, Nairobi, 1994
Blunt, Robert. ' "Satan is an imitator": Kenya's recent cosmology of corruption' in B. Weiss (ed.), *Producing African Futures: Ritual and reproduction in a neoliberal age*, Leiden, 2004, pp. 294–328

Boone, Catherine. *Political Topographies of the African State: Territorial authority and institutional choice*, Cambridge, 2003

Branch, Daniel. 'The search for the remains of Dedan Kimathi: The politics of death and memorialization in colonial Kenya', *Past and Present*, 206(supplement 5) (2010), pp. 301–20

Branch, Daniel and Nic Cheeseman. 'Using opinion polls to evaluate Kenyan politics, March 2004 – January 2005', *African Affairs*, 104(415) (2005), pp. 326–36

— 'The politics of control in Kenya: Understanding the bureaucratic-executive state, 1952–78', *Review of African Political Economy*, 107 (2006), pp. 11–31

— 'Democratization, sequencing, and state failure in Africa: Lessons from Kenya', *African Affairs*, 108(430) (2009), pp. 1–26

Bratton, Michael and Mwangi Kimenyi. 'Voting in Kenya: Putting ethnicity in perspective', *Journal of Eastern African Studies*, 2(2) (2008), pp. 272–89

Bravman, Bill. *Making Ethnic Ways: Communities and their transformations in Taita, Kenya, 1800–1950*, Oxford, 1998

Brennan, James. 'Lowering the sultan's flag: Sovereignty and decolonization in Coastal Kenya', *Comparative Studies in Society and History*, 50(4) (2008), pp. 831–61

Bridger, Gordon. *Harambee Settlement Schemes: An evaluation*, Nairobi, 1968

Brown, Stephen. 'Authoritarian leaders and multiparty elections in Africa: How foreign donors help to keep Kenya's Daniel arap Moi in power', *Third World Quarterly*, 22(5) (2001), pp. 725–39

— 'From demiurge to midwife: Changing donor roles in Kenya's democratisation process' in G. Murunga and S. Nasong'o (eds), *Kenya: The struggle for democracy*, London, 2007

Brownhill, Leigh. *Land, Food, Freedom: Struggles for the gendered commons in Kenya 1870 to 2007*, Trenton, NJ, 2009

Carotenuto, Matthew. '*Riwruok E Teko*: Cultivating identity in colonial and postcolonial Kenya', *Africa Today*, 53(2) (2006), pp. 53–74

Catholic Bishops of Kenya. *Kenya 1992: Looking towards the future with hope*, Nairobi, 1992

— *A Call to Justice, Love and Reconciliation*, Nairobi, 1992

Central Depository Unit. *Ghasia Watch: CDU report on electoral violence in Kenya January–December 2002*, Nairobi, 2003

Chabal, Patrick and Jean-Pascal Daloz. *Africa Works: Disorder as political instrument*, Oxford, 1999

Chande, Abdin. 'Radicalism and reform in East Africa' in Nehemia Levtzion and Randall Pouwels (eds), *The History of Islam in Africa*, Oxford, 2000, pp. 349–69

Cheeseman, Nic. 'The Kenyan elections of 2007: An introduction', *Journal of Eastern African Studies*, 2(2) (2008), pp. 166–84

Cheeseman, Nic and Blessing-Miles Tendi. 'Power-sharing in comparative perspective: The dynamics of "unity governments" in Kenya and Zimbabwe', *Journal of Modern African Studies*, 48(2) (2010), pp. 203–29

Chege, Michael. 'Introducing race as a variable into the political economy of Kenya debate: An incendiary idea', *African Affairs*, 97(387) (1998), pp. 209–30

— 'Kenya: Back from the brink?', *Journal of Democracy*, 19(4) (2008), pp. 125–39

Chweya, Ludeki (ed.). *Electoral Politics in Kenya*, Nairobi, 2002

Clough, Marshall. 'Mau Mau and the contest for memory' in E.S. Atieno Odhiambo and John Lonsdale (eds), *Mau Mau and Nationhood: Arms, authority and narration*, Oxford, 2003, pp. 251–67

Cohen, David William and E.S. Atieno Odhiambo. *Burying S.M.: The politics of knowledge and the sociology of power in Africa*, London, 1992

— *The Risks of Knowledge: Investigations into the death of the Hon. Minister John Robert Ouko in Kenya, 1990*, Athens, OH, 2004

Collier, Paul. *War, Guns and Votes: Democracy in dangerous places*, London, 2009

Committee of Inquiry into the Post-Election Violence. *Commission of Inquiry into the Post-Election Violence Report*, Nairobi, 2008

Committee for the Release of Political Prisoners in Kenya. *Law as a Tool of Political Repression in Kenya*, London, 1982

— *Release the Political Prisoners in Kenya*, London, 1982

— *University Destroyed: Moi crowns ten years of government terror in Kenya*, London, 1983

Commonwealth Observer Group. *Kenya General Election 27 December 2007: The report of the Commonwealth Observer Group*, London, 2008

Convention on Social and Economic Development in the Emerging Kenya Nation. *The Kenya We Want: Report of the Convention on Social and Economic Development in the Emerging Kenya Nation*, Nairobi, 1962

Cooper, Frederick. *On the African Waterfront: Urban disorder and the transformation of work in colonial Mombasa*, New Haven, CT, 1987

— 'Conflict and connection: Rethinking African colonial history', *American Historical Review*, 99(5) (1994), pp. 1516–45

— *Decolonization and African Society: The labor question in French and British Africa*, Cambridge, 1996

— *Africa Since 1940: The past of the present*, Cambridge, 2002

— 'Possibility and constraint: African independence in historical perspective', *Journal of African History*, 49 (2008), pp. 167–96

Cronk, Lee. *From Mukogodo to Maasai: Ethnicity and cultural change in Kenya*, Boulder, CO, 2004

Cross, Sholto. 'L'Etat c'est Moi: Political transition and the Kenya general election of 1979', discussion paper no. 66, University of East Anglia, April 1983

Currie, Kate and Larry Ray. 'State and class in Kenya: Notes on the cohesion of the ruling class', *Journal of Modern African Studies*, 22(4) (1984), pp. 559–93

Dianga, James. *Kenya 1982, the Attempted Coup: The consequences of a one-party dictatorship*, London, 2002

Dolan, Catherine. 'Contested terrain: Gender, labor and religious dynamics in horticultural exporting, Meru District, Kenya', working paper no. 501, Institute of Development Studies, University of Nairobi, 1995

Dowden, Richard. *Africa: Altered states, ordinary miracles*, London, 2008

Dudziak, Mary. *Exporting American Dreams: Thurgood Marshall's African journey*, Oxford, 2008

Dutto, Carl. *Nyeri Townsmen, Kenya*, Kampala, 1975

Eaton, Dave. 'The business of peace: Raiding and peace work along the Kenya–Uganda border (part I)', *African Affairs*, 107(426) (2008), pp. 89–110

— 'The business of peace: Raiding and peace work along the Kenya–Uganda border (part II)', *African Affairs*, 107(427) (2008), pp. 243–59

Ellis, Stephen. 'Writing histories of contemporary Africa', *Journal of African History*, 43(1) (2002), pp. 1–26

— *Season of Rains: Africa in the world*, London, 2011

Ellis, Stephen and Gerrie ter Haar. 'Religion and politics in sub-Saharan Africa', *Journal of Modern African Studies*, 36(2) (1998), pp. 175–201

Episcopal Conference of Kenya. *Justice and Peace Commission: Pastoral letter of the bishops of Kenya*, Nairobi, 1988

European Union Election Observation Mission. *Kenya: Final report general elections 27 December 2007*, Brussels, 2008

Evans, Emmit. 'Sources of socio-political instability in an African state: The case of Kenya's educated unemployed', *African Studies Review*, 20(1) (1977), pp. 37–52

Fleisher, Michael. *Kuria Cattle Raiders: Violence and vigilantism on the Tanzania/Kenya border*, Ann Arbor, MI, 2000

Floris, Fabrizio. *Puppets or People?: A sociological analysis of Korogocho slum*, trans. S. Gibbins, Nairobi, 2006

Fraser, Nancy. 'From redistribution to recognition: Dilemmas of justice in a "post-socialist" age', *New Left Review*, 212(1) (1995), pp. 68–93

Furedi, Frank. *The Mau Mau War in Perspective*, London, 1989

Gaddis, John Lewis. *We Now Know: Rethinking Cold War history*, Oxford, 1997

Gatheru, Mugo. *Child of Two Worlds*, London, 1966

Gecaga, Margaret. 'Religious movements and democratisation in Kenya: Between the sacred and the profane' in G. Murunga and S. Nasong'o (eds), *Kenya: The struggle for democracy*, London, 2007

Gertzel, Cherry. *The Politics of Independent Kenya, 1963–8*, Nairobi, 1970

Gertzel, Cherry, Maure Goldschmidt and Donald Rothchild (eds). *Government and Politics in Kenya: A nation building text*, Nairobi, 1969

Geschiere, Peter. *The Perils of Belonging: Autochthony, citizenship, and exclusion in Africa and Europe*, Chicago, 2009

Ghai, Yash. 'Devolution: Restructuring the Kenyan state', *Journal of Eastern African Studies*, 2(2) (2008), pp. 211–26

Gifford, Paul. *Christianity, Politics, and Public Life in Kenya*, London, 2009

Ginzburg, Carlo. *The Cheese and the Worms: The cosmos of a sixteenth-century miller*, Baltimore, 1992

Githii, David. *Exposing and Conquering Satanic Forces over Kenya*, Nairobi, 2008

Godfrey, E.M. and G.C.M. Mutiso. 'The political economy of self-help: Kenya's "Harambee" institutes of technology', *Canadian Journal of African Studies*, 8(1) (1974), pp. 109–33

Goldsworthy, David. 'Ethnicity and leadership in Africa: The "untypical" case of Tom Mboya', *Journal of Modern African Studies*, 20(1) (1982), pp. 107–26

— *Tom Mboya: The man Kenya wanted to forget*, London, 1982

Gona, George. 'Changing political faces on Kenya's Coast, 1992–2007', *Journal of Eastern African Studies*, 2(2) (2008), pp. 242–53

Good, Kenneth. 'Kenyatta and the organization of KANU', *Canadian Journal of African Studies*, 2(2) (1968), pp. 115–36

Goodstein, Laurie. 'The trouble in Kenya', *Index on Censorship*, 11(4) (1982), pp. 49–50

Grignon, François. 'Understanding multi-partyism in Kenya: The 1990–1992 years', working paper no. 19, Institut Français de Recherche en Afrique, Nairobi, September 1994

Grignon, François, Marcel Rutten and Alamin Mazrui. 'Observing and analysing the 1997 general elections: An introduction' in M. Rutten, A. Mazrui and F. Grignon (eds), *Out for the Count: The 1997 general elections and prospects for democracy in Kenya*, Kampala, 2001

Gwyer, G.D. 'The agricultural labour markets for two smallholder areas of Kenya', staff paper no. 94, Institute for Development Studies, University of Nairobi, October 1971

Hake, Andrew. *African Metropolis: Nairobi's self-help city*, London, 1977

Harbeson, John, Donald Rothchild and Naomi Chazan (eds). *Civil Society and the State in Africa*, Boulder, CO, 1994

Haugerud, Angelique. 'Land tenure and agrarian change in Kenya', *Africa*, 59(1) (1989), pp. 61–90

— *The Culture of Politics in Modern Kenya*, Cambridge, 1995

Hempstone, Smith. *Rogue Ambassador: An African memoir*, Sewanee, TN, 1997

Herbst, Jeffrey. *States and Power in Africa: Comparative lessons in authority and control*, Princeton, NJ, 2000

Heyer, Amrik. ' "Nowadays they can even kill you for that which they feel is theirs": Gender and the production of ethnic identity in Kikuyu-speaking Central Kenya' in

Vigdis Broch-Due (ed.), *Violence and Belonging: The quest for identity in post-colonial Africa*, Abingdon, 2005

Hilton, Michael. 'Malcolm MacDonald, Jomo Kenyatta and the preservation of British interests in Commonwealth Africa, 1964–68', unpublished MPhil dissertation, University of Cambridge, 2009

Himbara, David. 'Myths and realities of Kenyan capitalism', *Journal of Modern African Studies*, 31(1) (1993), pp. 93–107

Holmquist, Frank. 'Matunwa Farmers Cooperative Society and the cooperative farming experiment in Kisii District', staff paper no. 106, Institute for Development Studies, University of Nairobi, July 1971

— 'Self-help: The state and peasant leverage in Kenya', *Africa*, 54(3) (1984), pp. 72–91

Holmquist, Frank and Michael Ford. 'Kenya: State and civil society the first year after the election', *Africa Today*, 41(4) (1994), pp. 5–25

Hornsby, Charles. 'The social structure of the National Assembly in Kenya, 1963–83', *Journal of Modern African Studies*, 27(2) (1989), pp. 275–96

— 'Election day and the results' in M. Rutten, A. Mazrui and F. Grignon (eds), *Out for the Count: The 1997 general elections and prospects for democracy in Kenya*, Kampala, 2001

Hoskyns, Catherine (ed.). *Case Studies in African Diplomacy*, Number II: *The Ethiopia-Somali-Kenya dispute 1960–67*, Dar es Salaam, 1969

Hughes, Lotte. 'Malice in Maasailand: The historical roots of current political struggles', *African Affairs*, 104(415) (2005), pp. 207–24

Human Rights Watch. *Kenya's Unfinished Democracy: A human rights agenda for the new government*, New York, 2002

— *Playing with Fire: Weapons proliferation, political violence, and human rights in Kenya*, New York, 2002

— *'All the Men Have Gone': War crimes in Kenya's Mt Elgon conflict*, New York, 2008

— *Ballots to Bullets: Organized political violence and Kenya's crisis of governance*, New York, 2008

— *'Why am I Still Here?': The 2007 Horn of Africa renditions and the fate of those still missing*, New York, 2008

— *'Bring the Gun or You'll Die': Torture, rape, and other serious human rights violations by Kenyan security forces in the Mandera Triangle*, New York, 2009

— *'Welcome to Kenya': Police abuse of Somali refugees*, New York, 2010

Hurd, David. *Kidnap at Kiunga*, London, 1967

Hutton, Pat and Jonathan Bloch. 'How the West established Idi Amin and kept him there' in E. Ray, W. Schapp, K. Van Meter and L. Wolf (eds), *Dirty Work 2: The CIA in Africa*, London, 1980

Hyden, Goran and Colin Leys. 'Elections and politics in single-party systems: The case of Kenya and Tanzania', *British Journal of Political Science*, 2(4) (1972), pp. 389–420

Iliffe, John. *Africans: The history of a continent*, Cambridge, 2007

Independent Review Commission on the General Elections. *Independent Review Commission on the General Elections held in Kenya on 27 December 2007*, Nairobi, 2009

Institute for Education in Democracy. *Enhancing the Electoral Process in Kenya: A report on the transition general elections 2002*, Nairobi, 2003

Institute of Economic Affairs and Kenya National Commission on Human Rights. *Kenyan's Verdict: A citizen's report card on the Constituencies Development Fund (CDF)*, Nairobi, 2006

International Commission of Jurists (Kenya Chapter). *The Political Economy of Ethnic Clashes in Kenya*, Nairobi, 2000

International Labour Organization. *Employment, Incomes and Equality: A struggle for increasing productive employment in Kenya*, Geneva, 1972

Jonyo, Fred. 'The centrality of ethnicity in Kenya's political transition' in W. Oyugi, P. Wanyande and C. Odhiambo Mbai (eds), *The Politics of Transition in Kenya: From KANU to NARC*, Nairobi, 2003

Kagwanja, Peter. 'Facing Mount Kenya or facing Mecca? The Mungiki, ethnic violence and the politics of the Moi succession in Kenya, 1987–2002', *African Affairs*, 102(406) (2003), pp. 25–59

— ' "Power to *Uhuru*": Youth identity and generational politics in Kenya's 2002 elections', *African Affairs*, 105(418) (2006), pp. 51–75

Kagwanja, Peter and Roger Southall (eds). *Kenya's Uncertain Democracy: The electoral crisis of 2008*, London, 2010

Kahora, Billy. 'The fire next time or a half-made place: Between Tetra Paks and plastic bags', *Kwani?*, 5(2) (2008), pp. 8–12

— *The True Story of David Munyakei: Goldenberg whistleblower*, Nairobi, 2008

Kaiser, John. *If I Die*, Nairobi, 2003

Kamande, James. *The Devil's House: Nyayo House Nazi chambers and devil worship*, Nairobi, 2003

Kanogo, Tabitha. *Squatters and the Roots of Mau Mau*, London, 1987

Kantai, Parselelo. 'Comrade Lemma and the Black Jerusalem Boys' Band' in *Seventh Street Alchemy: A selection of writings from the Caine Prize for African writing 2004*, Johannesburg, 2005

Kanyinga, Karuti. 'Struggles of access to land: The land question, accumulation, and changing politics in Kenya', working paper no. 54, Institute of Development Studies, University of Nairobi, 1996

— *Re-Distribution from Above: The politics of land rights and squatting in Coastal Kenya*, Uppsala, 2000

Kanyinga, Karuti, Winnie Mitullah and Sebastian Njagi. *The Non-Profit Sector in Kenya: Size, scope and financing*, Nairobi, 2007

Kareri, Charles. 'Sermon preached by the Very Rev. Charles M. Kareri', in order of service, *The State Funeral for His Excellency the Late Mzee Jomo Kenyatta*, Nairobi, 1978

Karimi, Joseph and Ochieng' Philip. *The Kenyatta Succession*, Nairobi, 1980

Kariuki, G.G. *Illusion of Power: Fifty years in Kenya politics*, Nairobi, 2001

Kariuki, J.M. 'Assistance for emergency widows and orphans' in Kareithi Munuhe (ed.), *J.M. Kariuki in Parliament*, Nairobi, 1974

— *J.M. Speaks His Mind*, Nairobi, 1974

— *'Mau Mau' Detainee: The account by a Kenya African of his experiences in detention camps, 1953–1960*, Nairobi, 1975

Kariuki-Machua, Rosemary. *I am My Father's Daughter: Over 30 years later JM Kariuki daughter's quest for truth and justice revealed*, Nairobi, 2008

Karume, Njenga. *Beyond Expectations: From charcoal to gold*, Nairobi, 2009

Kenya African National Union. *What a KANU Government Offers You*, Nairobi, 1963

Kenya Human Rights Commission. *Haven of Repression: A report on the University of Nairobi and academic freedom in Kenya*, Nairobi, 1992

— *The Fallen Angel: A report on the performance of Amos Wako in promoting human rights and democracy as Kenya's attorney general*, Nairobi, 1993

— *Licence to Kill: Police shootings in Kenya*, Nairobi, 1995

— *Ours by Right, Theirs by Might*, Nairobi, 1996

— *Kayas of Deprivation, Kayas of Blood: Violence, ethnicity and the state in Coastal Kenya*, Nairobi, 1997

— *Kayas Revisited: A post-election balance sheet*, Nairobi, 1998

— *Where Terror Rules: Torture by Kenyan police in North Eastern Kenya*, Nairobi, 1998

Kenya Human Rights Commission and Article 19 International Centre against Censorship. *Media Watch: Media monitoring in Kenya December 1997*, Nairobi, 1998

Kenya National Commission on Human Rights. *An Evening with Tom Mboya*, Nairobi, 2006

— *Referendum Report*, Nairobi, 2006

— *Preliminary Report on Alleged Executions and Disappearances of Persons Between June and October 2007*, Nairobi, 2007

— *'Still Behaving Badly': Second periodic report of the election-monitoring project*, Nairobi, 2007

— *'The Cry of Blood': Report on the extra-judicial killings and disappearances*, Nairobi, 2008

— *On the Brink of the Precipice: A human rights account of Kenya's post-2007 election violence*, Nairobi, 2008

Kenyans for Peace, Truth and Justice. 'Unfinished business from Kriegler's IREC', *Wajibu*, 24(1) (2009).

Kihoro, Wanyiri. *Never Say Die: The chronicle of a political prisoner*, Nairobi, 1998

— *The Price of Freedom: The story of political resistance in Kenya*, Nairobi, 2005

Kimenyi, Mwangi and Njuguna Ndung'u. 'Sporadic ethnic violence: Why has Kenya not experienced a full-blown civil war?' in Paul Collier and Nicholas Sambanis (eds), *Understanding Civil War: Evidence and analysis*, Volume 1: *Africa*, Washington, DC, 2005

Kindy, Hyder. *Life and Politics in Mombasa*, Nairobi, 1972

King, Kenneth. *Jua Kali Kenya: Change and development in an informal economy, 1970–95*, London, 1996

Kinyanjui, Kabiru. 'Justice, peace and reconciliation: The challenge to the church today' in S. Kobia and G. Ngumi (eds), *Together in Hope: The official report of the Mission Conference 1989*, Nairobi, 1991

Kipkorir, Benjamin. *Descent from Cherang'any Hills: Memoirs of a reluctant academic*, Nairobi, 2009

Kipkorir, Benjamin, R.C. Soper and J.W. Ssennyonga (eds). *Kerio Valley: Past, present and future*, Nairobi, 1983

Kitching, Gavin. *Class and Economic Change in Kenya: The making of an African petite-bourgeoisie*, New Haven, CT, 1980

Kizito, Sabala. 'The proliferation, circulation and use of illegal firearms in urban centres: The case of Nairobi, Kenya', unpublished paper presented to United Nations Economic Commission of Africa and International Resource Group on Disarmament and Security in the Horn of Africa conference on 'Curbing the Demand Side of Small arms in the IGAD States: Potentials and Pitfalls', Addis Ababa, 26 April 2001

Klopp, Jacqueline. 'Pilfering the public: The problem of land grabbing in contemporary Kenya', *Africa Today*, 47(1) (2000), pp. 7–26

— ' "Ethnic clashes" and winning elections: The case of Kenya's electoral despotism', *Canadian Journal of African Studies*, 35(3) (2001), pp. 473–517

— 'Can moral ethnicity trump political tribalism? The struggle for land and nation in Kenya', *African Studies*, 61(2) (2002), pp. 269–94

— 'Violence and elections: Will Kenya collapse?', *World Policy Journal*, 24(4) (2007/8), pp. 11–18

Klopp, Jacqueline and Janai Orina. 'University crisis, student activism, and the contemporary struggle for democracy in Kenya', *African Studies Review*, 45(1) (2002), pp. 43–76

Knighton, Ben. 'Going for *Cai* at Gatundu: Reversion to a Kikuyu ethnic past or building a Kenyan national future' in D. Branch, N. Cheeseman and L. Gardner (eds), *Our Turn to Eat: Kenyan politics since 1950*, Berlin, 2009

Kombani, Kinyanjui. *The Last Villains of Molo*, Nairobi, 2004

Kroll Associates. 'Project KTN: Consolidated report', 27 April 2004.

Kyle, Keith. *The Politics of the Independence of Kenya*, New York, 1999

Lamb, Geoff. *Peasant Politics*, Lewes, 1974

Laurence, Tony. *The Dar Mutiny of 1964: And the armed intervention that ended it*, Brighton, 2007

Leo, Christopher. *Land and Class in Kenya*, Toronto, 1984

Leonard, David. *African Successes: Four public managers of Kenyan rural development*, Berkeley, CA, 1991

Lesorogol, Carolyn. *Contesting the Commons: Privatizing pastoral lands in Kenya*, Ann Arbor, MI, 2008

Lewis, Ioan. *Understanding Somalia and Somaliland*, London, 2008

Leys, Colin. 'Politics in Kenya: The development of peasant society', *British Journal of Political Science*, 1(3) (1971), pp. 307–37

— 'Interpreting African underdevelopment: Reflections on the ILO report on employment, incomes and equality in Kenya', *African Affairs*, 72(289) (1973), pp. 419–29

— *Underdevelopment in Kenya: The political economy of neo-colonialism 1964–1971*, Nairobi, 1975

Lonsdale, John. 'The moral economy of Mau Mau: Wealth, poverty and civic virtue in Kikuyu political thought' in B. Berman and J. Lonsdale, *Unhappy Valley: Conflict in Kenya and Africa*, Oxford, 1992

— 'Kikuyu Christianities', *Journal of Religion in Africa*, 29(2) (1999), pp. 206–29

— 'Agency in tight corners: Narrative and initiative in African history', *Journal of African Cultural Studies*, 13(1) (2000), pp. 5–16

— 'Jomo Kenyatta, God and the modern world' in J.-G. Deutsch, P. Probst and H. Schmidt (eds), *African Modernities: Entangled meanings in current debate*, Oxford, 2002

— 'Soil, work, civilisation, and citizenship in Kenya', *Journal of Eastern African Studies*, 2(2) (2008), pp. 306–15

Lukalo, Fibian Kavulani. 'Extended handshake or wrestling match?: Youth and urban culture celebrating politics in Kenya', discussion paper no. 32, Nordiska Afrikainstitutet, Uppsala University, 2006

Luongo, Katherine. 'Polling places and "slow punctured provocation": Occult-driven cases in postcolonial Kenya's high courts', *Journal of Eastern African Studies*, 4(3) (2010), pp. 577–91

Lynch, Gabrielle. 'The fruits of perception: "Ethnic politics" and the case of Kenya's constitutional referendum', *African Studies*, 62(2) (2006), pp. 233–70

— 'Negotiating ethnicity: Identity politics in contemporary Kenya', *Review of African Political Economy*, 33(107) (2006), pp. 49–65

— 'Courting the Kalenjin: The failure of dynasticism and the strength of the ODM wave in Kenya's Rift Valley Province', *African Affairs*, 107(429) (2008), pp. 541–68

— *I Say to You: Ethnic politics and the Kalenjin in Kenya*, Chicago, 2011

Maathai, Wangari. *The Green Belt Movement: Sharing the approach and the experience*, New York, 2003

— *Unbowed: One woman's story*, London, 2008

Macarthur, Julie. 'How the west was won: Regional politics and prophetic promises in the 2007 Kenya election', *Journal of Eastern African Studies*, 2(2) (2008), pp. 227–41

Macharia, Kinuthia. 'Social networks: Ethnicity and the informal sector in Nairobi', working paper no. 463, Institute for Development Studies, University of Nairobi, August 1988

Makokha, Kwamschetsi and Rosemary Okello Orlale. *In the Shadow of Death: My trauma, my experiences, voices of Kenyan women from post-election violence*, Nairobi, 2009

Mars Group Kenya. *The Case Against the Members of the 9th Parliament of Kenya: A critique of the 9th parliament of Kenya (2003–2007)*, Nairobi, 2007

Matiangi, Fred and Wanja Muguongo. *Institutional Management of Election Violence in Kenya*, Nairobi, 2005

Matiba, Kenneth. *A Dream for Kenya*, Nairobi, 1992

— *Aiming High: The story of my life*, Nairobi, 2000

Maughan-Brown, David. *Land, Freedom and Fiction: History and ideology in Kenya*, London, 1985

Maupeu, Herve, Musambayi Katumanga and Winnie Mitullah (eds). *The Moi Succession: Elections 2002*, Nairobi, 2005

Maupeu, Herve and Patrick Mutahi (eds). *Wahome Mutahi's World*, Nairobi, 2005

Maxon, Robert. 'Social and cultural changes' in B. Ogot and W. Ochieng (eds), *Decolonization and Independence in Kenya: 1940–93*, London, 1995

Mazrui, Ali. 'On heroes and Uhuru-worship', *Transition*, 11 (1963), pp. 23–8

— 'Thoughts on assassination in Africa', *Political Science Quarterly*, 83(1) (1968), pp. 40–58

— 'Tom Mboya, underdevelopment, and I', *East Africa*, 6(9) (1969), pp. 19–29

— 'Academic freedom in Africa: The double tyranny', *African Affairs*, 74(297) (1975), pp. 393–400

Mboya, Tom. *Conflict and Nationhood: The essentials of freedom in Africa*, London, 1963

— 'The future of Kenya', *African Affairs*, 63(250) (1964), pp. 6–12

— *Freedom and After*, Nairobi, 1986

— *The Challenge of Nationhood: A collection of speeches and writings*, Nairobi, 1993

Mburu, Nene. 'Contemporary banditry in the Horn of Africa: Causes, history and political implications', *Nordic Journal of African Studies*, 8(2) (1999), pp. 89–107

— *Bandits on the Border: The last frontier in the search for Somali unity*, Trenton, NJ, 2005

McIntosh, Janet. *The Edge of Islam: Power, personhood, and ethnoreligious boundaries on the Kenya Coast*, Durham, NC, 2009

Middleton, John. *The World of the Swahili: An African mercantile civilization*, New Haven, CT, 1992

Miller, Norman and Rodger Yeager. *Kenya: The quest for prosperity*, Boulder, CO, 1994

Ministry of Finance and Economic Planning, *An Economic Appraisal of the Settlement Schemes: 1964/5–1967/8, Farm Economic Survey Report No. 27*, Nairobi, 1972

Mitullah, Winnie. 'Lake Victoria's Nile perch fish industry', working paper no. 519, Institute for Development Studies, University of Nairobi, 2000

Mitullah, Winnie, Lawrence Mute and Jackson Mwalulu (eds). *The People's Voice: What Kenyans say*, Nairobi, 1997

Mkutu, Kennedy Agade. *Guns and Governance in the Rift Valley: Pastoralist conflict and small arms*, Oxford, 2008

Morrison, Lesa. 'The nature of decline: Distinguishing myth from reality in the case of the Luo of Kenya', *Journal of Modern African Studies*, 45(1) (2007), pp. 117–42

Morton, Andrew. *Moi: The making of an African statesman*, London, 1998

Mueller, Susanne. 'Government and opposition in Kenya, 1966–9', *Journal of Modern African Studies*, 22(3) (1984), pp. 399–427

— 'The political economy of Kenya's crisis', *Journal of Eastern African Studies*, 2(2) (2008), pp. 185–210

Muigai, Githu. 'Jomo Kenyatta and the rise of the ethno-nationalist state in Kenya' in B. Berman, D. Eyoh and W. Kymlicka (eds), *Ethnicity and Democracy in Africa*, Oxford, 2004

Mungai, Joseph. *From Simple to Complex: An autobiography*, Nairobi, 2002

Munuhe, Kareithi (ed.). *J.M. Kariuki in Parliament*, Nairobi, 1974

Muriuki, Godfrey. *A History of the Kikuyu, 1500–1900*, Nairobi, 1974

— 'Central Kenya in the Nyayo era', *Africa Today*, 26(3) (1979), pp. 39–42

Murunga, Godwin. 'The state, its reform and the question of legitimacy in Kenya', *Identity, Culture, and Politics*, 5(1 & 2) (2004), 179–206

— 'Governance and the politics of structural adjustment in Kenya' in G. Murunga and S. Nasong'o (eds), *Kenya: The struggle for democracy*, London, 2007

Murungi, Kiraitu. 'The role of the I.C.J. (Kenya Section) in promoting the rule of law and protecting the enjoyment of human rights' in International Commission of Jurists (Kenya Section), *Law and Society: Selected papers from a seminar held 24–26 November 1988 at the Green Hills Hotel, Nyeri, Kenya*, Nairobi, 1989

— *In the Mud of Politics*, Nairobi, 2000

Musalia, Martha Wangari. *Archbishop Manasses Kuria: A biography – strong in the storms*, Nairobi, 2001

Mutahi, Patrick. *Political Violence in Marginal Areas: A case study of Samburu and Lamu districts*, Nairobi, 2003

Mutahi, Wahome. *Three Days on the Cross*, Nairobi, 1991

— *How to be a Kenyan*, Nairobi, 1996

— *Whispers and Camisassius*, Nairobi, 2002

Mutongi, Kenda. 'Thugs or entrepreneurs? Perceptions of matatu operators in Nairobi, 1970 to the present', *Africa*, 76(4) (2006), pp. 549–68

Mutua, Makau. *Kenya's Quest for Democracy: Taming Leviathan*, Boulder, CO, 2008

Mutunga, Willy. *Constitution-Making from the Middle: Civil society and transition politics in Kenya, 1992–1997*, Nairobi, 1999

Mwakenya. *Draft Minimum Programme: September 1987*, Nairobi, 1987

Mwangi, Esther. 'Subdividing the commons: The politics of property rights transformation in Kenya's Maasailand', working paper no. 46, CGIAR Systemwide Program on Collective Action and Property Rights, International Food Policy Research Institute, Washington, DC, January 2006

Nasong'o, Shadrack. 'Negotiating new rules of the game: Social movements, civil society and the Kenyan transition' in G. Murunga and S. Nasong'o (eds), *Kenya: The struggle for democracy*, London, 2007

National Assembly. *Report of the Select Committee on the Disappearance and Murder of the Late Member for Nyandarua North, the Hon. J.M. Kariuki, M.P.*, Nairobi, 1975

— *Report of the Parliamentary Select Committee to Investigate Ethnic Clashes in Western and Other Parts of Kenya*, Nairobi, 1992

— *Report on the Investigation into the Conduct of the 'Artur Brothers' and their Associates*, Nairobi, 2007

National Council of Churches of Kenya. *Who Controls Industry in Kenya?: Report of a working party*, Nairobi, 1968

— *A Report on the Church's Involvement in Development*, Nairobi, 1984

— *A Kairos for Kenya: NCCK reflection on the KANU review committee report and KANU special delegates conference resolutions on it*, Nairobi, 1991

— *Nairobi Demolitions: What next?* Nairobi, 1991

— *Why You Should Vote*, Nairobi, 1991

— *The Cursed Arrow: Contemporary report on the politicised violence in the Rift Valley, Nyanza and Western Provinces*, Nairobi, 1992

National Council of Churches of Kenya/Netherlands Development Corporation/Semi-Arid Rural Development Programme. *Pacifying the Valley: An analysis on the Kerio Valley conflict*, Nairobi, 2002

National Election Monitoring Unit. *Courting Disaster: A report on the continuing terror, violence and destruction in the Rift Valley, Nyanza and Western Provinces of Kenya*, Nairobi, 1993

— *The Multi-Party General Elections in Kenya 29 December, 1992: The report of the National Election Monitoring Unit*, Nairobi, 1993

Ndegwa, Duncan. *Walking in Kenyatta Struggles*, Nairobi, 2006

Ndegwa, Stephen. 'Citizenship and ethnicity: An examination of two transition moments in Kenyan politics', *American Political Science Review*, 91(3) (1997), pp. 599–616

— 'Kenya: Third time lucky?', *Journal of Democracy*, 14(3) (2003), pp. 145–58

Ndemo, Salim. *Epitome of State Power: The provincial administration in Kenya*, Nairobi, 2007

Ndigirigi, Gichingiri. *Ngugi wa Thiong'o's Drama and the Kamiriithu Popular Theater Experiment*, Trenton, NJ, 2007

Ndua, Gihiri and Njuguna Ng'ethe. 'The role of the informal sector in the development of small and intermediate size cities: Background information on Nakuru', working paper no. 416, Institute for Development Studies, University of Nairobi, November 1984

— 'The role of the informal sector in the development of small and intermediate size cities: The informal sector in Nakuru', working paper no. 417, Institute for Development Studies, University of Nairobi, November 1984

Ng'ang'a, Makaru. 'Machine politics and the electoral process: Background to the 1979 general elections in Murang'a', unpublished paper, Department of Government, University of Nairobi, January 1980

Njogu, Kimani (ed.). *Healing the Wound: Personal narratives about the 2007 post-election violence in Kenya*, Nairobi, 2009

Nkinyagi, J.A. 'The origins of student disturbances: The Kenyan case', working paper no. 378, Institute for Development Studies, University of Nairobi, February 1981

Northern Frontier District Commission. *Kenya: Report of the Northern Frontier District Commission*, London, 1962

Nugent, Paul. *Africa since Independence: A comparative history*, Basingstoke, 2004

Oba, Gufu. 'Ecological factors in land use conflicts, land administration and food insecurity in Turkana, Kenya', network paper no. 33a, Overseas Development Institute, Pastoral Development Network, London, December 1992

Ochieng', William. *The Third Word: More essays on Kenyan history*, Nairobi, 1984

— 'Structural and political changes' in B.A. Ogot and W.R. Ochieng' (eds), *Decolonization and Independence in Kenya: 1940–93*, London, 1995

— *The Black Man's Democracy: Kenya, the first five years after Moi, 2003–2007*, Kisumu, 2008

Odinga, Oginga. 'Let the people of Kenya, Africa and the world know', unpublished pamphlet, June 1962

— *Two Months in India*, Nairobi, 1965

— *Not Yet Uhuru*, Nairobi, 1967

— 'Letter to the delegation head, US Armed Services Committee', *Race and Class*, 24(3) (1983), pp. 317–20

Odinga, Oginga, Joseph Murumbi *et al. Pio Gama Pinto: Independent Kenya's first martyr*, Nairobi, 1966

Office of the Vice President and Ministry of Planning and National Development. *Nakuru District Development Plan 1994–1996*, Nairobi, 1994

— *Nandi District Development Plan 1994–1996*, Nairobi, 1994

— *Narok District Development Plan 1994–1996*, Nairobi, 1994

— *Trans Nzoia District Development Plan 1994–1996*, Nairobi, 1994

— *Uasin Gishu District Development Plan 1994–1996*, Nairobi, 1994

— *West Pokot District Development Plan 1994–1996*, Nairobi, 1994

Ogembo, Justus Mozart. 'The rise and decline of communal violence: Analysis of the 1992–94 witch hunts in Gusii, Southwestern Kenya', unpublished PhD thesis, Harvard University, 1997

Ogot, Bethwell. *A History of the Southern Luo*, Nairobi, 1967

— 'Tom Mboya: An appreciation', *East Africa*, 6(9) (1969), pp. 9–13

— *A History of the Luo-Speaking Peoples of Eastern Africa*, Kisumu, 2009

— *Who, if Anyone, Owns the Past? Reflections on the Meaning of 'Public History'*, Kisumu, 2010

Ogot, Grace. *The Promised Land*, Nairobi, 1966

Okoth Ogendo, H.W.O. 'The politics of constitutional change in Kenya since independence, 1963–69', *African Affairs*, 71(282) (1972), pp. 9–34

Ole Kantai, B.K. 'Ethnic land expansionism and electoral politics in Kenya: A case study of the Kikuyu of Central Province', working paper no. 2, Institute of Policy Analysis and Research, Nairobi, 2004

Ole Kaparo, Francis. 'The party as an instrument for promoting the democratic process' in International Commission of Jurists (Kenya Section), *Law and Society:*

Selected papers from a seminar held 24–26 November 1988 at the Green Hills Hotel, Nyeri, Kenya, Nairobi, 1989

Ole Karbolo, Mark. 'Facing modern land loss challenges: The Loita Maasai pastoralists and the recent controversy over the Naimina Enkiyio indigenous forest in Narok District', working paper no. 2, Arid Lands and Resources Management Network in Eastern Africa, Nairobi, 1999

Omolo, Ken. 'Political ethnicity in the democratisation process in Kenya', *African Studies*, 61(2) (2002), pp. 209–21

Orwa, Katete. 'Political recruitment in Mbita constituency: A study in election politics', seminar paper 3, Department of Government seminar series on general elections, University of Nairobi, 2 March 1984

Oucho, John. *Undercurrents of Ethnic Conflicts in Kenya*, Leiden, 2002

Ouko, Otumba. *The Trial of Jaramogi in the Underworld*, Kisumu, 2001

Ouko, Robert. 'Development – the challenge ahead', Second Tom Mboya Lecture, Kenya Institute of Management, July 1971

Oyugi, Walter. 'Ethnicity in the electoral process: The 1992 general elections in Kenya', *African Journal of Political Science*, 2(1) (1997), pp. 41–69

Oyugi, Walter, Peter Wanyande and Crispin Odhiambo Mbai (eds). *The Politics of Transition in Kenya: From KANU to NARC*, Nairobi, 2003

Parker, Ian. *What I Tell You Three Times is True: Conservation, ivory, history and politics*, Kinloss, 2004

Parkin, David. *Neighbours and Nationals in an African City Ward*, London, 2004

Parsons, Timothy. *The 1964 Army Mutinies and the Making of Modern East Africa*, Westport, CT, 2003

— 'The Lanet incident, 2–25 January 1964: Military unrest and national amnesia in Kenya', *International Journal of African Historical Studies*, 40(1) (2007), pp. 51–70

Patel, Zarina. *Unquiet: The life and times of Makhan Singh*, Nairobi, 2006

Percox, David. *Britain, Kenya, and the Cold War: Imperial defence, colonial security, and decolonisation*, London, 2004

Rasmussen, Jacob. 'Outwitting the Professor of Politics? Mungiki narratives of political deception and their role in Kenyan politics', *Journal of Eastern African Studies*, 4(3) (2010), pp. 435–49

Republic of Kenya. *African Socialism and its Application to Planning in Kenya*, Nairobi, 1965

— *On Economic Prospects and Policies*, Nairobi, 1975

— *Funeral Programme for the State Funeral of His Excellency the Late Mzee Jomo Kenyatta*, Nairobi, 1978

— *Bungoma District Development Plan 1979–1983*, Nairobi, 1980

— *Lamu District Development Plan 1979–1983*, Nairobi, 1980

— *Report of Judicial Commission Appointed to Inquire into Allegations Involving Charles Mugane Njonjo*, Nairobi, 1984

— *Report of the Judicial Commission Appointed to Inquire into Tribal Clashes in Kenya*, Nairobi, 1999

— *Comments by the Government on Report of the Judicial Commission Appointed to Inquire into Tribal Clashes in Kenya (Akiwumi Report)*, Nairobi, 1999

— *Report of the Commission of Inquiry into the Land Law System of Kenya on Principles of a National Land Policy Framework, Constitutional Position of Land and New Institutional Framework for Land Administration*, Nairobi, 2002

— *Report of the Commission of Inquiry into the Illegal/Irregular Allocation of Public Land*, Nairobi, 2004

— *Report of the Judicial Commission of Inquiry into the Goldenberg Affair*, Nairobi, 2005

— *Report of the Commission of Inquiry into the Sale of the Grand Regency Hotel*, Nairobi, 2008

Rogge, John. *The Internally Displaced Population in Kenya, Western and Rift Valley Provinces: A need assessment and a program proposal for rehabilitation*, Nairobi, 1993

Ross, Marc. 'Political alienation, participation, and ethnicity: An African case', *American Journal of Political Science*, 19(2) (1975), pp. 291–311

Ross, Stanley. 'The rule of law and lawyers in Kenya', *Journal of Modern African Studies*, 30(3) (1992), pp. 421–42

Rothchild, Donald. 'Kenya's Africanisation programme: Priorities of development and equity', *American Political Science Review*, 64(3) (1970), pp. 737–53

Ruteere, Mutuma. 'Dilemmas of crime, human rights and the politics of *Mungiki* violence in Kenya', occasional paper no. 1, Kenyan Human Rights Institute, 2008

Rutten, Marinus. *Selling Wealth to Buy Poverty: The process of individualization of landownership among the Maasai pastoralists of Kajiado District, Kenya; 1890–1990*, Saarbrücken, 1992

Sabar-Friedman, Galia. 'Church and state in Kenya, 1986–1992: The churches' involvement in the "Game of Change" ', *African Affairs*, 96(382) (1997), pp. 25–52

Sanger, Clyde and John Nottingham. 'The Kenya general election of 1963', *Journal of Modern African Studies*, 2(1) (1964), pp. 1–40

Schechter, Dan, Michael Ansara and David Kolodney. 'The CIA as an equal opportunity employer' in E. Ray, W. Schapp, K. Van Meter and L. Wolf (eds), *Dirty Work 2: The CIA in Africa*, London, 1980

Schmidt, Elizabeth. *Cold War and Decolonization in Guinea, 1946–1958*, Athens, OH, 2007

Scott, James. *The Art of Not Being Governed: An anarchist history of upland Southeast Asia*, New Haven, CT, 2009

Shachtman, Tom. *Airlift to America: How Barack Obama, Sr., John F. Kennedy, Tom Mboya, and 800 East African students changed their world and ours*, New York, 2009

Singh, Chanan. 'The republican constitution of Kenya: Historical background and analysis', *International and Comparative Law Quarterly*, 14(3) (1965), pp. 878–949

Singo, Mwachofi, Francis Wairagu and J.A.N. Kamenju. *Peace, Security and Development: An agenda for the North Rift Region of Kenya*, Nairobi, 2004

Smith, James. *Bewitching Development: Witchcraft and the reinvention of development in neoliberal Kenya*, Chicago, 2008

Solomon, Joel. *Failing the Democratic Challenge: Freedom of expression in multi-party Kenya – 1993*, Washington, DC, 1994

Southall, Aidan. 'The illusion of tribe' in P. Gutkind (ed.), *The Passing of Tribal Man in Africa*, Leiden, 1970

Spear, Thomas and Richard Waller (eds). *Being Maasai: Ethnicity and identity in East Africa*, Oxford, 1993

Stern, Chester. *Dr Iain West's Casebook*, London, 1997

Stewart, Frances. 'Note for discussion: Kenya, horizontal inequalities and the political disturbances of 2008', Centre for Research on Inequality, Human Security and Ethnicity, University of Oxford, March 2008

Swainson, Nicola. 'The rise of a national bourgeoisie in Kenya', *Review of African Political Economy*, 8 (1977), pp. 39–55

— 'State and economy in post-colonial Kenya, 1963–1978', *Canadian Journal of African Studies*, 12(3) (1978), pp. 357–81

— *The Development of Corporate Capitalism in Kenya, 1918–77*, London, 1980

Tamarkin, M. 'Tribal associations, tribal solidarity, and tribal chauvinism in a Kenya town', *Journal of African History*, 14(2) (1973), pp. 257–74

— 'The roots of political stability in Kenya', *African Affairs*, 77(308) (1978), pp. 297–320

— 'From Kenyatta to Moi: The anatomy of a peaceful transition of power', *Africa Today*, 26(3) (1979), pp. 21–37

Throup, David. 'The construction and destruction of the Kenyatta state' in M. Schatzberg (ed.), *The Political Economy of Kenya*, New York, 1987

— 'Elections and political legitimacy in Kenya', *Africa*, 63(3) (1993), pp. 371–96

Throup, David and Charles Hornsby. *Multi-Party Politics in Kenya: The Kenyatta and Moi states and the triumph of the system in the 1992 election*, Oxford, 1998

Tignor, Robert. *Capitalism and Nationalism at the End of Empire*, Princeton, NJ, 1998

Transparency International. *National Integrity Systems Transparency International Questionnaire: Kenya 2003*, Berlin, 2004

Umoja. *Struggle for Democracy in Kenya: Special report on the 1988 general elections in Kenya*, London, 1988

— *Moi's Reign of Terror: A decade of Nyayo crimes against the people of Kenya*, London, 1989

United Nations Development Programme. *Election 2007: Interim report on national voter bribery survey*, Nairobi, 2007

Van Zwanenberg, Roger. 'History and theory of urban poverty in Nairobi: The problem of slum development', working paper no. 26, Institute for Development Studies, University of Nairobi, April 1972

wa Githinji, Mwangi and Frank Holmquist. 'Kenya's hopes and impediments: The anatomy of a crisis of exclusion', *Journal of Eastern African Studies*, 2(2) (2008), pp. 344–58

wa Kinyatti, Maina. *Kenya: A prison notebook*, London, 1996

— *Mother Kenya: Letters from prison, 1982–1988*, London, 1997

wa Mungai, Mbugua and George Gona. 'Introduction' in M. wa Mungai and G. Gona (eds), *(Re)Membering Kenya*, Volume 1: *Identity, Culture and Freedom*, Nairobi, 2010

wa Thiong'o, Ngugi. *The River Between*, London, 1965

— *Homecoming: Essays on African and Caribbean literature, culture and politics*, London, 1972

— *Writers in Politics*, Nairobi, 1981

— *Detained: A Writer's Prison Diary*, Nairobi, 2000

— *Petals of Blood*, London, 2002

wa Thiong'o, Ngugi and Ngugi wa Mirii. *I Will Marry When I Want*, Nairobi, 2005

wa Wamwere, Koigi. *Conscience on Trial: Why I was detained, notes of a political prisoner in Kenya*, Trenton, NJ, 1988

— *I Refuse to Die: My journey for freedom*, New York, 2002

— *Negative Ethnicity: From bias to genocide*, New York, 2003

Wachtel, Eleanor and Andy Wachtel. 'Women's co-operative enterprise in Nakuru', discussion paper no. 250, Institute for Development Studies, University of Nairobi, March 1977

Wainaina, Binyavanga. 'Middle ground', *Kwani?*, 5(2) (2008), pp. 16–18

Waiyaki Otieno, Wambui. *Mau Mau's Daughter: A life history*, Boulder, CO, 1998

Waller, Richard. 'Ecology, migration, and expansion in East Africa', *African Affairs*, 84(336) (1985), pp. 347–70

Wallis, M.A.H. *Bureaucrats, Politicians and Rural Communities in Kenya*, Manchester, 1982

Wambua, Frederick. *The '82 Kenyan military coup: An airman's prison experience*, Kansas City, MO, 2003

Wanyande, Peter. 'State driven conflict in the Greater Horn of Africa', paper presented at USAID workshop on 'Conflict in the Great Horn of Africa', Nairobi, May 1997

Wasserman, Gary. *Politics of Decolonization: Kenya Europeans and the land issue, 1960–1965*, Cambridge, 1976

Wekesa, Bob. *The Road Not Taken: The biography of Michael Wamalwa Kijana*, Nairobi, 2004

Wekesa, Peter Wefula. 'Negotiating "Kenyanness": The "debates" ' in M. wa Mungai and G. Gona (eds), *(Re)Membering Kenya*, Volume 1: *Identity, Culture and Freedom*, Nairobi, 2010

Whittaker, Hannah. 'Pursuing pastoralists: The stigma of *Shifta* during the "*Shifta* War*" in Kenya, 1963–68', *ERAS*, 10 (2008)

Widner, Jennifer. *The Rise of a Party State in Kenya: From 'Harambee' to 'Nyayo'*, Berkeley, 1992

— (ed.). *Economic Change and Political Liberalization in Sub-Saharan Africa*, Baltimore, 1994

Willis, Justin. *Mombasa, the Swahili, and the Making of the Mijikenda*, Oxford, 1993

Wilson, Rodney. 'The economic implications of land registration in Kenya's smallholder areas', staff paper no. 91, Institute for Development Studies, University of Nairobi, February 1971

Wipper, Audrey. 'The Maendeleo ya Wanawake Organisation: The co-optation of leadership', *African Studies Review*, 18(3) (1975), pp. 99–120

Wolf, Thomas. 'Immunity or accountability? Daniel Toroitich arap Moi: Kenya's first retired president' in R. Southall and H. Melber (eds), *Legacies of Power: Leadership change and former presidents in African politics*, Cape Town, 2006

— ' "Poll poison"?: Politicians and polling in the 2007 Kenya election' in Peter Kagwanja and Roger Southall (eds), *Kenya's Uncertain Democracy: The electoral crisis of 2008*, Abingdon, 2010

World Bank. *The Economic Development of Kenya*, Washington, DC, 1963

— *Kenya: Into the second decade*, Baltimore, 1975

— *Population and Development in Kenya*, Washington, DC, 1980

— *Kenya Poverty Assessment*, Washington, DC, 1995

— *The Republic of Kenya Poverty Reduction Strategy Paper*, Washington, DC, 2004

— *Gender and Economic Growth in Kenya: Unleashing the power of women*, Washington, DC, 2007

— 'Republic of Kenya: Country social analysis', dissemination draft, Washington, DC, 2007

Wrong, Michela. *It's Our Turn to Eat: The story of a Kenyan whistle blower*, London, 2009

Young, Crawford. 'The end of the post-colonial state in Africa?: Reflections on changing African political dynamics', *African Affairs*, 103(410) (2004), pp. 23–49

Young, Tom. *Africa: A beginner's guide*, Oxford, 2010

ARCHIVE SOURCES

George Padmore Institute, London
Papers of the Committee for the Release of Political Prisoners in Kenya

Herskovits Library, Northwestern University, Evanston
Vertical file

Library of Congress, Washington, DC
African pamphlet collection, African and Middle East Reading Room

Kenya National Archives, Nairobi
Assorted personal papers and manuscripts, MSS 8, 12, 35 & 61

District Commissioner Garissa, DC/GRS

District Commissioner Isiolo, DC/ISO

District Commissioner Lamu, DC/LMU

District Commissioner Nandi, DC/KAPT
District Officer Eldama Ravine, DO/ER
District Officer Lokitaung Sub-District, DC/LOK
Ministry of Economic Planning and Development, AE
Ministry of Information, Broadcasting and Tourism, AHC
Murumbi Africana Collection, MAC/KEN
Office of the President, GO & KA
Provincial Commissioner Central Province, VQ
Provincial Commissioner Coast Province, CA & CO
Provincial Commissioner Eastern Province, BB & PC/EST
Provincial Commissioner North Eastern Province, PC/GRSSA
Provincial Commissioner Nyanza Province, HT & PC/NZA

The National Archives, Public Record Office, Kew, London
Commonwealth Relations Office and Commonwealth Office, DO 213 & DO 226

Foreign and Commonwealth Office, FCO 31 & FO 1110

Prime Minister's Office, PREM

National Archives II, College Park, Maryland
General Records of the Department of State, Record Group 59

NOTES

INTRODUCTION: THE PARTY

1. Ruchti to Secretary of State, 3 July 1963; POL 2 General Reports & Statistics, Records of the Bureau of African Affairs (RBAA) 1958–66; Record Group 59 (RG 59); National Archives II, College Park (NACP).
2. Benjamin Kipkorir, *Descent from Cherang'any Hills: Memoirs of a reluctant academic*, Nairobi, 2009, p. 146.
3. MacDonald to Bottomley, 5 May 1965, 4; National Archives, Public Record Office (TNA: PRO) DO 213/65.
4. David Goldsworthy, *Tom Mboya: The man Kenya wanted to forget*, Nairobi, 1982, p. 4.
5. Ruchti to Secretary of State, 3 July 1963; POL 2 General Reports & Statistics, RBAA 1958–66; RG 59; NACP.
6. Duncan Ndegwa, *Walking in Kenyatta Struggles*, Nairobi, 2006, p. 250.
7. George Bennett and Carl Rosberg, *The Kenyatta Election: Kenya 1960–1961*, London, 1961, p. 203.
8. Murumbi to Koinange, 18 January 1961; Kenya National Archives (KNA) MAC/KEN/73/3.
9. Musa Amalemba, 'Buluyia Political Union visits Jomo Kenyatta at Maralal on Tuesday, 11th July 1961'; KNA MSS 12/21.
10. *Ibid.*
11. Minutes of KANU backbenchers' meeting, 6 August 1964, 2; KNA KA/2/14.
12. Tom Mboya, *The Challenge of Nationhood: A collection of speeches and writings*, Nairobi, 1993, pp. 266–78.
13. Musa Amalemba, 'Buluyia Political Union visits Jomo Kenyatta at Maralal on Tuesday, 11th July 1961'; KNA MSS 12/21.
14. E.S. Atieno Odhiambo, 'The formative years: 1945–55' in Bethwell Ogot and William Ochieng (eds), *Decolonization and Independence in Kenya: 1940–93*, London, 1995, p. 44.
15. Hyder Kindy, *Life and Politics in Mombasa*, Nairobi, 1972, p. 188.
16. *Ibid.*, p. 188.
17. David Anderson, ' "Yours in the struggle for Majimbo": Nationalism and party politics of decolonization in Kenya, 1955–64', *Journal of Contemporary History*, 40(3) (2005), p. 552.

18. Untitled minutes of meeting of Nandi District Independent Party, 4 September 1959; KNA DC/KAPT/1/10/21.
19. KADU, 'Land tenure and agricultural and pastoral development for independent Kenya', July 1962, 3; KNA MAC/KEN/36/7.
20. 'Speech by Hon. John Konchellah at opening session of conference of delegates of tribes resident in Rift Valley Region at Nakuru', 1963, 1; KNA MAC/KEN/36/7.
21. Oginga Odinga, *Not Yet Uhuru*, Nairobi, 1967, p. 229.
22. Vass to Secretary of State, 18 May 1963; POL Political Affairs Kenya, RBAA 1958–66; RG 59; NACP.
23. Oluoch to Minister of Information, Broadcasting and Tourism, 22 October 1963; KNA AHC/1/33.
24. Michemi to President, Central Region, 30 April 1964; KNA VQ/10/12.
25. Kisiero to Tengut, 13 December 1963; KNA DO/ER/2/14/10.
26. Ochieng to Kenyatta, 9 September 1963; KNA KA/6/28.
27. O'odang'a to Murumbi, 22 July 1964; KNA KA/6/33.
28. Kisaka to Kenyatta, 4 December 1963; KNA KA/6/33.
29. Ole Kimelonganai to Kenyatta, 10 September 1963; KNA KA/6/32.
30. Civil Secretary North Eastern to Permanent Secretary, Ministry of Local Government, 16 July 1964; KNA DC/GRS/3/7/12.
31. Mboya, *Challenge*, pp. 46–7.
32. David William Cohen and E.S. Atieno Odhiambo, *The Risks of Knowledge: Investigations into the death of the Hon. Minister John Robert Ouko in Kenya, 1990*, Athens, OH, 2004, pp. 28–9.
33. Nancy Fraser, 'From redistribution to recognition: Dilemmas of justice in a "post-socialist" age', *New Left Review*, 212(1) (1995), p. 68.
34. Bethwell Ogot, *Who, if Anyone, Owns the Past? Reflections on the meaning of 'public history'*, Kisumu, 2010, p. 153.
35. Mugo Gatheru, *Child of Two Worlds*, London, 1966, p. v.
36. Mwai Kibaki, 'Where are we going?', May 1964, 2; KNA MAC/KEN/77/4.
37. John Iliffe, *Africans: The history of a continent*, Cambridge, 2007, pp. 251–2.
38. E.S. Atieno Odhiambo, 'Democracy and the ideology of order in Kenya' in Michael Shatzberg (ed.), *The Political Economy of Kenya*, New York, 1987, pp. 177–202.
39. 'Kenya becomes a one-party state by law', *Weekly Review*, 11 June 1982, p. 4.
40. Roger Cohen, 'How Kofi Annan rescued Kenya', *New York Review of Books*, 14 August 2008, available at: www.nybooks.com/articles/archives/2008/aug/14/how-kofi-annan-rescued-kenya/?pagination=false
41. Carlo Ginzburg, *The Cheese and the Worms: The cosmos of a sixteenth-century miller*, Baltimore, 1992, p. xxi.
42. Binyavanga Wainaina, 'Middle ground', *Kwani?*, 5(2) (2008), p. 17.
43. Robert Bates, *When Things Fell Apart: State failure in late-century Africa*, Cambridge, 2008.
44. Frederick Cooper, *Africa Since 1940: The past of the present*, Cambridge, 2002, pp. 156–90.
45. Nhan to Okello, 21 October 1963; KNA KA/4/7.
46. Moni to Murumbi, 4 November 1963; KNA KA/4/7.

CHAPTER 1: FREEDOM AND SUFFERING, 1963–69

1. Lumumba Institute, untitled pamphlet, 1964, 8; KNA MSS/35/2.
2. Pink, 'Independence day in Lamu and district', 27 November 1963; KNA DC/LMU/2/11/27.

3. James Scott, *The Art of Not Being Governed: An anarchist history of upland Southeast Asia*, New Haven, 2009.
4. DC Lamu to PC (Provincial Commissioner) Coast, 24 June 1968; KNA CA/41/3.
5. Ruchti to Secretary of State, 18 December 1963; POL 2 General Reports & Statistics Kenya, RBAA 1958–66; RG 59; NACP.
6. Frederick Cooper, 'Conflict and connection: Rethinking African colonial history', *American Historical Review*, 99(5) (1994), p. 1519.
7. DC Lamu, Lamu District Security Report 16 June–30 June 1967, 4; KNA CA/41/1.
8. Ndegwa, *Walking*, p. 349.
9. Ernest Bevin, 'Mr. Bevin's proposal' in Catherine Hoskyns (ed.), *Case Studies in African Diplomacy*, Number II: *The Ethiopia-Somali-Kenya Dispute 1960–67*, Dar es Salaam, 1969, p. 9.
10. Somali Government, 'A people in isolation: Statement by the Somalis of the Kenya Northern Frontier District, March 1962' in Hoskyns, *Case Studies*, p. 21.
11. Vass to Secretary of State, 18 May 1963; POL Political Affairs Kenya, RBAA 1958–66; RG 59; NACP.
12. *Hansard*, House of Lords Debate, 3 April 1963, vol. 248, c. 603.
13. Kenyan delegation to the African Summit Conference, 'Memorandum submitted to the conference by the Kenya Delegation and entitled "Pan African Unity and the NFD Question in Kenya" ' in Hoskyns, *Case Studies*, p. 39.
14. Northern Frontier District Commission, *Kenya: Report of the Northern Frontier District Commission*, London, 1962, pp. 18–19.
15. Progressive Party to Secretary of State for the Colonies, 22 July 1963; KNA GO/3/2/81.
16. John Drysdale, 'The Somali way of life' in Hoskyns, *Case Studies*, p. 2.
17. Office of the Director of Intelligence and Security to Civil Secretary Eastern, 15 February 1964, 18–19; KNA BB/1/156.
18. DO Garba Tula, untitled statement, May 1966; KNA/DC/ISO/4/7/14.
19. Sworn statement by Eketoei Ngalup, undated; KNA DC/ISO/4/7/14.
20. Sworn statement by Lokui Longomo, undated; KNA/DC/ISO/4/7/14.
21. Kenya Government Information Services North Eastern Province (NEP), *Garissa Handout*, 13 July 1966; KNA PC/GRSSA/3/21/1.
22. Ministry of Economic Planning and Development, 'Development in North-Eastern Province and Isiolo and Marsabit Districts of Eastern Province', 1967, 1; KNA AE/19/34.
23. DC Mandera, Mandera District Annual Report 1967, 3; KNA PC/GRSSA/3/3/3.
24. Kenya Government Information Services NEP, *Garissa Handout*, 24 August 1966; KNA PC/GRSSA/3/21/1.
25. Kenya Government Information Services NEP, *Garissa Handout*, 16 August 1966; KNA PC/GRSSA/3/21/1.
26. Ferguson to Secretary of State, 21 June 1967; POL Kenya-Somalia, Central Foreign Policy Files 1967–1969 (CFPF 1967–69); RG 59; NACP.
27. Ruora to Permanent Secretary, Ministry of Information, Broadcasting and Tourism, 9 September 1964; KNA DC/GRS/2/7/14.
28. Kenya Government Information Services NEP, *Garissa Handout*, 27 April 1966; KNA PC/GRSSA/3/21/1.
29. DC Mandera, Monthly Report, January 1968, 1; KNA PC/GRSSA/3/21/25.
30. DC Lamu to PC Coast, 20 September 1968; KNA CA/41/3.
31. Modogashe Police Station to Divisional Police Headquarters, Isiolo, 8 December 1967; KNA DC/ISO/4/7/14.
32. Memorandum of conversation between Abdi Haji Ahmed, John Atchley and Robert Blackwill, 6 May 1971; POL Kenya 1970, Subject Numeric Files, 1970–73 (SNF 1970–73); RG 59; NACP.

33. Imray to Hickman, 25 January 1964; TNA: PRO DO 213/65.
34. Elizabeth Schmidt, *Cold War and Decolonization in Guinea, 1946–1958*, Athens, OH, 2007, pp. 4–5.
35. Odinga, *Not Yet Uhuru*, p. 296.
36. Mboya, speech delivered at Africa Freedom Day rally, 17 April 1961; KNA MAC/KEN/70/1.
37. Odinga, *Not Yet Uhuru*, p. 279.
38. Director of Intelligence, Weekly Intelligence Report, 31 March–6 April 1964, 1; KNA BB/1/156.
39. Republic of Kenya, *African Socialism and its Application to Planning in Kenya*, Nairobi, 1965, p. i.
40. 'Kenya official assures U.S. on investments, trade', *New York Times*, 20 December 1963, p. 43.
41. Tom Mboya, *Freedom and After*, Nairobi, 1986, p. 143.
42. Nalle, 'Problems relating to Kenya students in the United States', 5 November 1965; EDX 10 Educational and Cultural Exchange, Foreign Student Program (Student Incident); RBAA 1958–66; RG 59; NACP.
43. Joint Soviet-Kenyan Communique, April 1964; KNA MAC/KEN/89/7.
44. Garvey to Butler, 27 May 1964; TNA: PRO DO 213/214.
45. UK High Commission Nairobi to Commonwealth Relations Office, 19 May 1964; TNA: PRO DO 213/214.
46. Cabinet Joint Intelligence Committee, 'The outlook for British interests in Kenya up to 1975', 27 May 1970, 2; TNA: PRO PREM 15/509.
47. Foreign and Commonwealth Office, 'Leading personalities in Kenya', 1972, 5; TNA: PRO FCO 31/1192.
48. Richard Dowden, *Africa: Altered states, ordinary miracles*, London, 2008, p. 44; Pat Hutton and Jonathan Bloch, 'How the West established Idi Amin and kept him there' in Ellen Ray, William Schaap, Karl van Meter and Louis Wolf (eds), *Dirty Work 2: The CIA in Africa*, London, 1980, p. 177.
49. MacLaren to Ure, 17 March 1966; TNA: PRO FO 1110/2090.
50. MacLaren to Ure, 14 August 1965; TNA: PRO FO 1110/1967.
51. 'Indication of an early swing to left in Kenya', 12 August 1963, 4; TNA: PRO FO 1110/1704.
52. *Ibid.*
53. Oginga Odinga, 'Let the people of Kenya, Africa and the world know', unpublished pamphlet, June 1962, p. 10.
54. Barclay to Armitage-Smith, 23 September 1963; TNA: PRO FO 1110/1704; Ure to Simmons, 16 March 1965; TNA: PRO FO 1110/1967.
55. Garvey to Foreign Office, 13 May 1964; TNA: PRO DO 213/214.
56. Wortoel to Secretary of State, 16 September 1964; POL 2 Kenya Political Affairs & Relations, Kenya-USSR; RBAA 1958–66; RG 59; NACP.
57. Kenya Police Special Branch, Weekly Intelligence Report, 17–23 March 1964, 2; KNA BB/1/156.
58. Odinga, *Not Yet Uhuru*, pp. 277–8.
59. Director of Intelligence, Special Branch Weekly Intelligence Report, 14–20 September 1965, 1; KNA BB/1/158.
60. Director of Intelligence, Special Branch Weekly Intelligence Report, 27 April–3 May 1965, 1; KNA BB/1/158.
61. Nalle, 'Countering Chicom intrusion: Kenya', 18 May 1965; POL 2 Kenya Political Affairs & Relations, China-Kenya Relations; RBAA 1958–66; RG 59; NACP.
62. Odinga, *Not Yet Uhuru*, p. 277.
63. British Land Forces Kenya to Ministry of Defence, 12 October 1964; TNA: PRO DO 213/159.

64. Ruchti, 'The U.S. position in Kenya', 24 December 1964; POL 1 Kenya – General Policy Background; RBAA 1958–66; RG 59; NACP.
65. MacDonald to Bottomley, 12 May 1965; TNA: PRO DO 213/65.
66. Ferguson to Secretary of State, 4 June 1967; POL 12; RBAA 1958–66; RG 59; NACP.
67. MacDonald to Secretary of State for Commonwealth Relations, 5 May 1965, 2–3; TNA: PRO DO 213/65.
68. Oginga Odinga *et al. Pio Gama Pinto: Independent Kenya's first martyr*, Nairobi, 1966.
69. Pinto to all KANU members of House of Representatives, 29 May 1963, 2; KNA MAC/71/1.
70. Ruchti, 'The U.S. position in Kenya', 24 December 1964, 3–4; POL 1 – General Policy Background; RBAA 1958–66; RG 59; NACP.
71. Minutes of KANU Backbenchers Group meeting, 1 March 1965; KNA KA/2/14.
72. O'Neill to Mulcahy, 26 February 1965; POL 6-1 Pinto; RBAA 1958–66; RG 59; NACP.
73. William Attwood, *The Reds and the Blacks: A personal adventure*, New York, 1967, p. 245.
74. 'How Pinto murder was plotted . . . and Kisilu framed', *The Nation*, 19 June 2000.
75. Luke Obok, 'Motion for the adjournment under Standing Order 14: Attack on Mr and Mrs B.M. Kaggia' in *National Assembly Debates (Hansard)*, 14 December 1967; 3332.
76. Allinson to Dawbarn, 7 March 1973; TNA: PRO FCO 31/1496.
77. Murumbi, 'Funeral oration', 1965; KNA MAC/KEN/71/5.
78. MacDonald to Secretary of State for Commonwealth Relations, 29 June 1965, 1–2; TNA: PRO DO 213/65.
79. Minutes of Cabinet Defence and Policy Committee, 12 April 1965; TNA: PRO CAB 148/18.
80. Attwood, *Reds and the Blacks*, p. 246.
81. Lador, untitled memorandum, 14 April 1965; POL 23-7 Kenya Subversion, Espionage, Sabotage; RBAA 1958–66; RG 59; NACP.
82. Ruchti, 'The U.S. position in Kenya', 24 December 1964, 5; POL 1 Gen. Policy Background Kenya; RBAA 1958–66; RG 59; NACP.
83. Ruchti, 'The U.S. position in Kenya', 24 December 1964, 1; POL 1 Gen. Policy Background Kenya; RBAA 1958–66; RG 59; NACP.
84. John Lewis Gaddis, *We Now Know: Rethinking Cold War History*, Oxford, 1997, p. 188.
85. Stanley to Aspin, 12 April 1965; TNA: PRO DO 213/65.
86. 'Kenya: Arms and Odinga', *Time*, 23 April 1965.
87. MacKnight to Williams, 15 April 1965; POL 23-7 Kenya Subversion, Espionage, Sabotage; RBAA 1958–66; RG 59; NACP.
88. Foreign Office to certain of Her Majesty's representatives, 5 May 1965; TNA: PRO FO 1110/1967.
89. Walker to Commonwealth Relations Office, 15 April 1965; Kenya Misc. Old 1965; RBAA 1958–66; RG 59; NACP.
90. Foreign Office Information Research Department to Chancery *et al.*, 22 April 1965; TNA: PRO FO 1110/1967.
91. Lumumba Institute, untitled pamphlet, 1964, 13; KNA MSS/35/2; Foreign Office Information Research Department to Chancery *et al.*, 22 April 1965; TNA: PRO FO 1110/1967.
92. Lumumba Institute, untitled pamphlet, 1964, 3; KNA MSS/35/2.
93. Kenya News Agency handout no. 223, 'Assistant minister speaks at the Lumumba Institute', 8 April 1965; TNA: PRO DO 213/65.
94. US Embassy to Secretary of State, 3 May 1965; EDU 3 Educational and Cultural Affairs Kenya, Lumumba Institute; RBAA 1958–66; RG 59; NACP.

95. Attwood, *Reds and the Blacks*, p. 249.
96. Director of Intelligence, Special Branch Weekly Intelligence Report, 30 June–6 July 1965, 1; KNA BB/1/158.
97. Otuko to Permanent Secretary, Ministry of External Affairs, 15 July 1965; KNA AE/28/2.
98. MacKnight to Trimble, 2 August 1965; POL 2 Kenya General Reports & Statistics; RBAA 1958–66; RG 59; NACP.
99. Director of Intelligence, Special Branch Weekly Intelligence Report, 30 March – 5 April 1965, 1; KNA BB/1/158.
100. Director of Intelligence, Special Branch Weekly Intelligence Report, 9–15 February 1965, 1; KNA BB/1/158.
101. Kamumba to Kenyatta, 19 October 1965; KNA KA/6/24.
102. Kagunda to Kenyatta, 23 July 1965; KNA KA/6/27.
103. Robert Bates, *Beyond the Miracle of the Market: The political economy of agrarian development in Kenya*, Cambridge, 2005, p. 69.
104. McBain to Tesh, 4 May 1965; TNA: PRO DO 213/65.
105. Ruchti to Wild and Culpepper, 7 November 1964; POL 6-1 Political Affairs & Relations Kenya, Odinga, Oginga; RBA 1958–66; RG 59; NACP.
106. Mahihu to Ndegwa, Permanent Secretary, Office of the President, 15 May 1965; KNA BB/1/158.
107. Republic of Kenya, *African Socialism*.
108. William R. Ochieng', 'Structural and political changes' in B.A. Ogot and W.R. Ochieng' (eds), *Decolonization and Independence in Kenya: 1940–93*, London, 1995, p. 85.
109. Jomo Kenyatta, address on Jamhuri Day, 12 December 1968, 15; KNA KA/4/17.
110. Director of Intelligence, Special Branch Weekly Intelligence Report, 20–26 April 1965, 1; KNA BB/1/158.
111. Kenyatta, address to nation on Independence Day, 12 December 1967, 7–8; KNA KA/4/16.
112. Kenyatta, speech at opening of Mwea rice mill, 14 February 1969, 9–10; KNA KA/4/17.
113. Quoted in Cherry Gertzel, Maure Goldschmidt and Donald Rothchild (eds), *Government and Politics in Kenya: A nation-building text*, Nairobi, 1969, pp. 83–4.
114. Mboya to Kenyatta, 21 September 1965; KNA KA/11/4.
115. Ochok to Kenyatta, 14 November 1965; KNA KA/6/28.
116. DC Kilifi, Secret Intelligence Report, 15 November–15 December 1965, 1–3; KNA CA/41/1.
117. MacDonald to Bottomley, 5 February 1966; TNA: PRO DO 213/66.
118. Minutes of KANU Re-Organisation Conference, 11–13 March 1966, 5; KNA KA/2/14.
119. Minutes of KANU Re-Organisation Conference, 11–13 March 1966, 5–7; KNA KA/2/14.
120. Oneko, 'Why I have decided to resign', April 1966; KNA MAC/KEN/73/1.
121. KANU, 'KANU statement on Mr. Oneko's resignation', 25 April 1966; KNA KA/11/4.
122. Maranga and Kola to Kenyatta, 15 March 1966; KNA KA/11/4.
123. Shitemi to Permanent Secretary, Ministry of Defence, 6 June 1966; KNA PC/NZA/4/20/1.
124. DC Lamu, Lamu District Security Report, 1–15 June 1966, 2; KNA CA/41/1.
125. District Assistant Faza to DC Lamu, 20 June 1966; KNA CA/41/1.
126. Gachogo, 'Press statement', 21 April 1966; KNA KA/11/4.
127. Bates, *Beyond the Miracle*, pp. 63–4.

128. Peck to Bottomley, 1 July 1966; TNA: PRO DO 213/188.
129. Oginga Odinga, 'Message to Wananchi of Kenya on Madaraka Day 1967', *Ujamaa*, 1 June 1967; POL 12 Kenya; RBAA 1958–66; RG 59; NACP.
130. Clerk of the National Assembly, 'Programme of parliamentary business for week commencing 11 July 1967', 3; KNA AE/28/9.
131. Oneko to Kenyatta, October 1966; KNA MAC/KEN/73/1.
132. Kenyatta, speech on Labour Day, 1 May 1968, 5–6; KNA KA/4/16.
133. De Ling to Reid, 4 September 1967; TNA: PRO FCO 31/206.
134. US Embassy to Secretary of State, 28 April 1968; POL 15-2 Kenya; CFPF 1967–69; RG 59; NACP.
135. Ferguson to Secretary of State, 1 June 1968; POL 14 Kenya; CFPF 1967–69; RG 59; NACP.
136. US Embassy to Secretary of State, 20 March 1968; POL 14 Kenya; CFPF 1967–69; RG 59; NACP.
137. US Embassy to Secretary of State, 2 April 1968; POL 15-1 Kenya; CFPF 1967–69; RG 59; NACP.
138. Coote to Secretary of State, 17 August 1968; POL 14 Kenya; CFPF 1967–69; RG 59; NACP.
139. Goodall to Tallboys, 21 August 1968; TNA: PRO FCO 31/206.
140. Coote to Secretary of State, 28 August 1968; POL 14 Kenya; CFPF 1967–69; RG 59; NACP.
141. Funk to Secretary of State, 3 April 1971; POL 29 Kenya; SNF 1970–73; RG 59; NACP.
142. Brighty, 'Record of a private conversation between the Secretary of State and Mr. Bruce McKenzie, Kenya Minister of Agriculture', 30 August 1968; TNA: PRO PREM 13/2743.

CHAPTER 2: THE BIG MAN, 1968–69

1. Tom Mboya, *Conflict and Nationhood: The essentials of freedom in Africa*, London, 1963, p. 6.
2. Ferguson to Secretary of State, 6 May 1968; POL 15-1 Kenya; CFPF 1967–69; RG 59; NACP.
3. 'When Jomo "died" before', *Hull Daily Mail*, 25 August 1978.
4. Ferguson to Secretary of State, 30 May 1968; POL 15-1 Kenya; CFPF 1967–69; RG 59; NACP.
5. Ferguson to Secretary of State, 13 June 1968; POL 15-1 Kenya; CFPF 1967–69; RG 59; NACP.
6. Stanley to Aspin, 29 January 1964; TNA: PRO DO 213/65.
7. Greatbach to Scott, 26 March 1968; TNA: PRO FCO 31/209.
8. Ferguson to Secretary of State, 13 June 1968; POL 15-1 Kenya; CFPF 1967–69; RG 59; NACP.
9. Greatbach to Scott, 8 May 1968; TNA: PRO FCO 31/209.
10. Dan Schechter, Michael Ansara and David Kolodney, 'The CIA as an equal opportunity employer' in E. Ray, W. Schaap, K. van Meter and L. Wolf (eds), *Dirty Work 2: The CIA in Africa*, London, 1980, pp. 58–60.
11. Imray, 'Notes on politics in Nyanza', 15 October 1965, 2; TNA: PRO DO 213/65.
12. Mboya, *Challenge*, p. 66.
13. Office of the Director of Intelligence, Special Branch Weekly Intelligence Report, 28 September–5 October 1965, 1; KNA BB/1/158.

14. Office of the Director of Intelligence, Special Branch Weekly Intelligence Report, 10–16 August, 1; KNA BB/1/158.
15. Roger van Zwanenberg, 'History and theory of urban poverty in Nairobi: The problem of slum development', working paper no. 26, Institute for Development Studies, University of Nairobi, April 1972, p. 1.
16. E.P. Wilkinson, 'Nairobi's population growth and the problem of housing', c.1963, 3; KNA KA/1/52.
17. Minutes of meeting on 'Immediate public health measures to be taken against cholera in Nairobi City', City Hall, Nairobi, 16 March 1971; KNA KA/1/52.
18. DC Nairobi, 'Illegal squatting in Nairobi', February 1965; KNA KA/1/52.
19. Lenayiarra to Kenyatta, 25 July 1970; KNA KA/6/52.
20. Koinange, 'Brief on memorandum by the Meru people for Sunday, 23 March 1969', 1; KNA KA/6/22.
21. Cheboiwo to Bomett, 5 August 1967; KNA KA/6/14.
22. Kenyatta, speech at the official opening of the Provincial Administration Seminar at the Kenya Institute of Administration, Kabete, 5 May 1969; KNA KA/4/17.
23. Minutes of the KANU Parliamentary Group meeting, 20 December 1966, 5; KNA KA/2/14.
24. Mbogoh to Moi, 7 August 1967; KNA KA/6/22.
25. Mboya to Jahazi et al., 3 October 1965; KNA KA/11/9.
26. Ferguson to Secretary of State, 29 February 1968; POL 15 Kenya; CFPF 1967–69; RG 59; NACP.
27. Anon., 'Jodong Luo Oromo gi Jaduong' Jomo Kenyatta', 21 June 1967; KNA MAC/KEN/70/2.
28. US Embassy to Secretary of State, 14 February 1968; POL 15-1 Kenya; 1967–69; RG 59; NACP.
29. Hughes to Secretary of State, 25 April 1968; POL 15-1 Kenya; CFPF 1967–69; RG 59; NACP.
30. Hughes to Secretary of State, 25 April 1968; POL 15-1 Kenya; CFPF 1967–69; RG 59; NACP.
31. Ling to Tallboys, 31 July 1968; TNA: PRO FCO 31/206.
32. Ferguson to Secretary of State, 13 July 1968; POL 15-1 Kenya; CFPF 1967–69; RG 59; NACP.
33. Ferguson to Secretary of State, 3 July 1968; POL 15-1 Kenya; CFPF 1967–69; RG 59; NACP.
34. Ferguson to Secretary of State, 13 July 1968; POL 15-1 Kenya; CFPF 1967–69; RG 59; NACP.
35. Ferguson to Secretary of State, 8 January 1969, 2; POL 15-1 Kenya; CFPF 1967–69; RG 59; NACP.
36. Coote to Secretary of State, 23 April 1969; POL 14 Kenya; CFPF 1967–69; RG 59; NACP.
37. Coote to Secretary of State, 16 May 1969; POL 14 Kenya; CFPF 1967–69; RG 59; NACP.
38. Allinson to Holmes, 31 May 1971; TNA: PRO DO 226/13.
39. 'The last few minutes of minister's life', East African Standard, 7 July 1969.
40. US Embassy to Secretary of State, 7 July 1969; POL 15-1 Kenya; CFPF 1967–69; RG 59; NACP.
41. Coote to Secretary of State, 10 July 1969; POL 15-1 Kenya; CFPF 1967–69; RG 59; NACP.
42. US Embassy to Secretary of State, 7 July 1969; POL 15-1 Kenya; CFPF 1967–69; RG 59; NACP.
43. Coote to Secretary of State, 10 July 1969; POL 15-1 Kenya; CFPF 1967–69; RG 59; NACP.

44. Coote to Secretary of State, 10 July 1969; POL 15-1 Kenya; CFPF 1967–69; RG 59; NACP.
45. Coote to Secretary of State, 10 July 1969; POL 15-1 Kenya; CFPF 1967–69; RG 59; NACP; Norris to FCO, 10 July 1969; TNA: PRO FCO 31/356.
46. Coote to Secretary of State, 14 July 1969; POL 15-1 Kenya; CFPF 1967–69; RG 59; NACP.
47. Bethwell Ogot, *A History of the Luo-Speaking Peoples of Eastern Africa*, Kisumu, 2009, p. 783.
48. Coote to Secretary of State, 11 July 1969; POL 15-1 Kenya; CFPF 1967–69; RG 59; NACP.
49. Norris to Johnston, 16 July 1969; TNA: PRO FCO 31/356.
50. Goodall to Tallboys, 23 July 1969; TNA: PRO FCO 31/356.
51. Edis to Purcell, 20 August 1969; TNA: PRO FCO 31/356.
52. Goodall to Purcell, 27 August 1969; TNA: PRO FCO 31/356.
53. Goodall to Tallboys, 23 July 1969; TNA: PRO FCO 31/356.
54. Foreign and Commonwealth Office, 'Leading personalities in Kenya, 1972', 111; TNA: PRO FCO 31/1192.
55. Ferguson to Secretary of State, 28 September 1968; POL 12 Kenya; CFPF 1967–69; RG 59; NACP.
56. Hughes to Secretary of State, 25 April 1968; POL 15-1 Kenya; CFPF 1967–69; RG 59; NACP.
57. Ferguson to Secretary of State, 28 September 1968; POL 12 Kenya; CFPF 1967–69; RG 59; NACP.
58. Goodall to Purcell, 27 August 1969; TNA: PRO FCO 31/356.
59. Denney to Secretary of State, 11 September 1969; POL 12 Kenya; CFPF 1967–69; RG 59; NACP.
60. Allinson to Dawbarn, 7 March 1973; TNA: PRO FCO 31/1496.
61. Edis to Purcell, 3 September 1969; TNA: PRO FCO 31/356.
62. Goodall to Purcell, 27 August 1969; TNA: PRO FCO 31/356.
63. Edis to Purcell, 12 September 1969; TNA: PRO FCO 31/356.
64. Edis to Purcell, 15 October 1969; TNA: PRO FCO 31/356.
65. Goodall to High Commission, 15 September 1969; TNA: PRO FCO 31/356.
66. Norris to FCO, 19 November 1969; TNA: PRO FCO 31/356.
67. Hart to Hunt, 28 January 1977; TNA: PRO FCO 31/2121.
68. PC Rift Valley to Kariithi, 14 August 1969; KNA KA/6/52.
69. Ngugi to Koinange, 18 July 1969; KNA KA/6/52.
70. Coote to Secretary of State, 24 September 1969; POL 17 Kenya; CFPF 1967–69; RG 59; NACP.
71. Ben Knighton, 'Going for *Cai* at Gatundu: Reversion to a Kikuyu ethnic past or building a Kenyan national future' in D. Branch, N. Cheeseman and L. Gardner (eds), *Our Turn to Eat: Kenyan politics since 1950*, Berlin, 2009, p. 117.
72. 'Kenya: Ominous oaths', *Time*, 15 August 1969, available at: www.time.com/time/magazine/article/0,9171,901233,00.html (accessed 1 April 2011).
73. McIlvaine to Secretary of State, 22 October 1969, 8; POL 14 Kenya; CFPF 1967–69; RG 59; NACP.
74. US Embassy to Secretary of State, 17 September 1969; POL 17 Kenya; CFPF 1967–69; RG 59; NACP.
75. Kosanga to Kenyatta, 15 September 1966; KNA KA/11/9.
76. Mitei, 'Nandi Hills Declaration', 27 July 1969; KNA KA/11/9.
77. McIlvaine to Secretary of State, 28 October 1969; POL 23-2 Kenya; CFPF 1967–69; RG 59; NACP.
78. McIlvaine to State Department, 29 October 1969; POL 23-2 Kenya; CFPF 1967–69; RG 59; NACP.

CHAPTER 3: THE FALLEN ANGEL, 1970–75

1. Gakinye *et al.* to DC Nyeri, 14 November 1970; KNA VP/1/12.
2. Newman to High Commissioner *et al.*, 7 March 1972; TNA: PRO FCO 31/1191.
3. Rengontia *et al.* to Motoku, 10 December 1963; KNA KA/4/7.
4. Christopher Leo, *Land and Class in Kenya*, Toronto, 1984, pp. 126–9.
5. Gitathu to Kenyatta, 23 October 1964; KNA VQ/10/3.
6. Ministry of Finance and Economic Planning, *An Economic Appraisal of the Settlement Schemes: 1964/5–1967/8: Farm economic survey report No. 27*, Nairobi, 1972, p. 7.
7. Mau Mau War Council to Prime Minister Kenyatta, 21 January 1964; KNA KA/6/32.
8. Leo, *Land and Class*, 129–30.
9. Edis to Steele, 15 September 1970; TNA: PRO FCO 31/597.
10. J.M. Kariuki, 'Assistance for emergency widows and orphans' in Kareithi Munuhe (ed.), *J.M. Kariuki in Parliament*, Nairobi, 1974, p. 30.
11. O'Neill to Attwood, 27 July 1965; Ruchti to O'Neill, 3 September 1965; POL 6-1 Kariuki; RBAA 1958–66; RG 59; NACP.
12. Steele to Arthur *et al.*, 24 September 1970; TNA: PRO FCO 31/597.
13. Karuga to Odinga, 25 August 1965; Permanent Secretary, Office of the President to Karuga, 7 September 1965; KNA VQ/10/12.
14. Angaine to Ngureti, 5 March 1964, KNA VQ/10/12.
15. Mugo and Muhoro to Kenyatta, 6 August 1973; KNA KA/6/16.
16. Manby, Weekly Personal Report by the Director of Intelligence, 17 August 1963; TNA: PRO CO 1035/188.
17. Colin Leys, *Underdevelopment in Kenya: The political economy of neo-colonialism 1964–1971*, Nairobi, 1975, p. 63.
18. Gavin Kitching, *Class and Economic Change in Kenya: The making of an African petite-bourgeoisie*, New Haven, CT, 1980, p. 325.
19. World Bank, *Kenya: Into the second decade*, Baltimore, 1975, p. 5.
20. Henry Bienen, *Kenya: The politics of participation and control*, Princeton, NJ, 1974, p. 21.
21. Kitching, *Class and Economic Change*, pp. 372–3.
22. Leys, *Underdevelopment in Kenya*, p. 78.
23. Bellers to Counsell, 23 April 1971; TNA: PRO FCO 31/852.
24. Newman to UK High Commissioner, 9 November 1971; Newman to Le Tocq, 20 December 1971; TNA: PRO FCO 31/865.
25. Clay to Joy, 9 September 1971; TNA: PRO FCO 31/870.
26. Clay to Joy, 2 June 1971; TNA: PRO FCO 31/854.
27. Office of the Vice President and Ministry of Planning and National Development, *Uasin Gishu District Development Plan 1994–1996*, Nairobi, 1994, p. 11.
28. Office of the Vice President and Ministry of Planning and National Development, *Trans Nzoia District Development Plan 1994–1996*, Nairobi, 1994, p. 73.
29. Hart to Head of Chancery, 5 August 1972; TNA: PRO DO 226/16.
30. Clay to Joy, 12 November 1971; TNA: PRO FCO 31/865.
31. M.A.H. Wallis, *Bureaucrats, Politicians and Rural Communities in Kenya*, Manchester, 1982, p. 72.
32. Kangu to Kenyatta, 18 December 1971; KNA KA/6/21.
33. Norris to Secretary of State for Foreign and Commonwealth Affairs, 8 December 1971, 2; TNA: PRO FCO 31/854.
34. McIlvaine to Secretary of State, 31 March 1971; POL Kenya; SNF 1970–73; RG 59; NACP.
35. McIlvaine to Secretary of State, 9 May 1970; POL Kenya; SNF 1970–73; RG 59; NACP.

36. Ferguson to Secretary of State, 13 July 1968; POL 15-1 Kenya; CFPF 1967–69; RG 59; NACP.
37. Norris to Foreign and Commonwealth Office, 26 March 1971; TNA: PRO FCO 31/856.
38. Walker to Douglas-Home, 10 August 1971; TNA: PRO FCO 31/856.
39. Bellers to Counsell, 28 April 1971; TNA: PRO FCO 31/854.
40. US Embassy to Secretary of State, 21 June 1971; POL 29 Kenya; SNF 1970–73; RG 59; NACP.
41. McIlvaine to Secretary of State, 9 June 1971; POL 29 Kenya; SNF 1970–73; RG 59; NACP.
42. Walker to Douglas-Home, 10 August 1971, 5; TNA: PRO FCO 31/856.
43. US Embassy to Secretary of State, 23 June 1971; POL 29 Kenya; SNF 1970–73; RG 59; NACP.
44. Walker to Douglas-Home, 10 August 1971, 8; TNA: PRO FCO 31/856.
45. US Embassy to Secretary of State, 23 April 1967; POL 6 Kenya; CFPF 1967–69; RG 59; NACP.
46. Allinson to Bellers, 2 June 1971; TNA: PRO FCO 31/854.
47. Hart to Hunt, 28 January 1977; TNA: PRO FCO 31/2121.
48. Office of the President, 'Loyalty and unity demonstration Sunday June 27th, 1971', 26 June 1971; KNA KA/15/11.
49. US Embassy to Secretary of State, 1 July 1971; POL 15-2 Kenya; SNF 1970–73; RG 59; NACP.
50. Bellers to Duggan, 30 June 1971; TNA: PRO FCO 31/856.
51. Clay to Joy, 2 June 1971; TNA: PRO FCO 31/854.
52. Ferguson to Secretary of State, 12 November 1967; POL 15-3 Kenya; CFPF 1967–69; RG 59; NACP.
53. McIlvaine to Secretary of State, 28 October 1972; POL Kenya; SNF 1970–73; RG 59; NACP.
54. McIlvaine to Secretary of State, 9 December 1972; POL 12 Kenya; SNF 1970–73; RG 59; NACP.
55. Mansfield to Ewans, 7 May 1974; TNA: PRO 31/1707.
56. Hannam to Symons et al., 20 December 1973; TNA: PRO DO 226/13.
57. Bellers to Joy, 24 November 1971; TNA: PRO FCO 31/853.
58. McIlvaine to Secretary of State, 19 August 1970; POL 15-1 Kenya; SNF 1970–73; RG 59; NACP; Clay to Purcell, 30 March 1971; TNA: PRO 31/852.
59. Clay to Joy, 15 July 1971; TNA: PRO FCO 31/852.
60. Coote to Secretary of State, 21 February 1971; POL 15-2 Kenya; SNF 1970–73; RG 59; NACP.
61. McIlvaine to Secretary of State, 7 November 1970; POL Kenya; SNF 1970–73; RG 59; NACP.
62. Memorandum of conversation, J.M. Kariuki and Alan Lukens, 17 May 1971; POL Kenya-US; SNF 1970–73; RG 59; NACP.
63. McIlvaine to Secretary of State, 27 February 1971; POL 12 Kenya; SNF 1970–73; RG 59; NACP.
64. Bellers to Head of Chancery et al., 12 February 1971; TNA: PRO FCO 31/854.
65. McIlvaine to Secretary of State, 7 November 1970; POL Kenya; SNF 1970–73; RG 59; NACP.
66. Memorandum of conversation, J.M. Kariuki and Alan Lukens, 17 May 1971; POL Kenya-US; SNF 1970–73; RG 59; NACP.
67. Edis to Steele et al., 15 September 1970; TNA: PRO FCO 31/957.
68. Clay to Joy, 19 October 1971; TNA: PRO FCO 31/853.
69. McIlvaine to Secretary of State, 7 November 1970; POL Kenya; SNF 1970–73; RG 59; NACP.
70. Edis to Purcell, 30 June 1970; TNA: PRO FCO 31/596.

71. Hall to Darling, 26 July 1973; TNA: PRO FCO 31/1498.
72. Hall to Darling, 5 October 1973; TNA: PRO FCO 31/1498.
73. Hart to Wigan, 1 June 1976; TNA: PRO FCO 31/2019.
74. Hall to Darling, 17 October 1973; TNA: PRO FCO 31/1499.
75. J.M. Kariuki, *J.M. Speaks His Mind*, Nairobi, 1974, p. 3; Pamphlets Kenya – Speeches, African and Middle Eastern Pamphlet Collection, Library of Congress.
76. Kariuki, *J.M. Speaks His Mind*, p. 4.
77. *Ibid.*, p. 11.
78. Hart to Head of Chancery, 17 March 1975; TNA: PRO DO 226/15; Hart to Longrigg, 29 November 1978; TNA: PRO FCO 31/2324.
79. Carl Dutto, *Nyeri Townsmen, Kenya*, Nairobi, 1975, p. 177.
80. International Labour Organization, *Employment, Incomes and Equality: A strategy for increasing productive employment in Kenya*, Geneva, 1972.
81. Hannam to MacMahon, 7 December 1973; TNA: PRO FCO 31/1506.
82. Ministry of Finance and Planning, 'Quarterly economic report – December 1974'; TNA: PRO FCO 31/1892.
83. 'Kenya's inflation: How to beat it', *Weekly Review*, 3 March 1975, p. 5.
84. Republic of Kenya, *On Economic Prospects and Policies*, Sessional Paper No. 4, Nairobi, 1975.
85. Duff to Head of Chancery, 3 March 1975; TNA: PRO DO 226/15.
86. Jon Tinker, 'Who's killing Kenya's jumbos?', *New Scientist*, 22 May 1975, pp. 452–5.
87. Mansfield to Ewans, 12 February 1975; TNA: PRO FCO 31/1887.
88. Kelly to Hart *et al.*, 22 January 1975; TNA: PRO DO 226/17.
89. Fingland to Secretary of State for Foreign and Commonwealth Affairs, 2 January 1976; TNA: PRO FCO 31/2020.
90. 'Bombings shock', *Weekly Review*, 3 March 1975, p. 8.
91. National Assembly, *Report of the Select Committee on the Disappearance and Murder of the Late Member for Nyandarua North, the Hon. J.M. Kariuki, M.P.*, Nairobi, 1975, p. 19.
92. Hart to Head of Chancery, 12 September 1975; TNA: PRO DO 226/17.
93. Mansfield to High Commissioner *et al.*, 25 March 1974; TNA: PRO DO 226/15.
94. National Assembly, *Report of the Select Committee*, p. 21.
95. Hart to Head of Chancery, 10 March 1975; TNA: PRO DO 226/15; National Assembly, *Report of the Select Committee*, p. 25.
96. National Assembly, *Report of the Select Committee*, p. 25.
97. *Ibid.*, p. 29.
98. Hart to Head of Chancery *et al.*, 31 July 1975; TNA: PRO DO 226/16.
99. Hart to Holmes *et al.*, 11 March 1975; TNA: PRO DO 226/15.
100. Hart to Wigan, 1 June 1976; TNA: PRO FCO 31/2019.
101. Mansfield to Ewans, 5 March 1975; TNA: PRO DO 226/15.
102. Duff to Head of Chancery, 1 April 1975; TNA: PRO DO 226/15.
103. Mansfield to High Commissioner, 17 March 1975; TNA: DO 226/15.
104. National Assembly, *Report of the Select Committee*, p. 3; Africana Vertical File, Herskovits Library of African Studies, Northwestern University.
105. National Assembly, *Report of the Select Committee*, p. 6.
106. John Barry, 'The killing of Kenyatta's critic', *Sunday Times*, 10 August 1975; Hart to Wigan, 1 June 1976; TNA: PRO FCO 31/2019.
107. Hart to Holmes *et al.*, 7 July 1975; TNA: PRO DO 226/16.
108. National Assembly, *Report of the Select Committee*, p. 3.
109. *Ibid.*, p. 5.
110. Hart to Holmes *et al.*, 7 July 1975; TNA: PRO DO 226/16.
111. National Assembly, *Report of the Select Committee*, p. 36.
112. *Ibid.*, pp. 31, 37.

113. Hart to Wigan, 1 June 1976; TNA: PRO FCO 31/2019.
114. Hart to Hunt, 22 September 1977; TNA: PRO FCO 31/2121.
115. Hart to Head of Chancery, 17 July 1975; TNA: PRO DO 226/16; Barry, 'The killing of Kenyatta's critic'.
116. Marshall to Secretary of State, 7 March 1975; National Archives Access to Archival Databases (NAAAD) website, available at: http://aad.archives.gov/aad/ (accessed 1 March 2010); Hart to Head of Chancery, 10 March 1975; TNA: PRO DO 226/15.
117. Kenya Police, Daily Crime and Incident Report, 16, 18 and 21 March 1975; KNA MSS/8/35.
118. Hart to Holmes *et al.*, 10 April 1975; TNA: PRO DO 226/15.
119. Kenya Police, Daily Crime and Incident Report, 18 March, 19 March and 25 April 1975; KNA MSS/8/35.
120. Duff to Head of Chancery, 2 April 1975; TNA: PRO DO 226/15.
121. Duff to Head of Chancery, 2 April 1975; TNA: PRO DO 226/15.
122. Marshall to Secretary of State, 21 March 1975; NAAAD.
123. Marshall to Secretary of State, 17 March 1975; NAAAD.
124. Holmes to Head of Chancery *et al.*, 11 April 1975; TNA: PRO DO 226/15.
125. Duff to Head of Chancery, 2 April 1975; TNA: PRO DO 226/15.
126. Barry, 'The killing of Kenyatta's critic'.
127. Marshall to Secretary of State, 20 November 1975; NAAAD.
128. Marshall to Secretary of State, 22 September 1975; NAAAD.
129. Marshall to Secretary of State, 31 October 1975; NAAAD.
130. 'At last the national service scheme is here', *Weekly Review*, 7 April 1975.
131. Hart to Hunt, 27 June 1977; TNA: PRO FCO 31/2121.
132. Marshall to Secretary of State, 16 October 1975; NAAAD.
133. Crabbie to Wigan, 15 September 1976; TNA: PRO FCO 31/2019.
134. Hart to Head of Chancery, Wallis and Deputy High Commissioner, 17 July 1975; TNA: PRO DO 226/17.
135. Sigsworth to Mansfield, 15 July 1975; TNA: PRO DO 226/16.
136. Hart to Head of Chancery, 11 July 1975; TNA: PRO DO 226/16.

CHAPTER 4: FOOTSTEPS, 1975–82

1. Charles Kareri, 'Sermon preached by the Very Rev. Charles M. Kareri', *The State Funeral for His Excellency the Late Mzee Jomo Kenyatta*, Nairobi, 1978, p. 9.
2. Bruce Loudon, 'Oginga Odinga, the bitter enemy, pays homage to Kenyatta', *Daily Telegraph*, 26 August 1974.
3. 'Thousands at Kenyatta funeral', *The Scotsman*, 1 September 1978.
4. Jean-François Bayart, 'Africa in the world: A history of extraversion', *African Affairs*, 99(395) (2000), pp. 217–67.
5. National Christian Council of Kenya (NCCK), *Who Controls Industry in Kenya?: Report of a working party*, Nairobi, 1968.
6. Allinson to Dawbarn, 7 March 1973; TNA: FCO 31/1496.
7. East African Department, FCO, 'Kenya: Mr Udi Gecaga – recent activities', 3 April 1978; TNA: PRO FCO 31/2322.
8. Ngugi wa Thiong'o, *Petals of Blood*, London, 2002, p. 409.
9. Goodall to Tallboys, 20 January 1969; TNA: PRO FCO 31/352.
10. Ngugi wa Thiong'o, *Detained: A writer's prison diary*, Nairobi, 2000, p. 15.
11. Ngugi wa Thiong'o and Ngugi wa Mirii, *I Will Marry When I Want*, Nairobi, 2005.
12. Ngugi, *Detained*, p. 74.

13. Gichingiri Ndigirigi, *Ngugi wa Thiong'o's Drama and the Kamiriithu Popular Theater Experiment*, Trenton, NJ, 2007, p. 85.
14. 'Ngugi wa Thiong'o still bitter over his detention', *Weekly Review*, 5 January 1979, pp. 30–1.
15. Ngugi, *Detained*, pp. 75–80.
16. David Bevan, Paul Collier and Jan Willem Gunning with Arne Bigsten and Paul Horsnell, *Peasants and Governance: An economic analysis*, Oxford, 1989, pp. 39–41.
17. McIlvaine to Secretary of State, 8 August 1970; POL Kenya 12-2; SNF 1970–73; RG 59; NACP.
18. Crabbie to Wigan, 17 March 1976; TNA: PRO FCO 31/2019.
19. Hall to Darling, 14 May 1973; TNA: PRO FCO 31/1499.
20. Ewans to Campbell, 18 January 1974; TNA: PRO FCO 31/1707.
21. Bellers to Wallace, 26 April 1972; TNA: PRO FCO 31/1191.
22. McIlvaine to Secretary of State, 20 May 1972; POL Kenya 15-1; SNF 1970–73; RG 59; NACP.
23. Hart to Hunt, 11 March 1977; TNA: PRO FCO 31/2121; Hart to Hunt, 22 September 1977; TNA: PRO FCO 31/2121; Hart to Carter, 18 July 1978; TNA: PRO FCO 31/2322.
24. Hart to Hunt, 19 October 1976; TNA: PRO FCO 31/2019.
25. Fingland to Watts and Crabbie, 13 October 1976; TNA: PRO FCO 31/2019.
26. 'GEMA speaks out on politics', *Weekly Review*, 19 May 1975, p. 4.
27. Hall to Darling, 30 May 1973; TNA: PRO FCO 31/1498; 'Please cool it', *Weekly Review*, 10 November 1975, p. 4.
28. Hannam to High Commissioner, 24 April 1975; TNA: PRO DO 226/17.
29. Njenga Karume, *Beyond Expectations: From charcoal to gold*, Nairobi, 2009, p. 158.
30. Crabbie to Wigan, 18 August 1976; TNA: PRO FCO 31/2019.
31. Allinson to High Commissioner, 9 August 1972; TNA: PRO FCO 31/1193.
32. Karume, *Beyond Expectations*, p. 173.
33. Fingland to Secretary of State for Foreign and Commonwealth Affairs, 6 January 1977; TNA: PRO FCO 31/2120.
34. Joseph Karimi and Philip Ochieng, *The Kenyatta Succession*, Nairobi, 1980.
35. *Ibid.*, p. 132.
36. Crabbie to East African Department, FCO, 2 August 1978; TNA: PRO FCO 31/2322.
37. Fingland, 'Note of informal talk between the Secretary of State for Foreign and Commonwealth Affairs and the Kenyan Attorney-General', 12 January 1978; TNA: PRO FCO 31/2336.
38. Ian Black and Benny Morris, *Israel's Secret Wars: A history of Israel's intelligence services*, New York, 1991, p. 342.
39. Fingland to FCO, 22 August 1978; TNA: PRO FCO 31/2315.
40. Fingland to Foreign Office, 23 August 1978; TNA: PRO FCO 31/2323.
41. Daniel Arap Moi, eulogy at state funeral of Jomo Kenyatta, 31 August 1978; KNA KA/4/21.
42. Daniel Arap Moi, speech to delegation from Central Bank of Kenya, 15 September 1978; KNA KA/4/21.
43. Daniel Arap Moi, speech at passing-out parade of National Youth Service, Gilgil, 28 November 1978; KNA KA/4/21.
44. Interview with Charles Njonjo, 'Focus on Africa', BBC World Service, broadcast 15 December 1978; TNA: PRO FCO 31/2324.
45. Hughes to Secretary of State, 9 December 1968; POL Kenya 12; CFPF 1967–69; RG 59; NACP.
46. Crabbie to Longrigg, 19 December 1978; TNA: PRO FCO 31/2324.
47. Fingland to Munro, 5 October 1978; TNA: PRO 31/2324.
48. Crabbie to Longrigg, 5 December 1978; TNA: PRO FCO 31/2324.

49. 'A lesson to others: Prosecution has no room for technicalities', *Weekly Review*, 2 February 1979, pp. 8, 11.
50. 'Kimani in trouble: Charges of misdeeds', *Weekly Review*, 16 March 1979, p. 19.
51. 'Purge is on: Wanted: "Nyayo" promoters', *Weekly Review*, 11 May 1979, p. 6.
52. 'Njenga Karume gets major political boost', *Weekly Review*, 11 November 1981, p. 6.
53. 'Karume triumphs in leadership tussle', *Weekly Review*, 1 January 1982, pp. 6–7.
54. 'Suit and countersuit: Gecaga takes Lonrho to court', *Weekly Review*, 16 October 1981, p. 28.
55. 'Shikuku is back on the old trail', *Weekly Review*, 11 January 1980, p. 5.
56. 'Early comeback', *Weekly Review*, 5 January 1979, p. 11.
57. 'Ex-detainees to stage a comeback: Will Kanu allow them to run?', *Weekly Review*, 25 May 1979, p. 4–7.
58. 'Ex-KPU leaders, Anyona barred', *Weekly Review*, 5 October 1979, p. 4.
59. Oginga Odinga, 'Letter to the delegation head, US Armed Services Committee', *Race and Class*, 24(3) (1983), pp. 317–20.
60. 'Battling on: Kibaki reassures Law Society', *Weekly Review*, 22 February 1980, p. 24.
61. Gichiri Ndua and Njuguna Ng'ethe, 'The role of the informal sector in the development of small and intermediate size cities: Background information on Nakuru', working paper no. 416, Institute for Development Studies, University of Nairobi, November 1984; 'The role of the informal sector in the development of small and intermediate size cities: The informal sector in Nakuru', working paper no. 417, Institute for Development Studies, University of Nairobi, November 1984.
62. 'Continued smuggling causes food crunch', *Weekly Review*, 5 December 1980, p. 26.
63. Anonymous, *Independent Kenya*, London, 1982, pp. 115–16.
64. CIA, 'East Africa: Accumulating economic woes', June 1982, 1–4; CIA Records Search Tool (CREST) Database, NACP.
65. 'Murder most foul: Killers were never caught', *Weekly Review*, 9 March 1979, pp. 14–15.
66. 'Ngugi wa Thiong'o still bitter over his detention', *Weekly Review*, 5 January 1979, pp. 30–1.
67. Sholto Cross, 'L'etat c'est Moi: Political transition and the Kenya general election of 1979', discussion paper no. 66, University of East Anglia, April 1983, p. 9.
68. 'Six expelled: Students back to work', *Weekly Review*, 9 November 1979, pp. 5–6.
69. Anonymous, *Independent Kenya*, pp. 117–19.
70. World Bank, *Population and Development in Kenya*, Washington, DC, 1980.
71. 'Expensive drain: Moi suggests competitive consultancy', *Weekly Review*, 23 November 1981, pp. 24–5.
72. 'Riot costs: Students to pay huge damages', *Weekly Review*, 21 March 1980, p. 9.
73. 'Invisible masters: Moi charges campus is being used by foreigners', *Weekly Review*, 11 July 1980, pp. 13–15.
74. 'Low priority: President says ex-detainees will be last to get jobs', *Weekly Review*, 11 July 1980, pp. 12–13.
75. 'Kibaki's turn: Vice president hits at the press', *Weekly Review*, 4 July 1980, p. 10.
76. 'Trouble erupts again at varsity', *Weekly Review*, 18 July 1980, p. 4.
77. 'President Moi speaks out', *Weekly Review*, 25 July 1980, p. 9.
78. 'Firm without favour', *Weekly Review*, 25 July 1980, pp. 12–13.
79. 'What's going on? Moi in combative mood', *Weekly Review*, 7 November 1980, p. 10.
80. 'Serious accusations levelled on ministers', *Weekly Review*, 21 November 1980, pp. 4–5.

81. 'Early vacation: Lecturers criticise decision to close campus', *Weekly Review*, 6 March 1981, p. 19.
82. 'Odinga makes political gaffe', *Weekly Review*, 10 April 1981, pp. 4–5.
83. 'Same old story: Kanu bars Odinga from by-election', *Weekly Review*, 17 April 1981, p. 7.
84. 'Crack down at "Nation": "I have never known such torture all my life" ', *Weekly Review*, 29 May 1981, p. 34.
85. 'Silent hallways: Students sent home again after violent confrontations', *Weekly Review*, 22 May 1981, pp. 10–11.
86. 'Fiery Mutai once again in trouble', *Weekly Review*, 25 September 1981, pp. 5–6.
87. 'Studious silence: Ministers keep out of debate', *Weekly Review*, 12 February 1982, p. 7.
88. 'Detention threat: Moi warns potential dissidents', *Weekly Review*, 23 April 1982, pp. 7–9.
89. Alan Cowell, 'Multiparty system is under attack in Kenya', *New York Times*, 29 May 1982, p. 10.
90. 'Will Odinga now form another party?', *Weekly Review*, 21 May 1982, pp. 4–6.
91. 'Kanu backs Moi's expulsion of Odinga', *Weekly Review*, 28 May 1982, p. 9.
92. 'President expels Odinga from Kanu', *Weekly Review*, 21 May 1982, p. 4.
93. Wanyiri Kihoro, *The Price of Freedom: The story of political resistance in Kenya*, Nairobi, 2005, pp. 180–1.
94. 'Spotlight on lecturers: Moi speaks of guns plot', *Weekly Review*, 11 June 1982, p. 7.
95. *Pambana*, May 1982, reprinted in a special edition of *Race and Class*, 24(3) (1983), pp. 322–5. See also Laurie Goodstein, 'The trouble in Kenya', *Index on Censorship*, 11(4) (1982), pp. 49–50.
96. 'District visits: Moi keeps up momentum of warnings', *Weekly Review*, 25 June 1982, p. 6.
97. 'The coup broadcast', reprinted in a special edition of *Race and Class*, 24(3) (1983), pp. 325–6.
98. James Dianga, *Kenya 1982, the Attempted Coup: The consequences of a one-party dictatorship*, London, 2002; Fredrick Wambua, *The '82 Kenyan Military Coup: An airman's prison experience*, Kansas City, 2003, pp. 36–7.
99. Babafemi Badejo, *Raila Odinga: An enigma in Kenyan politics*, Lagos, 2006, pp. 95–8.
100. CIA, 'National intelligence daily (cable)', 2 August 1982, 5; CREST, NACP.
101. Amnesty International, *Torture, Political Detention and Unfair Trials*, London, 1987, pp. 3–4.
102. Republic of Kenya, *Report of Judicial Commission Appointed to Inquire into Allegations Involving Charles Mugane Njonjo*, Nairobi, 1984.
103. Karume, *Beyond Expectations*, pp. 244–5.

CHAPTER 5: LOVE, PEACE AND UNITY, 1982–88

1. CIA, Defense Intelligence Agency and Bureau of Intelligence and Research, State Department, 'Kenya: Prospects for stability', November 1982, 1; CREST, NACP.
2. BBC Monitoring, 'President Moi's inaugural speech', 14 October 1978; TNA: PRO FCO 31/2324.
3. Mwakenya, *Draft Minimum Programme: September 1987*, Nairobi, 1987, p. 7; papers of the Committee for the Release of Political Prisoners in Kenya, George Padmore Institute, London (CRPPK, GPI).

4. 'Moi is guilty of misrule', *Finance*, 16–31 December 1991.
5. Ogot, *Who, if Anyone*, p. 121.
6. Mwakenya, *Draft Minimum Programme*, pp. 13–15.
7. Dianga, *Kenya 1982*, pp. 227–32.
8. Mwakenya, *Draft Minimum Programme*, p. 20.
9. *Ibid.*, p. 33.
10. *Ibid.*, pp. 3–4.
11. Kiraitu Murungi, *In the Mud of Politics*, Nairobi, 2000, p. 10.
12. Amnesty International, *Torture, Political Detention and Unfair Trials*, p. 8.
13. Wanyiri Kihoro, *Never Say Die: The chronicle of a political prisoner*, Nairobi, 1998.
14. Mwakenya, *Draft Minimum Programme*, p. 17.
15. Ogot, *Who, if Anyone*, p. 121.
16. CRPPK, 'Political prisoners in Kenya', *Kenya News*, August 1986, pp. 3–4; CRPPK, GPI.
17. Amnesty International, *Torture, Political Detention and Unfair Trials*, p. 8.
18. *Ibid.*, pp. 17–18.
19. *Ibid.*, pp. 12–16.
20. *Ibid.*, p. 23.
21. Amnesty International USA, 'Human rights under serious attack in Kenya – Amnesty International cites government program to silence opponents', 21 July 1987; African pamphlet collection, Kenya – Politics and Government, African and Middle East Reading Room, Library of Congress.
22. BBC Monitoring Summary of World Broadcasts (SWB), 'Kenyan minister says reports of detainee's death "misleading" ', 25 March 1987.
23. Murungi, *Mud of Politics*, p. 11.
24. Amnesty International, *Torture, Political Detention and Unfair Trials*, pp. 11–12.
25. *Ibid.*, p. 40.
26. Maina wa Kinyatti, *Mother Kenya: Letters from prison, 1982–1988*, London, 1997, pp. 250–1.
27. Angelique Haugerud, *The Culture of Politics in Modern Kenya*, Cambridge, 1995, pp. 56–107.
28. CIA, 'National intelligence daily (cable)', 2 January 1982, 7–9; CREST, NACP.
29. CIA, 'Trends in the Horn of Africa', 27 September 1983, 11; CREST, NACP.
30. 'New explanation', *Weekly Review*, 21 November 1980, pp. 9–10.
31. BBC Monitoring SWB, 'Agreement between clans in north-eastern Kenya', 31 October 1983.
32. CRPPK, 'Press release: New wave of political detentions in Kenya', 8 February 1984; CRPPK, GPI.
33. BBC Monitoring SWB, 'Kenyan minister's statement on Wajir clashes', 12 April 1984.
34. *Ibid.*.
35. '2 Kenyan officials make massacre charge', *New York Times*, 29 February 1984; Edward Girardet, 'Notes from the border badlands', *Christian Science Monitor*, 24 September 1985. See also S. Abdi Sheikh, *Blood on the Runway: The Wagalla massacre of 1984*, Nairobi, 2007.
36. 'Genocide alleged', *Weekly Review*, 13 April 1984, pp. 15–19.
37. Bates, *Beyond the Miracle*, pp. 139–46.
38. BBC Monitoring SWB, 'Drastic reduction of harvest in Wajir district', 14 August 1984.
39. BBC Monitoring SWB, 'Wajir district calm', 6 October 1984.
40. Alastair Matheson, 'Reports of massacre surface in Kenya', *Globe and Mail*, 14 April 1985.
41. BBC Monitoring SWB, 'Kenya signs third oil exploration agreement with Amoco', 30 April 1985.

42. 'Background to a drastic measure', *Weekly Review*, 17 November 1989, pp. 19–20.
43. Daniel Arap Moi, address at provincial and district commissioners' meeting, 21 November 1978; KNA KA/4/21.
44. Jennifer Widner, *The Rise of a Party State in Kenya: From 'Harambee' to 'Nyayo'*, Berkeley, CA, 1992.
45. Katete Orwa, 'Political recruitment in Mbita constituency: A study in electoral politics', University of Nairobi, Department of Government seminar series on general elections, seminar paper 3, 2 March 1984, pp. 30, 35.
46. David Throup, 'The construction and destruction of the Kenyatta state' in M. Schatzberg (ed.), *The Political Economy of Kenya*, New York, 1987, pp. 60–1.
47. CIA, 'Sub-Saharan Africa report', 30 April 1981, 32–3; CREST, NACP.
48. Karume, *Beyond Expectations*, p. 242.
49. Amnesty International USA, 'Human rights under serious attack in Kenya: Amnesty International cites government program to silence opponents', 21 July 1987; African pamphlet collection, Kenya – Politics and Government, African and Middle East Reading Room, Library of Congress.
50. Committee for the Release of Political Prisoners in Kenya, 'Focus on human rights in Kenya', June 1988, 2; African pamphlet collection, Kenya – Politics and Government, African and Middle East Reading Room, Library of Congress.
51. Murungi, *Mud of Politics*, p. 10.
52. Atieno Odhiambo, 'Democracy and the ideology of order', pp. 177–201.
53. Herve Maupeu and Patrick Mutahi (eds), *Wahome Mutahi's World*, Nairobi, 2005.
54. Umoja, *Struggle for Democracy in Kenya: Special report on the 1988 general elections in Kenya*, London, 1988, pp. 15–16.
55. 'Steps towards taking Kanu to the people', *Weekly Review*, 5 February 1988, p. 4.
56. 'Cries of "unfair" ', *Weekly Review*, 26 February 1988, p. 13.
57. Umoja, *Struggle for Democracy*, p. 71.
58. Anonymous, 'The elections', 10 May 1988, 1; African pamphlet collection, Kenya – Politics and Government, African and Middle East Reading Room, Library of Congress.
59. 'Claims of coercion and rigging in nominations', *Weekly Review*, 4 March 1988, pp. 20–1.
60. 'Queuing has never been African', *Weekly Review*, 29 April 1988, p. 9.
61. Umoja, *Struggle for Democracy*, pp. 23–4.
62. Umoja, 'Umoja rejects the fraudulent general elections of March 21, 1988 in Kenya', 10 April 1988, 1; CRPPK, GPI.
63. Mwakenya, 'Moi-KANU regime has no legitimacy to rule Kenya', 29 March 1988; CRPPK, GPI.
64. 'The aim is positive patriotism', *Weekly Review*, 29 April 1988, p. 15.
65. Murungi, *Mud of Politics*, p. 17.
66. 'Memorandum of the Kenya Episcopal Conference to His Excellency Daniel T. Arap Moi, C.G.H., M.P., the President and Commander-in-Chief of the Armed Forces', 13 November 1986; Kenya: Catholic Church vertical file, Herskovits Library, Northwestern University.
67. 'Shall I ever have a say again?', *Weekly Review*, 29 April 1988, pp. 11–12.
68. 'Heretical statement', *Weekly Review*, 29 April 1988, p. 14.
69. Episcopal Conference of Kenya, *Justice and Peace Commission: Pastoral letter of the bishops of Kenya*, Nairobi, 1988.
70. Paul Vallely, 'Kenya's changing image: Church a lonely voice on Moi's totalitarian drift', *The Times*, 26 May 1987.
71. Widner, *The Rise of a Party State*, pp. 190–2.
72. NCCK, *A Report on the Church's Involvement in Development*, Nairobi, 1984, p. 53.
73. Ngugi wa Thiong'o, *Homecoming: Essays on African and Caribbean Literature, Culture and Politics*, London, 1972, p. 31.

74. Widner, *The Rise of a Party State*, p. 172.
75. Kiraitu Murungi, 'The role of the ICJ (Kenya Section) in promoting the rule of law and protecting the enjoyment of human rights' in International Commission of Jurists (Kenya Section), *Law and Society: Selected papers from a seminar held 24–26 November 1988 at the Green Hills Hotel, Nyeri, Kenya*, Nairobi, 1989, p. 10.
76. *Ibid.*, pp. 1–11.
77. J.R. Otieno, 'Has the system of a one party state outlived its usefulness in Africa?', *Nairobi Law Monthly*, July/August 1989, p. 7.
78. Murungi, 'Role of the ICJ'.

CHAPTER 6: THE WAR OF ARROWS, 1989–94

1. Wambui Waiyaki Otieno, *Mau Mau's Daughter: A life history*, Boulder, CO, 1998, p. 239.
2. Kabiru Kinyanjui, 'Justice, peace and reconciliation: The challenge to the Church today' in Samuel Kobia and Godffrey Ngumi (eds), *Together in Hope: The official report of the Mission Conference 1989*, Nairobi, 1991, p. 45.
3. *Ibid.*
4. BBC Monitoring SWB, 'Moi says advocates of pluralism "have masters abroad"', 15 January 1990.
5. Duff to Head of Chancery, 27 January 1975; TNA: PRO DO 226/17.
6. Neil Henry, 'World Bank urges steps to reverse Africa's economic decline', *Washington Post*, 22 November 1989, p. 17.
7. John Shaw, 'African Paradise Lost', *Sydney Morning Herald*, 26 August 1989, p. 71.
8. E.S. Atieno Odhiambo, 'Foreword: A critique of the postcolony of Kenya' in Waiyaki Otieno, *Mau Mau's Daughter*, p. xii.
9. Waiyaki Otieno, *Mau Mau's Daughter*, pp. 103–7.
10. David William Cohen and E.S. Atieno Odhiambo, *Burying S.M.: The politics of knowledge and the sociology of power in Africa*, London, 1992.
11. Waiyaki Otieno, *Mau Mau's Daughter*, p. 228.
12. Eleanor Wachtel and Andy Wachtel, 'Women's co-operative enterprise in Nakuru', discussion paper no. 250, Institute for Development Studies, University of Nairobi, March 1977.
13. Abantu for Development, *The Other Side of Prison: The role of women left behind*, Nairobi, 2004, p. 71.
14. Wangari Maathai, *Unbowed: One woman's story*, London, 2008, p. 221.
15. Robert Press, 'Kenyan democracy shows strains', *Christian Science Monitor*, 30 January 1990, p. 4.
16. BBC Monitoring SWB, 'Kenya's Ouko says Amnesty peddler of "Outright Lies"', 27 November 1989.
17. Chester Stern, *Dr Iain West's Casebook*, London, 1997, p. 99.
18. Smith Hempstone, *Rogue Ambassador: An African memoir*, Sewanee, TN, 1997, p. 65.
19. Jonah Anguka, *Absolute Power: The Ouko murder mystery*, London, 1998, p. 12.
20. Hempstone, *Rogue Ambassador*, pp. 69–70.
21. Cohen and Atieno Odhiambo, *Risks of Knowledge*, p. 32.
22. Kenneth Matiba and Charles Rubia, 'One party system stifles criticism ruthlessly', *Nairobi Law Monthly*, April/May 1990, p. 37.
23. Kariuki Gathitu, 'Kamukunji: The Kenyan Tiananmen', *Nairobi Law Monthly*, July 1992, p. 25.
24. 'Detentions and after: Crackdown on multi-party advocates is followed by riots in Nairobi and several other towns', *Weekly Review*, 13 July 1990, p. 4.

25. Africa Watch, *Kenya: Taking liberties*, New York, 1991, p. 61.
26. 'Detentions and after: Crackdown on multi-party advocates is followed by riots in Nairobi and several other towns', *Weekly Review*, 13 July 1990, p. 3.
27. 'Lobbying for dialogue', *Weekly Review*, 20 July 1990, p. 14.
28. 'Magugu's gaffe', *Weekly Review*, 20 July 1990, p. 15.
29. Wachira Maina and Chris Mburu, 'The Forum for Restoration of Democracy in Kenya', *Nairobi Law Monthly*, August 1991, p. 16.
30. 'FORD fights on', *Nairobi Law Monthly*, September 1991, p. 10.
31. Waiyaki Otieno, *Mau Mau's Daughter*, p. 210.
32. Hempstone, *Rogue Ambassador*, pp. 254–5.
33. BBC Monitoring SWB, 'Moi reportedly says multi-party system soon but says pluralism a luxury', 2 December 1991.
34. 'Kamukunji FORD rally attendance stuns Kenyans', *Nairobi Law Monthly*, January 1992, p. 20.
35. Catholic Bishops of Kenya, *Kenya 1992: Looking towards the future with hope*, Nairobi, 1992; Catholic Bishops of Kenya vertical file, Herskovits Library, Northwestern University.
36. *Ibid.*
37. Njehu Gatabaki, 'Peace: Interview – the Most Rev. Manasses Kuria', *Finance*, 16–31 October 1991, p. 37.
38. 'The Nandi clashes "a very dirty affair"', *Nairobi Law Monthly*, November 1991, p. 19.
39. National Election Monitoring Unit (NEMU), *Courting Disaster: A report on the continuing terror, violence and destruction in the Rift Valley, Nyanza and Western Provinces of Kenya*, Nairobi, 1993, p. 5.
40. Republic of Kenya, *Report of the Judicial Commission Appointed to Inquire into Tribal Clashes in Kenya*, Nairobi, 1999, p. 91.
41. NEMU, *Courting Disaster*, p. 12.
42. Patrick Chabal and Jean-Pascal Daloz, *Africa Works: Disorder as political instrument*, Oxford, 1999.
43. 'The Nandi clashes "a very dirty affair"', *Nairobi Law Monthly*, November 1991, pp. 19–20.
44. Kiraitu Murungi, 'Kenya's dirty war against multiparty democracy', *Nairobi Law Monthly*, January 1992, p. 29.
45. National Council of Churches of Kenya (NCCK), *The Cursed Arrow: Contemporary report on the politicised violence in the Rift Valley, Nyanza and Western Provinces*, vol. 1, Nairobi, 1992, p. 6.
46. Catholic Bishops of Kenya, *A Call to Justice, Love and Reconciliation*, Nairobi, 1992, pp. 4–5; Catholic Church Kenya vertical file; Herskovits Library, Northwestern University.
47. National Assembly, *Report of the Parliamentary Select Committee to Investigate Ethnic Clashes in Western and Other Parts of Kenya*, Nairobi, 1992, pp. 79–81.
48. NEMU, *Courting Disaster*, p. 9.
49. 'The Nandi clashes "a very dirty affair"', *Nairobi Law Monthly*, November 1991, pp. 19–20.
50. NCCK, *The Cursed Arrow*, p. 7.
51. African Rights, *Kenya Shadow Justice*, London, 1996, p. 81.
52. NEMU, *Courting Disaster*, p. 8.
53. NCCK, *Cursed Arrow*, p. 10.
54. National Assembly, *Report of the Parliamentary Select Committee*, p. 51.
55. 'Pokot elders want borders reviewed', *The Clashes Update*, June 1996, pp. 1–2.
56. Africa Watch, *Divide and Rule: State-sponsored ethnic violence in Kenya*, New York, 1993, p. 88.

57. Rodney Wilson, 'The economic implications of land registration in Kenya's smallholder areas', staff paper no. 91, Institute for Development Studies, University of Nairobi, February 1971, p. 21.
58. Republic of Kenya, *Report of the Commission of Inquiry into the Land Law System of Kenya on Principles of a National Land Policy Framework, Constitutional Position of Land and New Institutional Framework for Land Administration*, Nairobi, 2002, p. 7.
59. *Ibid.*, p. 78.
60. Jacqueline Klopp, 'Pilfering the public: The problem of land grabbing in contemporary Kenya', *Africa Today*, 47(1) (2000), pp. 7–26.
61. John Rogge, *The Internally Displaced Population in Kenya, Western and Rift Valley Provinces: A need assessment and a program proposal for rehabilitation*, Nairobi, 1993, p. 34.
62. John Kaiser, *If I Die*, Nairobi, 2003, pp. 27–8.
63. Office of the Vice President and Ministry of Planning and National Development, *Narok District Development Plan 1994–1996*, Nairobi, 1994, pp. 106, 109–11.
64. Africa Watch, *Taking Liberties*, p. 242.
65. NCCK, *Nairobi Demolitions: What next?* Nairobi, 1991.
66. Rogge, *Internally Displaced Population in Kenya*, p. 37.
67. Office of the Vice President and Ministry of Planning and National Development, *Nakuru District Development Plan 1994–1996*, Nairobi, 1994, pp. 105, 139.
68. Office of the Vice President and Ministry of Planning and National Development, *Uasin Gishu District Development Plan 1994–1996*, pp. 11, 19, 79–80, 125.
69. Office of the Vice President and Ministry of Planning and National Development, *Nandi District Development Plan 1994–1996*, Nairobi, 1994, pp. 146–7.
70. Rogge, *Internally Displaced Population in Kenya*, p. 34.
71. *Ibid.*, pp. 2–3.
72. *Ibid.*, p. 15.
73. International Commission of Jurists (Kenya Chapter) (ICJ-K), *The Political Economy of Ethnic Clashes in Kenya*, Nairobi, 2000, pp. 62–3.
74. Karume, *Beyond Expectations*, p. 262.
75. *Ibid.*, p. 263.
76. 'Kibaki's Democratic Party: A party the World Bank should like', *Nairobi Law Monthly*, January 1992, p. 25.
77. Karume, *Beyond Expectations*, p. 265.
78. Kenneth Matiba, *A Dream for Kenya*, Nairobi, 1992, p. 22.
79. *Ibid.*, pp. 25–7.
80. *Ibid.*, p. 28.
81. 'Interview with Oginga Odinga', *Nairobi Law Monthly*, January 1992, pp. 21–3.
82. David Throup and Charles Hornsby, *Multi-Party Politics in Kenya: The Kenyatta and Moi states and the triumph of the system in the 1992 election*, Oxford, 1998, p. 127.
83. Wangari Maathai, 'Kenya . . . Down the road', *Finance*, 31 January 1993, p. 21.
84. Gibson Kamau Kuria and Maina Kiai, 'The struggle continues', *Finance*, 31 January 1993, pp. 24–5.
85. 'A glance at the events in the hot spots', *The Clashes Update*, July 1993, p. 3.
86. 'No hope for victims in Nyayo regime – pastor', *The Clashes Update*, July 1993, p. 4.
87. 'Kibor sparks off violence', *The Clashes Update*, August 1993, pp. 1–7.
88. 'Maasais still attacking Kisiis', *The Clashes Update*, August 1993, p. 5.
89. 'Lotodo still determined to flush out non-Pokots: Kapenguria hospital is Lotodo's target', *The Clashes Update*, December 1993, pp. 7–8.
90. Africa Watch, *Divide and Rule*, p. 36.
91. 'Future of clash victims bleak', *The Clashes Update*, April 1993, p. 4.
92. 'Victims crying for security but state firm with deaf ear', *The Clashes Update*, April 1993, p. 7.
93. ICJ-K, *Political Economy of Ethnic Clashes*, p. 31.

94. Kaiser, *If I Die*, pp. 57–61.
95. NCCK, *Cursed Arrow*, p. 5.

CHAPTER 7: THE GOLDENBERG YEARS, 1993–2002

1. Kenya Human Rights Commission (KHRC), *Kayas of Deprivation, Kayas of Blood: Violence, ethnicity and the state in Coastal Kenya*, Nairobi, 1997, p. 60.
2. Richard Lyons, 'Oginga Odinga, 82, a longtime leader in Kenya's politics', *New York Times*, 22 January 1994, p. 10.
3. 'Timothy Njoya', *Finance*, 15 November 1994, p. 23.
4. Ogot, *Who, if Anyone*, p. 114.
5. François Grignon, Marcel Rutten and Alamin Mazrui, 'Observing and analysing the 1997 general elections: An introduction' in M. Rutten, A. Mazrui and F. Grignon (eds), *Out for the Count: The 1997 general elections and prospects for democracy in Kenya*, Kampala, 2001, p. 18.
6. Richard Dowden, 'Export scam robs Kenya of millions', *Independent*, 8 June 1993, p. 16.
7. Quoted in Billy Kahora, *The True Story of David Munyakei: Goldenberg whistle-blower*, Nairobi, 2008, p. 27.
8. *Ibid.*, p. 60.
9. Robert Press, 'Kenyan officials caught in export, bank scams', *Christian Science Monitor*, 17 August 1993, p. 7.
10. John Lonsdale, 'Agency in tight corners: Narrative and initiative in Africa history', *Journal of African Cultural Studies*, 13(1) (2000), pp. 5–16.
11. Ogot, *Who, if Anyone*, p. 153.
12. 'Clashes brewing up in Narok-Ngong diocese', *The Clashes Update*, April 1995, p. 6.
13. Karuti Kanyinga, *Re-Distribution from Above: The politics of land rights and squatting in Coastal Kenya*, Uppsala, 2000, p. 116.
14. Janet McIntosh, *The Edge of Islam: Power, personhood, and ethnoreligious boundaries on the Kenya Coast*, Durham, NC, 2009, p. 45.
15. KHRC, *Kayas of Deprivation*, pp. 12–16.
16. *Ibid.*, p. 12.
17. *Ibid.*, p. 25–7.
18. KHRC, *Kayas Revisited: A post-election balance sheet*, Nairobi, 1998, p. 9.
19. KHRC, *Kayas of Deprivation*, p. 38.
20. KHRC, *Kayas Revisited*, p. 39.
21. KHRC, *Kayas of Deprivation*, pp. 51–2.
22. Kenya Episcopal Conference, 'A message from the Catholic bishops of Kenya following recent events in Coast Province', 27 August 1997; Catholic Church Kenya vertical file, Herskovits Library, Northwestern University.
23. 'Clashes rage in border areas', *Update on Peace and Reconciliation*, November 1997, p. 5.
24. 'Security zoning criticised', *Update on Peace and Reconciliation*, December 1997, p. 12.
25. Charles Hornsby, 'Election day and the results' in M. Rutten, A. Mazrui and F. Grignon (eds), *Out for the Count*, p. 135.
26. Willy Mutunga, *Constitution-Making from the Middle: Civil society and transition politics in Kenya, 1992–1997*, Nairobi, 1999, p. 235.
27. 'Clashes hit Rift Valley again', *Update on Peace and Reconciliation*, January 1998, p. 4.
28. 'Why clashes erupted in Rift Valley', *Update on Peace and Reconciliation*, January 1998, pp. 5–6.
29. *Ibid.*
30. 'The quotes of the month', *Update on Peace and Reconciliation*, April 1998, p. 9.

31. Human Rights Watch, *Playing with Fire: Weapons proliferation, political violence, and human rights in Kenya*, New York, 2002, p. 7.
32. NCCK, Netherlands Development Corporation and Semi-Arid Rural Development Programme, *Pacifying the Valley: An analysis on the Kerio Valley conflict*, Nairobi, 2002.
33. 'Lotodo on cattle rustling', *Update on Peace and Reconciliation*, March 1999, p. 7.
34. Republic of Kenya, *Report of the Judicial Commission Appointed to Inquire into Tribal Clashes in Kenya*, pp. 286–91.
35. Republic of Kenya, *Comments by the Government on the Report of the Judicial Commission Appointed to Inquire into Tribal Clashes in Kenya (Akiwumi Report)*, Nairobi, 1999, p. 30.
36. Justus Mozart Ogembo, 'The rise and decline of communal violence: Analysis of the 1992–94 witch-hunts in Gusii, Southwestern Kenya', unpublished PhD thesis, Harvard University, 1997, pp. 168–9.
37. Paul Nugent, *Africa since Independence: A comparative history*, Basingstoke, 2004, pp. 336–7.
38. Murungi, *Mud of Politics*, p. 146.
39. Stephen Ellis and Gerrie ter Haar, 'Religion and politics in sub-Saharan Africa', *Journal of Modern African Studies*, 36(2) (1998), p. 177.
40. Paul Gifford, *Christianity, Politics, and Public Life in Kenya*, London, 2009, p. 119.
41. *Ibid.*, p. 117.
42. James Smith, *Bewitching Development: Witchcraft and the reinvention of development in neoliberal Kenya*, Chicago, 2008, p. 84.
43. Robert Blunt, ' "Satan is an imitator": Kenya's recent cosmology of corruption' in B. Weiss (ed.), *Producing African Futures: Ritual and reproduction in a neoliberal age*, Leiden, 2004, p. 319.
44. Gakiha Weru, 'Mungiki: Dangerous subversives?', *The Nation*, 28 June 1998.
45. Paul Harris, 'Religious cult inspired by bloody rebellion: "True sons of the Mau Mau" reject western culture in Kenya', *Ottawa Citizen*, 16 January 2000, p. 8.
46. Gakiha Weru, 'Mungiki: Dangerous subversives?', *The Nation*, 28 June 1998.
47. Muthui Mwai, 'What makes Mungiki tick?', *The Nation*, 23 October 2000.
48. Gakiha Weru, 'Mungiki: Dangerous subversives?', *The Nation*, 28 June 1998.
49. BBC Monitoring Africa, 'Police search MP's house for firearms', 25 November 1998.
50. Sabala Kizito, 'The proliferation, circulation and use of illegal firearms in urban centres. The case of Nairobi, Kenya', unpublished paper presented to United Nations and Economic Commission of Africa and International Resource Group on Disarmament and Security in the Horn of Africa at the 'Curbing the Demand Side of Small Arms in the IGAD States: Potentials and Pitfalls' conference, Addis Ababa, 26 April 2001, p. 3.
51. 'Matatu owners paying protection money', *The Standard*, 5 November 2001.
52. *Ibid.*
53. 'Deadly matatu wars', *The Standard*, 5 November 2001.
54. 'Three slain over commuter route dispute', *The Nation*, 18 September 2001.
55. David Anderson, 'Vigilantes, violence and the politics of public order in Kenya', *African Affairs*, 101(405) (2002), pp. 531–55.
56. 'Gov't blasted for continued operations of gangs', *The Standard*, 14 November 2001.
57. John Githongo, 'Why won't the state clip them dreadlocks?', *The East African*, 15 November 2000.
58. 'Mungiki sect to support Kanu, Saitoti and Uhuru in poll', *The Standard*, 4 March 2002.
59. 'Four people murdered in Dandora', *The Standard*, 3 February 2002.
60. '20 die in slum savage attack', *The Nation*, 5 March 2002.
61. 'Witnesses tell of death and violence', *The Nation*, 5 March 2002.

62. 'Police blamed over murders', *The Nation*, 8 March 2002.
63. 'Mungiki agenda in succession race', *The Nation*, 25 August 2002.
64. 'Mungiki officials call for a truce', *The Nation*, 6 February 2001.
65. James Orengo, 'Kenyans must act to rise out of reforms and economic mess', *The Nation*, 13 August 2000.

CHAPTER 8: NOTHING ACTUALLY REALLY CHANGED, 2002–11

1. Francis Openda, 'Minister: Standard rattled the snake', *The Standard*, 3 March 2006.
2. 'Moi names top four in succession line-up', *The Nation*, 9 March 2002.
3. Ranneberger to State Department, 13 November 2007; 07NAIROBI4427; Wikileaks cable viewer website, available at: http://213.251.145.96/origin/62_0.html (accessed 24 March 2011).
4. Republic of Kenya, *Report of the Commission of Inquiry into the Illegal/Irregular Allocation of Public Land*, Nairobi, 2004, Annexes, Volume 1, p. 485.
5. Fred Jonyo, 'The centrality of ethnicity in Kenya's political transition' in W. Oyugi, P. Wanyande and C. Odhiambo Mbai (eds), *The Politics of Transition in Kenya: From KANU to NARC*, Nairobi, 2003, p. 173.
6. 'Kanu nominates Uhuru Kenyatta', *The Standard*, 15 October 2002.
7. Ranneberger to State Department, 13 November 2007; 07NAIROBI4427; Wikileaks cable viewer website (accessed 24 March 2011).
8. Binyavanga Wainaina, 'Generation Kenya', *Vanity Fair*, July 2007, available at: http://www.vanityfair.com/culture/features/2007/07/wainaina200707?currentPage=1 (accessed 25 March 2011).
9. *Ibid.*
10. William Ochieng', *The Black Man's Democracy: Kenya, the first five years after Moi, 2003–2007*, Kisumu, 2008, p. 20.
11. 'Carnival mood after NARC boss takes over', *The Nation*, 31 December 2002.
12. *Ibid.*
13. Anthony Morland, 'Sunny outlook for Kenyan investment climate', Agence France Presse, 9 March 2003.
14. Karuti Kanyinga, Winnie Mitullah and Sebastian Njagi, *The Non-Profit Sector in Kenya: Size, scope and financing*, Institute for Development Studies, University of Nairobi, Nairobi, 2007, p. 16.
15. Institute for Education in Democracy, *Enhancing the Electoral Process in Kenya: A report on the transition general elections 2002*, Nairobi, 2003, pp. 3–4.
16. Joseph Ngure, 'Rift Valley MPs accuse Kibaki of favouritism', *The Nation*, 9 June 2003.
17. Parselelo Kantai, 'Comrade Lemma and the Black Jerusalem Boys' Band' in *Seventh Street Alchemy: A Selection of Writings from the Caine Prize for African Writing 2004*, Johannesburg, 2005, p. 73.
18. Kroll Associates, 'Project KTN: Consolidated report', 27 April 2004, available on Basel Institute of Governance website at: http://www.assetrecovery.org/kc/resources/org.apache.wicket.Application/repo?nid=a2925d58-c6c9-11dd-b3f1-fd61180437d9 (accessed 5 April 2011).
19. Transparency International, *National Integrity Systems Transparency International Questionnaire: Kenya 2003*, Berlin, 2004, p. 40.
20. Odhiambo Orale, 'Revealed: Scandal of the Sh.2.7 billion deal', *The Nation*, 21 April 2004.
21. Edward Clay, speech to British Business Association, Nairobi, 13 July 2004, reprinted as 'Britain takes tough stance on graft', *The Nation*, 15 July 2004.

22. Michela Wrong, *It's Our Turn to Eat: The story of a Kenyan whistle blower*, London, 2009.
23. Githongo to Kibaki, 22 November 2005; available on BBC News website at: http://news.bbc.co.uk/1/shared/bsp/hi/pdfs/09_02_06_kenya_report.pdf (accessed 25 March 2011).
24. Tony Kago, 'Clash killers will face the law, vows Kibaki', *The Nation*, 25 January 2005.
25. Ben Agina, 'MPs halt debate to discuss insecurity', *The Standard*, 13 April 2005.
26. Muchemi Wachira and Stephen Muiruri, '53 butchered as bandits raid town', *The Nation*, 13 July 2005.
27. KHRC, *The Fallen Angel: A report on the performance of Amos Wako in promoting human rights and democracy as Kenya's attorney general*, Nairobi, 1993, p. 9.
28. Bellamy to State Department, 24 February 2006; 06NAIROBI839; Wikileaks cable viewer website (accessed 24 March 2011).
29. Ranneberger to State Department, 25 May 2007; 07NAIROBI2240; Wikileaks cable viewer website (accessed 24 March 2011).
30. 'Communities strike deal over water', *The Standard*, 3 February 2005.
31. David Githii, *Exposing and Conquering Satanic Forces over Kenya*, Nairobi, 2008, p. 66.
32. 'Njoya criticises leaders of church in symbols row', *The Nation*, 16 December 2004.
33. Thomas Wolf, 'Immunity or accountability? Daniel Toroitich arap Moi: Kenya's first retired president' in R. Southall and H. Melber (eds), *Legacies of Power: Leadership change and former presidents in African politics*, Cape Town, 2006, p. 219.
34. 'Big debate goes live', *The Nation*, 19 October 2005.
35. *Ibid.*
36. Francis Openda, 'Minister: Standard rattled the snake', *The Standard*, 3 March 2006.
37. Bellamy to State Department, 10 March 2006; 06NAIROBI1114; Wikileaks cable viewer website (accessed 24 March 2011).
38. Bellamy to State Department, 10 March 2006; 06NAIROBI1114; Wikileaks cable viewer website (accessed 24 March 2011).
39. Kenya National Assembly, Joint Session of the Departmental Committees on Administration, National Security and Local Authorities, and Administration of Justice and Legal Affairs, 'Report on the investigation into the conduct of the "Artur Brothers" and their associates', July 2007, pp. 26–7, available on the Mzalendo Eye on Parliament website at: http://www.mzalendo.com/Files/Artur.pdf (accessed 28 March 2011).
40. *Ibid.*, p. 10.
41. Rowe to Department of State, 15 March 2006; 06NAIROBI1187; Wikileaks cable viewer website (accessed 24 March 2011).
42. Kenya National Assembly, 'Conduct of the "Artur Brothers" ', p. 39.
43. Bellamy to State Department, 9 January 2006; 06NARIOBI72; Wikileaks cable viewer website (accessed 24 March 2011).
44. Allan Odhiambo, 'Raila is challenged on mercenary allegations', *The Nation*, 5 March 2006.
45. Ogot, *Who, if Anyone*, p. 96.
46. World Bank, 'Republic of Kenya: Country social analysis', dissemination draft, August 2007, Washington, DC, p. viii.
47. *Ibid.*, p. 1.
48. 'Kibaki's pledge', *The Nation*, 1 October 2007.
49. Ochieng', *Black Man's Democracy*, p. 20.
50. Orange Democratic Movement, 'Mabadiliko Times', Western edition, election pamphlet, 2007.

51. Andrew Kipkemboi, 'Rift Valley is astir, so which way for region?', *The Standard*, 19 December 2007.
52. Gitau Warigi, 'Mystical rock where many seek solace', *The Sunday Nation*, 9 December 2007.
53. BBC Worldwide Monitoring, 'Kenyan "vote-rich basket" province split ahead of election – TV analysis', 18 December 2007.
54. Andrew Kipkemboi, 'Rift Valley is astir, so which way for region?', *The Standard*, 19 December 2007.
55. Patrick Mayoyo and Abdulsamad Ali, 'Raila pledges to fuel growth in Coast', *The Sunday Nation*, 2 December 2007.
56. Human Rights Watch (HRW), *'Why Am I Still Here?': The 2007 Horn of Africa renditions and the fate of those still missing*, New York, 2008.
57. 'Revealed: Raila's real MoU with Muslims', *The Nation*, 28 November 2007.
58. Daniel Otieno and Anthony Njagi, 'ODM to push for majimbo as church demonises system', *The Nation*, 28 October 2007.
59. Kenya National Commission on Human Rights (KNCHR), *'The Cry of Blood': Report on the extra-judicial killings and disappearances*, Nairobi, 2008, p. 5.
60. *Ibid.*, p. 5.
61. International Republican Institute, 'Preliminary findings of IRI's international election observation mission', press release, December 2007.
62. Kwamschetsi Makokha and Rosemary Okello Orlale, *In the Shadow of Death: My trauma, my experiences, voices of Kenyan women from post-election violence*, Nairobi, 2009, p. 9.
63. European Union Election Observation Mission, *Kenya: Final report general elections 27 December 2007*, Brussels, 2008.
64. Kimani Njogu (ed.), *Healing the Wound: Personal narratives about the 2007 post-election violence in Kenya*, Nairobi, 2009, p. 27.
65. *Ibid.*
66. Makokha and Orlale, *In the Shadow of Death*, p. 9.
67. Roger Cohen, 'How Kofi Annan rescued Kenya,' *New York Review of Books*, 14 August 2008.
68. Ranneberger to State Department, 29 January 2008; 08NAIROBI1312; Wikileaks cable viewer website (accessed 24 March 2011).
69. Ranneberger to State Department, 17 January 2008; 08NAIROBI199; Wikileaks cable viewer website (accessed 24 March 2011).
70. Ranneberger to State Department, 25 May 2007; 07NAIROBI2240; Wikileaks cable viewer website (accessed 24 March 2011).
71. Ranneberger to State Department, 17 January 2008; 08NAIROBI199; Wikileaks cable viewer website (accessed 24 March 2011).
72. Makokha and Orlale, *In the Shadow of Death*, p. 3.
73. Njogu, *Healing the Wound*, p. 52.
74. Commission of Inquiry into the Post-Election Violence, *Commission of Inquiry into the Post-Election Violence Report*, Nairobi, 2008, p. 417.
75. Billy Kahora, 'The fire next time or a half-made place: Between Tetra Paks and plastic bags', *Kwani?*, 5(2) (2008), pp. 8–12.
76. Njogu, *Healing the Wound*, pp. 67–8.
77. Barnabas Bii and Peter Ngetich, 'Raid on displaced families that shocked the world', *The Nation*, 6 January 2008.
78. Ranneberger to State Department, 3 June 2009; 09NAIROBI1083; Wikileaks cable viewer website (accessed 24 March 2011).
79. Njogu, *Healing the Wound*, p. 147.
80. Barnabas Bii and Peter Ngetich, 'Raid on displaced families that shocked the world', *The Nation*, 6 January 2008.

81. Parselelo Kantai and Patrick Smith, 'Kenya: No country for young men', *Africa Report*, 11, June/July 2008, p. 41.
82. Njogu, *Healing the Wound*, p. 68.
83. *Ibid.*, p. 56.
84. *Ibid.*, p. 147.
85. 'State "sanctioned" Kenyan clashes', BBC News, 5 March 2008, available at: http://news.bbc.co.uk/1/hi/world/africa/7279149.stm (accessed 18 December 2010).
86. Parselelo Kantai and Patrick Smith, 'Kenya: No country for young men', *Africa Report*, 11, June/July 2008, p. 43.
87. 'State "sanctioned" Kenyan clashes', BBC News, 5 March 2008.
88. Makokha and Orlale, *In the Shadow of Death*, p. 15.
89. Njogu, *Healing the Wound*, p. 167.
90. *Ibid.*, p. 143.
91. Ranneberger to State Department, 29 January 2008; 08NAIROBI1311; Wikileaks cable viewer website (accessed 24 March 2011).
92. Ranneberger to State Department, 5 February 2008; 08NAIROBI378; Ranneberger to State Department, 8 February 2009; 08NAIROBI420; Wikileaks cable viewer website (accessed 24 March 2011).
93. Ranneberger to State Department, 29 January 2008; 08NAIROBI1312; Wikileaks cable viewer website (accessed 24 March 2011).
94. Roger Cohen, 'How Kofi Annan rescued Kenya', *New York Review of Books*, 14 August 2008.
95. *Ibid.*
96. Parselelo Kantai, 'African "Deal Democracy" on trial', *Africa Report*, 16, April/May 2009, p. 31.
97. HRW, *'All the Men Have Gone': War crimes in Kenya's Mt Elgon conflict*, New York, 2008, pp. 16–17.
98. *Ibid.*
99. Ranneberger to State Department, 29 January 2008; 08NAIROBI1312; Wikileaks cable viewer website (accessed 24 March 2011).
100. Kenyans for Peace, Truth and Justice, 'Unfinished business from Kriegler's IREC', *Wajibu*, 24(1) (2009), p. 7.
101. Ranneberger to State Department, 3 June 2009; 09NAIROBI1083; Wikileaks cable viewer website (accessed 24 March 2011).
102. Muthoni Wanyeki, 'Hats off to Waki and his team', *The East African*, 19 October 2008.
103. Lucas Barasa, 'Vote for constitution, urge leaders', *The Nation*, 15 May 2010.
104. Lucas Barasa, 'No team confident of referendum win', *The Nation*, 9 June 2010.
105. Ouma Wanzala, 'Draft "violates rights of some religious groups" ', *The Nation*, 15 April 2010.
106. 'Kenya's post-election violence: ICC prosecutor presents case against six individuals for crimes against humanity', ICC press release, 15 December 2010, available at: http://www.icc-cpi.int/NR/exeres/BA2041D8-3F30-4531-8850-431B5B2F4416.htm (accessed 18 December 2010).
107. Ranneberger to State Department, 2 June 2009; 09NAIROBI1080; Wikileaks cable viewer website (accessed 24 March 2011).
108. Ranneberger to State Department, 24 March 2009; 09NAIROBI579; Wikileaks cable viewer website (accessed 24 March 2011).
109. Horand Knaup, 'Deep-seated corruption in Kenya a cause for US concern', *Der Spiegel*, 9 December 2010, available at http://www.spiegel.de/international/world/0,1518,733824,00.html (accessed 18 December 2010).
110. King'ara to Minister for National Security *et al.*, 14 October 2008; Wikileaks website, available at: wikileaks.org (accessed 25 July 2010).

111. Ranneberger to State Department, 2 June 2009; 09NAIROBI1077; Wikileaks cable viewer website (accessed 24 March 2011).
112. Peter Orengo, 'Ntimama claims assassination in Narok killings', *The Standard*, 9 December 2010.

CONCLUSION

1. Dave Opiyo, 'Joy and wine flow at Raila victory party', *The Nation*, 17 August 2010.
2. Mukhisa Kituyi, 'After rebirth of our nation comes the hard part', *The Nation*, 28 August 2010.
3. Joseph Karimi, 'This is how we know it is General Mathenge', *The Standard*, 22 January 2002.
4. Mburu Mwangi and Tigist Kassa, 'The puzzle remains as "Gen Mathenge" comes home', *The Nation*, 31 May 2003.
5. *Ibid.*
6. Patrick Mathangani and Muchemi Wachira, 'I am not Mathenge, says Ethiopian man', *Daily Nation*, 2 June 2003.
7. Peter Wafula Wekesa, 'Negotiating "Kenyanness": The "debates" ' in Mbugua wa-Mungai and George Gona (eds), *(Re)Membering Kenya*, Volume 1: *Identity, Culture and Freedom*, Nairobi, 2010, p. 57.
8. Kahora, 'The fire next time', p. 9.
9. Parselelo Kantai and Patrick Smith, 'Kenya: No country for young men', *Africa Report*, 11, June/July 2008, p. 43.
10. John Lonsdale, 'The moral economy of Mau Mau: Wealth, poverty and civic virtue in Kikuyu political thought', in B. Berman and J. Lonsdale, *Unhappy Valley: Conflict in Kenya and Africa*, Oxford, 1992, pp. 315–504.
11. Tom Young, *Africa: A beginner's guide*, Oxford, 2010, p. 150.
12. Kinuthia Macharia, 'Social networks: Ethnicity and the informal sector in Nairobi', working paper no. 463, Institute for Development Studies, University of Nairobi, August 1988.
13. Author's notes on Kenyans for Peace, Truth and Justice symposium, 'Combating Corruption in Kenya', Hilton Hotel, Nairobi, 20 August 2008.
14. Kahora, 'The fire next time', pp. 8–10.
15. Frances Stewart, 'Note for discussion: Kenya, horizontal inequalities and the political disturbances of 2008', Centre for Research on Inequality, Human Security and Ethnicity, University of Oxford, March 2008.
16. Matiba, *A Dream*, pp. 25–6.
17. Kahora, 'The fire next time', p. 8.
18. Binyavanga Wainaina, 'Generation Kenya', *Vanity Fair*, July 2007.
19. Ngugi wa Thiong'o, 'Protect your families: Vote for an MP with integrity', 14 December 2007, Ngugi wa Thiong'o's website, available at: http://ngugiwathiongo.com/kenya/kenya-home.htm (accessed 20 December 2010).
20. Njogu, *Healing the Wound*, p. 70.
21. Ranneberger to State Department, 11 June 2009; 09NAIROBI1168; Wikileaks cable viewer website (accessed 24 March 2011).
22. Stephen Brown, 'From demiurge to midwife: Changing donor roles in Kenya's democratisation process', in G. Murunga and S. Nasong'o (eds), *Kenya: The struggle for democracy*, London, 2007, p. 323.
23. Author's notes on 'Combating Corruption in Kenya' symposium.

INDEX